Frontiers of Financial Management

SECOND EDITION

SELECTED READINGS

WILLIAM J. SERRAINO
Chairman, Department of Finance
Miami University
Oxford, Ohio

SURENDRA S. SINGHVI
Manager, Financial Planning and Analysis
Armco Steel Corporation
Middletown, Ohio
and
Adjunct Professor of Finance
Miami University
Oxford, Ohio

ROBERT M. SOLDOFSKY
Professor of Finance
University of Iowa
Iowa City, Iowa

Published by

F26 **SOUTH-WESTERN PUBLISHING CO.**

CINCINNATI   WEST CHICAGO, ILL.   DALLAS   PELHAM MANOR, N.Y.
PALO ALTO, CALIF.   BRIGHTON, ENGLAND

PREFACE

In selecting the 34 articles for this revised collection of readings on financial management, the authors used the same three major criteria that guided the selection of articles for the first edition. These criteria are a managerial viewpoint, a concern for real and relevant problems that financial managers and other top-level managers must confront, and a judicious introduction of newer approaches to subjects including new models and techniques. A new item prepared by a partner of one of the "Big Eight" CPA firms discusses "What a Chief Executive Should Know About Financial Modeling." Even though many of the articles are at the frontiers of financial management, none of them includes statistical or mathematical techniques above the level of training received in undergraduate business schools or by first-year graduate students in business. The problems, practices, and theories discussed in this collection should be very useful at least into the 1980s.

This revised collection includes 11 of the items from the first collection and 23 new articles. New problems and newer theoretical developments quite understandably lead to changes in any collection of articles in any area of concern. The 34 articles are grouped under ten different headings. A balance in the topics selected was maintained so that instructors could find one or two articles to assign each week to supplement and enrich their regular textbook.

This collection of articles may be categorized in many different ways such as the position or experience of the authors; the use of models, surveys, or other relevant experience; and the number of sources from which they are drawn. Many of the articles do not fall neatly into any simple classification. At least 15 of the articles were prepared by people outside of academic institutions. These people work for consulting firms, major accounting firms, nonprofit business research organizations, very large banks, and large corporations.

At least 10 of the articles utilize equations or models of varying degrees of complexity. These include simulation and decision tree models for capital investment, financial expansion models, tests of dividend models, normative dividend models, control limits models for cash management, and utility curves. Several articles report and interpret important surveys, extensive data collection, and direct experience with the topic being presented. The 34 articles are drawn from 24 different sources. The only journals represented more than once are the

Financial Executive, Financial Management, Fortune, Harvard Business Review, Journal of Finance, and *MSU Business Topics.*

Some of the topics and areas covered will be of increasing importance for years to come. The declining prices of small computers and the very rapidly growing use of time-sharing computers will place increasing numbers of financial managers in the position of needing to know more about what computerized financial models can do for them. Computerized, probabilistic investment decisions (Article 6) and abandonment decisions (Article 7) are discussed. The problems of financing during periods of tight money, high interest rates, and low stock prices (Article 11) will recur from time to time. The utilization of the new, widely accepted stock valuation model, D/MP + g, is discussed (Article 13), as well as the decision to repurchase stock when its price is low (Article 15) and bond refunding decisions (Article 16) that will be faced with increasing frequency. Many large corporations are concerned with how their bonds are rated (Article 18) and the use of leases (Article 19); the value of leased assets is growing at about 20 percent per year. Some developments in working capital theory and practice are introduced in Part VI (Articles 20, 21, and 22). Mergers and acquisitions will continue to roll through the economy in waves and the problems of financing caused by inflation (Article 30) will rise and fall in intensity but will not disappear. International financial management (Article 32) continues to increase in importance and specialized problems such as those relating to the decision to expand into a foreign market (Article 33) will be of concern to more and more businesses.

The number of articles included in this collection is limited for obvious and realistic reasons. We hope that those selected will help to enrich, widen, and deepen undergraduate courses in financial administration. The book should be especially useful at the graduate level because of its coverage of topics and decision-making orientation.

W. J. S.

S. S. S.

R. M. S.

CONTENTS

PART IV.   DIVIDEND POLICY AND VALUATION

Article   **Page**

PART V.   LONG-TERM FINANCING

PART VI.   WORKING CAPITAL MANAGEMENT

PART VII.   MERGERS AND ACQUISITIONS

PART VIII. APPROACHES TO FINANCIAL PLANNING

Article   **Page**

PART IX. FINANCIAL IMPACT OF ACCOUNTING

PART X. INTERNATIONAL FINANCIAL MANAGEMENT

ABOUT THE AUTHORS*

Richard M. Adams—Tennant Company.

Guy J. Agrati—Manager-Control, Chemical Bank.

Douglas V. Austin—Chairman, Department of Finance, College of Business Administration, University of Toledo.

Oswald D. Bowlin—Professor of Finance, College of Business Administration, Texas Tech University.

Robert A. Bullington—Assistant Secretary, Irving Trust Company.

Ronald M. Copeland—Professor of Accounting, College of Business Administration, University of South Carolina.

John S. Fielden—Dean, School of Business, University of Alabama.

E. Stuart Files—Vice President and Secretary, A. T. Kearney & Co., Inc.

James M. Fremgen—Professor of Accounting, Naval Postgraduate School, Monterey, California.

Clark A. Hawkins—Professor of Finance, College of Business and Public Administration, University of Arizona.

John Heath, Jr.—Vice President, Marshall and Stevens Incorporated.

David B. Hertz—Director, McKinsey and Company.

F. Edward Lake—Treasurer, The Greyhound Corporation.

Roderic C. Lancey—Corporate Planner, International Minerals and Chemical Corporation.

Carol J. Loomis—Board of Editors, *Fortune*.

Robert K. Mautz—Partner, Ernst & Ernst; formerly Professor of Accounting, Graduate School of Business, University of Illinois.

Merton H. Miller—Edward Eagle Brown Professor of Finance and Economics, Graduate School of Business, University of Chicago.

Michael L. Moore—Assistant Professor of Accounting, College of Business Administration, The University of Texas at Austin.

---

*The position of some of the authors has changed since the date of their articles. The present position is given where it is known to the editors.

Roger F. Murray—S. Sloan Colt Professor of Banking and Finance, Graduate School of Business, Columbia University. Served also as a Director of College Retirement Equities Fund.

John J. Neuhauser—Chairman, Computer Science Department, Boston College.

Daniel Orr—Professor of Economics, University of California at La Jolla.

Robert M. Pennell—Manager of Corporate Finance, Optron, Inc.

James R. Piper, Jr.—Management Consultant, Theodore Barry and Associates.

Sidney M. Robbins—Professor of Finance, Graduate School of Business, Columbia University.

Alexander A. Robichek—Professor of Finance, Graduate School of Business, Stanford University.

John J. Scanlon—Vice President and Treasurer, American Telephone and Telegraph Company.

Michael Schiff—Ross Professor of Accounting, Graduate School of Business, New York University.

Marvin Schiller—Vice President, Eastern Division, A. T. Kearney & Co., Inc.

Joseph J. Seneca—Associate Professor of Economics, Rutgers University.

Michael A. Simkowitz—Associate Professor of Finance, Graduate School of Business, Indiana University.

Surendra S. Singhvi—Manager of Financial Planning and Analysis, Armco Steel Corporation, and Adjunct Professor of Finance, Miami University.

Donald J. Smalter—Corporate Director of Strategic Planning, International Minerals and Chemical Corporation.

Donald R. Smith—Partner, Price Waterhouse & Co.

Robert M. Soldofsky—Professor of Finance, College of Business Administration, The University of Iowa.

Ezra Solomon—Dean Witter Professor of Finance, Graduate School of Business, Stanford University. Member, Council of Economic Advisers, 1971–73.

Joel M. Stern—Vice President, Corporate Financial Research Division, Chase Manhattan Bank.

Robert B. Stobaugh—Professor of Business Administration, Harvard Business School, Harvard University.

Robert F. Vandell—Professor of Business Administration, Graduate School of Business, University of Virginia.

Peter Vanderwicken—Associate Editor, *Fortune.*

James C. Van Horne—Professor of Finance, Graduate School of Business, Stanford University.

Joseph Van Vleck, 3rd—Vice President, The Travelers Insurance Company.

Jerry A. Viscione—Associate Professor of Finance, Graduate School of Business, Boston College.

James E. Walter—Professor of Finance, Wharton School of Commerce and Finance, University of Pennsylvania.

Mervin H. Waterman—Professor Emeritus of Finance, Graduate School of Business, University of Michigan.

Edward E. Williams—Associate Professor of Finance, McGill University.

Lawrence H. Wortzel—Professor of Marketing, Boston University.

PART I. PERSPECTIVES IN FINANCIAL MANAGEMENT

Since its appearance as a separate branch of institutional economics around the turn of the century, financial management has changed in both its academic definition and in its practical application. Historically, it has been preoccupied with the procurement of funds, but there has been an evolutionary change toward a broader definition emphasizing the effective utilization of funds. The problems that were emphasized in each era reflected the political, economic, and social preoccupations of that period. The present development and increasing use of statistical and mathematical analysis in many areas of business, government, science, and human concern are the results of such profound movements as the growth in educational levels, new theoretical developments, increases in population and wealth, and the impact of computer technology. The articles of this section provide a proper perspective in financial management.

Professor Ezra Solomon's paper discusses trends and developments in academic and professional thinking on the subject of financial management. He observes that a growing analytical content that started to develop in the 1950's is displacing the traditional descriptive treatment as the center of emphasis in the field of business finance. He traces the evolution of the finance field from the turn of the century to the present time and discusses the implications of this evolution. Solomon distinguishes very lucidly between the traditional approach, which is still widely used, and the analytical approach, which is taking over. The traditional approach to finance represents a body of descriptive knowledge and a branch of institutional economics, and it is largely concerned with the process of raising funds and with the liability side of the balance sheet. The newer approach is more a way of thinking and an extension of the microeconomic theory of the firm; it is largely concerned with the optimal usage of funds and with the asset side of the balance sheet. In brief, the old question in finance was, How should a firm raise funds? The new question in finance is, How should a firm make decisions to commit funds for specific purposes and set standards against which it can assay the use of funds? The rapid changes in the field of finance have tremendous significance for investment, money and banking, and international business finance. Therefore, the student of finance must be prepared to enter a discipline which is increasingly analytical and international and which is rapidly changing in scope.

1

Professor Roger F. Murray reflects on the critical role of the securities industry in the allocation of a high but inadequate volume of savings which will have to be allocated among strongly competing investment opportunities during the current decade. He discusses the role of markets as allocators of capital with an illustrative example of the role played in the first half of the sixties versus the role played in the second half of the sixties. He comments correctly that business is facing a decade of growth and expansion with real savings depleted by inflation, reduced liquidity, and extended capital structures.

Professor Murray finds it disappointing that little is available in the way of objective standards by which one can appraise the efficiency with which the market mechanism allocates equity capital among competing uses. He comments on the "slow pace" of resources allocations, the instability of valuation, and the new issues markets. In his concluding remarks he suggests steps which can be taken to realize improvements necessary for the securities markets to function more efficiently.

Mr. Marvin Schiller and associates examine the concerns of today's financial executives. The authors divide these concerns into three parts: the financial executive's concern for his own performance and how he might increase his performance effectiveness; the development of the finance function and how it might improve its services to the rest of the organization; and a concern for the perpetuation of the organization itself.

The authors observe that the modern financial executive is aware of the scientific revolution and its impact on management and he is aware of the ever-greater impact that will be forthcoming in future years. Further, the use of new quantitative tools by leading consulting firms and graduate schools of business raise the question of whether new types of formal and informal education will be needed. All of these developments raise the question as to whether new men with different types of personalities, men who are more company oriented rather than finance-accounting oriented, will be required. The authors believe that training of future successful financial officers will require a blending of the humanities, accounting, other business functions plus various other disciplines. They recognize the need for graduate education but observe that the universities cannot hope to prepare a man for a lifetime of work in a period of ever-increasing change. Thus the individual and the corporation must play an important role in this educational process.

1. RECENT TRENDS AND DEVELOPMENTS IN ACADEMIC AND PROFESSIONAL THINKING ON THE SUBJECT OF FINANCIAL MANAGEMENT*

EZRA SOLOMON†

The subject matter of financial management is in the process of very rapid change. What appears to be happening is that a growing analytical content virtually nonexistent ten years ago is displacing the traditional descriptive treatment as the center of emphasis in the field. This change is taking place rapidly, both in the academic world and in the professional world, and is taking place both in the United States and abroad.

My talk today falls into two unequal parts: first, I am going to try to outline the nature of the changes that are taking place in the field of financial management; toward the end I shall discuss the implications of these changes for academic courses in finance and perhaps for academic courses in other related fields.

Finance is probably the oldest of the functional fields. Financial management, or corporation finance, as it was then more generally called, emerged as a separate branch of economics around the turn of the century. This was the age of institutional economics in this country. It was also the age in which our giant national corporations were being formed out of financial mergers and consolidations.

In this context, the original purpose of corporation finance as a separate subject was to describe and document the rapidly evolving complex of institutions, instruments, and practices in the capital market. As one of the earlier texts written soon after the turn of the century said: "Corporation finance aims to explain and illustrate the methods employed in the promotion, capitalization, financial management, consolidation and reorganization of business corporations."

By and large, the field continued to use this basic structure and content for nearly 50 years. It might be interesting to determine why. I think there were three factors involved. When academic work in business administration and, of course, in finance developed on a large scale in the 1920's, it simply adopted the early definition of the scope and method of the subject that I have outlined.

Secondly, the wide growth in security ownership after World War I increased public interest in corporations, in corporate securities, and in the network of institutional arrangements through which corporations obtained their funds from the public.

The third factor at work was the publication in 1920 of Arthur Stone Dewing's celebrated book, *The Financial Policy of Corporations*. This great book established the then-existing pattern of treatment firmly by

---

*From the *AACSB Bulletin* (October, 1965), pp. 1-8. Reprinted by permission.
†Dean Witter Professor of Finance, Graduate School of Business, Stanford University.

providing a definitive and scholarly text and a definitive and scholarly basis for academic courses in the field. The book itself dominated academic work in the field for at least 30 years.

I am not suggesting that this traditional treatment—I think we were all brought up on it—went unchallenged, but almost all of the challenges posed against it concerned matters of emphasis or matters of treatment. Several of these challenges are worth noting.

In the 1930's we had a huge upsurge of legislation and social controls, so we added large segments to the field of finance dealing with social control and legislative and regulatory aspects of finance. Also, in the '30's we had a large wave of reorganizations and bankruptcies, so quite naturally this topic was added. Thus at the end of fairly familiar chapter headings came a large section on bankruptcy and reorganization.

In the early years after World War II, a switch from external financing to internal financing combined with the freeing of interest rates and some degree of tightening in the money market made the whole question of working capital management more important. Consequently, there was a switch in emphasis from the question of long-term financing to working capital financing and working capital management. At the same time, there began a broadening of the subject away from corporation finance as such to business finance. When you deal with stocks and bonds and convertible debentures, you are dealing explicitly with corporations. When you talk about working capital management, you can be talking about noncorporate businesses.

A fourth kind of challenge to the content of the field emerged largely through the case method of instruction. The traditional textbook treatment was too much, as Pearson Hunt put it, "from the outside looking in." This investment banker point of view naturally involved heavy emphasis on a description of markets and institutions. When cases began to deal with decisions from the inside looking out, you got away somewhat from the descriptive body of treatment to the more typically case type decision situations.

In summary, throughout its 50 years of dominance, the traditional treatment of the field was criticized as being too descriptive, too much like an encyclopedia, and not sufficiently analytical.

Students complained about it and teachers complained about it. But very little change took place in spite of these complaints. This was because the basic assumption of the traditional approach was not questioned. This basic assumption was that the central emphasis of finance is on the procurement of funds and, hence, on the instruments, institutions, and practices through which funds are obtained in the marketplace and, by extension, on the legal and accounting relationships between a company on the one hand and its sources of funds on the other.

During the past ten years, and particularly the past five years, we have seen one more challenge to the traditional approach, but, unlike the previous challenges, this hits right at the basic assumption of the traditional approach —the basic assumption regarding the proper content of finance. The traditional assumption that the proper content of finance has to do with the procurement of funds has been questioned and rejected.

In its place we now have a much broader view. This view is that financial management is an integral part of overall management rather than a staff specialty concerned with fund-raising operations. In this new view, the central issue is the wise usage of funds. The central process involved is some sort of rational matching of the advantages of potential fund uses on the one hand against the cost of funds on the other; more properly speaking, against the cost of alternative potential sources of funds.

To state it another way, the present scope of the subject goes much further than the original question. The old basic question was: How should a company raise funds? The new questions are much broader. How should a company make decisions to commit funds for certain purposes? In other words, it is a discussion of the investment decision as such, which in turn involves the question of how we measure the profitability of committing funds in this direction versus another direction. How should a company set standards against which it can assay the use of funds? In other words, what is the minimum yardstick by which a company decides whether this usage is appropriate or not appropriate? And this body of analysis is being applied not only to normal profit-seeking companies but to other enterprises as well. I think you all saw a recent issue of *Time* magazine which reported that the planners in the Soviet Union are now grappling with this question of what minimum financial standards to set for the usage of funds by one state enterprise versus another state enterprise.

Thus, finance is involved not only with measuring profitability but with setting standards, minimum standards for profitability, and hence with the whole question of measuring the cost of capital for any given society or any given industry. This issue in turn leads to the third major question: How does the cost of capital vary with the financing mix which is used? Finally, and only in this context, can one ask the old traditional question: Given the foregoing set of theories or facts or inferences, how should a company go about its task of raising funds at any time in any given capital market?

You might ask whence these new questions have been borrowed. Has finance simply adopted as its subject matter questions that are properly in someone else's domain? The answer, surprisingly enough, is that these questions have not heretofore been studied systematically. It is not that businessmen have not been making these decisions; they have. Decisions to invest funds, decisions about the minimum standard required have been made for thousands of years, but they have been made way at the top, and how they have been made has neither been written down nor discussed. I suppose they were made by judgment of some kind or other. The academic version of finance itself never pondered these questions.

Academic and professional people in finance are now definitely asking these questions and pondering their appropriate solutions. You cannot walk within 20 feet of any finance classroom these days in the United States, or in Britain for that matter, and not hear the words, "the cost of capital." In contrast, look at anything written prior to 1955, and you will not find the phrase mentioned, let alone discussed. One might also ask: Since part of the new and broader view of finance has to do with the older question, how should a company raise funds, is there not a major overlap between the traditional and the new? Again the answer is no.

Taken in isolation, the narrow question, how should a company raise funds, had to devolve into a descriptive treatment of markets and institutions and practices. Taken in the broader context of the new definition of finance, it can be far more analytical. The turning point here came in the now celebrated article by Modigliani and Miller, published, I think, in 1958, which for the first time seriously and analytically tackled the question of optimal fund mixture.

One might also ask why 50 years went by before the scope and method of the subject of finance were redefined. I do not know the answer to this. All one can do is point out the many reasons that existed in the late '50's and in the early '60's for an emphasis on the kinds of questions implied by the new content of finance.

In one sense the developments I have been discussing represent a logical extension of the general scientific management movement into a field which previously had been reserved for judgment at the top. Although the most vigorously decentralized corporations have tended to keep financial decisions at the top, it was natural that scientific management, which began first at the factory level, should extend its way of thinking and its approach to the top itself. I also think that the move from implicit to explicit reasoning has been hastened by the computer. Computers do not take answers like, "Well, you use a little judgment." Computers like numbers, and so we have to find and use these numbers!

I think the implications of these changes in finance are very big, not only for top management but in many other matters. One important area other than top management is the field of utility regulation. Here, while the questions I am discussing have not been asked, the answers have been assumed. Utility regulators have measured the cost of capital without defining it. The other significant area or implication is for government investment of various kinds. I am talking now on a universal basis; in so many countries where state-owned enterprises are trying to maximize human welfare in some way, the older habit simply of engaging in pet projects is giving way now to the questions of engaging in economically feasible and desirable projects. The old capitalistic trick of maximizing wealth is being invoked within socialist economies or within socialist sectors of capitalistic economies, and this depends very much on answers to the financial questions involved.

Let me summarize the differences between what I call the older and the traditional approach, which still dominates the field in a numerical sense, and the new approach, which is taking over. The old approach was a body of knowledge. The new approach is more a way of thinking.

The older approach was concerned with the process of raising funds. The new approach is concerned with the optimal usage of funds—optimal with respect to volume, composition, and timing of both sources and uses.

The old approach was concerned very largely with the liability side of the balance sheet; it was concerned with the asset side of the balance sheet only where it involved cash and securities. The new approach is concerned with a balance between the assets and liabilities sides of the balance sheet.

The old approach was heavily descriptive. The new approach is largely analytical—more an exercise in inference than an exercise in description.

In the older approach, specialized description of corporation law and corporate accounting as they related to specific financing episodes, such as promotion, merger, consolidation, and reorganization, was a very big part of the subject. In the new approach, these episodic phenomena are treated as special aspects of a unifying basic problem, and this basic problem is simply the question of financial evaluation in an uncertain world.

Finally, the older approach represented a branch of institutional economics. The new approach represents much more an extension of the micro-economic theory of the firm; whereas the theory of the firm, price theory as we know it, is concerned largely with the relationship of profits to the level of output with level of capital taken as given, financial theory is concerned with the relationship between profits and a changing level of capital input.

Let me turn to the possible impact of this newer framework, this newer definition of the scope and method of finance. Apart from changing the subject itself, what are its implications? One important one is that it seems to have made the subject a lot more exciting, both to students and to teachers. There is a feeling of excitement within the field now.

Twenty years ago there was almost nothing being done in the way of doctoral dissertations in this field. This was true even ten years ago and five years ago. In other words, in a typical doctoral seminar, given the choice, students would write on then jazzier subjects like monetary theory, international finance, the balance of payments, and so on; very few of them selected topics within corporate financial management proper. This is no longer the case. At Stanford this last year I have had a group of about 15 doctoral students, each one reading and writing on a self-selected topic for the seminar. Only one subject has been outside the field of corporation finance. This was on the balance of payments issue. The other 14 have been within the subject of financial management proper. This is a big switch.

The development of subject matter is taking place at an extremely rapid pace. The young people now working in the field remind me of an incident in the Navy I should like to relate. After getting out of Burma the wrong way—across the mountains on foot—I was tired of land and joined the British Navy and was assigned to a ship run by an old fogey, a sort of universal Queeg. We used to refer to him as "the old woman" because he always seemed to be bothered about little things. About three years later, at the ripe age of 24, I had command of a ship myself, and I was standing up on the deck feeling the usual loneliness of the man at the top when through the speaker tube I heard two midshipmen talking about me; they were referring to me as that "old woman."

I feel that way about finance today. Just a few years ago I was a young Turk trying to overthrow the past. When I hear these young students discussing some of their ideas, I already feel a little out of date. I think in five years I am going to have to quit teaching finance.

In spite of very rapid change and a great deal of controversy, brought on in part by the rapid new quantitative methods and computer technology, the mainstream of the new finance is now reaching that degree of certainty and lucidity which I think makes it quite suitable for undergraduate courses in the field. I also feel that if undergraduate courses in the field of finance were to adopt the new approach, everybody would be better off.

In the first place, the questions it addresses are more universal. It is not confined to particular problems or a particular form of business called a corporation but rather deals with any form of enterprise. Furthermore, it deals with ongoing problems, rather than episodic problems. In short, it is less specialized; more general.

Secondly, it is more analytical and thus challenges and exercises the brain more. It is less a question of memory and learning facts; more a question of inference and thinking and logic.

Finally, I think the new look in finance ties in much better with the other parts of the curriculum in business administration. It ties in beautifully with production, problems of inventory control, and operations research. It ties in very well with business economics. It ties in with management accounting and with business policy.

For all these reasons it does provide a better basis of instruction at the undergraduate level. So while the subject will remain full of controversy and noise and argument for many years to come, there is already sufficient at the core for the new approach to be adopted as the basis for the curriculum in the field.

As far as implications for other subjects are concerned, time does not allow me to go into that in any detail. I do think that two implications are worth noting. I think what has happened in the field of corporation finance or financial management proper has tremendous significance for the field of investment. This highly respected field is one which has not changed very much in 30 years and about which there is a lot of deep discontent at the practitioner level today. Financial analysts feel that the academician has not done his stuff, that he is giving them recipes and not theories, and they want theory, better theory. I think there is a revolution coming in the field of investment. If there are any young faculty interested in working in this field, they should be given free rein. Let them have their heads. Let them experiment, get away from the present format of the field.

I also think that the new emphasis in financial management has some implications for the courses in money and banking which are taught in business schools. This is that they should have somewhat less emphasis on money and banking in the traditional sense and somewhat more emphasis on money in the capital markets in the broader sense; that we need to discuss more than the rate of interest on money—we need to discuss the whole structure of rates in the entire capital markets. This trend has been in existence for a long time, but it is going to be accelerated by developments in financial management.

Finally, there is the new field of international business. With multi-national operations increasing rapidly, business schools have been concerned about this new dimension that should be added to the business curriculum. If finance had not changed in the directions I have indicated, very clearly there should be a field of international business finance, for the simple reason that the older style domestic corporation finance dealt almost solely with Americana. Obviously it does little good to talk about convertible debenture bond issues in Malaya or any other country which does not have a capital market. Insofar as the older content of finance was heavily larded with Americana, it was hardly suitable training for people engaging in business overseas.

But this statement is no longer true with the new finance. The content is far more universal, far more abstracted from instruments and practices in a particular market, and definitely more theoretical and analytical. The fact that domestic financial courses now have developed this analytical core means that they are also suitable for students who wish to practice business overseas or in multinational corporations. The need for separate courses in international business finance or multinational business finance is far less than it would have been.

It is true that the different environments in different parts of the world do require somewhat different emphasis in terms of context. For example, at home we face a single type of capital rationing problem. We ration dollars among different projects, whereas in many countries abroad which have exchange control, they have a dual rationing problem. They are rationing domestic savings, and they are also rationing scarce foreign exchange among different projects. In many ways it is a far more difficult problem. On the other hand, because it is a difficult analytical dual rationing problem, it ought to be a part of our domestic curriculum.

Another kind of major difference that is worth noting between conditions here and abroad is that, in many countries abroad, inflation, or the pace of inflation, is a far more serious issue. It, therefore, has to be taken into account explicitly in financial analysis and financial evaluation.

But, by the same token, this is an interesting thing for us to do here anyway, because we too have some rate of inflation, and there may come a time when we have a faster rate of inflation. We ought to be thinking in terms of financial analysis within an inflationary economy.

What I am trying to say is that we can have one integrated course that serves the purposes of both the domestic student and the student who has a multinational interest, and this has been made possible by the fact that finance itself has changed in content and scope and emphasis. A financial management course which is ideal for persons interested in multinational operations comes pretty close to a financial management course which is ideal for people who never intend to leave the United States.

2. THE SECURITIES INDUSTRY: ITS CRITICAL ROLE IN A DECADE OF CAPITAL SCARCITY*

ROGER F. MURRAY†

For the American economy to achieve its strong growth potential for the 1970's, a high level of public and private investment is clearly essential. This is especially true because of the size of the household capital investment boom which is potentially inherent in the present population mix. In addition, the demands for public investment in housing, transportation, environmental protection, and government facilities are likely to be expanding throughout the decade at rates in excess of the growth in aggregate output.

Without even looking beyond our national borders, therefore, we can anticipate at least for the current decade a situation in which a high but inadequate volume of savings will have to be allocated among strongly competing investment opportunities. Sustainable growth without inflation can be achieved only if this allocation process is accomplished with maximum efficiency. The urgency of this task prompts these reflections on the critical role of the securities industry in this process.

MARKETS AS ALLOCATORS OF CAPITAL

There is no disagreement, I presume, with the proposition that an efficient market for securities makes them more attractive assets to hold because it imparts more liquidity or shiftability to them and reduces transaction costs. This function of providing a good secondary market needs no elaboration these days in view of the extensive reports, studies and hearings on market structures now in progress. The difficulty, perhaps, is that we have become so absorbed in this aspect of our securities markets that we have neglected to think seriously enough about their role in the allocating of capital to the most productive uses through the pricing of securities.

The scarcity of long-term savings relative to insistent investment demands in the years ahead places a new emphasis on the process and gives a new urgency to our collective efforts to improve the workings of our securities markets. The importance of this topic can be measured specifically in terms of the amounts of equity capital being raised.

During the first half of the 1960's, from 1961 through 1965, the average yearly amount of new equity capital provided to American non-

*From a booklet presenting the text of the first annual Buttonwood Lecture (January, 1972), pp. 1-11, sponsored by the Graduate School of Business, Columbia University, and The New York Stock Exchange, Inc. Reprinted by permission of the author.
†S. Sloan Colt Professor of Banking and Finance, Graduate School of Business, Columbia University.

financial corporations was $14.8 billion.[1] This comfortably supported a net addition to long-term debt averaging $13.5 billion a year. In the aggregate, therefore, American business was financing its growth with about $1.10 of equity for every dollar of additional debt.

In the second half of the 1960's, from 1966 through 1970, yearly additions to equity capital averaged only $19.2 billion compared with average net additions to long-term debt of $29.7 billion a year. This represented only 64 cents of new equity for each new dollar of debt. The result of this slowdown in growth of the equity base is the now familiar phenomenon of a deterioration in credit worthiness and a widespread reduction in corporate liquidity.

There is no mystery about this record of the 1960's. Funds provided by new equity security flotations increased from a level of $0.8 billion a year in the first half of the decade to an average of $2.8 billion a year in the second half; but the major source of equity capital, retained earnings, increased only from $13.9 billion to $16.5 billion a year during the comparable periods.

For our purposes, of course, there is no distinction to be made between new equity security issues and retained earnings, apart from the underwriting and distribution costs incurred in the former method of raising capital. We know that a dollar of retained earnings is just the same as a dollar raised through a preemptive rights offering fully subscribed by existing stockholders. The investor who accepts a current return of 3 percent from cash dividends does so only because he expects, say, 6 percent a year or more of growth in the value of his shares to reflect the value of the retained earnings. This enhancement in market value must be provided through the market mechanism to reward the investor for foregoing current income from dividends.

Our conventional description of what is happening to stock ownership is that individuals are selling stocks to institutional holders on balance. We would be much more accurate if we described this process as individuals saving a portion and liquidating a portion through the marketplace of their growing equities in corporate enterprise. Acceptance of the corporate retention of earnings as an efficient mechanism for raising equity capital is conditioned on the ability to obtain fair value for such accumulations.

The correct measurement of the net equity capital allocations made through the securities markets in a year, therefore, is more like $20 billion than the modest $2 billion of net new equity flotations of recent years. In a very real sense, the securities industry is making the markets in equity capital without regard to the number of stock certificates but only in relation to total equities in corporate enterprise.

---

[1]These and subsequent data are derived from the flow of funds accounts prepared by the Board of Governors of the Federal Reserve System and published regularly in the *Federal Reserve Bulletin.*

THE PRESENT POSITION OF CORPORATE BUSINESS

The performance of the past few years can only be described as dismal. While new equity raised by nonfinancial corporations in the noninflationary period of the mid-1960's averaged 3.4 percent of Gross National Product originating in the private sector, this relationship averaged only 2.1 percent during the latter years of the decade. This comparison suggests that the cumulative deficiency in corporate equities may have reached $30 to $40 billion by the end of last year. Such an estimate is exceedingly rough, but it serves to illustrate the point.

The truth of the old textbook adage that inflation impoverishes an economy has been demonstrated once again. The real savings of corporate business have been confiscated by the taxation of fictitious profits, eroded by the rising costs of corporate activities, and left unprotected by corporate managements who were victimized by the familiar "money illusion." As a consequence, we find business facing a decade of growth and expansion with liquidity reduced, capital structures extended, and real savings depleted by inflation. This unfavorable situation from which we start the decade of the 1970's gives further emphasis to the need for greater efficiency in allocating scarce equity capital in the years ahead.

MEASURING EFFICIENCY

In these days of intensive efforts to measure performance, it is natural that we should seek a standard for appraising the efficiency with which the market mechanism allocates equity capital among competing uses. It is disappointing that we have so little to offer in the way of objective standards. When we examine rates of return on total capital, we find a downward drift during the inflation period. We also observe that there are wide differentials between major industries and companies. These disparities in profitability suggest a slow rate of resource shifting to more productive areas; but there are serious measurement problems with the data. I should like to suggest, however, three observations which indicate the existence of considerable room for improvement in the allocation of capital, especially equity capital.

The first of these is the existence and persistence, for long periods of years prior to takeovers or liquidations, of business firms which are given access to equity capital through earnings retention in spite of low levels of productivity as measured by average profitability. The market mechanism is demonstrably too slow in bringing about a shift in resource utilization. There is no need for citing specific examples because the data are readily available showing returns on capital employed.

Secondly, there is scanty evidence that the market's continuing valuation of expected returns to investors is becoming more precise and reliable. Wide swings in share prices during short periods of time suggest unstable, uncertain, and unreliable appraisals of future profitability and efficiency in the use of real resources. Any blame for the lack of striking gains in the accuracy of this appraisal process can be shared generously by the investing community.

Thirdly, the record of the new issue market raises some serious questions about efficiency in resource allocations. The record of the 1967-1969 "hot" new issue market is not yet completely written. However, we still have the record from the 1950's to study. The score card for 960 small companies going public from 1952 to 1962 was as follows at the time of the SEC's *Special Study of Securities Markets*[2] in 1963:

Inactive, liquidated, or in reorganization	37%
Merged with other companies	5
Still in business but operating at a loss............	24
In business and operating at a profit	34
	100%

A failure rate as high as this one reflects some serious deficiencies in the abilities of financial analysts and underwriters to identify firms which have earned a right of access to the public markets for long-term risk capital.

These three observations do not provide neat documentation of deficiencies in the market's allocative efficiency, nor do they lend themselves to any form of precise measurement. They are offered, therefore, simply as evidence that opportunities for improvements clearly exist. They also form the basis for my concluding remarks on the directions in which I believe the securities industry should move in order to enhance its contribution to the process of increasing economic efficiency and growth in the American economy.

THE SLOW PACE OF RESOURCES REALLOCATION

Returning now to the first observation, which can be described as the problem of institutionalized inefficiency, it is obviously difficult to precipitate changes in corporate enterprises which are firmly locked into less productive activities. The fact that the market reduces the value of retained earnings substantially to zero and creates low or negative holding period returns for investors is productive of dissatisfaction and stockholder restlessness but seldom, except after long delays, do these developments produce material changes in the employment of physical and human resources.

---

[2]Part 1, p. 551. For a subsample of 504 "promotional" companies (i.e., those organized shortly before the offering and without an earnings record), the comparable statistics were even worse. The last category of profit-making firms was less than 15 percent, while the first category of failing firms exceeded 54 percent.

The pressure generated by declining stock prices must be reinforced by direct action. The company's investment bankers frequently have a clear responsibility to take steps to precipitate change. An example was the long and difficult task of restructuring the J. I. Case Corporation undertaken by the firm which has sponsored its securities over the years. In other cases, the profit motive may be sufficient to energize members of securities firms to act on behalf of investors in bringing about those changes in corporate strategies and managements which may reverse the trend toward declining profitability long before the company becomes reduced to being a target for radical reorganization or takeover.

Not for a minute can we forget that such direct action will incur criticism of "banker domination," "financial power," and the like; but this is one of the prices to be paid for successfully achieving leadership in the securities industry. Besides, not every instance of direct action involves conflicts, tensions, and unfavorable publicity. Furthermore, the rewards in terms of both profits and prestige are generous compensation for performing the unpleasant duty of unseating entrenched incompetence in the executive suite.

This function of the securities industry has become more important than ever as institutional investors have increased their ownership positions without a corresponding willingness to exercise their rights of ownership. They are afraid to act in concert with other investors, find their individual efforts to bring about change largely unproductive, and finally just liquidate their positions. The only likely prospect for successfully mobilizing the institutional investors is the capable, experienced, and respected investment banker.

THE INSTABILITY OF VALUATIONS

My second observation relates to how deficiencies in the market's allocative efficiency call for a joint effort on the part of both investors and the securities industry. The process of arriving at meaningful, stable valuations of corporate enterprise suffers from at least three major defects:

1. Despite the progress made over the last several decades, we still face serious problems in the lack of comparability over time and across industries of financial information. Generally accepted accounting principles are still inadequate standards or guides for financial analysis.
2. The integration of economic analysis and financial analysis is still in its infancy. As a result, the time horizon of forecasts and valuations is much too short to reflect the underlying continuity of a business enterprise and its economic worth.

3. The emphasis on instant performance in portfolio management has placed an artificial premium on news items and transitory developments affecting short-run price movements at the expense of depth in the analysis of fundamental industry and company characteristics.

Both the securities firms which supply investment information to investors and money managers are seriously engaged in a disciplined approach to making selections on the basis of relative values. The presumption is that all of the parties are engaged in bringing prices into line with economic values. Until this presumption is much more of a reality, our markets will not be performing efficiently their functions of pricing the cost of capital to different users of equity and of allocating it to the most productive areas through this process.

Over the years, tremendous progress has been made in the discipline of security analysis. When Benjamin Graham and David L. Dodd first offered their course under this title in Columbia University's Business School more than forty years ago, the quality of financial information was unbelievably bad and the analytical approach rudimentary. The past contributions of these distinguished pioneers, a growing number of other able academic minds, and many exceedingly capable practitioners have brought security analysis to a level of real proficiency. We have the capability to arrive at much more rational and stable valuations of corporate business. But both the securities industry and the investing community will have to exercise more disciplined control over their activities to prevent the periodic speculative binges to which the financial community seems to be addicted from distorting equity capital valuations and flows.

THE NEW ISSUE MARKET

Finally, as to my third observation, it is apparent that the securities industry is not, and has not been, adequately screening the new ventures coming to the public markets. The investment banking function includes, it seems to me, a careful appraisal of whether new and growing enterprises have established their viability sufficiently for them to qualify as a reasonable risk for public investors. All too often, when the "hot" new issue market is boiling, it appears that even the flimsiest ventures, lacking both capital and experience, can find distributors of their issues. All too often also, the major purpose of the public offering is to permit the organizers to realize a major fraction of their gains from the promotion, rather than simply to provide new capital to the firm.

Responsible firms decry some of these practices in the new issue market but exercise no visible leadership in checking them. Somehow the full disclosure requirements of the Securities Act of 1933 are expected to relieve the industry of expressing its expert opinion on whether or not a company is ready for public ownership. An industry which is committed to the concept of self-regulation simply cannot obtain public acceptance of this position.

It is much easier, of course, to voice this criticism than to suggest a feasible remedy. Because of the highly competitive nature of the underwriting business and the rewards for bringing a successful venture to the public market, it is asking too much of the individual firm to enforce standards on itself which other firms are free to ignore. For this reason, an industry agency may have to take part. The least that might be done is to investigate and publicize flagrant cases of using the public market to float totally untried and untested ventures. The announced intentions of the SEC to launch a study of the "hot" new issue market is the final and conclusive reason for the industry to do something on its own initiative.

SOME CONCLUDING THOUGHTS

If we were not anticipating a decade of capital scarcity, one might look tolerantly at these deficiencies on our securities markets' efficiency as allocators of equity capital. One might defensively point with pride to the fact that our capital markets are absolutely unique in their capacity to handle a huge volume of diverse transactions. One can also assemble persuasive evidence of progress on these and other fronts.

But such comforting thoughts and acceptance of the status quo are not responsive to the potential for real living standard improvements which many of us believe to be inherent in the attainment of greater precision, responsiveness, and reliability in the allocation of resources through the marketplace. Those who argue that we cannot do much better are those with only a half-hearted conviction that this process can work with real efficiency.

On the other hand, those who are determined to realize improvements recognize that all of the easy steps were taken long [ago]. I have suggested the application of efforts to materially strengthening the accountability of corporate managements, greatly improving the quality of pricing securities, and seriously policing the new issue market. None of these is a particularly easy or welcome assignment. Possibly my selections of these three objectives do not even reflect the correct priorities. Nevertheless, in the decade of the 1970's our impatient, insistent society will be looking to the securities markets to function more efficiently than ever before. These expectations require a response commensurate with what is at stake.

3. THE DEVELOPMENT OF FINANCIAL MANAGERS (SELECTED EXCERPTS)*

MARVIN SCHILLER†
E. STUART FILES††
JOHN S. FIELDEN†††
LAWRENCE H. WORTZEL††††

Today's alert financial executive is concerned about the future. This concern runs in three interrelated directions. First, he is concerned about his own performance and how he might increase his contribution and performance effectiveness. Second, he is concerned about the development of the financial function and the degree to which it can improve its services to the rest of the organization. And, finally, he is concerned about the perpetuation of the organization itself.

In preparing for the future, the financial executive is interested in gaining a better understanding of the type of men which have been, which are being, and which will be attracted into the financial function. He is concerned about the kinds of formal education these future managers have received prior to their entrance into corporate life and the kind of professional training and development they receive after entering their organization. He is keenly interested in determining whether some classes of industry offer greater opportunities for growth than others. Also, he is vitally concerned about the expectations that managers have of themselves and of their subordinates, knowing that the corporate climate these expectations produce will affect him as well as his successors. Further, he is concerned as to whether the entire financial function with which he has allied himself is moving in directions required by the realities of tomorrow's business world.

The modern financial executive realizes that the scientific revolution has already made a decided impact on the practice of management, and he knows that an ever-greater impact is going to be made in each of the years ahead. He wonders what effect the computer will have on the practice of financial management and what will be the reaction to the new quantitative tools which are promulgated by leading consulting firms and graduate schools of business. He wants to know if new types of formal and informal education will be required. Will different forms of management development programs be evermore necessary in this

* From *The Development of Financial Managers* (New York: Financial Executive Research Foundation, 1970), pp. 3, 67, 69, 127 and 131. Reprinted by permission.
† Vice President, Eastern Division, A. T. Kearney & Co., Inc.
†† Vice President and Secretary, A. T. Kearney & Co., Inc.
††† Dean, School of Business, University of Alabama.
†††† Professor of Marketing, Boston University.

process of evolution? In fact, will a new and more scientific management norm require different types of personalities, men with the flexibility necessary to cope effectively with the challenges and changes of the future? . . .

It should also be recognized, as has been reported by other research that the increased knowledge and skill of the financial executive in his company is not acquired in isolation. His growth is becoming more and more typical of the kind of growth and development occurring in other functional groups in the organization. He is becoming technically proficient as a financial executive, but this does not mean technically proficient as an accountant. The range of his skills, the breadth of his exposure, the sphere of his influence and the concentration of his effort go well beyond the normal boundaries of the finance-accounting department. In effect, the financial executive, as he rises to meet the challenges which will prove him successful, becomes company-oriented rather than finance-accounting oriented in his thinking. He becomes a generalist by being a broadened specialist. He builds greater understanding and acceptance of his staff function by the line and, in turn, plays a more critical role in coordinating the efforts of others. He becomes an analyzer of business problems and progress and as an interpreter of the meaning and solution to the company's ebb and flow in its industry. . . .

On the technical side information, technology and the computer will exert tremendous direct and indirect pressures on future financial executives. The financial executive will constantly face the challenge of, and must be involved in the development of, information systems by which data can be made available in a timely fashion and in a form which will fulfill managerial decision making requirements. Part of this challenge is the development of more practical analytical techniques by which this cascading flood of data can be analyzed and made more accurately predictive for management decisions outside the financial sphere. The feeling of most top financial executives interviewed was that these related demands will require the financial executive of the future, as a minimum, to be aware of the important uses of computers in technical and operations research areas and to assume leadership to bridge the growing gap between the applications that are feasible and the development of meaningful ways to exploit these capabilities.

The belief of most of the financial executives interviewed was that the successful financial executive of the future, like his present counterpart, must have adequate grounding in accounting and finance disciplines. Furthermore, it was apparent to the respondents that if a financial officer seeks broader opportunities to contribute to overall corporate direction and profits, he can do so from his present vantage point. He must, however, first of all execute the traditional responsibilities and functions of his position. True, some of the problems will be different (such as internationalization of business, increasing attempts by the government to regulate or limit profits, justification of mergers and acquisitions, etc.) but the professionally trained financial managers will adequately cope with these issues as they are merely extensions or outgrowths of similar problems presently confronting him.

It seems clear that in the future the financial executive will be involved more deeply in long-range planning, both strategic and tactical, which are logical extensions of budgeting. Such planning is, in a sense, a logical extension of budgeting, but because of the time span involved, forecasts and decisions must be made under conditions of greater uncertainty and greater risks must be assumed. In this area, there is a real need for special or increased knowledge of the newer analytical techniques, and how and where to use them in order to participate most effectively. This refers to the management sciences or quantitative analysis techniques, such as simulation, the development and use of mathematical models, linear programming, etc., which are finding increasing practical use as tools of management to improve decision making. . . .

. . . we believe (and the weight of opinion of top management executives supports this belief) that education for future successful financial executives must contain the necessary training in accounting, but more must also be added. There should also be a generous blending

---

COLLEGE PERFORMANCE

How good a predictor of success is the executive's performance in college? We found that the respondent's standing in his undergraduate class—and the honors he may have achieved in undergraduate school—*do* have significant bearing on success as a financial executive. Some 60 percent of the respondents with college degrees stated they finished college in the top quarter of their class.

More significance is given to college performance, however, when the college graduate respondents are divided into success categories. Then we see that the percentage claiming high performance ranges from 70 percent of the highly successful people to just 36 percent of the less successful executives.

The same holds true when we consider academic honors. The significant correlation between undergraduate honors and later success is shown by the fact that 54 percent of the highly successful respondents, versus just 28 percent of the less successful executives attained some honor during undergraduate school.

of the humanities, the other business functions, the quantitative sciences, economics, and the social and behavioral sciences. Furthermore, we doubt whether all this can be accomplished in four years; therefore, graduate education must be recommended. . . .

But we must recognize that colleges and graduate schools only have the man for from four to six years. He will spend forty-five years in industry. In this period of ever-increasing change, how can the university ever hope to prepare a man for a lifetime of work? Obviously, this is impossible. Hence, the challenge, like a torch, is passed from the university to the individual and his corporation. . . .

PART II.   CAPITAL BUDGETING

Capital budgeting, a critical area of financial management, has received considerable attention in recent years. Decisions concerning long-term capital expenditures are of paramount importance to the long-run welfare of the firm. These decisions involve large sums of money, and mistakes cannot be rectified easily. Efficient and effective capital expenditures require a comprehensive program readily understood by personnel at all levels of management.

Professor James Fremgen conducted a survey of two hundred and fifty business firms to determine the actual capital budgeting practices being utilized. He received one hundred and seventy-seven usable responses. The survey complements and adds realism to the usual topics covered by textbook material on capital budgeting. It included such topics as the methods actually being used in evaluating the profitability of proposed capital investments, analysis of mutually exclusive alternatives, capital rationing, risk analysis, and nonfinancial justification for making the investment. If more than one evaluation method was being used, the respondent was asked which method he deemed to be the most important.

Professor Fremgen expanded the questions to cover more than just the methods of financial analysis. He identifies two other areas: project definition and estimation of cash flows, and project implementation and review. These two additional areas add a new dimension to the usual textbook approach.

Professors Neuhauser and Viscione conducted a survey to determine the degree of use of various analytical techniques in the capital budgeting processes of very large firms. In addition to examining the degree of use, this study was designed to determine the reasons for the continued skepticism and indifference toward them. The results of the survey have important implications for both the practicing managers and the academicians.

The questionnaires were sent to the chief financial officers of the five hundred largest firms listed in *Fortune* and usable responses were received from one hundred and seventy-four companies. As might be expected, companies with larger capital budgets tended toward greater acceptance of the discounting approach, although they did not abandon the more traditional methods.

The interesting question raised is why the more advanced techniques strongly recommended by the better-known business schools have not been accepted by the practicing manager. The authors categorize the responses to this question into three basic types of objections upon which they elaborate. They conclude that managers can be faulted for not appreciating the value of these techniques as adjunct to rather than as a replacement for judgment and decision making. They believe that academicians can be criticized to some extent for treating capital investment decisions in a vacuum and not bringing the complexities of the business environment into the teaching process.

David B. Hertz explains how management is able to utilize computer simulation in examining the risk consequences of various investment policies for individual investments. He concludes that a good investment policy should include the determination of risk profiles for all investments, the use of a discounting measure (either discounted internal rate of return or an equivalent net present value) for assessing the merit of an investment proposal, the establishment of alternative screening rules for investment proposals, and the determination of risk boundaries for the alternative policies.

After reviewing the conventional means of dealing with uncertainty, he presents a discussion of a method called risk analysis. This method involves the identification of leverage factors which will influence key variables determining future costs and revenues. The method involves the development of uncertainty profiles for each key variable and the use of computer simulation. A detailed outline of a seven-step simulation and the results of a simulation are presented.

Professors Alexander A. Robichek and James C. Van Horne show how a simulation approach can be developed for incorporating the effects of abandonment into the information provided for the investment decision. Monte Carlo simulation, which is used in the article, is a technique to investigate the implications of uncertainty in a systematic manner.

The consideration of possible future abandonment is a dimension frequently omitted from capital-budgeting analysis. Abandonment value can be defined as the net disposal value of the project that would be available to the company in either cash or cash savings. This article examines the importance of abandonment value to capital budgeting, analyzes its effect on a project's expected return and risk, and proposes a framework for taking account of this neglected dimension.

What effect does the incorporation of abandonment value have on a capital budgeting decision? The authors show that a previous "no-invest" decision can be completely reversed when abandonment value is considered. They also show that such measures of risk as the variance, the standard deviation, and the semi-variance are actually more favorable when abandonment value is incorporated in the decision-making process. Significant abandonment value for a project may result in a higher expected net-present value or internal rate of return and lower expected risk than would be the case if the project had no abandonment value over its economic life. The appendix to the article describes the Simulation Model as used to analyze such decisions.

Professor Clark Hawkins and Richard Adams explore very recent developments of goal programming as it applies to capital budgeting. In their article the authors indicate how goal programming might aid the firm in more realistic approaches to decision analysis and point out areas such as probabilistic projections and benefit-cost programs which could be the basis for further study. They review the earlier works of some authors with linear programming and then refer to a model which has been developed that reorganizes the existence of multiple conflicting goals. This model was first introduced in the 1960's and is appropriately called goal programming. They set out to show that this more realistic model can be reconstructed for application to capital budgeting problems. The authors suggest that the introduction of goal programming into capital budgeting presents the possibility of extending goal planning into the public sector.

4. CAPITAL BUDGETING PRACTICES: A SURVEY*

For the past two decades, the literature of accounting, finance, and economics has dealt extensively with the subject of capital budgeting. Most of this literature has been prescriptive in nature. That is, it has advised the reader how to do his capital budgeting—what techniques and practices he should use. This emphasis is appropriate in a practice-oriented discipline, for the goal of the published literature should be to develop and improve practice. At the same time, however, it is also useful to observe the state of current practice. Such observations permit one to determine those areas of practice that conform to published recommendations and those that do not. In this article we will report the results of a survey of American business firms which was made to determine the capital budgeting methods that they are actually using.

METHODS OF FINANCIAL ANALYSIS

Before we discuss the details of the survey, a word about the more popular capital budgeting methods is in order. The majority of all published materials dealing with capital budgeting has focused primarily on the financial methods used by management to assess the profitability of an investment. There is general agreement that the superior methods are those that recognize the time value of money. The first three methods below are the most common ones.

Discounted Rate of Return

This is the true interest rate expected to be earned on an investment. It is that discount rate at which the present value of the cash receipts from an investment are just equal to the present value of the cash outlays for it. This measure is also known as the internal rate of return, the yield, and the DCF (discounted cash flows) method.

Net Present Value

This is a dollar amount, the difference between the present value of the cash receipts and the present value of the cash outlays for an investment. The discount rate used is normally the cost of capital or some other predetermined cutoff rate required for acceptable investments.

---

*From *Management Accounting* (May, 1973), pp. 19–25. Reprinted by permission.
†Professor of Accounting, Naval Postgraduate School, Monterey, California.

Present Value Index

This is a ratio, computed by dividing the present value of cash receipts by the present value of cash outlays. The discount rate is the same as that used in determining the net present value. Other terms sometimes used for this method are the profitability index and the discounted benefit/cost ratio.

Although any method of investment analysis that fails to recognize the time value of money is thereby deficient, there are two such methods that are frequently discussed in the literature and used in practice:

Simple Rate of Return

Computationally, this is similar to the return on investment in assets calculated from financial statements at the end of a year. It is the expected average annual net income from an investment divided by the initial outlay for that investment. It is sometimes referred to as the accounting or the financial statement method of computing rate of return.

Payback Period

This is the time required for the cumulative sum of the cash receipts from an investment just to equal the amount of the initial outlay. Colloquially, it is the time that it takes an investment to pay for itself. Although the payback period can be computed by using appropriately discounted cash flows, it usually is not.

At best, the simple rate of return is an approximation of the discounted rate of return. It is not a reliable substitute for the latter, however, and ought not be used. The payback period, also, is not a measure of investment profitability, and it should not be used by itself as a criterion for investment selection. If used in conjunction with one or more of the time-value methods, however, it may be a useful supplementary index of an investment's desirability. Other things being equal, a shorter payback period suggests less risk of loss of invested capital.

THE SURVEY

During the spring of 1971, a questionnaire containing 25 questions about capital budgeting practices was sent to financial executives of 250 business firms. One hundred and seventy-seven usable responses were received; this is a response ratio of almost 71 percent. The firms in the sample were selected randomly from the 1969 edition of Dun and Bradstreet's *Reference Book of Corporate Managements*. Questionnaires were sent to companies engaged in manufacturing, retailing, mining, transportation, land development, entertainment, and various other services as well as to public utilities and conglomerates. Only financial institutions, such as banks and insurance companies, were specifically excluded from the sample. The capital investment practices of these institutions may be so dominated by considerations peculiar to investments in loans and other securities as to inhibit useful comparisons with the practices of the firms surveyed.

The respondents were not asked to identify themselves or their firms. They were asked, however, to indicate the sizes of their firms' annual capital budgets. This measure of size was chosen in preference to the more familiar ones (sales volume, total assets, and number of employees) because it seemed likely to be most pertinent to capital budgeting practices. As a matter of fact, few significant relationships appeared between the size of the annual capital budget and the capital budgeting methods used.

METHODS IN ACTUAL USE

Respondents to the questionnaire were asked which of the five methods described above (or what other methods) they actually used in evaluating the profitability of a proposed capital investment. Their responses are summarized in Exhibit 4-1.

An inspection of Exhibit 4-1 shows that the most popularly used single method is the "Discounted rate of return," which recognizes the time value of money. However, next in order of popularity are the two methods that do not recognize this time value, "Payback period" and "Simple rate of return." Incidentally, only 76 percent of the firms used at least one of the three time-value methods.

Respondents who used analytical methods other than the five principal ones listed were asked to specify what they were. The "Other methods" reported are as follows:

1. Lifetime cost
2. Minimum life required to achieve a predetermined discounted rate of return

EXHIBIT 4-1
METHODS IN ACTUAL USE

Size of Annual Capital Budget	Discounted Rate of Return	Net Present Value	Present Value Index	Payback Period	Simple Rate of Return	Other Methods
Over $100 million	78%	34%	9%	72%	60%	14%
$50-$100 million	79%	21%	10%	62%	55%	3%
$10-$50 million	64%	14%	2%	68%	44%	11%
Under $10 million	67%	0%	5%	52%	33%	0%
No size given	67%	33%	0%	67%	0%	33%
All respondents	71%	20%	6%	67%	49%	10%

3. Rate of return on sales
4. Revenue required to cover average annual costs including depreciation and interest on the investment
5. Rate of return calculation required by the Federal Power Commission
6. Payback period based on discounted cash flows
7. Effect of the investment on earnings per share
8. MAPI formula
9. Necessity to maintain current operations or product lines
10. Requirements of new products
11. Future corporate needs
12. Safety
13. Management judgment

Although the question specified methods of financial analysis, the last five responses on this list are obviously nonfinancial criteria. Management judgment, of course, should be exercised in every decision. However, it is reasonable for management to want the type of information that can be obtained from using one or more of the analytical methods before making a judgment.

By adding the percentages in Exhibit 4-1 horizontally, we find that they add up to considerably more than 100 percent in every case. This reflects the fact that most of the respondents used two or more different methods for analyzing investment proposals. In this connection, the size of the annual capital budget did make a difference. Firms with larger capital budgets consistently used a larger variety of methods than those with smaller budgets.

If a respondent stated that his firm used more than one method of investment analysis, he was asked to indicate which was considered most important in the decision making process. Responses to this question are summarized in Exhibit 4-2.

This time, the percentages add up to less than 100 percent horizontally (except in the category of the firms with the smallest capital budgets). This is because all the respondents who use more than one method did not answer this particular question. It is possible that no single method is always considered to be most important.

A comparison of the percentages in Exhibit 4-2 with those in Exhibit 4-1 is also interesting. Although discounted rate of return is still the most popular method, the payback period has declined dramatically in frequency of mention. And, although 67 percent of all firms used it, only 14 percent considered it the primary indicator of an investment profitability. This is consistent with the notion that the payback period is not a valid index of investment profitability by itself, but it may be a useful supplementary tool.

EXHIBIT 4-2

MOST IMPORTANT METHOD

Size of Annual Capital Budget	Discounted Rate of Return	Net Present Value	Present Value Index	Payback Period	Simple Rate of Return	Other Methods
Over $100 million	34%	5%	0%	2%	31%	7%
$50-$100 million	38%	7%	3%	7%	14%	0%
$10-$50 million	39%	3%	0%	23%	18%	5%
Under $10 million	47%	0%	5%	24%	24%	0%
No size given	0%	0%	0%	33%	0%	33%
All respondents	38%	4%	1%	14%	22%	5%

ANALYSIS OF MUTUALLY EXCLUSIVE ALTERNATIVES

A potentially troublesome type of investment decision is one that requires the investor to choose between two or more mutually exclusive alternative projects. A familiar example is the choice among several different models of a machine when only one machine can be used. If each alternative involves the same initial capital investment, the financial dimensions of this choice are not unduly complex. If, however, different alternatives entail significantly different outlays, the choice may be complicated. If an alternative requiring a larger initial outlay is chosen, less capital may be available for other investments. There is general agreement in the literature that the choice among mutually exclusive alternatives should be based on an analysis of the incremental cash flows determined by subtracting the cash flows associated with one alternative from those related to another. If there are more than two alternatives, there will be more than one set of incremental cash flows, and each set will have to be compared with the others until the most advantageous alternative is identified.

The survey of current practice showed that this analysis of incremental cash flows is made by only 29 percent of the responding firms. Most of the respondents stated that, in choosing among mutually exclusive alternatives, they looked for that alternative with the best rating as determined by the index of financial attractiveness which they regularly used to evaluate investment proposals. Thus, referring to Exhibit 4-1, the alternatives with the highest discounted rate of return or with the shortest payback period might be selected. It is entirely possible, of course, that the same decision would be made as a consequence of using the latter approach as would be made after an analysis of incremental cash flows. Such a happy coincidence of outcomes cannot be relied upon, however. Analysis of incremental cash flows is still the best way of dealing with the problem.

MULTIPLE RATES OF RETURN

The discounted rate of return method suffers from a technical deficiency that may, in some cases, significantly impair its usefulness. Under certain conditions, this method may produce not one but two or more different rates of return. That is, there may be two or more discount rates at which the present value of the cash receipts is equal to the present value of the cash outlays for an investment. This result may occur when there is a mixed sequence of receipts and outlays in successive years over the life of the investment. For a simple investment there is an initial cash outlay followed by a series of net cash receipts in all successive periods. In a more complex case, however, there may be periods with net cash outlays interspersed with those having net receipts. It is in this latter situation that multiple rates of return may appear. In some cases, however, it may be possible to isolate just one economically meaningful rate of return; but one cannot always expect such a happy resolution of the problem.[1] It is obvious then, that the practical utility of the discounted rate of return as a criterion for investment decision making is affected by the frequency of occurrence of the multiple-rate problem.

In the survey questionnaire, respondents were asked two questions. First, how frequently did they actually encounter investments with mixed sequences of cash receipts and outlays (the condition necessary for multiple rates)? Second, if they used the discounted rate of return method, how frequently had they actually experienced investments with multiple rates of return? The answers to these two questions are summarized in Exhibit 4-3. The first column shows the percentages of firms in the entire group of respondents that encountered mixed sequences of receipts and outlays with four verbally defined degrees of frequency. The second column shows percentages of those respondents that stated they did use the discounted rate of return method and the frequency with which they encountered the multiple-rate problem. An examination of the data suggests that the multiple rate of return problem is not purely academic. The condition in which it may occur is encountered frequently by a significant minority of the firms. Moreover, among those firms using the discounted rate of return, the actual incidence of multiple rates is sufficient to warrant explicit attention to the problem. On the other hand, it would not appear that the problem is so prevalent as to invalidate any use of the discounted rate of return method in investment analysis.

---

[1]A more extensive discussion of the multiple-rate problem and of practical means of dealing with it may be found in G. David Quirin, *The Capital Expenditure Decision*, Richard D. Irwin, Inc., Homewood, Ill. 1967, pp. 49-57.

EXHIBIT 4-3

MIXED SEQUENCES AND MULTIPLE RATES

	Incidence of Mixed Sequences of Cash Flows	Incidence of Multiple Rates of Return
Never	3%	21%
Rarely	62%	52%
Fairly frequently	29%	13%
Very frequently	3%	2%
No response	3%	12%

RATE OF RETURN ON REINVESTMENT

Use of the time-value-of-money methods entails an implicit assumption that the cash receipts from the investment proposal under consideration will be reinvested and that a specific rate of return will be earned. That is, all cash receipts over the life of an investment will be reinvested at once, as earned, and will earn an assumed rate of return in each remaining period through the end of the original investment's life. In each case, the assumed reinvestment rate of return is the same discount rate used in the basic mechanics of the particular analytical technique. Thus, the discounted rate of return method implicitly assumes that cash receipts from the investment under study will be reinvested to yield the same rate of return as that realized on the original investment. The computations for both the net present value and the present value index implicitly assume that cash receipts will be reinvested to earn a rate of return equal to the cost of capital. These reinvestment rates are implicit in the mathematics of the three methods.[2] However, it should be pointed out that, if management believes that some other explicit reinvestment rate assumption is more appropriate, that assumption can be incorporated in the financial analysis of the investment.

Respondents to the survey were asked whether they made any explicit assumption about the rate of return to be earned on reinvestment of cash receipts. Twenty-nine percent of the firms indicated that they did. Most of these firms stated that they explicitly assumed that the reinvestment rate would be equal to either the rate of return on current investments or the current average cost of capital. In other words, most of the explicit assumptions seemed to accept the nature of the implicit assumptions. A few firms, however, attempted explicitly to estimate either a future rate of return or the future cost of capital and

---

[2]Gerald A. Pollack, "The Capital Budgeting Controversy: Present Value vs. Discounted Cash Flow Method," *NAA Bulletin*, November, 1961, pp. 11-16.

to use this as their assumed reinvestment rate on the current investments' cash receipts. The important thing here is that, even if these assumed future interest rates prove to be incorrect, they will have involved management in the very useful exercise of studying those factors that will determine future rates.

RISK AND UNCERTAINTY

In any decision-making situation, there is risk associated with whatever alternative may be chosen. The decision maker may expect a particular outcome from a particular course of action, but he knows that there is some probability that the actual outcome will be different. Moreover, there is inevitably some element of uncertainty surrounding any estimate of future quantities. For example, in capital budgeting, there will be uncertainty about estimates of future cash flows, about estimates of a project's economic life, and even about the firm's cost of capital. There is no way that risk and uncertainty can be eliminated from a decision problem, but they can be recognized explicitly in the analysis of that decision.

Sixty-seven percent of the firms responding to the survey questionnaire stated that they considered risk and uncertainty explicitly in the analysis of individual capital investment proposals. This was true somewhat more frequently in firms with larger annual capital budgets than in those with smaller budgets.

Exhibit 4-4 summarizes the methods used by the respondents to allow for risk and uncertainty in investment analyses. Percentages in this table are based on the number of firms that stated they did adjust for risk and uncertainty, not on the total number of firms in the survey. Many of the firms reported use of two or more methods of allowing for risk and uncertainty. Hence, the figures in Exhibit 4-4 add up to considerably more than 100 percent.

Among the "Other methods" mentioned were the following:

1. Sensitivity analysis of critical variables
2. Monte Carlo simulation

EXHIBIT 4-4
ADJUSTING FOR RISK AND UNCERTAINTY

Requirement of a higher-than-normal index or profitability	54%
Requirement of a shorter-than-normal payback period	40%
Adjustment of estimated cash flows by use of quantitative probability factors	32%
Purely subjective, nonquantitative adjustment	29%
Other methods	8%

3. Comparative analysis of results at high and low estimates of benefits
4. Analysis of project profitability over an arbitrarily assumed shorter life

The most popular methods of dealing with the problem appear to be to place more stringent requirements on the customary financial criteria for investments. For example, a relatively risky investment is expected to offer a higher rate of return, a higher present value index, or perhaps, a shorter payback period than a safer investment. There is some intuitive logic in this approach. Greater potential benefits should be the investor's compensation for taking greater risks. However, how much higher must the rate of return on a risky investment be? Is a single "risk premium" satisfactory, or must there be different premiums to reflect differing degrees of risk?

Perhaps the most significant deficiency of this logic is that it does not permit the investor to adjust directly for varying degrees of risk in the different cash flows projected for a single investment project. For example, management may be very confident of its estimate of the initial outlay for an investment and, perhaps, of certain subsequent outlays; but the greatest uncertainty may surround estimates of cash receipts in the future. This is sometimes taken into account by the use of probability factors to adjust the several different cash flows, and these factors do permit some flexibility. Of course, the problem of determining just what probability should be assigned to each possible value for each of the different cash flows still remains. Nevertheless, the effort to identify these probabilities is likely to be very helpful to management in refining its analysis of an investment and in reaching an ultimate decision.

NONFINANCIAL JUSTIFICATION OF INVESTMENTS

One might think that the appropriate decision rule is to make all investments that are determined to be financially profitable and to reject all others or, under conditions of capital rationing, to make the most profitable investments that are possible within the constraint of limited capital. Indeed, such a decision rule would be consistent with a purely economic view of the organization. However, there is substantial evidence that suggests that business firms respond also to noneconomic motivation and pursue noneconomic goals. Hence, the firms surveyed were asked whether they included investments that failed to meet established financial criteria in their approved capital budgets. Ninety-seven percent of the firms stated that they did approve capital investments that were apparently unprofitable but were justified on other grounds. Exhibit 4-5 details the nonfinancial justifications offered by

EXHIBIT 4-5

NONFINANCIAL CONSIDERATIONS

Safety of employees or the public	92%
Necessity of maintaining existing programs or product lines	79%
Employees' convenience or comfort	77%
Social concern or enhanced community relations	69%
Pollution control	10%
Legal requirements	7%
Unmeasurable long-term potential (e.g., in research and development programs)	5%
Contractual commitments	2%
Protection of property	1%

respondents for accepting investments that failed to meet profitability standards and the frequency with which those justifications were mentioned. The percentages in this table are based on the total number of firms in the survey.

An important observation should be made about these nonfinancial justifications. Just because an investment does not meet a test of profitability does not necessarily mean that it is, in fact, unprofitable. It may simply mean that the relevant profit potential cannot be assessed at the time the decision is made. For example, investments in pollution control equipment may forestall taxes or penalties on pollution or may prevent the forced closure of a profitable plant, but there may be no reasonable way of measuring such potential financial losses. Similarly, very costly investments in research projects may be approved in the expectation of future profits, but no attempt to measure those profits in advance may be made.

One very commonly mentioned nonfinancial justification is difficult to understand, however. It is the necessity to maintain existing product lines which ought to be supported by profit projections. Why would a firm wish to maintain a product line that is not expected to be profitable? (Remember, a true loss leader is really profitable if it does stimulate sales of other product lines.) And, if a product line is profitable, investments necessary to sustain it should be quite easily justified financially.

Finally, some readers may be surprised to learn that, in today's atmosphere of environmental concern, only 10 percent of the firms indicated that pollution control was regarded as suitable justification for a capital investment. Actually though, the true percentage may be higher than that, for some respondents may have included pollution control within the scope of social concern or safety of the public. On the other hand, some firms may have found that pollution control investments are actually profitable.[3]

---

[3]See, for example, "Dow Cleans up Pollution at No Net Cost," *Business Week*, January 1, 1972, pp. 32-35; and "Turning Pollution Control into an Asset," *Ibid.*, September 9, 1972, pp. 96-97.

CAPITAL RATIONING

One of the major objectives of the survey was to determine the incidence of and the causes for capital rationing and to observe the practices used by management in dealing with that condition. Capital rationing may be defined as a situation in which an organization does not have and cannot obtain enough capital to make all of the investments that are available to it. In other words, capital rationing requires the investor to reject investment projects that otherwise meet his financial or nonfinancial requirements for acceptance. This situation complicates the investment decision process, for the investor must not merely determine whether an investment is profitable, but he must also decide how profitable it is in relation to other investments.

Incidence of Capital Rationing

Respondents to the survey questionnaire were asked about their experiences with capital rationing. The questions sought to determine whether firms actually do encounter the problem, how regularly they do, and how tight the capital constraint is. Seventy-three percent of the business firms in the survey reported that they did experience capital rationing. While this suggests that capital rationing should be regarded as the general case, a significant minority of the firms apparently are free of this capital constraint. A majority, 64 percent, of those firms that did experience capital rationing stated that it was a restriction with which they had to contend every year. The other 36 percent encountered the problem only in certain years. Finally, 87 percent of the firms faced with capital rationing indicated that the capital limitation was not a single, fixed-dollar amount but was a somewhat inexact amount within a recognized range. This is not surprising. One would expect that the limit on the capital available to a firm at any given time is somewhat flexible. An absolutely fixed-dollar limitation would seem most consistent with a situation in which a firm's capital budget is determined by higher authority, as in a subsidiary where the budget allowance is fixed by the parent corporation. However, only 56 percent of the firms reporting a fixed-dollar capital limit stated that it was caused by a restriction imposed by higher management.

Causes of Capital Rationing

Capital rationing may be caused by conditions external to the firm, by internal factors, or by a combination of both. Indeed, certain possible causes of rationing actually reflect internal perceptions of external constraints (e.g., management's assessment of the capital markets). Exhibit 4-6 summarizes the causes of capital rationing reported in this

EXHIBIT 4-6

CAUSES OF CAPITAL RATIONING

Basically external causes:	
Limit on new debt imposed by some agreement with outside parties (e.g., a bond indenture)	41%
Limit imposed by higher authority outside the reporting organization (e.g., corporate management, when the respondent is a division or subsidiary)	36%
Lack of free access to capital markets for some other reason	6%
Basically internal causes:	
Limit on new borrowing imposed by management	67%
Management's desire to maintain a regular dividend policy and, thus, to restrict retained earnings available for new investment	29%
Management's goal of maintaining some specific earnings per share or price-earnings ratio and, thus, a policy of restricting issuance of additional shares of common stock	21%
Some other restriction on issuance of new shares of common stock (e.g., a desire to maintain close control of a corporation)	15%
Inadequate cash flow from operations to finance new investments	3%
Other causes	8%

survey. The percentages in the exhibit add up to much more than 100 percent, since most of the respondents reported more than one cause for their capital restrictions. Some of the "Other causes" mentioned were essentially variations on causes listed in the table. Others were not clear as to their meaning and cannot be interpreted further.

Clearly, the most prevalent cause of capital rationing is a limitation on borrowing, whether that limitation is imposed by management or by external market conditions. As a matter of fact, any distinction between internal and external restrictions on borrowing is questionable. Management, aware of the capital market's reactions to various levels of debt in a company, places apparently internal limitations on new borrowing because of perceived external conditions. Capital restrictions imposed by higher, outside management are most likely secondary causes of capital rationing. That is, corporate management limits the amount of funds available to subsidiaries or divisions because of other limitations faced at the corporate level. Nevertheless, it is top management's decision that is the effective constraint as far as the divisional managers are concerned.

Ranking of Investment Proposals

Capital rationing requires the investor to reject some of the investments that meet his usual criteria of profitability or of nonfinancial justification. Hence, all possible investments are, in effect, alternatives to one another. Consequently, management must find some reasonable means of comparing the various alternatives and of choosing the best ones. One common way of making this comparison is to rank all investments that meet the basic profitability standard in the order of their profitability. If investments are also approved on the basis of non-financial criteria, it would be useful if they could be ranked also in the order of their nonfinancial attractiveness. However, this latter ranking would be complicated by the lack of any standard unit of measure, and intermixing the two sets of rankings would be practically impossible except on a purely judgmental basis.

Sixty-five percent of the firms in the survey that did experience capital rationing stated that they ranked all investment opportunities in order of profitability. Not surprisingly, most of these respondents ranked projects according to one or more of the financial methods used earlier to determine whether or not investments were profitable. Only seven percent of the firms introduced a new financial criterion for purposes of this ranking. Once again, the discounted rate of return was the most popular index; it was used by 60 percent of the firms that ranked investments. Following in order of frequency of use were the payback period (46 percent of the firms), the simple rate of return (40 percent), the net present value (11 percent), other methods (seven percent), and the present value index (four percent). The most commonly mentioned "Other method" for ranking was the priority of the project. This, of course, is not a financial index at all, but a subjective assessment of relative importance.

Linear Programming

Many writers have suggested that the best method of selecting investments under the constraint of capital rationing is to use linear programming. In this method, the objective is to maximize the net present value of the total "package" of investments made, subject to the constraint of limited capital. However, only 19 percent of the firms experiencing capital rationing said that they had ever used linear programming in their investment analysis. And only 17 percent of this number said that they used it regularly. The remainder had used it only occasionally in special situations. Of course, linear programming is still a relatively new management tool. A similar survey 10 or 20 years from now might show substantially increased usage of this procedure.

THREE STAGES OF THE CAPITAL BUDGETING PROCESS

Most of the questions in this survey have focused on the methods of financial analysis and on the selection of investments to be undertaken Without doubt, these are very important considerations, but they are not all there is to capital budgeting. For purposes of this study, two other stages in the total capital budgeting process were defined. Essentially, these two additional stages include what must precede financial analysis and project selection and what ought to follow it. Thus, the total process was described as follows:

1. Project definition and estimation of cash flows
2. Financial analysis and project selection
3. Project implementation and review

Obviously, a project must be defined as a potential capital investment and the pertinent cash flows must be estimated before any financial analysis or decision making can occur. Similarly, once a project has been approved, it must be implemented and should subsequently be reviewed to determine whether the projected benefits have actually been achieved. Subsequent reviews, or post-completion audits, at the very least should improve future investment decision making. More immediately, such reviews may lead to the reinforcement of successful projects and the salvaging of failing projects.

Survey respondents were asked to consider the three stages of capital budgeting outlined above and to indicate which one they believed was most critical to the success of an investment and which one was the most difficult to accomplish. Their responses are summarized in Exhibit 4-7. Percentages in this exhibit add up to slightly more than 100 percent because a few respondents felt that two or, in one case, all three stages were equally critical or difficult. What is most striking about these answers is that the phase of capital budgeting that receives most attention in the literature is regarded as neither most critical nor most difficult. Actually, these results should not be too surprising. If project definition and cash flow estimation is not done well, subsequent financial analysis will be largely meaningless and decision making will be haphazard.

Exhibit 4-7
The Most Critical and Difficult Stages

	Most Critical	Most Difficult
Project definition and estimation of cash flows	51%	44%
Financial analysis and project selection	27%	12%
Project implementation and review	23%	44%
No response	2%	1%

CONCLUSION

One conclusion that might be drawn from this survey is that the literature might better serve practice if it devoted more attention to the first and third stages of capital budgeting. As these two stages are less structured than the second, it would be more difficult to develop general theoretical frameworks for them. Nevertheless, they are inescapable parts of the total capital budgeting process. They are real management problems and must be faced. How well management copes with these problems and how well they are solved may determine how successful the capital investment program will be.

5. HOW MANAGERS FEEL ABOUT ADVANCED CAPITAL BUDGETING METHODS*

JOHN J. NEUHAUSER†
and JERRY A. VISCIONE††

The vitality of a company depends to a great extent on its ability to renew itself through capital expenditures. Because these investments in new plants and machinery and other improvements involve some of the largest financial commitments a firm will make, the measurements that management applies to evaluating them are extremely important. If these measurements are inadequate, a company risks the possibility of spending vast amounts on projects that return too little and too late on the investment.

Since the 1950s, many academicians in business schools have been trying to tell practicing managers that the most common techniques applied to capital investment evaluations are indeed inadequate. They have proposed alternative methods that promise sounder capital investment decisions. But much to their bewilderment, practicing managers have remained largely indifferent to these new approaches.

Studies conducted in the early 1960s indicated that management was adopting these advanced evaluation techniques very slowly. Perhaps because of the rise of operations research and the attention that this new discipline has given to capital budgeting, later surveys found an increase in the use of these techniques; but their acceptance by the world of business is still far from widespread.

To find out why, we conducted our own study recently to investigate the use of various analytic techniques in the capital budgeting processes of large, well-established firms. Besides examining degree of use, our study focused on high-level executives' appraisals of these techniques in an effort to uncover the reasons for the continued skepticism and indifference towards them.

The results of our research hold important lessons both for academicians and for practicing managers. Before describing them, however, let us briefly define some of the old and new capital budgeting evaluation techniques that we are talking about.

Two of the most traditional approaches are the *payback* method and the *average rate of return*. The payback method measures the time required for the cash income from a project to return the initial investment.

° From *Management Review* (November, 1973), pp. 16-22. © 1973 by AMACON, a division of American Management Associations. Reprinted by permission.
† Chairman, Computer Science Department, Boston College.
†† Associate Professor of Finance, Graduate School of Business, Boston College.

The average rate of return is the ratio of the average net income after taxes promised by a project to its average book value.

Academicians have criticized these methods because they do not consider both the magnitude and the timing of cash returns. A number of techniques were developed that overcame these deficiencies, two of the most important being the *net present value* method and the *internal rate of return.*

Under the net present value method, the firm discounts the expected cash income from a project by its hurdle rate, which is the minimum acceptable rate of return that all company projects must meet. (The hurdle rate that should be used in making capital budget decisions is a weighted average cost of capital, which is a rate of return that will leave unchanged the market value of the firm's common stock.) The net present value is equal to the present value of the cash income minus either the cost of the project or—if the investment is spread out over time—the present value of the cash outflows. If the net present value is more than the cost, then the project is acceptable. [Editor's Note: Sentence should read, "If the net present value is zero or positive, then the project is acceptable."] The internal rate of return method equates the present value of the cash income from a project to its cost—or the present value of that cost if the investment is spread out over time. If the return is greater than the firm's hurdle rate, the project is acceptable.

Our study investigated whether the use of specific investment analysis methods was related to the size of a firm's annual capital budget and whether such methods become more applicable as investments take on a longer run or a more strategic nature. The techniques investigated involved those measuring return on investment, those based on hurdle rates, those dealing with explicit measures of risk, and certain operations research models. In addition, an open-ended question was included in the questionnaire as to why theoretical developments were being accepted so slowly. We sent our questionnaires to the chief financial officers of the 500 largest industrial firms listed in *Fortune* and received usable responses from 174 companies, about 35 percent of the sample.

ACCEPTANCE OF NEW TECHNIQUES

Responses concerning the degree of use of discounting techniques such as net present value and internal rate of return showed that firms have now generally accepted the appropriateness of such methods. Companies with larger capital budgets seem to show greater acceptance of discounting than those with smaller budgets, no matter how the investment might be classified. For instance, approximately 85 percent of the corporations with annual capital budgets over $100 million employed internal rate of return in all but their routine investments. Only

60 percent of the firms with capital budgets under $25 million used internal rate of return for the same type of investment.

While the firms with the larger capital budgets did show greater acceptance of the newer techniques, they did not abandon the more traditional methods. These latter methods were used just as heavily for strategic decisions as for everyday replacement decisions. This is not surprising when one considers that these older methods are generally easy to apply, especially when data have already been generated for use in the more advanced approaches. The maintenance of these older methods provides a natural link to older evaluations, and there is reason to believe that managers themselves are much more comfortable with the conclusions reached if they can also see these more familiar evaluation schemes.

We also inquired about the type of hurdle rate employed to justify a particular capital investment decision. Many executives stated that they did not rely on a fixed required rate because investments being considered served different purposes and corporate needs. Only a few respondents found that an industry average or the cost of the financial source of the investment was an adequate hurdle rate. For most corporations, past experience coupled with a weighted average cost of capital seemed the prevalent method employed. The larger firms, we found, were heavier users of the weighted-average approach.

Our survey found that only a few firms have procedures for incorporating risk into a decision process. But when firms do employ risk assessment techniques, they tend to use the entire spectrum of possible methods. It seems plausible that once managers have been convinced of the feasibility and effectiveness of such techniques for producing better decisions, they are quite willing to accept a wide range of usage.

Along the same line, we investigated the acceptance of a sample of operations research techniques, including linear programming (a mathematical method of allocating resources subject to certain monetary, supply, and other constraints), critical path analysis (a means of determining the sequence of activities critical to completion of a project on schedule), and simulation (the construction of a mathematical model of a process or even an entire firm expressed as a series of relationships on a computer). While some firms noted that they were just beginning to employ operations research techniques, some of these techniques were used quite heavily in the larger firms. For instance, 63 percent of the larger firms employ simulation, and 49 percent use linear programming. In the smaller firms, these same techniques, respectively, are used by 19 percent and 5 percent of the organizations.

Much of this concentration in the larger corporations may be explained by the increased likelihood of these firms to have suitable problems and large numbers of staff specialists to handle them.

WHY AREN'T THE TECHNIQUES USED MORE?

While these facts do indicate a growing use of advanced techniques, they do not explain why their nonacceptance is still substantial. For some time, academicians, especially at the better-known universities, have been telling their students that these analytic techniques are *sine qua non* for a modern manager. Obviously, practicing managers do not agree. Many firms ignore operations research and still succeed even in capital budgeting, which has received so much attention from OR people. We felt it important to ascertain why managers were not using these more advanced methods, so we included the following question in our survey:

"Many managers seem to reject the use of quantitative capital budgeting techniques, or, at least, they do not place great reliance on the output produced by such techniques. In your opinion, what is the basis for such rejection?"

Approximately 80 percent of the respondents answered this question. Although there was no notable difference in type of response among different-sized firms, it was interesting to find that the corporations that most heavily relied on these techniques provided the most telling criticism. It is difficult to summarize and categorize the many comments that were made, but we concluded that there were three basic types of objections:

1. The most common criticism was that much of the required data are approximate and inevitably deal with future uncertainties; yet the output of sophisticated methods, which is often computer-generated, gives an illusion of exactness down to the "nth" decimal point. The old aphorism, "garbage in, garbage out," certainly is true, but as executives become more comfortable in dealing with outputs from these models, we think they will be less concerned with the apparent over-emphasis on exactness and more concerned with the underlying assumptions.

2. Another objection was that, because these techniques emphasize data without concern for a management "feel" for the situation, they often seem to downgrade the human element in decision making. Managers seemed concerned that if younger executives became too dependent on decisions generated by mathematical models, they would neglect vital elements of experience, opinion, and other less quantitative but certainly important decision aids.

3. Many respondents stated that no one has proved that the use of the recommended procedures will improve performance. This is a telling criticism addressed to academicians, because if these techniques themselves are not deemed cost-effective, we cannot expect managers to employ them just because they are the "state of the art."

The statements of two respondents are typical of the first objection. A food-packing company executive commented:

> "The quantifications are based on estimates. If the estimates are wrong, so will be the results. The quantification leaves one with a false sense of precision since the number can be extended to "x" number of decimal points. When results are disappointing because of false assumptions or estimates the executive feels betrayed. Logically, he knows quantification is beneficial, but subliminally he is disappointed. He questions if the program is worth the effort."

An executive of a metal processing company has this to say:

> "If there is a weakness in exotic evaluation systems, it is probably the fallacy that sophisticated mathematics can convert approximate data into highly accurate information. We have seen two-digit data manufactured into answers with five 'significant' figures."

A large number of respondents apparently believe that these procedures tend to ignore judgment and experience, which in their view are much more important than a quantitative analysis. They sincerely doubt that their subordinates will develop properly if they become accustomed to "mechanical" approaches to decision making. The priority they give to the human element was clearly expressed by the following response from a chief executive of a very large, diversified manufacturing firm:

> "Many capital investment decisions hinge on the personal enthusiasm for the project as expressed by the initiator and his associates and by the effectiveness in the way the project is presented to various approval levels. To the extent that this is wholly applicable, quantitative techniques may be either unnecessary or only supportive. Projects implemented via the 'enthusiasm route' have greater likelihood of success than those with equal quantitative evaluation but little or no support."

The executives were skeptical of the benefits to be derived from switching to the more sophisticated techniques, and they questioned the value of these techniques in terms of improving profit performance. The following statement from an executive of a large chemical corporation was typical of this point of view:

> "Perhaps the basis for this rejection is that the academicians have not presented convincing evidence to managers illustrating that the use of these quantitative techniques will improve their success in achieving their profitability objectives. The literature usually presents these techniques from a theoretically based argument, using abstract and over-simplified situations. These articles attempt to appeal to the manager's intellect rather than appealing to his mission; they are not really results oriented. Managers need to be shown with specific, pragmatic examples in a real business environment how these techniques will improve their performance."

One respondent (who obviously did not have a high regard for academicians) felt that the very fact some techniques were not developed in industry precluded their being useful:

> "Academicians are full of prune juice. I never met one who could run a candy store. If we use 'academic techniques,' it means (1) we devised them and proved them, and then the academics learned from us, or (2) we are wasting our time."

The results of this study hold important lessons for both operating managers and business schools. Managers can be faulted for not appreciating the true value of advanced capital budgeting techniques as an adjunct to, rather than a replacement for, judgment and decision making. Top management should recognize that these techniques require specialized staffs and a certain managerial orientation, both of which take time to develop. If managers are uncomfortable with these techniques because they do not understand them, then the burden is on them to attempt to develop the necessary understanding.

Academicians can be criticized to some extent for treating capital investment decisions in a vacuum and ignoring the complexities of the business environment. But more importantly, they can be castigated for ignoring the real needs expressed by managers.

It is clear that a more open and lively exchange is needed between the theoreticians and the practitioners. An exchange of viewpoints in the journals that serve each side of the profession could certainly serve this end better than the present situation where academic journals are strictly academic and business periodicals strictly business. Another approach might be for both business schools and managements to promote internships whereby academicians could take leave from their schools every four years or so to serve as line managers. Also, the schools could expand their practice of having operating managers serve on their faculties.

At present, both sides are talking to themselves rather than each other, and, like all people who talk to themselves, they are finding the conversation too agreeable for their own good. Such conversations do little to bridge a gulf.

6. INVESTMENT POLICIES THAT PAY OFF*

DAVID B. HERTZ †

In the next 12 months, U.S. businessmen, acting for the most part on the basis of painstaking staff analyses, will commit an estimated $65 billion to promising new capital investment projects. Two or three years later, when the long-term financial results of those investments are beginning to take shape, a good many of these same businessmen will be suffering the pangs of the big loser at Las Vegas. For, despite all the high-priced staff time and the board-level soul-searching that go into them, most capital investment decisions remain an incongruous blend of the slide rule and the roulette wheel. Consider some recent evidence:

The president of a big international corporation told me recently, "I can't understand why our investment policy hasn't worked the way we expected." Some years ago, he explained, the executive committee had decided that every capital investment, to be acceptable, would have to show an estimated before-tax average annual return on capital of 20 percent. The rule had been scrupulously followed; yet actual results had averaged 14 percent. "And we've got some of the best analysts in the business," added the frustrated president.

In another large and sophisticated company engaged in diversified manufacturing operations, barely half of the new investments during the past ten years are now expected to reach the break-even point, and less than half of those will reach or exceed their predicted return on investment. (On the other hand, some of the winners will be much larger than anticipated.)

The executive committee of a major chemical company is facing a real dilemma. It currently requires each proposed capital project to show an expected return of at least 12 percent after taxes (16 percent for high-risk investments). Applying this policy, the executive committee has not turned down a single capital investment proposal for the past two years. Results from recent investments, however, have been alarmingly uneven. To provide a better screen for future proposals and hopefully to improve investment results, a new policy requiring a three-year payback period plus a discounted cash flow return of 8 percent has been recommended to the committee. The members of the committee do not know what to do.

Capital investment decisions, it would seem, are still more art than science—and often more gamble than art. The reasons, moreover, are fairly obvious.

Any investment decision is (or should be) concerned with a choice among the available alternatives, and it is always subject to an unknown

*Reprinted from *The Harvard Business Review* (January-February, 1968) pp. 96-108: © 1968 by the President and Fellows of Harvard College; all rights reserved.

†Director, McKinsey and Company.

future environment. Actual future costs, markets, and prices will inevitably differ from any single set of assumptions used as a framework for weighing proposals. Moreover, a variety of criteria—payback, average annual return, net present value, internal ROI—may be used as yardsticks for proposals. And, despite much theoretical discussion, it has been hard for management to guess what difference, if any, the choice of a particular yardstick would make in actual long-term dollars-and-cents results. In short, lacking any way to test out the ultimate financial impact of a given investment policy, management literally has had no way of knowing whether it might have done better.

Research results recently obtained by McKinsey & Company through analysis and computer simulation of the investment process indicate that there is a practical way for most companies to make sure that the policies they do choose have the greatest chance of meeting their objectives. Specifically, management can answer these questions with confidence:

Historically, has our investment policy given us the highest possible return, consistent with the risks we have accepted?

How much risk have we been accepting in our investment decisions? Is this consistent with the risks that top management really wants to accept?

Have we been using the best criteria for investment selection, considering long-term corporate objectives? Have we been taking adequate account of uncertainty?

Given the investment alternatives that are available to us and the risks we are willing to accept, what *investment policy* will maximize the earnings-per-share performance of our investments over the long run?

To understand how these questions can be answered and to clarify the methods and results of our research, it will be useful to compare some current approaches to risk and then to explore the concept of an effective investment policy.

RISK AND THE FUTURE

The exact course of future events is unknown when investment choices are made, and uncertainty creates risk. There are two conventional ways of dealing with risk and uncertainty and one less conventional method that is gaining acceptance.

Best-guess Estimates

A simple, widely used conventional approach is to express one's assumptions about the key variables affecting future costs, revenues, and investment requirements in terms of single-point estimates based on the best information available to management at the time the forecast is made. The calculated outcome of the investment, based on these "best guesses," is judged acceptable if it exceeds a specified criterion of return or payback. If the project is considered particularly risky, the hurdle may be raised—in effect, requiring a *risk premium*, an idea carried over from the early days of insurance.

Exhibit 6-1 shows how difficult it is to determine an acceptable risk premium, even in a simple case. Using very reasonable ranges for each of the variables involved (e.g., a best guess of 200,000 units for sales volume, with a range from 175,000 to 225,000 units), it demonstrates that the outcome, in terms of average return on investment, may vary anywhere from 0 percent to 56.5 percent. Thus, as Exhibit 6-1 demonstrates, this approach has a fatal weakness: if the actual outcome for any variable is significantly different from the estimate, the actual results of the investment may be *very* much different from those projected; simply raising the hurdle may not help much.

Exhibit 6-1
Drawbacks of Single-point Estimates

$$\text{ROI} = \frac{(\text{Price} \times \text{Unit sales}) - (\text{Costs})}{(\text{Investment})}$$

Best-guess estimates: Likely ranges:
Price = \$5.00   Price = \$5.00 to \$5.50
Costs = \$800,000   Costs = \$700,000 to \$875,000
ROI = 20%   Sales = 175,000 to 225,000 units
Sales = 200,000 units   Investment = \$950,000 to \$1,100,000
Investment = \$1,000,000

Worst case: $\dfrac{5.0 \times 175,000 - 875,000}{1,100,000} = \dfrac{0}{1,100,000} = $ **0% ROI**

Best case: $\dfrac{5.5 \times 225,000 - 700,000}{950,000} = $ **56.5% ROI**

In an attempt to overcome this weakness, many managements follow the practice of supplementing their best-guess estimates with other values for each variable, e.g., a high (optimistic) and a low (pessimistic) value. By permuting the values for each variable in repeated calculations, it is then possible to see what variations might occur if the best guesses are not all on target—as, in fact, they are highly unlikely to be.

With no information as to the *likelihood* of a given outcome, however, the decision maker has not added much to his assessment of the uncertainty. He has a better idea of what he may be letting the company in for, but he has little real information about what he ought to *expect*. To be sure, managements can and do try out various investment criteria, e.g., payback period, ROI, and net present value, to see whether each seems to yield good results under varying conditions. But they have not really been able to predict the ultimate financial results of using particular criteria.

Forced Fit Forecasts

The second conventional way around the difficulties of an unknown future—a way that seems to have special appeal to marketing-oriented companies—is to acknowledge freely all the uncertainties surrounding the estimated outcome of a new investment and then to wave them away on the grounds that the actual outcome can be forced to fit the estimate. For example, if sales fall short of target, various measures—ranging from heavier advertising to a shake-up of the sales force—can be applied to get the desired results. And since the precise circumstances in which these tactics might be applied cannot be known in advance, there is no point in worrying until the time comes; "something will always turn up."

Of course, this micawberish view completely misses the point. If one can be certain of achieving a particular set of results, the uncertainty disappears and so, in large measure, does the problem of investment policy. If one cannot, the uncertainty and the problem remain. The striking proportion of marketing failures among new products (estimates range from 30 percent to 80 percent, depending on definitions) belies the optimism of the micawbers.

Risk-based Profiles

A third method of dealing with uncertainty, which is less conventional but more sophisticated, has recently been gaining adherents. Some years ago I suggested that the risks inherent in an investment could be directly assessed through computer simulation.[1] In this method, called risk analysis, the first step is to identify the leverage factors that will influence the key variables determining future costs and revenues. For example, capacity will influence sales volume; timing of market entry will influence price; and so forth. The next step is to weigh all of the available information—e.g., historical trends, growth of markets, likely price changes—about each of these leverage factors and then, from this information, to develop the *uncertainty profile* for each key variable.

Estimates of revenues from a proposed new plant, for example, might indicate that there is a two-thirds chance of their falling within ± $40,000 of an *expected*—or average over the long run—$250,000 a year, that there is only one chance in ten of their falling below $180,000, but that there is also one chance in ten that they will exceed $350,000. These estimates are used to define a probability distribution curve for future revenues, which is called the uncertainty profile. These profiles for the elements that enter into an investment project are sometimes determined from historical or other objective data, but they are more likely to be subjective estimates by those most familiar with the various parts of the overall proposal.

Gathering and analyzing the data needed to construct such uncertainty profiles may pose difficult communications problems, it should be noted.

---

[1] See my article "Risk Analysis in Capital Investment," *Harvard Business Review* (January-February, 1964), p. 95.

EXHIBIT 6-2
EXAMPLE OF RISK-ANALYSIS SIMULATION

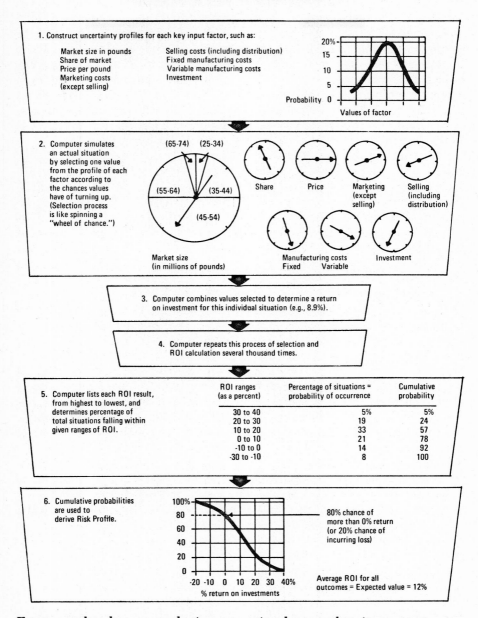

For example, does a marketing executive know what it means to say, "Product A has at least a 90 percent chance of achieving a 15 percent return on investment five years out"? Can he learn to think in these terms? Solving such communications problems is part of the process of developing a rational and effective investment policy. It is not, however, the issue addressed in this article.

Once an "uncertainty profile" has been established for each key investment project variable, we can repeatedly sample from the distributions of these variables shown in their uncertainty profiles. Using a computer, we calculate the financial outcome of the combined variables each time we sample and thus simulate the range of probable outcomes from the proposed investment in terms of the particular investment criterion to be used or tested. From the results of these simulations, a probability distribution or *risk profile* of the criterion can be built up.

Exhibit 6-2 shows the steps employed in simulating the possible outcomes of a given investment and in determining the risk profile. Such profiles can be developed for any criterion that management may wish to use. Exhibit 6-3 shows the payback, average ROI, and discounted ROI profiles of a hypothetical investment.

Of two investments, one is clearly better than the other if it offers a greater probability of achieving any given level of return. In this situation risk analysis permits management to distinguish without question among more and less desirable investments. For example, in Part I of Exhibit

EXHIBIT 6-3
RISK-ANALYSIS RESULTS USING DIFFERENT CRITERIA

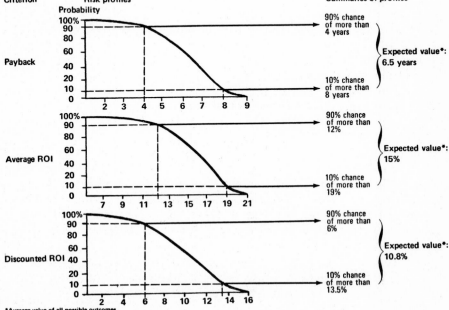

*Average value of all possible outcomes.

6-4, we see that Investment A is a better bet than Investment B at all values of return—that is, it *dominates* Investment B.

But one investment alternative is *not* always dominant. Consider the case of Investments X and Y in Part 2 of Exhibit 6-4. Here, Investment X is more likely than Investment Y to attain at least a 10 percent return on investment but less likely to bring in a 40 percent return. In cases of this kind—and they are numerous—the questions of which investment to select and how to go about establishing a policy to guide the choice have hitherto gone unanswered.

EXHIBIT 6-4
EXAMPLES OF BEST-CHOICE INVESTMENT ALTERNATIVES

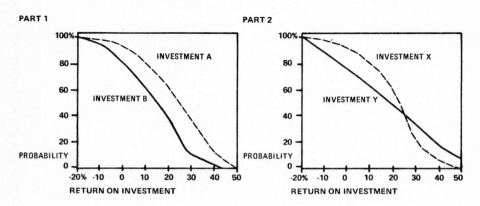

To be sure, in using risk profiles management is availing itself of all, not just part, of the quantitative information that can be put together on the investment possibilities. And more information in the hands of management should mean better decisions. But the question of how to use this information remains. Before it can be answered, we need a clear conception of the nature and function of an investment policy.

NATURE OF POLICY

Any investment policy, if it is to guide management's choices among available investment alternatives, must embody two components: (1) *one or more criteria* by which to measure the relative economic attributes of investment alternatives, and (2) *decision rules,* which may or may not make use of risk analysis or otherwise seek to take uncertainty into account, for selecting "acceptable" investments.

The criteria have been the subject of much analysis and discussion. They include: payback period, which is simply the number of years required for the investment to return its costs; average annual percent return on average funds employed; net present value measures; and internal rates of return, calculated on a discounted cash-flow basis.[2] On the other hand, the rules for making choices, particularly under uncertainty, have been largely left up in the air.[3] Of course, no preestablished policy can take into account all the considerations—human, organizational, strategic, and financial—that typically enter into a major capital investment decision. In this article, however, I am concerned strictly with the question of financial policy, which does lend itself to rigorous formulation.

Dual Role

A consistent and adequate investment policy has a double function. In the short run, it should indicate which investments should be chosen to achieve the financial objectives of the corporation. In the long run, it should serve as a basis for identifying or developing investment alternatives that are likely to match the policies selected. In other words, it serves as a basis for both (a) *acting on* and (b) *communicating about* investment alternatives.

Screening proposals. In the first instance, an investment policy may be regarded as a screen which will pass certain investment proposals and reject others. The screen may be coarse or fine, tight or loose, high risk or low risk, depending on management's knowing or unknowing choice. Through the screen will pass the acceptable investment proposals that will form management's investment set.

Once it is understood that a risk profile attaches, willy-nilly, to all investments and that this profile varies with the criteria chosen even though based on the same estimates of underlying real-world phenomena, it becomes clear that a policy with a determinate, or single-point-based, decision-rule component is a very coarse screen indeed, if it can be called a screen at all. In any case, as we shall see, such a determinate policy is ineffective; it will not guide management to making the best use of its investment funds, no matter what the company's financial objectives may be.

Risk-based policies, on the other hand, may specify how management would prefer to trade off the chances of low return against the chances of high return. For example, would it prefer a virtual certainty of no loss coupled with a virtual ceiling on gains over 20 percent after taxes, or would it accept a one-in-ten chance of significant loss for the sake of a one-in-ten chance of very high gain?

Exhibit 6-5 shows how one specific policy may be defined by the criterion to be used and the rules to be followed in screening investments in

---

[2]For a comprehensive discussion of these measures and their relative merits, see Harold Bierman, Jr. and Seymour Smidt, *The Capital Budgeting Decision* (New York: The Macmillan Company, 1966).

[3]An interesting and provocative discussion of such rules will be found in R. M. Adelson, "Criteria for Capital Investment: An Approach Through Decision Theory," *Operational Research Quarterly*, Vol. 16, No. 1; Adelson approaches the problems suggested in this article and provides, along with a useful list of references, an excellent analytical discussion of the difficulties in presently used methods.

terms of their risk profiles. These rules, which make explicit management's entrepreneurial or risk-taking attitudes, do allow consistent investment choices.[4] The methods described in this article assume that uncertainty—that is, the spread of distribution of potential returns around the expected value, or average of all outcomes—is a useful measure of risk. It is generally accepted that the further the return might exceed the expected value, the further it could also fall short, and lucky indeed is the company to which this principle does not apply.

EXHIBIT 6-5
EXAMPLE OF RISK-BASED INVESTMENT POLICY

1. Criterion to be used as a measure of investment worth: Before-tax return on investment, on a discounted cash flow basis
2. Rules to be used to screen investments based on risk profiles of proposed projects:
   Accept proposals that have—
   a. Expected value (average of all outcomes) of 5% or greater
   b. One chance in ten that the ROI will exceed 25%
   c. Nine chances in ten that the ROI will exceed 0%

Communicating alternatives. In the second instance, an investment policy can be a powerful communications tool. It enables top management to make known in advance to those responsible for developing investment proposals what sort of projects the company seeks. The object is to control the selection and development of alternatives so that they reflect the gains the company wants to make and the risks it is willing to undergo to achieve them.

In theory, of course, this function could be served by policy statements such as, "All investments must have an estimated average return on capital employed at 12 percent or more after taxes." But, on the practical level, the complexity of most present-day investment projects and the multitude of future variables to which they are subject rob such statements of most of their usefulness. This is why top management today, confronted with requests for capital, so often finds that the only significant response it can make is to approve the results of all the analyses that have previously taken place at divisional and staff levels.

With a risk-based policy, using one or more criteria and such rules as shown in Exhibit 6-5, management still has no guarantee that all or any of the available investments will pass through the screen. But it does have a better, more specific means for discriminating among proposed investments. And it also has a tool for testing out its own procedures for developing investment proposals and for checking out alternative policies. To analyze its own past investments and requests for capital, a company can estimate the risk profiles of these past investments and determine (a) whether it has been consistent in its past selections and (b) what changes in the mix selected would be indicated by different policy choices.

---

[4]See Ralph O. Swalm, "Utility Theory—Insights Into Risk Taking," *Harvard Business Review* (November-December, 1966), p. 123.

This analysis, however, still will not indicate what is the best overall investment policy, that is, what impact the choice of a particular criterion, such as net present value, payback, or return on investment, has on the likely outcome of specific real-world variables, such as costs and revenues, or what differences there are (again, in terms of real-world financial results) between high-risk and low-risk screens. In this connection I think it is important to note that the criteria are mathematically derived in fairly complicated ways from real-world events, such as sales, price changes, equipment installations, and so on. Since the uncertainty profiles of the events must be used to determine the final risk profile of the criterion, simulation methods are required.

EFFICIENCY CONCEPT

Most managements would like to have investment policies that both maximize financial results over the long run and minimize uncertainty or risk. Seeking additional returns, however, normally entails accepting additional uncertainty, that is, risk. If two policies produce the same average result, e.g., the same average earnings per share over a 5-year period, the one that involves less "variability" (or uncertainty as to the outcome), for the same yield is a more desirable or "efficient" policy. Conversely, of two policies entailing the same variability, the one producing the higher expected return ("expected" meaning the average of all outcomes) is obviously the better policy. Variability is best measured in terms of the probability distribution of the values within which the actual results are likely to fall.

Standard Deviation

The spread or variability of risk profile can be measured by the size of the standard deviation, which represents the spread around the expected value of the criterion encompassing two thirds of all the actual outcomes. Thus, if one can simulate the financial results of investments selected on the basis of a particular policy, the expected return, along with the standard deviation of the financial results obtained with that policy, will indicate the "efficiency" of the investment project set selected under that policy. (With this simulation, the distributions of the uncertainty profiles of revenues, costs, and investments in a specific year are combined. These combinations are linear, and we can expect the results to be normally distributed.)

The expected return and the standard deviation can be plotted on a graph to show the effectiveness of any policy, and a line can then be drawn through the points of greatest yield for a given standard deviation. This line is called the *efficiency frontier* because it represents the best return management can get for a given variance, unless, of course, management either (a) finds a policy that will yield a greater return on investment for no more variance or (b) develops investment proposals with different uncer-

Exhibit 6-6
Comparing Investment Policies

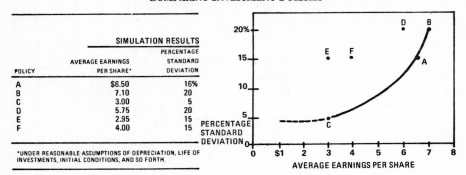

POLICY	SIMULATION RESULTS	
	AVERAGE EARNINGS PER SHARE*	PERCENTAGE STANDARD DEVIATION
A	$6.50	16%
B	7.10	20
C	3.00	5
D	5.75	20
E	2.95	15
F	4.00	15

*UNDER REASONABLE ASSUMPTIONS OF DEPRECIATION, LIFE OF INVESTMENTS, INITIAL CONDITIONS, AND SO FORTH.

tainty profiles that provide project choices with less variance for equivalent returns.

Exhibit 6-6 illustrates how the average returns, in this case, earnings per share, are plotted against the standard deviation of those earnings to give an efficiency frontier.[5] Each point on the graph represents the financial results to be expected from a combination of investments selected by passing the same group of proposals through the screen of a particular investment policy. (The results shown in this exhibit were obtained by simulating the operation of a company using this policy for 15 years.)

Policies A, B, and C lie on the efficiency frontier because each produces the maximum earnings per share for a given degree of risk. Policies D, E, and F do not lie on the frontier because none of them produces, for a given standard deviation, as much earnings as management could obtain by using a different policy. Policy F, for example, is better than E because it earns $4.00 against $2.95 for the same risk (15 percent standard deviation), but it is worse than A, which produces earnings of $6.50 at a standard deviation of 16 percent. An efficient policy at 15 percent standard deviation should produce average earnings of approximately $6.25 per share.

Specific policies can, of course, be developed to fill in the entire efficiency frontier curve. For example, the simulation can take into account the capital structure of a real or hypothetical firm, both currently and in the (uncertain) future, thereby dealing effectively with the problem of the marginal cost of capital.

If the objective of an investment policy is to maximize average long-term earnings or yield for a given variation of those earnings or that yield, there is literally no reason why a management that has calculated its own efficiency frontier should use a policy that is not on that frontier. By

[5]In *Portfolio Selection: Effective Diversification of Investments* (New York: John Wiley & Sons, Inc., 1959), Harry M. Markowitz develops a similar concept; the method he describes does not, however, select investments with reference to their risk characteristics; see Michael L. Kirby, "The Current State of Chance-Constrained Programming," *Systems Research Memorandum No. 181.* (Evanston, Ill.: The Technological Institute, Northwestern University Press, August, 1967).

EXHIBIT 6-7

EXAMPLES OF INVESTMENT POLICIES (AFTER TAX)

Criterion	Conservative policy			High-risk policy		
	90% probability of doing better than	Expected value better than	10% probability of doing better than	90% probability of doing better than	Expected value better than	10% probability of doing better than
1. Payback (years to recover investment)	7	5	—	10	4	2
2. Average annual proceeds/investment (percent)	15%	20%	—	− 5%	15%	45%
3. ROI-dcf (percent)	10%	15%	—	−10%	10%	35%
4. NPV-dcf° Discount rate:						
10	1.0					
15		1.0			1.0	
45						1.0

°The indicated values are ratios of NPV of cash flow at the specified discount rates, divided by the present value of the investment.

definition, such a policy entails more variability in investment results and/or a lower expected return than the company is in fact obliged to accept. A management that wants to invest rationally, that is, wants to optimize results, has every reason, therefore, to locate its efficiency frontier and continually strive to improve it.

RESEARCH RESULTS

How practicable is the concept of efficient investment sets (on the efficiency frontier) and effective investment policies that will lead to a choice of such sets? In terms of actual investment results, what light does it throw on the choice of particular investment criteria, such as payback period, average annual return, and the like? To help answer these questions, a computer model was developed that made it possible to simulate the effects of various policies, operating over a period of years, on the financial results of a hypothetical company which selects annually from a wide range of investment proposals. Generally acceptable accounting procedures were used to determine financial results. Straight-line depreciation was used, and a fixed percentage dividend, along with a constant allowable debt ratio, was required to be paid where profits were available. At initial start-up each simulation run had standard conditions of assets, earnings, and so forth.[6]

Seven-step Simulation

As input to the computer simulation model, we developed three sets of 37 hypothetical investments. Each of the hypothetical investments, in turn, was characterized by uncertainty profiles for each of the three key variables for each year of the particular investment: sales, costs, and investment requirements. The computer simulation involved seven steps:

[6]This simulation was programmed for an IBM 7094 computer by my colleague at McKinsey & Company, Joan Morthland Bush.

1. Choose an investment policy by (a) selecting financial criterion or criteria and (b) establishing decision rules. Except in the case of single-point estimates, these rules specified criterion values, along with a minimum expected value, at the 10 percent and 90 percent probability points on the criterion-risk profile (see Exhibit 6-5).
2. From the uncertainty profiles of key variables for each investment given in the available investment set, develop risk profiles for each.
3. Screen investments against policy and accept all those that pass the screen, subject to realistic constraints on size and number of investments to be made in a given year.
4. Simulate the financial performance of the chosen investments over a 15-year period, selecting at random the operating results for each year from the individual uncertainty profiles for the investment project in order to obtain one set of operating results for that investment for each year.
5. Combine the various revenues, costs, and investment requirements for each of the years and then compute the yearly financial results for this investment set.
6. Repeat the entire process until a stable distribution of the financial results for the policy chosen and the investments available has been built up. Determine the average or expected value and the standard deviation of the key financial results.
7. Repeat for other policies and other sets of investment alternatives.

Policies Tested

For each of the three investment sets, investment policies covering conservative, medium-risk, and high-risk screens were tested. The conservative ones required a very high probability of no loss along with moderate expectations, while the high-risk ones accepted significant chances of loss but required good chances of high gains.

Exhibit 6-7 shows the nature of the policies used for the test, illustrating the low-risk and high-risk policies. (Note that single-point determinate policies, not shown on the exhibit, were also included in the tests.) The investments available were varied, ranging from short-term to longer term payouts, with cash investment requirements sometimes extending into later years.[7] The simulation was repeated 500 times for each policy and each set of investments, and the financial results were calculated for each year of a 15-year period. The average of each financial result and its standard deviation was determined for each year and for the combination of the last five years of the runs.

---

[7]On a single-point basis, the investments ranged from 1.9 years to 6.8 years for payback, from 16.9 percent to 47.2 percent average annual return, and from 7.5 percent to 77 percent ROI-dcf.

General Findings

Exhibit 6-8 shows the results of all the runs, plotted on a standard index basis, for the new investments selected. As can be seen, these results permit us to draw at least four general conclusions.

First, there is a wide gap in financial performance between some commonly used investment policies and those policies that lie on the efficiency frontier.

Second, risk-based policies consistently give better results than those using single-point, determinate decision rules. Using determinate decision rules, one cannot compensate for high risk by raising the level-of-return hurdle; single-point estimates produce, at best, half the return for a given degree of risk, no matter how the required return level is raised or lowered.

Third, long-term financial results are highly dependent on the risk accepted for a given return or on the return achieved for a given degree of risk. Thus, on the efficiency frontier, to get a long-term average of $6 per share, management would have to accept fluctuations on the order of 45 percent in two years out of three, whereas it could get only $3 if it decided to accept a probable fluctuation no greater than 10 percent.

EXHIBIT 6-8
INVESTMENT POLICY SIMULATION

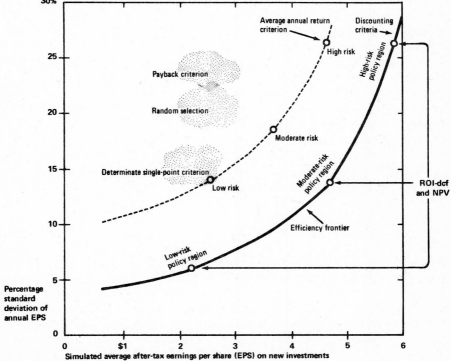

EXHIBIT 6-9
DETERMINING RISK BOUNDARIES ON THE EFFICIENCY FRONTIER

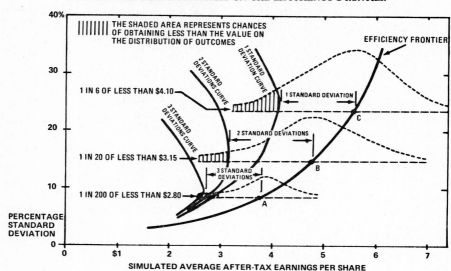

Fourth, some investment criteria are empirically better than others. Whenever growth is a goal, that is, whenever results are measured on an earnings-per-share (EPS) basis, net present value (NPV) and internal discounted cash flow return (ROI-dcf), both of which are based on discounting future returns, are superior to criteria, such as average annual return, which do not take the time value of money into account. At 25 percent annual standard deviation, for example—that is, accepting one chance in three of the results falling outside ± 25 percent of the expected values in any given year—the discounting criterion gives expected EPS of $5.50 while the nondiscounted criterion gives $4.10, or 25 percent less.

Policies that produce equivalent financial results for NPV and ROI-dcf can also be developed. That is, by specifying appropriate values for (a) the discount rate and (b) the probability of achieving a particular ratio of the NPV of the cash flow stream to the NPV of the investment, one can obtain exactly the same screen for investments as is provided by specific risk-based values of the ROI-dcf criterion.

Although payback period is still an extremely popular criterion, it turns out to be an extremely crude, inconsistent, and inefficient yardstick from the standpoint of actual financial results. Thus all the investments selected with payback criteria showed higher variances and lower returns than the others.

A more general conclusion to be drawn from this simulation project is that the same approach can profitably be used by management to evaluate its past investments, to determine its efficiency frontier, and to select efficient investment policies that more accurately reflect its risk preferences.

Note that the results shown in Exhibit 6-8 are charted in terms of standard deviation. That is, the vertical coordinate of any point on the chart represents the range of variation that may be expected *two thirds of the time* in the results of a particular policy. If management is unwilling to accept one chance in six of results falling below this range, it will have to accept a lower average return.

How much lower depends, of course, on what odds are acceptable. If, for example, assurance is wanted that results will fall above a given boundary five sixths of the time, *one standard deviation* must be subtracted from average earnings per share for each policy on the efficiency frontier, thereby creating a new curve inside the efficiency frontier as shown in Exhibit 6-9. Or, if management has a still more conservative attitude toward risk and wants a 19-to-1 probability of a given range of results— that is, an assurance that results will fall below the range indicated for a given return only one time in 20—*two standard deviations* may be subtracted, giving still another curve along which the returns offered by particular policies can be located.

Of significance here is the fact that different risk preferences, as exemplified by different risk boundaries, dictate different investment policy choices. Thus, in the situation illustrated by Exhibit 6-9, Policy C provides an expected return of $5.50 with a ± 25 percent standard deviation. Since these are typical Gaussian or normal distributions, we know that one standard deviation (25% × $5.50) subtracted from the mean will give a value —approximately $4.10 in this case—below which no more than one sixth of the possible future values may be expected to fall. Two standard deviations subtracted would mean no more than a 1-in-20 chance of getting less than $2.70.

In the example a *very* conservative management might wish to accept no more than a 1-in-200 risk. In this case Policy A would offer the best return possible; all others would give less after subtracting three standard deviations. For a management inclined to moderate risk, however, Policy B is the best choice; it offers a 19-in-20 chance of getting $3.15 or better.[8]

Which risk boundary is used determines which investment policy is best; which boundary to select depends on management's willingness to assume risk. Moreover, the risk aversion inherent in any policy can be assessed by determining the risk boundary on which that policy gives better results than all others. The fewer standard deviations one must subtract to define a frontier on which a given policy is best, the greater is the indicated willingness to accept risk.

---

[8]William J. Baumol has suggested a somewhat similar approach to stock portfolio selection in "An Expected Gain-Confidence Limit Criterion for Portfolio Selection," *Management Science* (October, 1963), p. 174.

CONCLUSION

Computer simulation offers corporate management, for the first time, a tool that will enable it to examine the risk consequences of various investment policies. As the research reported in this article shows, the development of a good investment policy involves four requirements:

1. The determination of risk profiles for all investments.
2. The use of a discounting measure (either discounted internal rate of return or an equivalent net present value) for assessing the merit of an investment proposal.
3. The establishment of alternative screening rules for investment proposals.
4. The determination of risk boundaries for the alternative policies.

It should be clear that the same policy will not necessarily show the same risk characteristics (or risk boundaries) when used to screen different classes of investments. In one application, for example, a diversified chemical company found that the projects proposed by various divisions—overseas, heavy chemical, and so on—varied widely in their efficiency frontiers and, therefore, entailed different risks for the same policies. Having decided what level of risk it wished to assume for each of the businesses, management was able to choose its policies accordingly.

Moreover, the company was able to determine the level of investment in each class of projects that would combine with investment levels and risks in other classes to maximize its chances of achieving its long-range growth goals. With the aid of simulation, it was able to establish ceilings and targets in the various investment classes and to describe in detail the screens or policies to be used to make choices in each of them. This enabled division managers and staff personnel to understand management's objectives and to develop more appropriate and promising investment alternatives.

Using the same approach, other companies can now examine in detail the kind of investment opportunities generated by various segments of their businesses and select investment policies that will give them firmer control over their long-term growth. Top executives can analyze their own prejudices and test out the historical effects of inconsistent and irrational choices on their companies' long-term financial results. In short, top management can get back in the driver's seat, in charge of the most important element of the corporate future—effective investment for growth.

7. ABANDONMENT VALUE AND CAPITAL BUDGETING*

ALEXANDER A. ROBICHEK †
and JAMES C. VAN HORNE ††

In the appraisal of investment proposals, insufficient attention in the literature is paid to the possibility of future abandonment. Customarily, projects are analyzed as though the firm were committed to the project over its entire estimated life. However, many projects have significant abandonment value over their economic lives; and this factor must be considered in the capital-budgeting process if capital is to be allocated optimally. This paper will examine the importance of abandonment value to capital budgeting, analyze how it can affect a project's expected return and risk, and propose a framework for taking account of this seldom considered dimension. In this regard, a simulation method is developed for incorporating the effects of abandonment into the information provided for the investment decision.

THE INVESTMENT DECISION

The current literature in the field of capital budgeting favors the use of the discounted cash-flow approach to project selection. The basic decision rule given by this approach can be stated in one of two ways: 1) accept a project if the present value of all expected cash flows, discounted at the cost of capital rate, is greater than, or equal to, zero; and 2) accept a project if the internal rate of return (i.e., the discount rate which equates the present value of expected cash inflows with the present value of expected cash outflows) is greater than, or equal to, the firm's cost of capital.[1]

These two rules will lead to the same optimal selection of investment proposals if the following conditions hold:

1. A meaningful cost of capital rate does exist in the sense that the firm has access to capital at this cost.
2. There is no capital rationing. If a project meets the acceptance criterion, capital is available at the cost of capital rate to finance the project.
3. All projects, existing as well as proposed, have the same degree of risk, so that the acceptance or rejection of any project does not affect the cost of capital.
4. A meaningful, unique internal rate of return exists.

---

* From the *Journal of Finance* (December, 1967), pp. 577-590; and (March, 1969), pp. 96 and 97. Reprinted by permission.
† Professor of Finance, Graduate School of Business, Stanford University.
†† Professor of Finance, Graduate School of Business, Stanford University.
[1] See, for example, Solomon, reference [13]; and Bierman and Smidt, reference [1], especially Chapters 2 and 3.

In the absence of these assumptions, the capital-budgeting decision becomes considerably more complex.[2] Inasmuch as the resulting problems do not affect the central thesis of this paper, we assume initially all four of the conditions listed above.

THE ABANDONMENT OPTION

The economic rationale behind the capital-budgeting decision rule can be applied directly to the abandonment decision. We submit that a project should be abandoned at that point in time when its abandonment value exceeds the net-present value of the project's subsequent expected future cash flows discounted at the cost of capital rate.[3] Using the internal rate of return method, the decision rule would be to abandon when the rate of return on abandonment value is less than the cost of capital. In either case, funds will be removed from a project whenever their incremental return is less than the minimum acceptable standard—namely, the cost of capital.[4]

Although the abandonment concept itself is quite simple, problems of measurement exist in estimating cash flows and abandonment value. Fortunately, the measurement of these factors has been analyzed ably elsewhere;[5] consequently, in this paper we shall not be concerned with how they may be determined. "Cash flows" are assumed to be all cash revenues that would be lost by abandonment less all cash expenses avoided. Abandonment value is assumed to represent the net disposal value of the project that would be available to the company in either cash or cash savings.[6]

EFFECT OF ABANDONMENT

When the possibility of future abandonment is recognized, what effect does it have upon project selection? We suggest that the effect may be quite dramatic and that altogether different selection decisions may be reached when abandonment is considered explicitly. To illustrate, consider the following example: Project A, costing $4,800 at time 0, is expected to generate cash flows over three years, after which time, there is no expected salvage value. The cash flows and their respective probabilities are shown in Table 7-1.[7] There are 27 possible sequences (or branches) of cash flows over the 3-year period. For instance, sequence No. 11 represents a cash-flow pattern of $2,000 in year 1, $1,000 in year 2, and $1,000 in year 3. The joint probability of each sequence of cash flows is shown in the last column of the table. For sequence No. 11, the probability of occurrence

[2]See Lorie and Savage, reference [6]; Teichroew, Robichek, and Montalbano, reference [14]; and Weingartner, reference [16].

[3]Dean, reference [2] discusses this problem in the Appendix to this book.

[4]The existence of the abandonment possibility may affect the "riskiness" of the project. This aspect is considered in detail later in the paper.

[5]For an excellent discussion on measuring cash flows and abandonment value, see Shillinglaw's two articles, references [11] and [12]. For a somewhat related discussion involving replacement, see Moore, reference [9].

[6]See Shillinglaw, reference [11], p. 270.

[7]For additional discussion of decision trees, see Magee, reference [7].

is $(1/2 \times 1/4 \times 1/2 = 1/16 = 4/64)$. The abandonment value at the end of each period is shown below the cash flows; this value is \$3,000 at the end of the first year, \$1,900 at the end of the second, and zero at the end of the third year.[8] After the third year, the project is not expected to provide any cash flow or residual value.

If we assume that the firm's cost of capital is 10 percent, then the expected net-present value of Project A can be computed.[9] The procedure involves the following steps: (1) compute the net-present value for each cash flow sequence; (2) obtain the *expected* net-present value by multiplying the computed net-present value by the probability of occurrence of that sequence;[10] and (3) add the expected net-present values for all sequences.

When we follow this procedure for Project A, we find that the expected net-present value is —\$144.23. Since this value is less than zero, the project is unacceptable under conventional standards. However, when we allow for abandonment, the results for the project are changed. Recall that the decision rule is to abandon a project if the abandonment value exceeds the expected cash flows for all subsequent periods, discounted at the cost of capital rate. Applying this rule to Project A, a revised set of relevant expected cash-flow sequences is obtained.[11] For example, if the cash flow in period 1 turned out to be \$1,000, the only relevant cash-flow sequences would be 1 through 9 in Table 7-1. The project would be abandonment at the end of period 1 because the sum of the expected net-present value of cash flows for sequences 1 through 9 for periods 2 and 3 discounted to period 1 (\$577.86) is less than the abandonment value at the end of period 1 (\$3,000). Consequently, for the "branch" encompassing sequences 1 through 9 in Table 7-1, the cash flow for period 1 becomes \$4,000 (i.e., the sum of the \$1,000 cash flow during the period plus the abandonment value of \$3,000); and there are no cash flows in the remaining two periods. Similarly, it is found that

---

[8]For simplicity, we assume that the abandonment values over time are known and invariant with respect to the cash-flow patterns. For many projects, these assumptions are not unreasonable. For example, general-purpose buildings and machine tools are likely to have abandonment values that are, to a great extent, invariant with the results of operations for which they are used. When the assumptions are inappropriate, the proposed approach can be modified by specifying probability distributions for the abandonment values.

The modifications would fall into two basic categories depending on whether the abandonment values: (a) vary independently of the expected cash-flow patterns; or (b) are correlated in some measure with them. In the first case, the decision rule is to abandon the project at that point in time when the *expected* abandonment value at the end of time t exceeds the present value of the project's expected subsequent cash flows. In the second case, different expected abandonment values would be projected for the different "branches" of cash flows. The decision rule would be to abandon a project at that point in time when the expected abandonment value *for the particular cash-flow branch* exceeds the present value of expected subsequent cash flows for that branch.

[9]While this example is analyzed in terms of the net-present value, it also could be analyzed in terms of the internal rate of return.

[10]For example, the expected net-present value for sequence No. 11 $(E(NPV_{11}))$ is determined as follows:

$$E(NPV_{11}) = \left[-4,800 + \frac{2,000}{(1+.10)} + \frac{1,000}{(1+.10)^2} + \frac{1,000}{(1+.10)^3} \right] (4/64) = -87.76.$$

[11]If the project is abandoned, the cash flows lost are those in Table 7-1.

abandonment takes place at the end of period 2 for the cash-flow sequences 10 through 12, 13 through 15, and 19 through 21 in Table 7-1. The expected net-present values of cash flows for the above three "branches" for period 3 discounted to period 2 ($909.09, $1,818.18, and $1,818.18 respectively) are less than the abandonment value at the end of period 2 ($1,900). For the branch encompassing cash-flow sequences 10 through 12, the cash flow for period 2 becomes $2,900; and for the two branches encompassing sequences 13 through 15 and 19 through 21, the cash flow becomes $3,900 for each branch. Taking account of these changes, the revised cash-flow sequences are shown in Table 7-2.

Based upon the cash-flow information in Table 7-2, the expected net-present value for Project A is now recalculated and found to be $535.25—a considerable improvement over the —$144.23 calculated before. Whereas the project would have been rejected previously, the consideration of the abandonment option results in the acceptance of the project.

The discussion so far serves to illustrate the importance of considering abandonment value when evaluating projects. The funds committed to

TABLE 7-1
EXPECTED FUTURE CASH FLOWS FOR PROJECT A

PERIOD 1		PERIOD 2		PERIOD 3		CASH FLOW SEQUENCE NUMBER	PROBABILITY OF SEQUENCE (IN 64ths)
CASH FLOW	PROBABILITY	CASH FLOW	CONDITIONAL PROBABILITY	CASH FLOW	CONDITIONAL PROBABILITY		
		0	.25	—$1,000	.25	1	1/64
				500	.50	2	2/64
				0	.25	3	1/64
$1,000	.25	$ 500	.50	— 500	.25	4	2/64
				0	.50	5	4/64
				500	.25	6	2/64
		1,000	.25	0	.25	7	1/64
				1,000	.50	8	2/64
				2,000	.25	9	1/64
		1,000	.25	0	.25	10	2/64
				1,000	.50	11	4/64
				2,000	.25	12	2/64
2,000	.50	2,000	.50	1,000	.25	13	4/64
				2,000	.50	14	8/64
				3,000	.25	15	4/64
		3,000	.25	2,000	.25	16	2/64
				3,000	.50	17	4/64
				4,000	.25	18	2/64
		2,000	.25	1,000	.25	19	1/64
				2,000	.50	20	2/64
				3,000	.25	21	1/64
3,000	.25	3,000	.50	2,000	.25	22	2/64
				3,000	.50	23	4/64
				4,000	.25	24	2/64
		3,500	.25	3,000	.25	25	1/64
				3,500	.50	26	2/64
				4,000	.25	27	1/64
ABANDONMENT VALUE AT END OF PERIOD $3,000		$1,900		0			

TABLE 7-2

EXPECTED FUTURE CASH FLOWS FOR PROJECT A WITH THE CONSIDERATION OF ABANDONMENT VALUES

Period 1 Cash Flow	Period 1 Probability	Period 2 Cash Flow	Period 2 Conditional Probability	Period 3 Cash Flow	Period 3 Conditional Probability	Cash Flow Sequence Number	Probability of Sequence (in 64ths)
$4,000	.25	0		0		1	16/64
2,000	.50	2,900	.25	0		2	8/64
		3,900	.50	0		3	16/64
		3,000	.25	2,000	.25	4	2/64
				3,000	.50	5	4/64
				4,000	.25	6	2/64
3,000	.25	3,900	.25	0		7	4/64
		3,000	.50	2,000	.25	8	2/64
				3,000	.50	9	4/64
				4,000	.25	10	2/64
		3,500	.25	3,000	.25	11	1/64
				3,500	.50	12	2/64
				4,000	.25	13	1/64

some projects may be far more flexible than those committed to others. Not to take account of the possible mobility of funds and to regard all outlays as sunk overlooks an extremely important dimension. Such an omission may provide very misleading information for decision making and may re--sult in capital-budgeting decisions that are sub-optimal.

SIMULATION AND THE ABANDONMENT OPTION

In the preceding section of this paper, the attempt was made to show how the possibility of abandonment may affect the investment decision. To illustrate the problem, a relatively simple example was used—Project A, which had a total of 27 possible cash-flow sequences. While this Project was useful for purposes of illustration, most projects under consideration are considerably more complex with respect to the possible number of cash-flow sequences. As a result, the approach illustrated above that evaluates each separate cash-flow sequence becomes unfeasible.

In practice, it is often true that management has reasonably good knowledge of the possible range of cash flows to be expected from a project.[12] If probability distributions of these cash flows over time can be specified, Monte Carlo simulation[13] may serve as a practical substitute for the "all inclusive" approach described earlier. To illustrate the application of simulation techniques to the problem at hand, consider Project B, which has an estimated life of ten years, no expected salvage value, and expected cash flows and abandonment values as shown in Table 7-3.

If no account is taken of the possibility of abandonment, the internal rate of return for this Project is 10 percent. If a discount rate of 8 percent is assumed, the Project has an expected net-present value of $565.

Assume now that the abandonment values and the cash outflow in year 0, shown in Table 7-3, are known with certainty but that the expected cash flows for years 1 through 10 are random variables distributed normally with a constant standard deviation of $100. We must specify also whether the yearly cash flows are independent of each other (i.e., the "actual" cash flows in any one period do not affect the cash flows of subsequent periods) or whether, in some measure, they are correlated over time.[14] The latter relationship is considered to be more representative of the real world; consequently, we specify in our simulation approach a provision to generate revised cash forecasts as "actual" simulated cash flows deviate from expected cash flows. The particular manner in which forecasts are revised is described fully in the Appendix.[15]

---

[12]For example, Grayson, reference [3], has been successful in obtaining probabilistic information relating to possible cash flows of oil exploration projects.

[13]Monte Carlo simulation is a technique which investigates the implications of uncertainty in a systematic manner. The readers who are unfamiliar with this approach will find it described in most basic operations research texts. For one such description, see Sasieni, Yaspan, and Friedman, reference [10], pp. 58-67.

[14]See Hillier, reference [5], especially pp. 447-449.

[15]The form of the cash-forecast revision rule was selected solely to illustrate the methodology of Monte Carlo simulation. We were not concerned particularly with the rule's realism, because in practice each project faces a distinct set of circumstances.

TABLE 7-3
EXPECTED CASH FLOWS AND ABANDONMENT VALUES FOR PROJECT B
(DOLLARS)

	0	1	2	3	4	5	6	7	8	9	10
					Year						
Expected Cash Flow	−6,145	1,000	1,000	1,000	1,000	1,000	1,000	1,000	1,000	1,000	1,000
Expected Abandonment Value		−6,200	5,700	5,180	4,580	3,980	3,300	2,570	1,780	920	0

The net-present value and the internal rate of return for Project B are simulated 100 times with the consideration of abandonment and 100 times without the abandonment option. We specified that in simulating with the abandonment option, the decision rule to abandon was identical in form to the one described in connection with Project A—abandon the project at the end of year t if the revised expected cash flows for years t + 1 through 10, discounted at 8 percent to year t, are less than the abandonment value at year t. A detailed description of this rule is given in the Appendix. The simulation results are summarized in Table 7-4.

TABLE 7-4
RESULTS OF SIMULATION FOR PROJECT B

	Net Present Value		Internal Rate of Return	
	Without Abandonment	With Abandonment	Without Abandonment	With Abandonment
Expected Value	$672	$991	9.83%	13.62%

Note that for the "without abandonment" option there are differences between the simulated expected values in Table 7-4 and the calculated expected values based upon the data in Table 7-3. For the net-present value case, the simulated mean value is $672, as compared with a calculated value of $565; for the internal rate of return, the simulated mean value is 9.83 percent, while the computed value is 10 percent. These differences are insignificant statistically,[16] and we conclude that the simulation technique described approximates fairly the actual distributions of net-present value and internal rate of return for Project B.

It is seen in Table 7-4 that explicit consideration of the abandonment

---

[16]The differences in means between simulated and calculated value is less than .08 standard deviations for the net-present value and about .03 standard deviations for the internal rate of return.

FIGURE 7-1
FREQUENCY OF ABANDONMENT OF PROJECT B BEFORE END OF ESTIMATED USEFUL LIFE

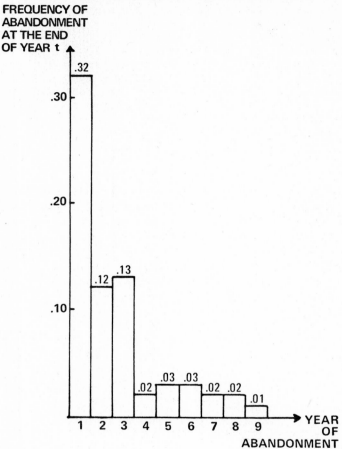

option results in a significant increase in Project B's expected value of return, whether this return is measured in terms of the net-present value or of the internal rate of return. Based upon the simulation undertaken, Figure 7-1 shows the frequency with which abandonment takes place for each year of Project B's life. For this particular simulation, the project is abandoned before the end of its originally estimated useful life in 70 percent of the cases. Clearly the abandonment results would be different under alternative assumptions as to: abandonment values; expected cash flows; distribution of cash flows; the manner in which forecasts are revised; and the discount rate.

THE ABANDONMENT OPTION AND PROJECT RISK

Our discussion thus far has been limited to capital-budgeting decisions solely based upon expected net-present value or internal rate of return.

TABLE 7-5
SELECTED VALUES FOR PROJECTS A AND B

	Without Abandonment	With Abandonment
Project A		
Net Present Value:		
Expected Value	$—144	$ 535
Standard Deviation	2,372	1,522
V/2SV	.945	1.29
Project B (Simulated Values)		
Net Present Value:		
Expected Value	$ 672	$ 991
Standard Deviation	1,422	888
V/2SV	1.01	2.96
Internal Rate of Return		
Expected Rate	9.83%	13.62%
Standard Deviation	5.31	2.25
V/2SV	.75	1.25

This limitation was in order because of our assumption that all projects are of "equal risk." Specifically, Projects A and B are assumed to be "equally risky," whether evaluated with or without the abandonment option. In this section it is demonstrated that the presence of abandonment value may reduce the "risk" of a project over that which would be present if there were no abandonment value. By a reduction in risk, we mean either or both of the following: (1) a lower variance of the probability distribution around the expected value of returns;[17] and (2) a shift in the skewness of the probability distribution toward the right, reducing both the range and the magnitude of undesirable returns, i.e., those to the left of the expected value of returns.

In order to evaluate the effect that abandonment value has upon risk, let us consider Projects A and B both with and without the abandonment option. In this regard, we can compute such measures of risk as the variance, V, the standard deviation, S, and the semi-variance, SV.[18] In addition, a

---

[17]For a discussion of expected return and variance as they relate to capital budgeting, see Hertz, reference [4], Hillier, reference [5], and Van Horne, reference [15].

[18]Semi-variance is the variance of the probability distribution to the left of expected net-present value and may be thought to represent a measure of downside risk. Mathematically, it can be expressed as

$$SV(X) = \sum_{i=1}^{m} \{[X_i - E(X)]^2 \, P(X_i)\}$$

where X_i is the observation, $E(X)$ is the expected net-present value, $P(X_i)$ the probability of the event X_i, and m denotes the number of observations to the left of the mean. See Markowitz, reference [8], p. 191.

measure of relative skewness can be obtained by computing the ratio V/2SV. For symmetrical probability distributions, V/2SV equals one; for distributions skewed to the right, it is greater than one; and for distributions skewed to the left, it is less than one.

In addition to the expected value of returns, S and the ratio V/2SV were computed for Projects A and B with and without the consideration of the abandonment option. The principal results are summarized in Table 7-5.

For Project A, note that when abandonment is considered not only does the expected net-present value increase from —$144 to $535 but the standard deviation decreases from $2,372 to $1,522. Also, the skewness of the probability distribution of net-present values changes from slightly negative to positive. This latter result suggests that much of the downside risk can be eliminated if the Project is abandoned when events turn unfavorable. Figure 7-2 illustrates this point graphically—it depicts the cumulative probability distribution for Project A with and without the consideration of abandonment. For example, with abandonment, there is a 48/64 probability that the Project will provide an expected net-present value of more than zero; without abandonment, the probability is only 40/64 that the net present value will be greater than zero. Moreover, with abandonment, there is no probability that the expected net-present value will be less than —$1,164; while without abandonment, there is an 18/64 probability that it will be less than this amount.[19] For a given probability, the expected net-present value is higher with abandonment value than without through probability 27/64, after which the expected net-present values are about the same for both distributions.[20]

For Project B, a comparison of the simulation results, with and without the abandonment option, yields conclusions similar to those arrived at from the analysis of data for Project A. Again, consideration of the abandonment option results in a number of desirable occurrences: the expected value of returns (either net-present value or internal rate of return) increases; the standard deviation decreases; and the skewness of the probability distributions shifts to the right. The distributions of individual simulation values for Project B follow the general pattern illustrated in Figure 7-2 for Project A, and we shall not reproduce them here.

In our analysis, the acceptance or rejection of any project was assumed not to change the discount rate, i.e., the firm's cost of capital. The effect that the acceptance of a project will have on the discount rate will depend upon the characteristics of existing investments, the manner in which the project's expected returns are related to the expected returns of other projects, and the expectations and preferences of investors and lenders. The

---

[19]Since Figure 7-2 is in terms of discrete probability distributions, this probability is denoted by the first dot to the left of the point where net-present value equals zero.

[20]For illustrative purposes, the same cost of capital rate was used to discount the subsequent cash flows for each event-tree. In practice, there may be situations when this approach is not completely appropriate.

FIGURE 7-2
CUMULATIVE PROBABILITY DISTRIBUTIONS
PROJECT A

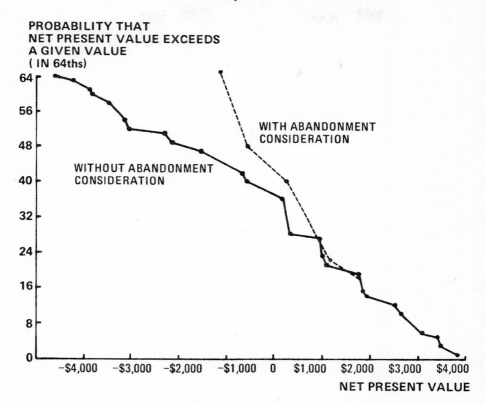

determination of this effect is extremely complex; and, inasmuch as it does not invalidate any of the basic tenets of this paper, we do not attempt to deal with it here.[21]　We would suggest, however, that the acceptance of Project A (or B) with the possibility of abandonment is likely to result in a more favorable change (if a change takes place) in the discount rate than would occur from the acceptance of Project A (or B) without the abandonment option.

CONCLUSIONS

Any estimate of future cash flows implies that a particular operating strategy will be followed. All too often, however, this strategy is not stated explicitly. Specifically, the consideration of possible abandonment is a dimension frequently omitted from capital-budgeting analysis. As illustrated in our examples, significant abandonment values for a project may

---

[21]In this paper, we do not consider the portfolio problem of risk to the firm as a whole. For an analysis of this problem, see Van Horne, reference [15].

result in a higher expected net-present value or internal rate of return and lower expected risk than would be the case if the project had no abandonment value over its economic life. It is important to take account of the fact that different investment projects provide different degrees of flexibility with respect to the possible mobility of funds if the project turns bad. To ignore these differences may result in sub-optimal investment decision. Since having the option to abandon never decreases project value, the typical consequences of ignoring the option would be to underestimate the value of a project. The framework proposed in this paper allows the firm to incorporate the possibility of abandonment into its capital-budgeting procedures.

APPENDIX

Description of the Simulation Model

Let

$EC_{t.\tau}$ = expected cash flow in year t as of year τ.

AV_t = abandonment value in year t.

AC_t = "actual" simulated cash flow in year t.

The values for AV_t and $EC_{t.o}$ are input as given in Table 7-3.

Rule to Generate Revised Cash Flow Forecasts

where

$$EC_{t.r} = EC_{t.r-1} [1 + X\alpha], \tag{1}$$

$$X = \frac{AC_r - EC_{r.r-1}}{EC_{r.r-1}},$$

and α varies depending on the values of X as shown below.

$$
\begin{array}{lllll}
& \text{If} & -.05 \leqslant X \leqslant .05 & \text{then } \alpha = & 0 \\
\text{If} -.10 \leqslant \alpha < -.05 & \text{or} & .05 < X \leqslant .10 & \text{then } \alpha = & .5 \\
\text{If} -.15 \leqslant \alpha < -.10 & \text{or} & .10 < X \leqslant .15 & \text{then } \alpha = & 1.0 \\
\text{If} -.20 \leqslant \alpha < -.15 & \text{or} & .15 < X \leqslant .20 & \text{then } \alpha = & 1.5 \\
\text{If} -.20 > X & \text{or} & X > .20 & \text{then } \alpha = & 2.0
\end{array}
$$

In words, the above rule revises the expected cash flow forecasts as of year τ for subsequent years if ($X\alpha$) differs from zero, where X represents the percentage difference between "actual" simulated cash flows and "expected" cash flows and α is a parameter dependent upon X. For example, if the "actual" cash flow in year 5 were 4 percent greater than the "expected" cash flow for year 5 as of year 4, α would be zero, and the expected cash flows for all subsequent years (as of year 5) would remain the same as of year 4. On the other hand, if the "actual" cash flows were 18 percent less than the "expected" cash flows, all subsequent cash flows would be revised downward by 27 percent.

$$[X\alpha = (-.18)(1.5) = -.27].$$

Decision Rule to Abandon

Given all $EC_{t.\tau}$ for $\tau < t \leqslant 10$, compute for all $\tau < 10$ the discounted present value of cash flows in Eq. 2:

$$PV_r = \sum_{t=r+1}^{10} \frac{EC_{t.r}}{(1 + .08)^{(t-r)}} \tag{2}$$

If $PV_\tau \geqslant AV_\tau$ then continue simulation.
If $PV_\tau < AV_\tau$ abandon project; in this case AC_τ (final) $= AC_\tau + AV_\tau$ and all $EC_{t.\tau} = 0$ for $t > \tau$.

Compute Net-Present Value and Rate of Return

After all the final cash flows are determined for each run j, compute the net-present value in (Eq. 3) and rate of return from (Eq. 4):

$$NPV_j = -6145 + \sum_{t=1}^{10} \frac{AC_t}{(1 + .08)^t}; \tag{3}$$

Solve for R_j in (Eq. 4)

$$6145 = \sum_{t=1}^{10} \frac{AC_t}{(1 + R_j)^t}. \tag{4}$$

Complete Simulation

Go to next simulation run. Run simulation 100 times and compute mean, variance, standard deviation, and semi-variance.

REFERENCES

1. Bierman, Jr., H., and S. Smidt. *The Capital Budgeting Decision.* New York: The MacMillan Company, 1966.
2. Dean, J. *Capital Budgeting.* New York: Columbia University Press, 1951, pp. 163-168.
3. Grayson, C. J. *Decision under Uncertainty.* Cambridge, Mass.: Harvard University Press, 1960.

4. Hertz, D. B. "Risk Analysis in Capital Budgeting," *Harvard Business Review*. Vol. XLII (January-February, 1964), pp. 95-106.
5. Hillier, F. S. "The Derivation of Probabilistic Information for the Evaluation of Risky Investments," *Management Science*. Vol. IX (April, 1963), pp. 443-457.
6. Lorie, J. H., and L. J. Savage. "Three Problems in Rationing Capital," *Journal of Business*. Vol. XXVIII (October, 1955), pp. 229-239.
7. Magee, J. F. "How to Use Decision Trees in Capital Investment," *Harvard Business Review*. Vol. XLII (September-October, 1964), pp. 79-96.
8. Markowitz, H. M. *Portfolio Selection*. New York: John Wiley & Sons, Inc., 1959.
9. Moore, C. L. "The Present-Value Method and the Replacement Decision," *Accounting Review*. Vol. XXXIX (January, 1964), pp. 94-102.
10. Sasieni, M., A. Yaspan, and L. Friedman. *Operations Research—Methods and Problems*. New York: John Wiley & Sons, Inc., 1959.
11. Shillinglaw, G. "Profit Analysis for Abandonment Decisions," *The Management of Corporate Capital*, edited by E. Solomon. Glencoe, Ill.: The Free Press of Glencoe, 1959, pp. 269-281.
12. ———————. "Residual Values in Investment Analysis," *The Management of Corporate Capital*, edited by E. Solomon. Glencoe, Ill.: The Free Press of Glencoe, 1959, pp. 259-268.
13. Solomon, E. "The Arithmetic of Capital-Budgeting Decisions," *Journal of Business*. Vol. XXIX (April, 1956), pp. 124-129.
14. Teichroew, D., A. A. Robichek, and M. Montalbano. "An Analysis of Criteria for Investment and Financing Decisions under Certainty," *Management Science*, Vol. XII (November, 1965), pp. 151-179.
15. Van Horne, J. C. "The Capital-Budgeting Decision Involving Combinations of Risky Investments," *Management Science*. Vol. XIII (October, 1966), pp. B84-92.
16. Weingartner, H. M. *Mathematical Programming and the Analysis of Capital Budgeting Problems*. Englewood Cliffs, N.J.: Prentice-Hall, Inc., 1963.

ABANDONMENT VALUE AND CAPITAL BUDGETING: REPLY*

The comment by Professors Dyl and Long (DL) is, for the most part, an appropriate modification of our procedure for evaluating the abandonment of an investment project. We accept their principal point—in our original paper[1] we omitted from consideration the possibility that future abandonment may be more desirable than either "present" abandonment or continuation of the project to the end of its economic life. In certain cases, deferral of abandonment to a future date may be the optimal alternative.

DL propose the following algorithm for the optimal abandonment decision rule:

Calculate:

$$\underset{\tau+1 \leqslant a \leqslant n}{\text{Max}} \quad PV_{\tau.a}, \tag{1}$$

where τ is the "current" period, a is any period of possible future abandonment, and n represents the life of the project. In determining the maximum

---

*This article appears at the request of the authors of Article 7. It originally appeared in *Journal of Finance*, XXIV (March, 1969), pp. 96-97.

[1] Alexander A. Robichek and James C. Van Horne, "Abandonment Value and Capital Budgeting," *Journal of Finance*, XXII (December, 1967), pp. 577-89.

$PV_{\tau.a}$, the algorithm requires that present values be computed under the assumption of abandonment in every period $\tau + 1 \leqslant a \leqslant n$.   In other words, n different $PV_{\tau.a}$'s are computed; $PV_{\tau.a}$ represents the abandonment value in period a plus the expected values of cash flows in the first a periods, all discounted to their present value at time τ.[2] Having calculated present values for all future a's, the largest such value is then compared with the current abandonment value. The decision rule is to abandon the project at time τ if the current abandonment value, AV_τ, exceeds the maximum $PV_{\tau.a}$. If AV_τ is less than (or equal to) the maximum $PV_{\tau.a}$, then the project should be held and abandoned at time a corresponding to the maximum $PV_{\tau.a}$.

The consideration of deferred abandonment, as proposed by DL, is important in situations where abandonment value and expected future cash flows do not decline rapidly over time. However, in cases where expected abandonment values decline significantly over time and where expected future cash flows deteriorate when a project turns bad, the possibility of deferred abandonment rarely will need be considered.

Operationally, the DL algorithm is cumbersome and, in a sense, incorrect. DL's rule (if $AV_\tau \leqslant$ max. $PV_{\tau.a}$, then the project should be held and abandoned at $\tau = a$) holds only under the condition of certainty with respect to future cash flows and abandonment values. Where uncertainty obtains, as it does in most problems affecting abandonment decisions, DL's rule is not correct. Consider the situation where $AV_\tau \leqslant$ max. $PV_{\tau.a}$. This result tells us *only* that the project should be held beyond period τ. The project may or *may not* be abandoned at time a for which $PV_{\tau.a}$ is maximum. Maximum $PV_{\tau.a}$ is computed at time τ using expected cash flows and abandonment values *estimated as of that time*. Because the project is held beyond time τ, expectations may (and probably will) change. As a result, a completely different set of values may have to be considered to reach an optimal decision at time a_{max}, or before if the project should be abandoned prior to that time.

Accordingly, we propose the following modified algorithm to be used in evaluating abandonment decisions:

(a) Compute $PV_{\tau.a}$ for a = n, where

$$PV_{T.a} = \sum_{t=T+1}^{a} \frac{EC_{t.T}}{(1+k)^{(t-T)}} + \frac{AV_{a.T}}{(1+k)^{(a-T)}}. \tag{2}$$

(b) If $PV_{\tau.n} > AV_\tau$,
     continue to hold project and evaluate it again at time $\tau + 1$, based upon expectations at that time.

---

[2]This assumes that abandonment values over time are known and invariant with respect to the cash-flow patterns. As noted in *ibid*. p. 579, probability distribution of future abandonment values could be incorporated into the analysis.

(c) If $PV_{\tau,n} \leqslant AV_\tau$,
compute $PV_{\tau,a}$ for $a = n - 1$.

(d) Compare $PV_{\tau,n-1}$ with AV_τ as in (b) and (c) above. Continue procedure until either the decision to hold is reached or $a = \tau + 1$.

(e) If $PV_{\tau,a} \leqslant AV_\tau$ for all $\tau + 1 \leqslant a \leqslant n$, then abandon project at time τ.

The algorithm described above will provide the optimal decision with respect to abandonment. It is also considerably less costly and time consuming than DL's procedure. In conclusion, we wish to thank Dyl and Long for pointing out an important omission in our previous paper.

8. A GOAL PROGRAMMING MODEL FOR CAPITAL BUDGETING*

CLARK A. HAWKINS†
and RICHARD M. ADAMS††

One of the earlier works dealing with linear programming (LP) in capital budgeting under conditions of certainty was that of Weingartner [9]. His model employed an objective function composed of net present values of investment proposals from which will be selected, under constrained financing, that combination bringing the highest return to the firm. Expressed mathematically, these well-known relationships are as follows:

$$\text{maximize} \quad \sum_{j=1}^{n} b_j x_j$$

$$\text{subject to} \quad \sum_{j=1}^{n} c_{tj} x_j \leq C_t$$

$$0 \leq x_j \leq 1,$$

where b_j is net present value of investment proposal j, x_j is an amount between 0 and 1 that is in this context the fraction of an investment proposal adopted, c_{tj} is the net cash outlay required for j in period t, and C_t is the budget constraint in period t [9, p. 17].

Baumol and Quandt [2] developed a seemingly different programming model which attempted to maximize shareholder wealth by providing the investor with an optimal dividend stream. This implies an objective function where future dividend payments are discounted using marginal utility as the appropriate discount factor and available cash as the constraint. Despite the introduction of utility, Myers [7] demonstrated that there is little difference in meaning between this model and the Weingartner model.

Among those who presented chance-constrained LP models were Naslund [8], and Byrne, Charnes, Cooper and Kortanek [3].

Naslund's model deals with deterministic data as do those previously mentioned models, except for net cash flows which he assumes to have a known normal distribution.

Byrne, Charnes, Cooper and Kortanek construct a model that incorporates the payback period as a device for filtering acceptable from unacceptable risk levels. They experiment with a model that applies a

°From *Financial Management* (Spring, 1974), pp. 52-57. Reprinted by permission.
†Professor of Finance, College of Business and Public Administration, University of Arizona.
††Tennant Company, Minneapolis, Minnesota.

strict payback condition to each investment proposal taken individually and then treat a portfolio of investment proposals for risk considerations using the payback as a decision rule. They also use liquidity constraints to monitor risk-taking activities. Specifically, their model assumes that some minimum level of liquidity must exist for the firm's owners to maintain control and for the firm to remain solvent, liquidity being defined as the level of a firm's quick assets. If an investment proposal does not meet this minimum, it is rejected.

A third type of programming model in capital budgeting is the integer programming model. This model, first introduced by Lorie and Savage [6] and later restated by Weingartner [9], differs in only one respect from the deterministic models previously described; a constraint has been added to this latter programming model that restricts the x_j value in the Weingartner formulation (shown above) to either 0 or 1, meaning that an investment is adopted wholly or rejected wholly. This restriction has intuitive appeal. There are a number of difficulties, however, in attempting to implement integer programming. The most important problem is that it may take an unmanageable number of iterations in order for the model to converge on a solution, and at times it will not converge at all. Also, because of the integer restriction, it is not possible to state the other restrictions to the problem. They must be generated during the computational process and once calculated often prove to be redundant [9, p. 45].

While the financial manager might well attempt to maximize shareholder wealth, as the three types of models previously mentioned suggest, in reality, his decisions are tempered by conflicting goals that other departments within the organization are seeking to achieve and, more importantly, by those objectives the firm pursues that do not further stockholder interests. If it is taken that the firm has multiple goals, a position that has gained some credence in recent years [1, 5], then the LP models previously presented are incapable of solving capital budgeting problems. However, non-profit maximizing theories of the firm do not often present fruitful lines of analysis. Therefore, although the prime goal of the financial manager may still be categorized as maximization of shareholder wealth, we will argue that this aim may not be pursued in the usual uni-directional manner postulated by theory. Rather it takes place on a more indirect route and in an environment of more constraints than the financial ones typically stated.

THE GOAL PROGRAMMING APPROACH

In recent years, a model has been developed that recognizes the existence of multiple conflicting goals. This model, first introduced by Charnes and Cooper [4], is appropriately called goal programming (GP). This more realistic model can be reconstructed for application to capital budgeting problems. To keep the exposition fairly simple, we will deal only with the certainty case in this paper.

As with other LP models, the GP model attempts to optimize subject to constraints. However, unlike other LP models, the GP model has a multidimensional objective function that seeks to minimize deviations from goals within a given set of constraints. The form of this function is as follows:

$$\text{minimize} \quad Z = \sum_{i=1}^{n} (d_i^+ + d_i^-),$$

where d_i^+ = deviations above specified goals, d_i^- = deviations below specified goals, and n = number of goals in the model.

If exact attainment of, say, goal 1 is desired, both d_1^+ and d_1^- must appear in the objective function, while if only underachievement is undesirable, only d_1^- must appear in the objective function.

The model allows the manager to make an ordinal ranking of goals according to the relative importance of their contribution to the organization, or according to their pressure on immediate operations and/or necessary action. The ranking of these goals is done by assigning each a weight in the objective function. This weighting is assigned to the deviations according to the importance of each. For example, if d_1^+ is twice as important as d_1^-, a coefficient of 2 is given to d_1^+ and a coefficient of 1 to d_1^-. In the solution, goals of a lower rank are satisfied after those with a higher weight have been satisfied. Because of this, it is possible for high priority goals to be incorporated so that they cannot be compromised by simply eliminating d^+ and d^- relating to them from the objective function.

GP obtains a simultaneous solution to a system of complex objectives rather than a single objective, and the complex objectives need not be measureable in the same units. The ordinal solution of GP is dependent on the ordinal statement of goals, as discussed above, dependent on the preferences of the decision maker. This presumably incorporates implicitly those preferences that would not preclude theoretically the ultimate goal of wealth maximization for stockholders, while at the practical level permitting the pursuit of intermediate goals appearing in conflict with the prime goal. In this sense, the ranking of goals in any situation would be derived from experience and judgement.

The constraint equations in the GP model are of two types. First, there are resource constraints—those in the familiar LP designation. In addition, constraint equations take the form of goals of the organization. In GP models the integer constraint is generally excluded from the analysis for reasons previously mentioned, and will be eliminated in the capital budgeting application. All other constraints will be developed to fit the problem analyzed.

GOAL PROGRAMMING APPLICATION
TO CAPITAL BUDGETING

Consider a well known problem presented by Lorie and Savage and reformulated in an LP format by Weingartner. The problem is one in which nine mutually exclusive projects are under consideration with given net present values for each proposal and a certain configuration of funds outlays over a two year period. The objective is to find an optimal combination of these investments in terms of present values, given a budget constraint of $50 for the first period and $20 for the second period. Exhibit 8-1 lists the investment proposals along with their net present values and the present values of outlays for each period.

EXHIBIT 8-1
INVESTMENT PROJECTS

Investment Project	PV of Outlay		PV of Investment
	Period 1	Period 2	
1	$12	$ 3	$14
2	54	7	17
3	6	6	17
4	6	2	15
5	30	35	40
6	6	6	12
7	48	4	14
8	36	3	10
9	18	3	12

Source: Lorie and Savage [6], Table 1, p. 234.

Reformulating this problem in a form adaptable to LP analysis, Weingartner arrived at the following model wherein the subscript numbering corresponds with numbering of investment projects in Exhibit 8-1.

maximize $Z = 14X_1 + 17X_2 + 17X_3 + 15X_4 + 40X_5 + 12X_6 + 14X_7 + 10X_8 + 12X_9$

subject to

$$12X_1 + 54X_2 + 6X_3 + 6X_4 + 30X_5 + 6X_6 + 48X_7 + 36X_8 + 18X_9 \leq 50$$

$$3X_1 + 7X_2 + 6X_3 + 2X_4 + 35X_5 + 6X_6 + 4X_7 + 3X_8 + 3X_9 \leq 20$$

$$1 \geq Xj \geq 0, Xj = 1, \ldots, 9.$$

Solving the program, the fraction of each investment proposal adopted is presented in Exhibit 8-2 as an Xj value. Utilizing Weingartner's criteria, it can be seen that all of projects 1, 3, 4, and 9 should be accepted, as well as 97% of project 6 and 4.5% of project 7, while re-jecting all other projects completely. To proceed, consider the modifica-tions to the Lorie and Savage problem presented in Exhibit 8-3 under the assumption that this is a manufacturing firm in which each invest-ment proposal is expected to yield a certain amount of revenue in each period and utilize a specified number of man-hours per day.

Exhibit 8-2

Weingartner Solution

$X_1 = 1.0$	$X_4 = 1.0$	$X_7 = .045$
$X_2 = 0$	$X_5 = 0$	$X_8 = 0$
$X_3 = 1.0$	$X_6 = .97$	$X_9 = 1.0$

Adapted from: Weingartner [9], Table 3.1, p. 18.

Assume that the following goals have been established by top management of the firm: (1) The projects as a whole must yield a net present value of at least $32.40. (2) In order to maintain an upward sales trend, the sales manager would like the first year to have as close to $70 in sales generated by the investments selected and at least a 20% growth in sales for the second year. The growth in sales from year 1 to 2 is determined to be four times as important as the initial sales goal. (3) The projects selected are desired to require as close to 40 man-hours of labor per day as possible in order to maintain the present level of employment and avoid having to rehire and retrain at a time when the labor supply may be low. These goals are determined to be equally im-portant as that of meeting the first year's sales goal.

Exhibit 8-3

Modified Investment Proposals

Investment Project	Sales		Man-hours	
	Period 1	Period 2	Period 1	Period 2
1	$14	$15	10	12
2	30	42	16	16
3	13	16	13	13
4	11	12	9	13
5	53	52	19	16
6	10	14	14	14
7	32	34	7	9
8	21	28	15	22
9	12	21	8	13

In the following, references by subscript to goal conform to the sequence listed in Exhibit 8-4 where results of solution of the modified problem are shown. Deviations d_4^- and d_4^+ refer to the first sales goal, viz., an increase of $70 in the first year. The goal of a growth of at least 20% in sales in the second year at least four times as important as the goal for the first year will appear in the objective function as $4d_5^-$. Reference to the first production goal will be made by the subscript 6 and to the second one by the subscript 7. With this notation the mathematical expression of this problem using goal programming is as follows:

minimize $Z = d_4^- + d_4^+ + 4d_5^- + d_6^- + d_6^+ + d_7^- + d_7^+$

subject to

$$14X_1 + 17X_2 + 17X_3 + 15X_4 + 40X_5 + 12X_6 + 14X_7 + 10X_8 \\ + 12X_9 \geqslant 32.4$$

$$12X_1 + 54X_2 + 6X_3 + 6X_4 + 30X_5 + 6X_6 + 48X_7 + 36X_8 \\ + 18X_9 \leqslant 50$$

$$3X_1 + X_2 + 6X_3 + 2X_4 + 35X_5 + 6X_6 + 4X_7 + 3X_8 + 3X_9 \leqslant 20$$

$$14X_1 + 30X_2 + 13X_3 + 11X_4 + 53X_5 + 10X_6 + 32X_7 + 21X_8 \\ + 12X_9 + d_4^- - d_4^+ = 70$$

$$15X_1 + 42X_2 + 16X_3 + 12X_4 + 52X_5 + 14X_6 + 34X_7 + 28X_8 \\ + 21X_9 + d_5^- = 84$$

$$10X_1 + 16X_2 + 13X_3 + 9X_4 + 19X_5 + 14X_6 + 7X_7 + 15X_8 \\ + 8X_9 + d_6^- - d_6^+ = 40$$

$$12X_1 + 16X_2 + 13X_3 + 13X_4 + 16X_5 + 14X_6 + 9X_7 + 22X_8 \\ + 13X_9 + d_7^- - d_7^+ = 40$$

$$X_1, X_2, \ldots, X_9 \geqslant 0$$

Solving this goal programming problem yields the optimal solution presented in Exhibit 8-4.

The net present value of this optimal investment strategy under goal programming is $70.566. This is essentially the same result which Weingartner achieved (the difference being the result of rounding). The

EXHIBIT 8-4

SOLUTION TO MODIFIED PROBLEM

$X_1 = 1.0$	$X_4 = 1.0$	$X_7 = 0$
$X_2 = .037736$	$X_5 = 0$	$X_8 = 0$
$X_3 = 1.0$	$X_6 = .99371$	$X_9 = 1.0$

	Goal Constraint	Optimal Solution
Net present value	$\geqslant 32.4$	70.5660
Budget constraint-1	$\leqslant 50$	49.9999
Budget constraint-2	$\leqslant 20$	19.9999
Sales goal-1	$= 70$	51.0691
Sales goal-2	$= 84$	79.2968
Production goal-1	$= 40$	54.5156
Production goal-1	$= 40$	65.5156

similarity can be explained by the fact that in the goal programming model such a high cost was placed on underachievement of the second period's sales goal, coupled with the presence of that impossibly high goal, that minimum deviations from goals could only be achieved by utilizing resource constraints to their optimum level.

Assume now that the organization feels it is much more important that employment goals be met in each of the two periods than it is that sales goals be met. The objective function then becomes:

minimize $Z = d_4^- + d_4^+ + 3d_5^- + 6d_6^- + 6d_6^+ + 6d_7^- + 6d_7^+$

subject to the same constraints.

The optimal solution to this problem is given in Exhibit 8-5. Notice that although the goals have not been altered from the original example, the optimal solution differs significantly. This, of course, is due to the re-ordering of the goal priorities. While the net present value of $48.67 is lower than in the original solution, it still far exceeds the minimum level established by management as a goal.

EXHIBIT 8-5

SOLUTION WITH EMPLOYMENT GOALS HIGH PRIORITY

$X_1 = 0$	$X_4 = .17066$	$X_7 = 0$
$X_2 = .57462$	$X_5 = .22754$	$X_8 = 0$
$X_3 = 1.0$	$X_6 = .85334$	$X_9 = 0$

	Goal Constraint	Optimal Solution
Net present value	$\geqslant 32.4$	48.6700
Budget constraint-1	$\leqslant 50$	49.9995
Budget constraint-2	$\leqslant 20$	19.9998
Sales goal-1	$= 70$	52.7088
Sales goal-2	$= 84$	65.9606
Production goal-1	$= 40$	39.9997
Production goal-2	$= 40$	39.9997

Consider an adjustment to this revised problem such that management reevaluates its sales goals and determines that they are too high. Specifically, they feel that these goals have been overestimated by 30%. The objective function will be the same as before, as well as all of the goals except the sales goals (fourth and fifth above), which will now be

$$14X_1 + 30X_2 + 13X_3 + 11X_4 + 53X_5 + 10X_6 + 32X_7 + 21X_8 + 12X_9 + d_4^- - d_4^+ = 53.8$$

$$15X_1 + 42X_2 + 16X_3 + 12X_4 + 52X_5 + 14X_6 + 34X_7 + 28X_8 + 21X_9 + d_5^- = 64.6$$

The optimal solution is given in Exhibit 8-6.

EXHIBIT 8-6

SOLUTION TO REEVALUATED SALES GOALS

$X_1 = .33307$	$X_4 = 0$	$X_7 = 0$
$X_2 = .53043$	$X_5 = .22205$	$X_8 = 0$
$X_3 = 1.0$	$X_6 = .78311$	$X_9 = 0$

	Goal Constraint	Optimal Solution
Net present value	≥ 32.4	48.9595
Budget constraint-1	≤ 50	49.9999
Budget constraint-2	≤ 20	19.9999
Sales goal-1	$= 53.8$	53.1755
Sales goal-2	$= 64.6$	65.7841
Production goal-1	$= 40$	39.9999
Production goal-2	$= 40$	39.9999

An interesting result is obtained by solving this revised problem. A seemingly paradoxical higher net present value is obtained by relaxing the sales goals. This can be explained by the fact that in the goal programming formulation, satisfaction of lower priority goals (i.e., those with the lowest "costs") is only attempted after higher priority goals are satisfied. In both Exhibits 8-5 and 8-6 the highest priority goals of employment maintenance are met. However, only in Exhibit 8-6 is the next priority goal of second period sales met. Therefore, it can be seen that in an effort to reach the values related to that goal, other goals which have already been exceeded (in this case only the net present value goal) are sacrificed in an attempt to reach that next priority goal. Under the example where there are relaxed goals, however (since the second period sales goal is met), satisfaction of the third priority goal—the first period sales goal—is attempted. The net present value total increases because the net present value of those investments which are newly introduced into the solution are greater than those that have left. For example, about one-third of X_1 (which has a net present value of 14) has been introduced into the solution in Exhibit 8-6, while what has been sacrificed is about 17% of X_4 (which has a net present value of 15), 7% of X_6 (which has a net present value of 14), and 4% of X_2 (which has a net present value of 17). Notice also that in comparing Exhibit 8-5 and Exhibit 8-6, there is a lower sales goal for the second period in the latter case. This makes sense since that particular goal has been satisfied, and as in the case above any excess over previously satisfied goals may be sacrificed in an effort to reach a lower priority goal.

CONCLUSIONS

This paper is necessarily an exploratory one, and has not been designed to be an exhaustive analysis of goal programming applied to capital budgeting. Instead, it has tried to indicate the usefulness of goal programming in capital budgeting and how it might aid in more realistic approaches to decision analysis of the firm.

It is useful to point out areas which this paper could not explore, and which could be topics in further studies.

The overriding unanswered question is what to do where an integer solution is required. It is difficult to develop a totally realistic capital budgeting model without being able to impose such a constraint efficiently. However, if and when such a solution is found to the integer programming problem, the integer constraint can be applied just as well to GP problems as to other types of LP models.

This paper also has not dealt with the conversion of the more complex probabilistic LP models into the goal programming formulation. This extension could be done as it has been for the LP models.

Finally, the introduction of goal programming into capital budgeting opens to further analysis the possibility of using goal programming to evaluate investment projects in the public sector. In this context, goal programming could be an adjunct to PPB (Planning-Programming-Budgeting) systems. The main problem in the public sector in evaluating investments is that the benefit-cost figures employed are frequently made to conform to political decisions already made. Using the benefit-cost framework then gives the effect of evading economic analysis while appearing to utilize it. Goal programming could provide a useful function by making it possible to explicitly incorporate criteria other than that of a benefit-cost nature into a programming model for the public sector.

REFERENCES

1. William J. Baumol. *Business Behavior, Value and Growth*. New York: Harcourt Brace & World, Inc., revised edition, 1967.
2. William J. Baumol and Richard Quandt. "Investment and Discount Rates Under Capital Rationing—A Programming Approach," *Economic Journal* (June, 1965), p. 317.
3. R. Bryne, A. Charnes, W. Cooper, and K. Kortanek. "A Chance Constrained Approach to Capital Budgeting with Portfolio Type Payback and Liquidity Constraints and Horizon Posture Controls." *Journal of Financial and Quantitative Analysis* (December, 1967), p. 339.
4. A. Charnes and W. Cooper. *Management Models and Industrial Applications of Linear Programming*. New York: John Wiley & Sons, Inc., 1961.
5. Richard M. Cyert and James G. March. *A Behavioral Theory of the Firm*. Englewood Cliffs, New Jersey: Prentice-Hall, Inc., 1963.
6. J. Lorie and L. Savage. "Three Problems in Capital Rationing." *Journal of Business* (October, 1955), p. 229.
7. Stewart C. Myers. "A Note on Linear Programming and Capital Budgeting." *Journal of Finance* (March, 1972), p. 89.
8. Bertil Naslund. "A Model of Capital Budgeting Under Risk." *Journal of Business* (April, 1966), p. 257.
9. H. M. Weingartner. *Mathematical Programming and the Analysis of Capital Budgeting Problems*. Englewood Cliffs, New Jersey: Prentice-Hall, Inc., 1963.

PART III. CAPITAL STRUCTURE AND COST OF CAPITAL

The effect of capital structure on the cost of capital has been closely studied since Modigliani and Miller's provocative work in 1958. Since then questions relating to leverage and the cost of capital for the firm have been set forth by both academicians and practitioners. With the cost of capital increasing, it is very important that financial executives reassess their capital structure planning. The articles included in this section expound on some of the aspects of this subject matter. (Readers will find Article 27 in Section VIII authored by Mr. Joel Stern useful in conjunction with the articles in this Part.)

Mr. Scanlon discusses the financial policies of the Bell System which he feels have offered the maximum possibility of acquiring capital across the entire spectrum of company circumstances and capital market conditions over several decades. He discusses the inherently different characteristics of the Bell System from those of unregulated business, the capital intensive nature of the business, the need to satisfy a large percentage of the need for funds in the capital markets, and the vast increase in the demand for communication service since the end of World War II.

The author also discusses the capital structure of the nation's largest firm. The beneficial aspects of debt include their associated cost and income tax reductions. He advises against excess use of debt which might erode investor confidence and impair the firm's ability to attract capital. Further, Mr. Scanlon, who is Treasurer of AT&T, traces the past financing efforts in detail and discusses the recent complications starting around 1965. He stresses that policies and goals designed to maintain a sound capital structure while achieving adequate levels of earnings are the approaches that have met the past challenges. AT&T's policies applied with sufficient flexibility and judgment will meet the need of the investors and customers in the future.

Professor Michael A. Simkowitz' objective is to communicate the practical impact of modern financial theory to the business community which, in his judgment, has not received adequate attention from academicians. He defines financial strategy as consisting of debt policy, dividend policy, and investment policy. He summarizes the theories in all of those areas and gives Modigliani and Miller credit for introducing the modern era of financial theory. The article covers a broad range of topics which one would expect to find in a discourse on modern financial theory including such topics as the maximization of owner's wealth assumption, perfect markets, and the advantage of corporate leverage as viewed from the point of modern theory.

Professor Simkowitz presents a clear, brief statement of modern financial theory. In concluding, he vividly indicates that modern financial theory points out that extraordinary opportunities are brought about by market imperfections, a point well recognized in both the marketing and production areas.

Professor Robert F. Vandell and Mr. Robert M. Pennell, Manager of Corporate Finance for Optron, Inc., discuss the profound changes in money market conditions and the impact of these conditions on financing an aggressive expansion program. Some authorities feel that the liquidity squeeze is not a thing of the past and the authors offer some guidelines to financial corporate officers for staying flexible in a period of tight-money conditions. They compare the effects of debt and equity financing under "easy money" and "tight money" conditions. In order to illustrate many of their points, they have "created an aggressively managed, medium-sized company with typical financing needs." Debt and equity financing is compared in terms of such factors as the effects on earnings per share, debt burden coverage, flexibility, debt capacity, and dividends.

The authors indicate that many corporate treasurers were caught unaware by the liquidity squeeze and many companies were required to refinance overburdened debt structures at a time when it was disadvantageous to raise equity capital. Despite this hard lesson, the authors indicate that the rules of thumb which were effective in past years are still being used. They conclude that these rules of thumb are "suspect" under tight money conditions.

9. BELL SYSTEM FINANCIAL POLICIES*

JOHN J. SCANLON†

It has been said that all business management is — although some facets of it are indirectly so — *financial* management. Further, the specific financial policies of any well-run business must derive from overall operating philosophy; indeed, they may reflect the basic character and purpose of the enterprise better than other measures of management activity. The primary financial goals of any company are to raise, at reasonable cost, the funds needed to meet corporate objectives, and to achieve an adequate level of earnings on these funds. Therefore, a most critical test of any company's financial policies is whether adherence to such policies has provided the capital required by the enterprise.

Corporate objectives can be explicit or implicit. The objectives of the Bell System are oft stated and well known: to provide the best possible communications services at the lowest cost consistent with responsibilities to employees and investors. Obviously, this fundamental commitment to service generates a need for capital — a need compounded by the basic characteristics of the communications industry. In the aggregate, these factors have resulted in a continuing need for large amounts of new capital. The financial policies followed by the Bell System have been those that appeared to offer the maximum possibility of acquiring this capital across the entire spectrum of capital market conditions and company circumstances. My purpose here is to discuss: (1) how the Bell System's financial policies have been shaped; (2) our past financing efforts as evidence that these policies have met the needs of our business; and (3) our recent and future financing efforts and their consistency with long-run financial objectives.

BASIC CORPORATE CHARACTERISTICS

As a public utility, the Bell System has characteristics inherently different from unregulated businesses. Service must be provided when and where requested. As part of the economy's infrastructure, communications service is required before other industrial and residential development can take place. Further, the communications business is extremely capital-intensive — i.e., large quantities of capital are required to meet service demands. Capital investment of over $2.60 is required to produce $1.00 of annual revenue (sales) — by contrast, the average manufacturing company needs about $.60 to produce a dollar of annual sales. Even the more capital-intensive industrial groups need considerably

---

*From *Financial Management* (Summer, 1972), pp. 16-26. Reprinted by permission.
†Vice-President and Treasurer, American Telephone and Telegraph Company.

less capital to generate a dollar of sales; aluminum companies need $1.30 on average, and petroleum companies need $1.00. (See Exhibit 9-1.) Moreover, it is necessary for us to satisfy about 50% of these capital needs in the capital markets. Again, this contrasts sharply with an average external requirement of only 20% for all industrial firms.

Demand for communications service since the end of World War II has resulted in an increase in Bell telephones in operation from 22.4 million to 100.3 million. During that same period, toll calls have increased 7-fold, from 948 million to nearly 7.8 billion per year. There are other measures of the demand for communications services, but these two are sufficiently representative. As a result, we have had to expend about $74 billion for facilities for new service, increased usage, and technological improvements. To finance this effort we were obliged to raise nearly $36 billion in "new" money from the capital markets—a large task by any standards.

There seems to be no let-up in this demand and hence no slackening in the need for capital to satisfy it. The Bell System construction program totaled $7.6 billion in 1971 and will be about $8.5 billion in 1972. We had to raise more than $4 billion from the capital markets in 1971 for this expansion. Our needs are expected to continue at about the same level, or somewhat higher.

The combined result of being highly capital-intensive, having experienced a high rate of growth in demand, and having a relatively low

EXHIBIT 9-1

CAPITAL PER $1.00 OF REVENUE—1971 . . .

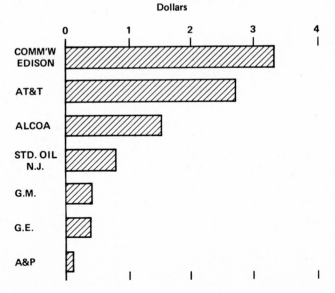

EXHIBIT 9-2

BELL SYSTEM AS A PERCENT OF . . .

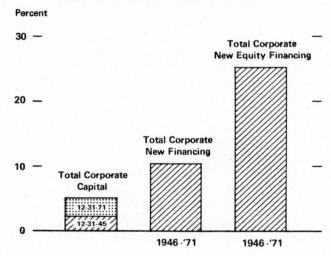

potential for internal generation of new capital needs has been that we have had to raise a disproportionate share of all new external capital. While the Bell System's total capital currently accounts for about 5% of total corporate capital in the United States, we have required about 12% of all corporate financing and 25% of all equity financing. (See Exhibit 9-2.)

Because of the persistent need for new funds, our securities offerings cannot be limited only to those periods when market conditions are favorable. We are not free, for example, to expand our service only when enthusiasm for AT&T stock favors an equity offer, or when interest rates on debt are at a relatively low level. On top of these needs to finance growth and improvements in the telecommunications system, we are at the threshold of an era in which we must refund increasing amounts of maturing debt issues.

From the very early days of the Bell System, these basic corporate characteristics and capital market considerations have necessitated adoption of policies that permitted utilization of all viable sources of funds and provided maximum flexibility of choice between modes of financing.

CAPITAL STRUCTURE

Any firm, but particularly one with heavy capital needs like the Bell System, would find it beneficial to use some debt because of the associated cost and income tax benefits. However, it is essential to avoid excessive use of debt; fixed charge coverage could be eroded and investor confidence in the financial viability of the firm could be destroyed. This would impair the firm's ability to attract capital and ultimately the ability to render adequate service. So the essential problem is to specify how much debt the Bell System should and can safely carry.

The specific level, or even the range, of debt that a firm can carry is not subject to precise determination. It is influenced by many considerations. Formulation of capital structure policy requires subjective evaluation of many factors — and a number of these cannot be quantified. Over time, corporate managements have arrived at quite different conclusions about appropriate levels of debt for their respective businesses. (See Exhibit 9-3.) Further, the amount of debt in a company's capital structure is not always a matter of management choice. It can be affected by capital market conditions, earnings levels, regulatory climate (in the case of utilities), and changes in investor preference. Debt ratio policies must be able to stand the test of time.

In determining how much debt a firm can safely carry, it is necessary to consider the basic risks inherent in that business. This varies considerably among industries and is related essentially to the nature

EXHIBIT 9-3

DEBT RATIOS VARY ACCORDING TO INDUSTRY . . .

AVERAGE 1960 - 1970

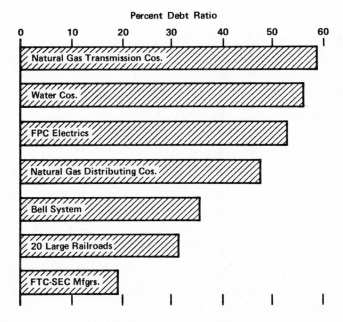

Percent Debt Ratio

and demand for an industry's product, the operating characteristics of
the industry, and its ability to earn an adequate return in an unknown
future. All of these factors have entered into determination of Bell System
debt ratio policy, and the judgments resulting therefrom have been
further evaluated in light of the ranges of debt found desirable in other
industries.

There is an additional important consideration that has influenced
Bell System debt ratio policy—the need to maintain high-grade credit
standing. High-grade credit ratings are granted, obviously, only to companies
that provide the lender the greatest safety of interest and principal.
Consequently, borrowers with the highest rating obtain the lowest
interest costs available at any given time in the marketplace. (Exhibit
9-4 depicts the extent to which debt costs have varied according to
quality ratings.) More importantly, however, high-grade credit assures
maximum breadth of access to capital, particularly in periods of stringent
market conditions. A top rating gives the Bell System flexibility in financing
by appealing to the broadest range of investors available in any

EXHIBIT 9-4

BOND YIELDS VARY ACCORDING TO QUALITY GROUPS...

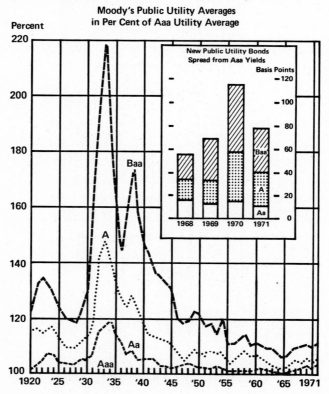

Moody's Public Utility Averages in Per Cent of Aaa Utility Average

situation. Our issues, because they stem from continuing capital needs, must be marketed virtually continually, even in times of extreme credit tightness or when the market is unreceptive for other reasons. It is precisely at such times that the broad appeal of a top credit rating is most valuable.

Because no one can predict either company circumstances or market conditions with complete accuracy, it is prudent financial practice to select an objective range for the ratio of total debt to total capital such that the upper end of the range affords some reserve or margin of borrowing power. If a firm's target debt ratio has been chosen in light of this, it will be able to exceed temporarily its stated target—i.e., "use up" some of the reserve borrowing power—without jeopardy to its credit rating.

All of the foregoing considerations led us to conclude, and reaffirm for a period of many years, that the proper range of our debt was 30% to 40% of total capital. Reasonable success in meeting financial needs under the diverse market and economic conditions that we have faced attest to the appropriateness of this conclusion. (See Exhibit 9-5 for a 50-year history of Bell System debt ratio.)

While financial policy must reflect consideration of long-run implications, it must also contain sufficient flexibility to cope with change. A capital structure should not be altered on a day-to-day or even year-to-year basis, but must be determined with full recognition of possible

EXHIBIT 9-5

BELL SYSTEM DEBT RATIO . . .

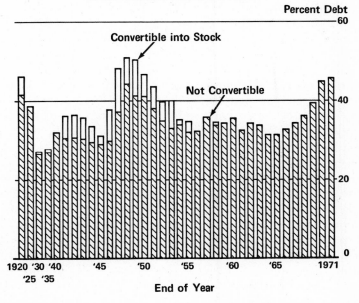

adversity, particularly those conditions beyond management's control. However, when basic circumstances do change, and there is adequate indication that such changes will persist, policy should be adjusted accordingly.

In the late 1950's, it became generally accepted that the dramatic depression-boom swings in our economy could be prevented or at least mitigated. This feeling pervades the 1959 report of the President's Council of Economic Advisers. The basic characteristics underlying this optimism were higher growth rates in our economy to achieve levels of full employment, and higher corporate profits to sustain that growth. Efforts of the government to embed these characteristics into our economy led corporations generally to conclude that a higher level of debt could be carried safely.

However, the Bell System delayed embarking on a program to raise its debt ratio until the middle 1960's because the market for AT&T stock was very favorable during the early 1960's. Two large equity offers were undertaken on extremely favorable terms. It is fortunate that a sizable amount of equity was floated during this period because the borrowing margin this afforded has been invaluable in meeting our recent capital requirements. After the successful completion in 1964 of the second of these offers, debt financing was used almost exclusively for nearly seven years with the intention of subsequent "testing" for the appropriate debt ratio under the then altered economic circumstances.

The results of the new course have been dramatic. At the end of 1964, the Bell System consolidated debt ratio was 32.7%. At the end of 1971, debt comprised 45.5% of total capital, and by the end of 1972, will account for over 47% of capital. There are many indications that we are approaching the limit that can prudently be maintained if we are to retain our high-grade credit. The circumstances surrounding recent downgrading of electric utility debt, as well as our own New England Telephone Company downgrading by Standard and Poor's in March, 1972, suggest that an objective debt ratio of about 45% is appropriate for today's circumstances. Coupled with achievement of adequate earnings levels, this should provide the interest coverage levels required to protect a high-grade quality rating for our debt issues.

Since 1971, we have also added preferred stock, both convertible and nonconvertible. Preferred stock has been utilized as a substitute for common equity. The use of preferred stock was necessitated by conditions that precluded issuance of common on reasonable terms. Moreover, these financings minimized the impact on per-share earnings growth and served to protect the high-grade credit rating of our debt issues.

To illustrate how these financial policies have played a major role in meeting the needs of the business, it would be helpful to recount some of the pertinent details of Bell System financings in several periods in the past.

PAST FINANCING EFFORTS

Immediately after World Wars I and II, we faced immense service needs that required large amounts of capital. Each time, inadequate earnings and a depressed market for AT&T stock presented financing problems. We persevered in (1) protecting our highgrade debt rating by various financing techniques, and (2) getting our earnings levels up. With adequate earnings restored, balanced financing was subsequently possible, borrowing margins were restored, and we were in a position to withstand the next period of adversity. We currently are faced with problems not unlike those of the two postwar periods. This situation began to take shape in the late 1960's and has significantly influenced our financing activities since 1967. Our current and future activities will also be shaped by these circumstances.

As the nation emerged from World War I, the rate of inflation was very high and wages and other costs were increasing rapidly. The Bell System was faced with a huge demand for new service—only about 30% of U.S. households had telephone service—that could only be met through massive (for that time) financing. But Bell System rates had not kept pace with increased costs and, as a result, earnings levels were completely inadequate. AT&T stock was selling below par, thus legally precluding issuance of additional equity. Shareowners were disenchanted with AT&T; they had subscribed to less than 25% of a 1918 issue of 6% convertible bonds, and the balance of the issue had to be sold to underwriters at $91.

Moreover, the debt ratio at the end of 1920, including the outstanding convertible debt, was 46%. Moody's Investors Service was citing an ominous parallel between the railroads and the Bell System. They noted deterioration in service and questionable quality of our bonds, some of which were rated Ba.

Improved earnings were critical to the new capital required. A round of rate cases was instituted and vigorously pursued. Earnings began to improve as early as 1921. Continuation of this rate program achieved equity earnings in the middle 1920's in parity with those of other corporations, and investor interest was rekindled.

Improving earnings made it possible to attract the required capital to meet service demands. During the 1920's, the Bell System was able to sell both equity and debt, and total capital increased by over 200%. In the process, equity financing was emphasized with the result that the debt ratio was reduced to the mid-30% level. This greatly improved the quality of both debt and equity, enhancing the attractiveness of AT&T security offers. By the end of the decade, AT&T shareowners had increased to 470,000 (from 140,000 in 1920) and the debt ratio was actually below 30%. Instead of increasing debt to boost equity earnings through "leveraging," the Bell System opted for the longer range objectives of a sound capital structure and a broad base of shareowners attracted by reasonable earnings and regular dividends.

When the Depression came and earnings declined, many regulated enterprises were overwhelmed by heavy debt and its fixed charges. As a result, many electric and railroad companies went bankrupt, wiping out whole classes of investors. The Bell System, however, survived the Depression even though its annual total income declined 40.1% (as opposed to a decline of only 16.3% for the electrics).

At the end of World War II, the situation was similar to that of 1920. There was surging inflation; despite wage and price controls during the war, the cost of living and cost of materials were up 40%-60% over pre-war levels. There was also widespread fear that the end of the war would trigger a postwar depression. In these circumstances, AT&T's main objective was to continue to pay the stable $9 annual dividend that had stood the test of time. This was the keystone of AT&T's successful financing in the early postwar period. We were literally "living on our reputation,"—i.e., the continuous $9 dividend paid throughout the 1920's and the Depression years.

In the early post-World War II years, AT&T's rate of return was at Depression levels. Telephone service was inadequate; the System had a backlog of almost two million unfilled orders for service. The first nation-wide telephone strike occurred in 1947. In such an environment AT&T could not issue stock; it would have seriously diluted earnings per share. The most feasible alternative seemed to be offers of straight debt—as long as the market was receptive—interspersed with offers of convertible debentures to shareowners to give the market a "rest." These convertibles differed in a significant way from those issued by most other firms. The conversion price was set *below* the then market price—but not as far below as would have been the case in a direct offer of common. This encouraged early conversion and brought some equity capital into the company as earnings began their slow recovery.

We again sought rate relief, but the rate case road was much rockier than during the 1920's. It was well into the 1950's before our rate activity, coupled with the effects of rapid technological improvements, achieved acceptable earnings levels. Meantime, our debt ratio soared to over 50%, convertibles included. Only the presence of this large quantity of convertible debt and the prospect that such debt would ultimately be converted convinced the marketplace that our capital structure goal continued to be 30%-40%, and prevented downgrading of our bonds. Between 1945 and 1955, we raised nearly $9 billion of new capital, with over $4 billion in equity through conversions. This approach restored our debt ratio to 35%, the middle of our objective range. Adequate earnings and restoration of a reasonable debt ratio set the stage for the balanced debt/equity financing during the next 10 years.

The latter half of the 1950's saw a gradual but pervasive change in the approach to investment decision making. While the concept of total returns—both dividend yield and market appreciation—had previously been recognized by some, it was not until 1958 that expectations of per-share earnings and market price growth drove common stock yields below those available on high-grade bonds. That year was also a turning point for AT&T; late in 1958 we increased the dividend for the first time since 1921, and also split the stock three for one.

Investors responded enthusiastically and the market price surged upward. In the early 1960's, our situation was enhanced by a generally favorable economy with stable interest rates, moderate inflation, and an improving stock market. Adequate earnings and strong equity markets afforded the opportunity to strengthen further our financial structure and to build in future borrowing margin.

In 1961 and 1964, we mounted common stock issues which produced about $2.25 billion of new equity. Moreover, strong demand for AT&T stock allowed setting favorable terms for both issues. The offering price was set sufficiently below market to provide attractive rights values, thus encouraging investor response. Yet there was still room to provide a significant premium above book equity, enhancing our per-share earnings growth.

After the 1964 stock issue, we began to rely almost exclusively on debt financing for reasons described earlier. Almost coincident with our move to increase our debt ratio, economic changes began to unfold that have complicated this process and that ultimately have led to the financing difficulties AT&T currently faces.

RECENT COMPLICATIONS

In 1965, the rate of inflation began to increase again, accelerated steadily until the summer of 1971, and is still well above the postwar average. This has had a dramatic impact on both our expenditures for new construction—specifically, the cumulative effect since 1965 has been in excess of $5 billion—and on our operating costs. The "bottom line" result has been a steady deterioration in our earnings; in 1971, earnings fell below 9% on average book equity for the first time in 13 years. This contrasts with the 10% we earned in 1960 and the 9.9% as recently as in 1966.

Further, equity investors recognize that high interest rates and the regulatory lag involved in attempts to achieve improved earnings through rate relief make it difficult to show competitive earnings improvement as long as inflation remains at or near current levels. These factors have resulted in a long period of depressed prices for AT&T stock. (See Exhibit 9-6.)

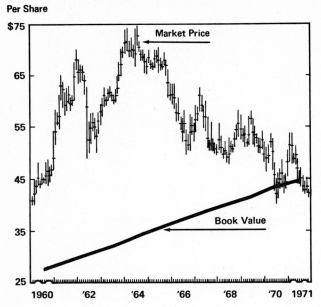

EXHIBIT 9-6

AT&T MARKET AND BOOK VALUES . . .

Even if we wanted to return to equity financing, our access to the equity markets has been effectively barred since 1968 by the price of our stock. Although the stock market was booming in the years 1966-1968, AT&T stock—along with the stocks of most other regulated utilities—was not following the trend. When the general market was hit badly in 1969-1970, AT&T performed even more poorly. In spite of the market rebound between May, 1970, and mid-1972, AT&T is still around its 1970 range, in the low 40's.

As recent growth in our construction program requirements has increased, our annual new money requirements moved from $1.5 billion to the $4 billion plus range. As a first step to meet this new level, we have steadily increased the frequency and size of our subsidiary company bond issues. During 1971 and the first half of 1972, we came to market nearly every three weeks with issues averaging between $125 and $150 million. Market experts tell us this is about as far as we can go without creating marked digestion problems for Bell System debt issues—digestion problems that would quickly be translated into cost penalties. As a result, we have found it necessary to utilize financing avenues beyond these straight debt issues.

Beginning in 1968, we undertook a program of borrowing in the short-term debt markets, i.e., bank loans and commercial paper. Our intention here was to mitigate drafts on the long-term markets, but we recognized that at best this would provide relief for only one or two years. By 1970, our level of short-term debt was up to about $2.0 billion, a prudent upper limit by all reasonable tests. Even after utilizing this relief measure, we find ourselves faced with a continuing need for around $1.5 billion of additional external financing each year.

But the debt financing we have done since 1964 has pushed our debt ratio to nearly 47%—notwithstanding $2 billion of preferred stock in the last year or so. As a result of this debt financing and high interest rates, our earnings coverage of annual debt charges fell in 1971 to less than four times pre-tax and three times post-tax (see Exhibit 9-7), our lowest levels since the early 1930's. We have used up most of our borrowing margin, and our earnings are inadequate to allow common equity financing on reasonable terms. At the same time, we are still faced with continuing large capital needs to meet service requirements.

In 1968, we started our current round of rate cases in order to improve our earnings posture. But this has been a long and tedious process. We have initiated over 70 cases thus far and intend to persevere in this effort—as well as in our efforts to increase operating efficiencies and introduce technological improvements—until adequate earnings levels are achieved. Meanwhile, we must continue to attract needed capital in the face of market and earnings constraints.

Our debenture with warrant issue in 1970, convertible preferred issue in 1971, and private placement early in 1972 were the most recent financing vehicles we selected to meet this need. Although vastly different in nature, the bonds with warrants and convertible preferred were both directed at our shareowners—a group we had not appealed to for capital since 1964. Both were equity-related, although the debenture

EXHIBIT 9-7

BELL SYSTEM INTEREST COVERAGE . . .

(PRE-TAX)

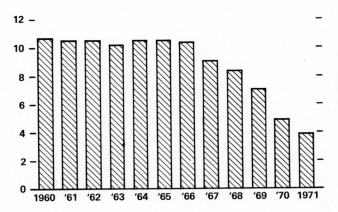

portion of the 1970 issue was designed and marketed to appeal in large part to debt investors other than our traditional market sources. Attractive terms were set on both issues; a full 8.75% coupon on the bonds and a $4.00 dividend rate on the $50 preferred. However, it is worthy of note that participation by our stockholders was significantly lower in both the 1970 and 1971 issues than in our stock issues of 1961 and 1964. Obviously, this is a situation that must be reversed if the equity offerings that will be required in the future are to be successful.

By late 1971, it was essential that we prevent further large increases in our debt ratio and halt the erosion in our interest coverage; preferred stock offered the most feasible means of accomplishing this. It was for this reason that $625 million of the $1 billion private placement was in the form of a straight preferred.

SUMMARY

In review, we have seen that it is the nature of our business that has been the main determinant of our capital structure goals and attendant financial policies for over a half-century. Our primary concern has been with the long-run financial health of the business. Although our financing decisions have had to adapt long-run objectives to contemporaneous conditions, we have tried to avoid short-term expedients which were contrary to our long-run goals. We have opted for financial policies which would maintain the integrity of an investment in AT&T over the years and enhance our appeal to our shareowners and a broad range of other investors on whom we must continually rely.

Embracing sound long-term goals has proved to be extremely important because economic and financial difficulties have a habit of reappearing. We may not be able to forecast their incidence precisely, but we can be assured these difficulties will return from time to time. So, too, will the problems of running a viable public utility in the face of difficulties — such as heavy service demand and large construction programs (particularly during accelerating inflationary periods), declining earnings, and poor market reception for AT&T stock. Moreover, the intensity of competition for investment capital is likely to accelerate.

Policies and goals aimed at maintaining a sound capital structure and achieving adequate levels of earnings are the approaches that have met past challenges — across a wide range of internal and external circumstances. Applied with sound judgment and sufficient flexibility to accommodate either basic changes or transient conditions, we believe they will meet the future needs of our customers and our investors.

10. MODERN FINANCIAL THEORY: IMPACT ON ANALYSIS OF STRATEGY*

New financial theories have been developed that have implications for financial strategy. The author first defines the area of strategy as consisting of debt, dividend, and investment policies. Modern theory holds that if we assume perfect capital markets, no taxes, and no growth, the financing decision cannot affect the total value of the firm. With respect to dividends, the theory argues that any artificial division of the benefit stream should have no material effect on the worth of the enterprise. As for investments, two firms in the same "equivalent return class" will maintain the relationship between their operating earnings regardless of other factors. In short, modern financial theory recognizes that extraordinary opportunities are exploitations of market imperfections.

The financial theory of the firm has evolved rapidly during the past two decades. To a large extent, the academic community has not conveyed to the business community the practical impact of these new theories. This article hopes to communicate to the business community the general nature of this modern theory and its impact upon financial strategy.

For the purposes of this article, it is important that the realm of decisions that make up financial strategy be carefully defined. Neither short-term decisions nor the specific tactics of long-range decisions will be dealt with; these decisions are determined largely by specific conditions. This is similar to the separation of military strategy and tactics. We will deal with strategy that is not dominated by specific firm situations or events.

FINANCIAL STRATEGY

In brief, financial strategy consists of debt policy (the proportion of the financing that should come from other than the stockholders, that is, debt of any form); dividend policy (the proportion or absolute amount of current profits that should be returned to the stockholders); and investment policy (the assets that should be owned by the corporation).

---

*From *Business Horizons* (February, 1972), pp. 89–96. Copyright, 1972 by the Foundation for the School of Business at Indiana University. Reprinted by permission.
†Associate Professor of Finance, Graduate School of Business, Indiana University.

Debt Policy

The corporation serves as a capital intermediary that receives funds from investors and converts them into real, productive assets. There are two broad classes of investments: loans on the basis of a contractual arrangement via debt, and investments that make the stockholder a residual beneficiary of the enterprise. In general, these are two distinct categories, but there is an overlap with such assets as investment vehicles, convertible securities, preferred stock, income bonds, and so on. For the purpose of our discussion, let us assume that there are just two distinct categories: debt and equity.

From the corporation's standpoint, debt and equity differ in two major ways. *First,* they differ in the degree of flexibility that management has in dealings with the existing holders of the corporation's stocks and bonds. The responsibility of the corporation to bondholders is defined explicitly in the bond indenture agreement. Other debt holders (trade creditors or suppliers of bank credit) have their relations defined either by similar contract or by the commercial code of the various states. Due to the nature of the agreement, any modification after the fact involves tenuous and formal negotiation; rarely does the corporation bargain from a position of strength. If the terms of the contract cannot be met or be modified to the satisfaction of the bondholders and the financial exigency of the corporation, bankruptcy or reorganization often results.

In contrast, the corporation's financial responsibility to its stockholders is defined in the broadest manner by the corporate charter, its amendments, and the bylaws of the corporation. These documents do little to specify the financial responsibilities of the corporation. The board of directors has the power to invest, pay dividends, and issue debt at its discretion. Only in the authorization of new stock certificates is there near universal need to obtain specific stockholder approval.

Second, debt and equity differ in tax treatment. The federal tax laws provide for the inclusion of interest as a deductible expense; payments to stockholders in the form of dividends are not deductible. This disparity of treatment is a fundamental factor in both the decisions of the practicing businessman and in the construction of the modern normative finance theory.

Thus, debt policy is the selection of the proper financing mix: bonds versus equity. The question of timing of the issues are decisions of a short-run nature and are more tactical than strategic.

Dividend Policy

Every corporation must decide how much capital it is going to return to its stockholders during a specific time period. Most firms have established policies that are publicly expressed as a certain dollar amount per quarter or year. But in the board rooms of corporations, there are discussions as to payout ratios, the proportion of earnings that are to be paid over some longer run. It is this decision that falls under the province of dividend strategies.

The strategies open to a corporation range from one extreme to the other—from no dividend payments at all to the pay-out of all earnings. At any point in time, we find corporations following strategies at various points across the whole spectrum. It is not the object of this article to explain or excuse these various behaviors, but to relate modern finance theory to the various options.

Investment Policy

Every corporation must invest the funds entrusted to it by its bond-holders and stockholders. It is the selection of the assets that a corporation holds that comprises its investment policy. The general thrust of modern theory is predicated on the assumption that the corporation's goal is the maximization of the wealth of its stockholders. This does not mean that the short-run interests of the stockholders are catered to at the expense of the interests of consumers, labor, management, society, and so on. Rather, it means that every alternative action or decision has some value to the stockholder, and the one chosen should be that which maximizes the present wealth of the stockholders.

For example, a foreman has a choice between production schedules A and B. A may have the lower cash and accounting costs but is extremely distasteful to the work force. Although A may minimize costs in the short run (and thus maximize short-run profits), it will also increase the probability of labor problems—strikes, slow-downs, damage, and so on. Thus, it is conceivable that B is the superior policy from the standpoint of the wealth maximization criterion.

The corporation, as it allocates its fund for the proper asset investment, should select those assets that will provide the maximum present value to the common stockholders. The present value of a specific choice depends upon the cash flows expected from the present to the end of the planning horizon. The reliability of these expectations determines the appropriate rate at which we will discount future cash flows. The less reliable the expectations and the riskier the alternative, the higher the discount rate. Thus, socially or politically hazardous choices may have low values because of either small expected future flows or the low level of reliability of the expectations or both.

It is commonly observed that a given investment is more attractive to some companies than others. This is due to the lack of perfect markets in both factor and product markets. These imperfections, plus the uniqueness of the managerial skill, explain the specialization of firms into particular industries.

MODERN THEORY

Debt

The modern era of finance theory can be dated from the publication of the first of a series of articles by Modigliani and Miller.[1] They advanced the theory that if we assume perfect capital markets, no taxes, and no growth, there is no way that the financing decision (bonds versus equity) can have any effect upon the total value of the firm.

The assumption of perfect capital [markets] is crucial to their analysis and, therefore, deserves some careful consideration. The necessary conditions for a perfect market are: (1) no transaction costs; (2) no barrier to entry; and (3) the inability of one buyer or seller to influence the price of the commodity. For any single financial asset, conditions (2) and (3) are met and (1), transaction costs, can be shown to be similar to transportation costs, which do not destroy the perfect market assumption. But Modigliani and Miller and later modern theorists go beyond this and state that all equities can be viewed as being traded in *one* perfect market. Since to the investor an investment in any financial asset provides the same kind of reward—an uncertain future return—there is a set of prices that can and would be set in the market place so that all equities are perfect substitutes for one another. The same argument can be applied to the bond market.

Thus, to the managerial investor all forms of debt become perfect substitutes for each other. Thus, the investor substitutes personal leverage in the form of margin notes or home mortgages for the debt of the corporations whose equities he holds. From the corporation's point of view, the perfect capital market assumption implies that there are no ways for it to differentiate its financial assets (common stock and bonds) from other financial assets given the investments of the corporation (the corporation's assets).

Thus, the corporation is an aggregation of real assets that generate a stream of net operating income. This stream and its risk characteristics determine the total value of the corporation as a going concern. If all forms of debt are perfect substitutes, then the corporation can neither adopt a debt policy that the investor cannot undo nor adopt a debt policy

---

[1]Franco Modigliani and Merton Miller, "The Cost of Capital, Corporation Finance, and the Theory of Investment," *American Economic Review* (June, 1958). The article attracted several worthwhile comments. The most widely noted are David Durand, "The Cost of Capital, Corporation Finance, and the Theory of Investment—Comment," *American Economic Review* (September, 1959); J. Fred Weston, "A Test of Capital Propositions," *Southern Economic Journal* (October, 1963). Later articles or comments by Modigliani and Miller appeared in the *American Economic Review* (September, 1958; June, 1963; and June, 1966), and in the *Journal of Business* (October, 1961).

Also see John Lintner, "Dividends, Earnings, Leverage, Stock Prices, and the Supply of Capital to Corporations," *Review of Economics and Statistics* (August, 1962), for a comprehensive but complex article taking issue with some of Modigliani and Miller's arguments. These articles represent but a fraction of the research in this area.

that the investor cannot arrange by himself. If two firms hold assets that are identical in terms of the expected returns and variation of these expectations, their worth will be proportionate to their size and independent of their financing. The important distinction to remember is that the modern theory states that the advantage of corporate leverage is provided by the tax code and possibility of bankruptcy and not by any mystical process where the sum of the parts (debt and equity) are worth more then the whole (the going concern value of the assets of the firm).

As an example of how Modigliani and Miller's theory would work, let us describe two firms, X and Y. We will assume that the two firms have had identical rates of return and identical uncertainty of that rate of return, and that there is a perfect capital market where all debt instruments are perfect substitutes for each other. Then it can be shown that the value of these two firms must, in equilibrium, be proportional to the size of their assets.

In order to show how this equilibrium would be maintained, we will start with a levered firm selling at a higher total value than its identical but unlevered counterpart (see Table 10-1). We will then describe the transactions that a rational investor in the "over-valued" security would undertake.

TABLE 10-1
COMPARISON OF COMPANIES X AND Y

	X	Y
Assets (book value)	$1,000,000	$1,000,000
Net operating income	150,000	150,000
Interest	30,000°	0
New income available for common stock	120,000	150,000
Dividends	120,000	150,000
Price of common earnings	12	10
Value of common stock	1,440,000	1,500,000
Value of bonds	500,000°	0
Total value of firm	*$1,944,000*	*$1,500,000*

°Total of $500,000 in bonds outstanding at 6 percent interest; assumes no taxes.

Assume that an investor owns $14,400 worth of stock in Company X; his income is $1,200 and, as a 1 percent owner, he is in essence a borrower of 1 percent of the debt of Company X or $5,000.

This investor can sell his $14,400 of Company X stock, borrow $5,000 at 6 percent from his bank, and purchase $19,400 of the common stock of Company Y. The investor's financial positions before and after this switch are summarized in Table 10-2.

If the above mechanism, which Modigliani and Miller call arbitrage, is available to the investors in the stock of Company X, they will have every incentive to attempt to use it. Table 10-2 shows how an investor

TABLE 10-2

EFFECTS OF SWITCH FROM X TO Y

	Before	After
Investor's equity	$14,400	$14,400
Debt via corporate ownership	5,000	0
Debt via personal borrowing	0	5,000
Stock held	14,400	19,400
Income received	1,200	1,940
Interest paid (personally)	0	300
Net income	1,200	1,640
Total debt equity	$5,000/14,400	$5,000/14,400

who originally had $14,400 invested in the equity of the levered Company X is in essence a borrower of $5,000 via his proxy, Company X. If he in turn can sell this investment, borrow $5,000 on his own, and buy $19,400 of Company Y stock after paying the interest on his loan, he has increased his net income by $440, while his total leverage has remained $5,000 in debt for a $14,400 equity investment.

Since it was assumed that X and Y were identical in the uncertainty of their net operating incomes, the investor's uncertainty as to his income streams is identical for both investors. Thus, we see that the rational investor in Company X will sell his stock and purchase stock on margin in Company Y. This process will go on as long as the total value of X is greater than Y. But this process will force the value of Company X down as investors sell, and the value of Company Y will rise as investors buy.

Thus, Modigliani and Miller described how, under their assumptions, an investor could in essence substitute his debt for the debt of a corporation so as to profit from any disparity in value between two firms identical in every way except the amount of debt in their capital structure. Most crucial to the analysis is the assumed indifference of an investor between borrowing personally and borrowing via the corporation. Since the latter method of borrowing places the corporate entity between the stockholder and the holder of debt instrument, the limited liability feature of the corporation makes borrowing via the corporation relatively more attractive.

Note that the theory initially assumed that there were no taxes, no growth, and perfect capital markets. In later writing, these assumptions were relaxed so that taxes, uncertainty, and growth were accounted for. The final status of the Modigliani and Miller theory is that as long as the threat or probabilities of bankruptcy exists, there is not a perfect substitutability of personal for corporate debt.

There is advantage for corporate debt via the income tax treatment of the corporation's interest expense. Because this expense is deductible, it is advantageous for firms to borrow as opposed to letting the individual "roll his own" leverage via margining his securities. The important distinction to remember is that the modern theory states that the advantage of corporate leverage is based on the tax code and possibility of bankruptcy, and not due to any mystical process where the sum of the parts (debt and equity) are worth more than the whole (the going concern value of the assets of the firm).

Dividends

With respect to dividend policy, Modigliani and Miller advanced the argument that any artificial division of the benefit stream, earnings into retained earnings, and dividends should have no material effect on the worth of the enterprise.[2] They proposed a mechanism similar to their arbitrage argument for debt: if a stockholder desires dividend larger than is currently being paid, he can sell some of his holdings to increase his current cash position at the expense of his investment position. Thus, the investor has control of his relative position of investment versus income. This argument is quite sound if we assume no transaction costs, no personal taxes, and no uncertainty as to future stock prices. The reverse procedure holds, that is, that if the dividend is too large, the investor can always reinvest some proportion of his quarterly dividend.

If the investor is in a high tax bracket, it will be advantageous for him to hold low dividend securities while those investors who look toward their security holdings as sources of current income have an incentive to hold high dividend securities. These incentives take the form of avoidance of the uncertainties of the stock market as mechanism for converting security wealth into cash, and the avoidance of the transaction costs incurred in the conversion. Thus, we can see that some investors may have strong preferences as to holding of equities of companies with a similar dividend policy.

The existence of these preferences does not mean that a corporation can increase its value by changing its dividend policy. As stated simply, the existence of these preferences does not necessarily imply that there is an optimal dividend policy for a firm.

Is this an anomaly? How can this be? First, let us assume that at the present the stock market is in equilibrium—money is not flowing from stocks with one kind of dividend policy into stocks with another. If this is true (Elton and Guber [*sic*] provide evidence of this[3]), then we can visualize that securities with a given dividend policy are held by investors who are satisfied with that particular policy. This effect is called

---

[2]Merton Miller and Franco Modigliani, "Dividend Policy, Growth, and the Valuation of Shares," *Journal of Business* (October, 1961).

[3]Edwin J. Elton and Martin J. Gruber, "Marginal Stockholder Tax Rates and the Clientele Effect," *Review of Economics and Statistics* (February, 1970), pp. 68-72.

the clientele effect; for each security there is a clientele that desires to hold it. In equilibrium there is nothing to be gained by a corporation from a change in its dividend policy, for when they do this they are abandoning their clientele in the hope of encroaching on another.

Why pay dividends at all? Why not let each would-be clientele make their own dividend policy via partial sales? The argument has been made that dividends, of and by themselves, are desirable, but yet many empirical studies have shown that the major value of a dividend payment is due to the information it conveys about the future earnings of the firm. This is known as the "informational contact" of dividends. The premise behind this is that the action of the board of directors in declaring and paying a dividend conveys confidence as to the viability of the assets and their profitability. It is this information that is valued and not the fact that the corporation has sent the stockholder a portion of his *own* wealth.

Investment Policy

The choice of assets has been traditionally linked to the area that most differentiates one corporate entity from another, and modern theory has not challenged this. Modigliani and Miller stated in their original article that the irrelevance of debt (assuming no taxes, perfect markets, and so on) depended upon the existence of "equivalent return classes."

These classes were made up of firms with operating incomes that differed only by a scale factor across all possible outcomes. This means that two firms in the same class will maintain the relationship between their operating earnings regardless of the state of the economy, interest rates, aggregate demand, income distribution, or any other factor. Obviously, this implies that firms in the same class have similar assets, and that the selection of assets determines the class and thus the value of the firm.

In a developed and diversified economy, such as ours, where some firms produce assets and others purchase them in order to produce either other goods (assets) or services, it is implied that the purchasing firm can use the asset to greater economic advantage than the seller. In other words, the purchaser places a higher value on the asset than the seller. This differential value exists because of imperfections in the economy. Thus, General Motors produces a truck and sells it to Yellow Freight because Yellow Freight, which has an existing fleet, routes, and terminals, can earn more by using the truck than can GM. These imperfections can be legal, economies of scale, patents, geographical location, unique sources of either raw material or labor inputs, or unique entrepreneurial skill.

It is possible for a firm to invade the domain of either its supplier or customer via vertical merger and integration. This path has been growing more difficult as the antitrust laws are applied more readily.

The expansion of a firm at a rate greater than its industry eventually will involve the absorption of some of its competitors through horizontal mergers. This route has also been narrowed by the antitrust activities of the Justice Department.

The most recent mode of expansion in the spotlight has been the conglomerate merger. When a firm purchases another whose business is not related (neither vertical or horizontal integration occurs) a conglomerate merger has taken place. These mergers have been relatively exempt from regulation since they do not appear a priori to lessen competition. The conglomerate merger is often defended and defined as being strictly a financial combination in which the stockholders of both firms benefit, leaving the customers and suppliers of both firms essentially unaffected. Modern finance theory has some relevant applications for this form of investment.

Modern theory predicates that a good decision is one which increases the wealth of the stockholder. Modigliani and Miller advocate that certain decision areas can be left to the stockholder if the capital markets are perfect markets, that is, if individual participants in the market, whether corporations or individuals, have equal and non-discriminatory access to the market. With these points in mind, let us view two firms, A and B. Firm A seeks to form a conglomerate with B. Both are valued in the stock market. Let us assume that A has a higher price earnings multiple than B, a common situation. The commonly accepted logic is that A buys B and that their combined earnings will be capitalized at the higher multiple.

If the capital markets are perfect, then the stockholders of A have always had the opportunity to become stockholders in B by the simple and direct method of individually adding the stock of B to their individual portfolios. If they have this opportunity, then it is not clear at all why it should be to their advantage for A, acting as their proxy, to purchase stock in B at a price higher than the prevailing price of B. The defense for evaluating the conglomeration A-B at a higher value than sum of the individual value of A and B is that, first, A will change the management and/or operation of B, and, second, the combination A-B will achieve financial diversification for the stockholders.

The answer to the first argument is that, if there is a management change or a classical turnaround situation, then there may be reason for increased value to be placed upon the conglomerate. But the past success of management changes has been far from assured and the resulting value is open to serious question. If the changes are of the nature of product or supply line assimilation, then we are really talking about either a horizontal or vertical merger, which do have value. The second point is answered by raising the counter question: if the capital markets are perfect, how can this diversification be purchased by A at a lower price than by the individual stockholders of A?

Thus, modern finance theory would say that a combination of A and B would not create additional value unless some change in the operations of the two firms takes place. A strictly financial combination cannot increase the value since the stockholders via their personal stock portfolios can always achieve this financial diversification.

Thus, there must be some imperfection in the capital market that can be exploited to justify the increase in value. The concept of financial synergism is based on the idea that a combination of two relatively independent but uncertain operations will produce a lower level of uncertainty in relationship to the gain. This lower relative risk can be translated into a debt policy question by showing that a combination can thus make greater use of debt and yet remain at the same total risk level. By doing this, the combination or conglomerate is in essence exploiting the tax advantage of debt.[4]

A related concept is that the combination has a lower probability of bankruptcy strictly due to the increased size.[5] This is analogous to the concept in inventory management that the safety stock of a good increases less than proportionate to the demand. Thus, a large grocery store with twice the demand for eggs as a small store does not have to stock daily twice the amount of eggs as the smaller store in order to maintain the same probability of stockout.

In the case of the financial conglomerate, bankruptcy is nothing more than a stockout of liquidity. Thus, the financial conglomerate may have a lower probability of bankruptcy than either firm individually. Funds or liquidity will flow more freely between the pseudo-independent entities of a conglomerate than they would if these units were truly independent. This condition is itself an imperfection in the capital market.

It is generally accepted that a corporation owes its existence to the fact that it can operate in the factor and product markets more efficiently than the individual investor. If this were not true, then the stockholders of GM, for example, could build cars in their backyards and have as high a return on their investment at as low a risk as they achieve via their investment in GM's stock. This is analogous to the conclusion on conglomerates: if the conglomeration is just a financial combination and capital markets are perfect, then the stockholders of A and B do not need their corporations serving as proxies.

---

[4]Robert Litzenberger and Donald Tuttle, "Financial Synergism and the Maximum Price for an Acquisition," presented before the Southern Finance Association, November, 1971.

[5]Haim Levy and Marshall Sarnat, "Diversification, Portfolio Analysis, and the Uneasy Case for Conglomerate Mergers," *Journal of Finance* (September, 1970). Also see Wilbur G. Lewellen, "A Pure Financial Rationale for the Conglomerate Merger," *Journal of Finance* (May, 1971); and John Lintner, "Expectations, Mergers, and Equilibrium in Purely Competitive Security Markets," *American Economic Review* (May, 1971).

The major impact of modern finance theory has been to make the analysis of strategy options more orderly. Knowledge that the capital markets are, in themselves, near perfect, forces the justification of basing many options on specific imperfections such as taxes and the risk of bankruptcy.

Thus, we see that modern financial theory has done nothing more than state that extraordinary opportunities are the exploitations of market imperfections. This is well recognized in both marketing and production where the function is to recognize and/or create imperfections (via marketing research, advertising, and research and development) and then exploit these through pricing and production. The same holds true in finance. The financial markets, by the very nature of their structure and the characteristics of their products—risk and return—are less likely to have major recognizable imperfections.

11. TIGHT-MONEY FINANCING*

ROBERT F. VANDELL†
and ROBERT M. PENNELL††

FOREWORD

Many corporate financial officers, accustomed to the unstrained financial atmosphere of the economic boom of the 1960's, experienced difficulties in their external financing during the recent liquidity squeeze. But those circumstances are not a thing of the past; and, as the authors of this article point out, some authorities predict that tight-money conditions will prevail throughout the current decade. Here the authors offer some guidelines for staying flexible in this environment. They compare debt and equity financing in terms of such critical factors as effect on earnings per share, internal funds flows, debt burden coverage, debt capacity, flexibility, and dividends.

The tight-money environment of 1970 was no doubt the severest that most senior corporate officers had experienced in their careers. Lenders not only had a limited supply of funds, but they were demanding high interest (the prime rate reached 8½% early last year), indirect compensation such as large compensating balances, and equity kickers. And they were paying closer attention to risk differentials.

Those companies that were pursuing the aggressive debt policies that had become fashionable during the 1960's found them to be inordinately expensive. In response to the changed conditions, corporate financial officers took a number of steps, including:

○ Use of short-term money to avoid long-term commitments at high rates.

○ Paying more attention to timing of debt issues to obtain more favorable rates.

○ Stressing equity and convertible funds in place of debt, and reducing debt-to-equity ratios to levels more consistent with the less aggressive policies of the 1950's.

○ Cutting back expansion plans in order to limit dependence on external sources of funds.

During the late 1960's, another fundamental change occurred. Price/earnings ratios declined in response to rises in interest rates and the poorer growth prospects of many larger companies. The cyclical

*From *Harvard Business Review* (September–October, 1971), pp. 82-97. © 1971 by the President and Fellows of Harvard College; all rights reserved. Reprinted by permission.
†Professor of Business Administration, Graduate School of Business, University of Virginia.
††Manager of Corporate Finance, Optron, Inc.

stock market adjustment in the spring of 1969 emphasized the more fundamental adjustment that had been taking place for several years (notwithstanding the wonder company "fads of the moment" that distracted the market from the long-term developments).

As a result, equity funds are now more difficult and expensive to raise. A number of companies are stuck with "hung" convertibles having greatly diminished chances of achieving conversion in the foreseeable future. And there have been other adverse complications as well. In short, financing a corporation's needs today is a new ball game.

Following a period in which credit was easier and the liquidity squeeze had subsided, interest rates, at this writing (May 1971), have started to rise again. Moreover, most financial experts are expecting tight-money conditions to become more or less normal in the current decade. That is the reason for our writing this article.

In the article we focus on the choice between debt and equity financing faced by a company in times of tight money, contrasted with the circumstances characterized by lower interest rates, such as prevailed in the late 1950's. (For convenience, we have labeled the latter period "easy money.")

As the model for our analysis we have created an aggressively managed, medium-sized company with typical financing needs. We have named it Universal Things, Inc. Universal is considering raising $10 million to finance its immediate and prospective needs. In Exhibit 11-1 we have outlined the factors which affect its funding requirements.

EXHIBIT 11-1
STARTING ASSUMPTIONS IN ANALYSIS OF UNIVERSAL THINGS, INC.

A. Factors Relatively Independent of Financial Market Conditions	
Initial capital	$100 million
Debt = 30% (unsecured debentures)	
Equity = 70% (2 million common shares)	
Annual capital requirements	12% of invested capital
Defensive or replacement = 6%	
Expansion requirements = 6%	
Annual depreciation	7% of invested capital
Average return on invested capital	16%
(cyclical range, 12% to 20%)	
Average dividend payout	60% of earnings
Tax rate (includes federal, state, and	
local taxes)	55%

B. Factors Varying with the Financial Climate		
	Easy Money	Tight Money
Price/earnings ratio	18	14
Effective interest rate on outstanding debt	5%	7%
Interest rate on new debt issues	6%	10%
New equity issue discount from market price	5%	7%

Historically, Universal's capital requirements have averaged 12% of its invested capital. About half of these funds have been necessary for replacement or defensive purposes in ways that do not add to earning power. (Since depreciation is determined by accounting convention, depreciation flows do not necessarily relate to actual replacement needs. Note that the funds required for Universal's replacement purposes amount to about 1% less than depreciation.)

EFFECTS ON INCOME FACTORS

With these general circumstances in mind, let us now look at the implications for income factors of raising the capital funds by means of either debentures or common stock under the two kinds of conditions.

Dilution of EPS

Naturally, Universal's management is concerned about the immediate dilution of earnings per share (EPS) caused by issuance of new securities. Exhibit 11-2 traces the impact of debt and equity financing on EPS during the year of issue.

We shall not dwell on the well-known diluting effect on EPS of new equity issues. New debenture issues also cause dilution, equaling the interest charges, stated net of taxes, divided by the shares outstanding. As Exhibit 11-2 shows, higher interest rates and lower price/earnings multiples increase dilution for both financing alternatives. Equity funds, however, are generally more costly than debt funding, and the exhibit bears this out.

A significant aspect of the calculations in this exhibit is the change in the *relative* impact of dilution. In times of easy money, under the fairly typical circumstances we are analyzing, the dilution from common stock financing is twice as great as that caused by debt (8.2% decline in EPS vs. 4.1%). But the change in conditions has decreased the relative advantage of the debt alternative to a point where the use of stock is now only 50% more diluting (7.2% vs. 10.9%). Furthermore, the dilution caused by high-interest debt in times of tight money approaches the dilution created in an easy-credit period by issuance of stock (7.2% vs. 8.2%).

Long-Term Impact on EPS

Now we shall examine the implications for EPS once Universal Things has employed the new capital. For purposes of comparison with Exhibit 11-2, we have drawn up Exhibit 11-3 on the assumption that the $10 million raised became immediately productive at the same rate as

EXHIBIT 11-2

SHORT-TERM EFFECTS OF FINANCING ON EARNINGS PER SHARE

[Dollar figures in thousands except for per-share figures]

Before Financing		Easy Money		Tight Money	
a. Earnings before interest and taxes (EBIT)		$16,000		$16,000	
b. Interest		1,500		2,100	
c. Profit before taxes (PBT)		$14,500		$13,900	
d. Taxes @ 55%		7,975		7,645	
e. Profit after taxes (PAT)		$ 6,525		$ 6,255	
f. Earnings per share (EPS)		$ 3.262		$ 3.127	

Financing Calculations	Debt	Equity	Debt	Equity
Equity				
g. Market price per share (*f* × P/E ratio)	°	$ 58.7	°	$ 43.8
h. New issue price per share (0.95 × *g*) and (0.93 × *g*)	°	$ 55.8	°	$ 40.7
i. New shares required ($10 million ÷ *h*)	°	179	°	246
j. Shares outstanding	2,000	2,179	2,000	2,246
Debt				
k. Interest on new debt	$ 600	°	$ 1,000	°
l. Total interest (*b* + *k*)	2,100	1,500	3,100	2,100
m. Adjusted PBT (*a* − *l*)	13,900	†	12,900	†
n. Adjusted taxes (0.55 × *m*)	7,645	†	7,095	†
o. Adjusted PAT	$ 6,255	$ 6,525	$ 5,805	$ 6,255

After Financing	Debt	Equity	Debt	Equity
p. EPS (*o* ÷ *j*)	$ 3.127	$ 2.994	$ 2.902	$ 2.785
q. Decrease in EPS (*p* − *f*)	0.135	0.268	0.225	0.342
r. Percentage decrease in EPS	4.1%	8.2%	7.2%	10.9%

° Not applicable.

† Same as before financing.

EXHIBIT 11-3

LONG-TERM EFFECTS ON EARNINGS PER SHARE

	Easy Money		Tight Money	
	Debt	**Equity**	**Debt**	**Equity**
Additional EBIT from new financing (in $ thousands)	$1,600	$1,600	$1,600	$1,600
EPS after financing	$3.487	$3.325	$3.262	$3.106
Increase (decrease) in EPS from initial estimate	$0.225	$0.063	$0.135	($0.021)
Percentage growth (decline)	6.9%	1.9%	4.3%	(0.7%)

the outstanding capital, 16% before taxes. (Since it takes most companies several years to digest capital additions and convert them to earning assets, this is an unrealistic assumption which we will not use subsequently.)

As might be expected, the growth in EPS is less with higher capital costs. Although the debenture alternative still enjoys a 16-cent (5%) differential over the use of stock, even the debentures offer little more than a 4% growth in EPS under circumstances of stringent credit.

In the real world, however, the effects of financing are not so clear-cut for the stockholders. Changes in earnings per share reflect not only financing transactions but also other forces and conditions affecting the company. To explore the implications of the "whole picture" on the shareholder's situation, in Exhibit 11-4 we have forecast EPS over five years under the various alternatives and conditions. There are three key assumptions in this analysis:

1. Universal's invested capital is expected to grow at a steady 6% rate over the five-year period. Unlike the example in Exhibit 11-3, the investments are turned gradually into earning assets. Although reinvestments will no doubt vary from year to year, we shall ignore that element for now.

2. The return on invested capital will follow a "typical" cyclical pattern over five years of "normal, good, excellent, poor, normal."

3. As for additional financing required and debt repayment, we shall defer consideration of these until later in the article.

The year-by-year EPS calculations summarized in Exhibit 11-4 show what would be expected, that growth in earnings per share is superior under the debt alternative. But the sharp impact of tight money on EPS growth potential is dramatized by the fact that the equity plan under easy-money conditions produces slightly better EPS than does undertaking debt when money is tight!

Exhibit 11-4

Financing Effects on Earnings Per Share Over Five Years

[Dollar figures, except for EPS, and numbers of shares in thousands]

Debt Financing

	Year 1	Year 2	Year 3	Year 4	Year 5
Easy money					
Total interest	$2,100	→			
Common shares	2,000	→			
EPS	$ 3.13	$3.82	$4.58	$2.74	$4.07
Percentage growth (decline)		22.2%	20.0%	(40.2%)	48.5%
Tight money					
Total interest	$3,100	→			
Common shares	2,000	→			
EPS	$ 2.90	$3.60	$4.36	$2.52	$3.85
Percentage growth (decline)		23.9%	21.3%	(42.3%)	52.7%

Equity Financing

	Year 1	Year 2	Year 3	Year 4	Year 5
Easy money					
Total interest	$1,500	→			
Common shares	2,179	→			
EPS	$ 2.99	$3.63	$4.33	$2.64	$3.86
Percentage growth (decline)		21.4%	19.3%	(39.0%)	46.1%
Tight money					
Total interest	$2,100	→			
Common shares	2,246	→			
EPS	$ 2.78	$3.40	$4.08	$2.44	$3.63
Percentage growth (decline)		22.3%	20.0%	(40.2%)	48.4%

Base Assumptions for Both Financing Alternatives

	Type of Year				
	Year 1, Normal	Year 2, Good	Year 3, Excellent	Year 4, Poor	Year 5, Normal
Pretax return on invested capital	16%	18%	20%	12%	16%
Total invested capital°	$100,000	$106,000	$112,400	$119,100	$126,200
EBIT†	$ 16,000	$ 19,080	$ 22,480	$ 14,292	$ 20,192
Percentage growth (decline)		19.3%	17.8%	(36.4%)	41.3%

°Growth rate of 6%.
†ROI times invested capital.

Since the investor in interested in growth prospects, the compound annual rates of growth are worth noting. Measuring EPS growth from Year 1 to Year 5 (which are two normal years, making comparisons appropriate) gives these results:

	Debt	Equity
Easy money	6.8%	6.5%
Tight money	7.3%	6.8%

Two things are noteworthy about these figures: (a) the post-dilution growth rate has *increased* with the rise in financing costs; (b) the differences between the financing alternatives and between the results under the differing conditions are *not great*. What has happened to the growth rates is the result of an aspect of leverage often overlooked: an increase in income-statement leverage due to costlier financing. This may seem strange to someone who is accustomed to thinking of financing leverage solely in terms of debt/equity ratios.

In reference to Universal's debt alternative, the balance sheet is the same under both financial conditions. And with stock financing, the number of shares increases as capital costs go up, thus *lowering* financial leverage. How, then, is increased leverage achieved? The principle is shown in Exhibit 11-5.

EXHIBIT 11-5

HYPOTHETICAL ILLUSTRATION OF INCOME STATEMENT LEVERAGE

	Year			Percent Change
	1	2	3	
EBIT	$10	$12	$14	40%
Small fixed charges	$ 2	$ 2	$ 2	
PBT	$ 8	$10	$12	
EPS°	$0.40	$0.50	$0.60	50%
Medium fixed charges	$4	$4	$4	
PBT	$6	$8	$10	
EPS°	$0.30	$0.40	$0.50	66⅔%
Large fixed charges	$8	$8	$8	
PBT	$2	$4	$6	
EPS°	$0.10	$0.20	$0.30	200%

°Tax rate of 50%; 10 shares of stock.

Thus, as fixed finance charges rise, the increase in income-statement leverage causes a more rapid increase in the rate of EPS growth. Even with a 5-to-1 EBIT coverage of fixed charges, EPS growth is 25% greater than EBIT over a three-year period (50% vs. 40%). With today's off-balance-sheet financing—for example, through leases and long-term rental contracts—and with the higher cost of debt financing, it is more important than ever to consider the income-statement leverage resulting from increases in fixed obligations.

Although the growth rate differentials in Universal's case appear small, it should be borne in mind that an EPS differential of one cent is equivalent to more than $20,000 in added profit. The differences in growth achievement between debt and common stock financing amount to about 25 cents a share by the fifth year. To make up this difference would require more than $500,000 in incremental profits *after* taxes!

Volatility Question.   A consideration often overlooked in determining suitable financing is the volatility of EPS. Financial officers know that the leverage that debentures add to the capital structure works for them when earnings are growing and magnifies the benefits of after-tax profit growth. On the other hand, leverage works against the company when profits are declining. How serious is adverse leverage?

Although it is hard to prove the hypothesis with market data, most investment analysts believe that the more erratic a company's earnings per share are—all else being equal (as it never is)—the lower its P/E ration will be. Since the importance of achieving a high P/E ratio is generally accepted, the effects of new financing on earnings per share volatility should be more commonly examined.

An analysis of this action can produce surprising results. Returning to Exhibit 11-4, we see that EPS volatility is not much greater than that for EBIT, in spite of the 30% to 36% debt financing. For example, when the basic profit declines 36% in Year 4, earnings per share decline 39% to 42%. Moreover, while debt in the debenture alternative grows by one third ($30 million to $40 million), this financing approach produces only slightly greater changes in earnings per share. These results, which are not atypical, underscore the fact that financial leverage is only one of several factors affecting EPS volatility, and often not the most important factor.

Dividend Prospects

Now we look at an aspect in which shareholders have a particular interest: What are the implications of the financial plans for dividend income? To ascertain this, we approached the question from two directions, total payout and risk. We shall defer consideration of the latter to the section on risk.

We chose a fairly typical, flexible dividend policy: Universal has a target payout of about 60% of its earnings. On the up side, it declares 40% of any indicated gain in earnings, provided that the increase amounts to 10 cents or more (rounded to the nearest 10 cents). On the down side, the dividend is cut only if the payout would thereby exceed 80% of net income, and the cut is as small as feasible to bring the payout near 80% (but still rounded to the nearest 10 cents). Exhibit 11-6 shows the results of this policy.

EXHIBIT 11-6

DIVIDEND PAYOUTS OVER FIVE-YEAR PERIOD

	Year					
	1	2	3	4	5	Total
Easy money						
Debt	$1.80	$2.00	$2.30	$2.20	$2.30	$10.60
Equity	1.80	2.00	2.20	2.10	2.20	10.30
Tight money						
Debt	1.80	1.90	2.20	2.00	2.10	10.00
Equity	1.80	1.90	2.10	2.00	2.10	9.90

Although the total dividends paid out amount to more under the common stock alternative because of the greater number of shares outstanding, the stockholder receives slightly greater benefit under the debt alternative. Nevertheless, it is prudent to question whether the marginal benefits with debenture financing (10 cents or 1% greater return over five years under tight-money conditions) are sufficient to compensate the stockholder for the marginal risks he incurs.

INTERNAL FUNDS FLOWS

Considering the effects of new financing on funds requirements —interest payments reducing the sources of capital within the company, for instance—what is the total effect on the company's ability to satisfy its future needs internally? The best way to answer this question is to forecast inflows and outflows in detail under a variety of circumstances. (In this article, however, we settle for a single source and application forecast.)

We should note here that the treatment of sinking funds solely as a cash outflow gives a shortsighted picture of the financial situation. Later, in the flexibility section of this article, we shall extend the discussion to include the impact of sinking funds on the company's ability to raise debt capital externally by reducing outstanding debt.

Retained Earnings

Using the same earnings and dividend streams as before, we can forecast the retention benefits of debt and equity financing under the two types of conditions. Here are the total retained earnings for the five-year period (in thousands of dollars):

	Debt	Equity
Easy money	$15,494	$15,599
Tight money	$14,430	$14,455

It is apparent that there is little to choose between methods of financing. There are two reasons for this:

1. Under the debenture alternative the higher per-share earnings create opportunities for increasing the dividend, which in turn reduces the retained earnings differential between the financing plans.

2. Under the common stock alternative, the number of shares outstanding is greater. Hence *total* retention is quite comparable.

At any rate, under tight-credit conditions, total retention has been reduced by more than $1 million because of higher interest costs, on the one hand, and equity dilution, on the other.

Uncommitted Earnings. It is even more important today than it once was to examine the future effects of financing. Lenders, having secured high interest rates on debt obligations, have not been anxious to see these loans repaid as long as the company appears financially sound. Sinking funds, for example, now rarely start before the sixth year of a long-term loan, and often the smaller part of the loan is amortized over its life—that is, the lender requires a higher balloon payment at maturity. Also, lenders try to make prepayments difficult, especially by refinancing (should interest rates fall dramatically).

To indicate the consequences of sinking funds on Universal, we have arbitrarily compressed our thinking into five years and assumed that a sinking fund of $400,000 commences on new debentures in the fourth year. The previously outstanding debt is assumed to have an annual sinking fund of $1.5 million.

Over five years the sinking-fund commitments will reduce Universal's internal funds available for investment purposes by $7.5 million in the case of the common stock alternative and by $8.3 million in the case of debentures. Universal's uncommitted earnings (retained earnings less sinking funds) under tight-money conditions amount to less than half of total retained earnings. Here are the uncommitted earnings as percentages of retained earnings:

	Debt	Equity
Easy money	46.4%	51.9%
Tight money	42.5%	48.5%

More critical than the effect on uncommitted earnings, however, is the impact of the sinking funds during a poor year (the fourth year). In all cases in the fourth year, the sinking-fund obligations exceeded the total addition to retained earnings. Sinking funds can create financial problems in years when the profit picture is very poor. As we shall see, it is often necessary to compensate for the risks inherent in this situation by preserving protective reserves.

Complete Picture

So far, we have been focusing on the funds-flow factors that are immediately affected by the financing decision. To obtain the complete picture, we need to add depreciation, capital expenditures, and working capital investment to the situation. This we have done graphically in Exhibits 11-7 and 11-8. To understand the source of funds flows shown, note that:

☐ Depreciation is forecast to be 7% of the invested capital defined in Exhibit 11-4.

☐ Renewal capital expenditures come to 6% of the invested capital. Failure to consider the size of investments necessary just to maintain the competitive status quo and preserve earning power—such as offsetting technical obsolescence—has all too often caused managements to overestimate the benefits of expansion. Therefore we have made renewal outlays a separate item.

☐ Expansion requirements amount to 6% of invested capital. They have been separated into plant and working capital components. While total investment for the five-year period remains consistent with that in Exhibit 11-4, we have changed the timing to reflect more closely the influence of cyclical circumstances on investment decisions. The method used to allocate the total expansion investment over five years was somewhat arbitrary, but, we think, realistic.

☐ We have assumed that Universal started the period with liquid reserves of $1 million in excess of the cash balances required for operating purposes (see Exhibit 11-8). Note that no additional financings are included. As a result, when liquid reserves fall below a target level (for the moment assumed to be zero), we have an indication of the amount and timing of future funding requirements.

An example will help to clarify Exhibit 11-8. In the first year, under tight-money conditions the common stock financing produces a net internal funds flow of $5.71 million. This, together with the opening liquid reserves of $1 million, results in liquid reserves of $6.71 million at the close of Year 1.

In Year 2, a net outflow of funds amounting to $3.75 million reduces the liquid reserves at year-end to just under $3 million. In Year 3, the continuing outflow ($3.8 million) results in negative closing reserves (of $0.84 million), which are augmented in the last two years.

The first notable conclusion to be drawn from those exhibits is how similar the fund requirement patterns are. In all cases, Universal will need a modest amount of external capital in the third year. The most serious fund drain takes place during recession, in the fourth year.

EXHIBIT 11-7

SOURCE AND APPLICATION OF FUNDS OVER FIVE-YEAR PERIOD

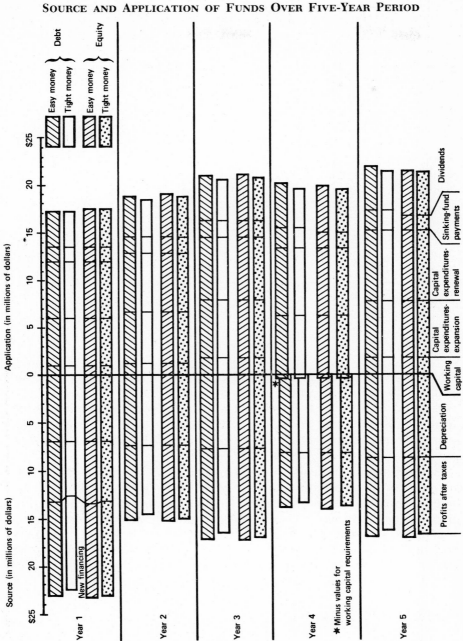

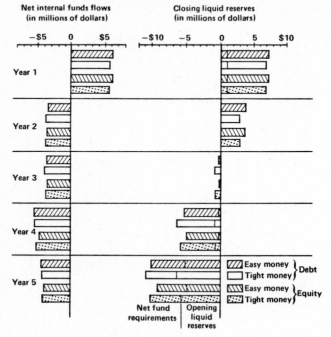

EXHIBIT 11-8

**NET INTERNAL FUNDS FLOWS AND CLOSING LIQUID RESERVES
OVER FIVE-YEAR PERIOD**

Somewhere between $10.1 million and $11.9 million must be furnished externally over the course of the five years to restore the liquid reserve of $1 million. If these data were extended for a longer period, they would show that the company has to raise about 10% of its then-existing capital about every three years to provide the funds necessary for expansion.

Additionally, under tight-money conditions, Universal must raise about $1 million more than in easy-credit times to service its expansion needs. The effects of costly capital show up not only in the initial dilution but also in terms of the amount of capital needed to finance operations over the long run. As might be expected, more external capital is required to underwrite operations under the debenture alternative because of the operation of sinking-fund payments, although the differential between debt and equity has declined somewhat.

Future Conditional

So far, we have examined the implications of just one set of business conditions for the amount and timing of fund requirements. But of course this is not an adequate picture for decision-making purposes.

In testing the adequacy of a financial program, consideration must be given to complications such as:

• How much extra funding might be necessary and when? The answer will depend very much on the opportunities and risks associated with the particular business.

• What can happen to reduce cash inflows? A strike? Increased competitive conditions, with lower margins on sales? The premature death of an important product in the line? An unusually severe dip in the business cycle?

• What can happen to warrant increased funds outflows? Availability of more attractive capital expenditure opportunities? A merger? More working capital needed to compete successfully?

It is difficult to forecast business conditions very far with accuracy. Nevertheless, to the extent that available data permit, it is advisable to test the implications of a financing plan over a 10-year period. As noted earlier, some important financing aspects, such as delayed sinking funds and balloon payments, do not manifest themselves until several years have gone by.

To gain a clearer perspective on the timing of needs, it is frequently desirable to trace requirements quarter by quarter rather than for a full year, as we have done. This enables the user to see, for example, how differently the late phases of a period of business growth can affect funds flows, compared with the early phases of a period of recession. Computer programs are available to make this task relatively easy, although "canned" programs obviously must be modified to fit a company's peculiarities.

RISK FACTORS

Financial risk analysis usually focuses on measuring a company's ability to meet payment requirements on its fixed obligations and testing whether any of the covenants in the debenture agreements are so tight that technical default is a material concern. In this section we shall explore these questions. Finally, we shall discuss the element of risk which new financings pose for the stockholder concerned about his investment.

Burden Coverage Ratios

The certainty of a company's earning power, both in degree and durability, is the most important ingredient in determining its ability to finance through senior securities. The primary measure of this ability is:

$$\text{Burden coverage ratio} = \frac{\text{EBIT}}{\text{Interest} + \text{sinking funds (tax adjusted)}}$$

(In some cases, it would be appropriate to include other fixed financial and operating commitments, such as leases or dividends, in the equation. For the sake of clarity, however, we assume that interest payments and sinking fund obligations are Universal's only fixed charges.)

Because debt contracts are written for long periods of time, the factors influencing the determination of "acceptable" servicing levels involve a number of fundamental considerations. Although many rules of thumb have been developed to test the adequacy of burden coverage ratios, use of these rules without regard to the underlying fundamentals can be very misleading. Questions like these must be asked:

○ How important are the products or product capabilities to the economy?

○ How strong is the company's present and prospective competitive position?

○ How skillfully has management anticipated change and capitalized on it?

○ How diversified is the company's earnings base?

○ Does the company have the size and soundness to withstand temporary shocks?

○ In the event of trouble, will the loans be backed by assets with enduring value?

In general, the more *durable* a company's earning power appears over time and the more certain that its earnings will stay above a specified level based on its earnings record (its so-called "profit life"), the lower the acceptable burden coverage ratio can be. Obviously, determining suitable coverage ratios requires sharp judgment.

We use two earnings levels to measure suitable coverage. The first relates to "normal" earning capacity—earnings in a year between the cyclical extremes of favorable and poor business conditions. The second measure is "depressed" earnings. These are not the worst earnings a company can expect to experience in a single year but, rather, the worst it is likely to average over three to five years of intensely competitive conditions, or some other adverse circumstances extending over several years.

This is our rule of thumb: debenture financing involves nominal risk as long as the normal burden coverage ratio exceeds 3.1× and the depressed coverage ratio exceeds 2.1× on average over a five-year period. This means that Universal probably would earn an "A" rating of moderate strength if Moody's were to rate its debentures.

If the company embarked on debt financing on the basis of lower coverage ratios, this would, in our opinion, entail enough additional risks to warrant careful consideration of the trade-offs in ratings and subsequent cost of debt. On the other hand, the unusual protection afforded by excessive coverage ratios is costly without providing value.

In our example, using a 16% ROI as a measure of "normal" and a 12% ROI to represent "protracted adversity," we projected earnings as a function of the invested capital shown in Exhibit 11-4. As expected, high interest rates noticeably hampered Universal's capacity to carry debt safely. Normal coverage under the debt alternative was reduced from an average of 3.2× under easy-money conditions to 2.8× under severe conditions—a clear sign of greater risk. The "depressed" coverage ratio (the more significant of the two) was still adequate (2.1×), but barely so. In a time of tight money, then, undertaking a new debt issue is much riskier.

Pro Forma Ratios. Coverage ratios based on existing sinking funds are becoming increasingly meaningless. Deferred sinking funds and partial amortization of the principal are partly to blame. Moreover, to avoid high-cost financing, many companies have borrowed from commerical banks on short-term schedules (which produce poor debt-servicing pictures), while intending to refinance the loans on a long-term basis. Many other distortions develop when sinking-fund requirements are used to measure safety.

As a result, we have developed a procedure that more realistically examines the potential impact of fixed-income securities. In effect, we take a company's outstanding debt in any year and amortize it on a straight-line basis over a period that represents a reasonable measure of its profit life. The resulting amortization becomes the sinking-fund requirement for that year. Interest on all debt is assessed at prevailing rates. We then calculate pro forma coverage ratios.

This procedure implicitly assumes total refinancing of the company's loans on a "more suitable" basis. Although complete refinancing is seldom practical, the procedure suggested here magnifies the long-term implications of current debt levels and highlights how risks change over time. Slavish adherence to the use of actual (often deferred) sinking-fund schedules in fixed-charge coverage analysis can lure an unsuspecting financial officer into a corner.

Cash Flow Ratios. With the greater emphasis on cash flow analysis in business, it is not surprising that corporate executives are increasingly using cash flow burden coverage. The most commonly used indicator for this coverage is:

$$\text{Cash flow burden coverage} = \frac{\text{Profits after taxes} + \text{depreciation}}{\text{Interest after taxes} + \text{sinking funds}}.$$

This ratio can be quite misleading. A company obviously must have adequate funds available to meet fixed obligations and maintain profitability, and it often requires depreciation funds to avoid profit erosion that would occur if no investments were made. So depreciation in this formula should be replaced by "uncommitted depreciation," which is

EXHIBIT 11-9
FORMULATING THE AVAILABLE FUNDS BURDEN COVERAGE RATIO

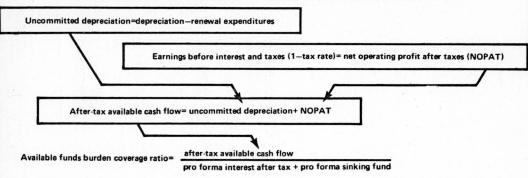

Uncommitted depreciation=depreciation—renewal expenditures

Earnings before interest and taxes (1—tax rate)= net operating profit after taxes (NOPAT)

After-tax available cash flow= uncommitted depreciation+ NOPAT

Available funds burden coverage ratio= $\dfrac{\text{after-tax available cash flow}}{\text{pro forma interest after tax + pro forma sinking fund}}$

depreciation minus capital expenditures required for profit renewal. The procedure for formulating the available funds burden coverage ratio is outlined in Exhibit 11-9.

In many companies, uncommitted depreciation is negative. In such a case, a company must generate funds in excess of depreciation just to maintain its competitive stance, which naturally diminishes its ability to borrow safely over the long run. In contrast, a positive balance will add to safe borrowing capacity.

Universal maintains a positive uncommitted depreciation throughout the five years examined. Understandably, then, the pro forma coverage ratios improve the debenture financing alternative under tight-money conditions, as Exhibit 11-10 shows.

Since the available funds ratio is a more significant indicator of risk, debt financing under these conditions, with a 3.0× average coverage ratio, would not be unduly risky by our rule of thumb.

EXHIBIT 11-10
UNIVERSAL'S PRO FORMA BURDEN COVERAGE RATIOS UNDER TIGHT-MONEY CONDITIONS, OVER FIVE-YEAR PERIOD

Year	Uncommitted Depreciation (in Thousands of Dollars)	Pro Forma Coverage Ratios° Earnings Basis	Available Funds Basis
1	$1,000	2.1×	2.4×
2	1,060	2.3×	2.7×
3	1,124	2.6×	2.9×
4	1,191	2.9×	3.3×
5	1,258	3.2×	3.7×
Average		2.6×	3.0×

° "Normal" (16%) return on invested capital and debt financing as previously defined.

Loan Covenants

Long-term debenture issues contain covenants that restrict management's freedom to act under certain conditions or bring the loan into technical default if unforeseen adversities develop. When corporate liquidity is squeezed, lenders usually are able to obtain tighter covenants.

A lender is likely to ask for more protective clauses than he needs rather than risk inadequate protection, since he knows he can waive any restrictions that prove to be unreasonably severe. Today he has more power to do so. Loan agreements frequently provide for restrictions on working capital, dividend payments, capital expenditures, additional indebtedness, disposition of assets, and mergers and acquisitions.

The impact of these covenants on a company's freedom of action or risk of default is not always clear. To test the seriousness of the restrictions and the circumstances under which they are likely to prove binding requires sophisticated, detailed analysis. Although full discussion of this subject is clearly beyond the scope of this article, we want to emphasize that explicit consideration of loan covenants should always be an integral part of a company's financial risk assessment.

Shareholder's Viewpoint

Fluctuations in the value of the stockholders' investment are often beyond the control of management. Naturally, however, stockholders are interested in avoiding situations under management's control that might jeopardize dividend income or the market value of the stock.

Dividend Income. Does debt financing tend to jeopardize the dividend more than does common stock? In terms of earnings coverage required for a target dividend, the reverse is true. Companies are usually better able to support their dividend requirements from earnings by using debt rather than issuing more common stock, because the interest on debt is less burdensome than dividends on new shares.

To look at dividend safety, we calculated the ROI necessary to cover a target dividend 1.25 times—that is, on an 80% payout. Starting with a dividend of $1.80, we adopted a minimum goal of increasing the payout by 10 cents each year. We worked backwards in this order:

1. The required EPS (1.25 × the target dividend).

2. EBIT necessary under each alternative to produce the per-share earnings

$$\left(\frac{\text{EPS} \times \text{total shares outstanding}}{1 - \text{tax rate}}\right).$$

3. The return on capital required to produce the EBIT (EBIT ÷ invested capital).

We came up with these results showing the average return on capital required to cover the target dividends:

	Debt	Equity
Easy money	11.7%	12.1%
Tight money	12.6%	13.0%

Lower returns on capital are required under debt financing in both kinds of circumstances to service the dividend, and the differential is about the same in both. More significant is the sharp increase in ROI requirements under tight-money conditions; the return must be 1% higher, on average, to ensure a steady growth in dividends. Attractive dividend growth is consequently more difficult to attain, and there is more risk that an earnings decline will necessitate a cut in dividends.

Market Value.   To analyze financial risk in terms of market value, we determined the minimum amount that must be earned on invested capital in a series of bad years to prevent a loss of more than 40% of the initial market value of Universal's stock. The results are shown in Exhibit 11-11. Note that we have worked through only a single set of assumptions here. In practice, the financial officer should be careful to explore the whole range of assumptions that he considers realistic.

Several surprising conclusions emerge from Exhibit 11-11:

• Stockholders are subject to serious loss in the market value of their investment long before the debtors start worrying about the safety of their investment. Burden coverage ratios exceed 2× in each example, even though the market value of the stock has declined by 40%.

Exhibit 11-11

Return on Capital Required to Prevent a Precipitous Loss in Market Value of Universal's Stock

[Dollar figures in thousands, except for per-share figures]

	Easy Money		Tight Money	
	Debt	Equity	Debt	Equity
a. Initial market price (see *Exhibit 11-2*)	$ 58.7	$ 58.7	$ 43.8	$ 43.8
b. 60% of market price (maximum decline)	$ 35.2	$ 35.2	$ 26.7	$ 26.7
c. Assumed P/E ratio (see *Exhibit 11-1*)	16×	16×	12×	12×
d. Necessary EPS ($b \div c$)	$ 2.20	$ 2.20	$ 2.22	$ 2.22
e. Shares outstanding (see *Exhibit 11-2*)	2,000	2,179	2,000	2,246
f. Necessary profit after taxes ($d \times e$)	$ 4,400	$ 4,790	$ 4,440	$ 4,990
g. Necessary PBT [$f \div (1 - \text{tax rate})$]	$ 9,800	$10,650	$ 9,860	$11,110
h. Interest°	$ 1,950	$ 1,350	$ 2,890	$ 1,890
i. Necessary EBIT ($g + h$)	$11,750	$12,000	$12,750	$13,000
j. Required return on capital ($i \div$ invested capital in year selected for interest)	10.5%	10.7%	11.3%	11.6%

°Actual interest in third year is shown, although relative results are the same in every year.

• The shareholder is less exposed to precipitous declines under the debt alternative. In other words, under the conditions we have outlined, debt is somewhat less risky from the shareholder's point of view than is common stock financing!

• The higher cost of money under tight-credit conditions makes it more difficult to protect the capital value of the shareholders' investment, regardless of what method of financing is used.

These findings, which have been confirmed in more extensive analyses that we have undertaken, raise questions about the adequacy of conventional definitions of financial risk.

Appreciation Potential. Before leaving the subject of risk factors, we should say a word about the problem of estimating future market prices. One of the critical aspects is the effect of financing on shareholders' impressions of risk. Do greater debt loads lead investors to consider the company to be riskier, and therefore place a lower P/E ratio on the stock? In our opinion, the stockholder's risk differentials we discuss in this article are not enough to justify a material reevaluation. In fact, the superior earnings growth rates under the debt alternatives are more likely to benefit than harm the P/E ratio.

In more elaborate analyses, using present-value techniques, it is possible to measure the returns on shareholders' investments after personal income taxes, in terms of both dividends and appreciation. Such analyses confirm that debt financing provides higher return prospects within the parameters being considered, but the high cost of debt reduces this benefit materially.

MAINTAINING FLEXIBILITY

The financial executive naturally wants to obtain the capital necessary to meet his requirements in adequate time on terms he considers reasonable. He can try to maintain flexibility either by raising the capital in advance and holding the funds as excess liquidity reserves, or by depending on his ability to raise funds from external sources on short notice.

Corporate treasurers taking the latter approach traditionally have depended on the debt markets. The equity markets are too volatile, they believe; reliance on them may necessitate financing under circumstances that are severely diluting, if it is even feasible. In contrast, by defining debt capacity conservatively and then operating at less than full utilization of it, treasurers have felt safe, knowing that the unused capacity was available on short notice, at not unreasonable cost.

This has been the general theory, at least before tight-money conditions developed. How has it changed?

Unused Debt Capacity

Debt capacity is a dynamic variable. Although it should always be defined conservatively—to make sure of meeting future financing requirements—it should also grow as the company's earning power grows. Likewise, it should be reduced if profits fall for a protracted period beyond the level of management's expectations.

Outstanding debt levels also change as debt is raised and repaid. So unused debt capacity (debt capacity minus outstanding debt) is constantly varying. Knowledge about the size of unused debt capacity is an item of financial information as critical for planning purposes as the forecast of liquid asset balances.

To illustrate the effects of changed financial conditions on debt capacity, we shall return to the affairs of Universal Things, Inc. Using a pro forma approach, we shall assume the following conditions:

○ Earnings for the first two years will remain at a "normal" level of 16% return on invested capital, then decline to 14% for the last three years as a result of some adversity.

○ Sinking funds amount to 4% of outstanding debt.

○ Interest is charged at the prevailing debt rates (6% in easy-money, 10% in tight-money times).

○ Uncommitted depreciation funds are available to service the debt.

○ The target available funds burden coverage (the minimum that Universal aims for if it is employing all its debt capacity) is 2.8×.

Additionally, to highlight the need for financial flexibility, we shall assume that our company has a new product in the research labs. If development is successfully completed, $7 million more will be needed during the third and fourth years. We shall assume that this need arises with no forewarning.

Exhibit 11-12 shows rather dramatically how high interest rates adversely affect debt capacity. Universal can borrow only 79% as much in times of scarce money as it could before, while providing the same coverage. Furthermore, under tight-credit conditions there is *less* unused debt capacity in the fourth and fifth years with equity financing (that is, with $30 million in debt) than there is under easy-money conditions with the debenture alternative (that is, with $40 million in debt).

Bottom-Side Flexibility

This change becomes critical when we consider the extra $7 million need in Years 3 and 4. In a time of easy credit, financing presents few problems. But under tight-money conditions, debt financing involves

EXHIBIT 11-12

UNIVERSAL'S DEBT CAPACITY, TOTAL AND UNUSED

[Dollar figures in millions]

	Easy Money					Tight Money				
	Year 1	Year 2	Year 3	Year 4	Year 5	Year 1	Year 2	Year 3	Year 4	Year 5
Debt capacity factors										
a. Available funds	$ 8.20	$ 8.69	$ 8.22	$ 8.71	$ 9.22	°	°	°	°	°
b. Target coverage ratio	2.8×				→	†	†	†	†	†
c. Feasible burden	$ 2.92	$ 3.10	$ 2.94	$ 3.12	$ 3.29	‡	‡	‡	‡	‡
d. Interest after taxes and sinking fund, as a percent of debt§	6.7%					8.5%				
e. Total debt capacity (c ÷ d)	$43.6	$46.3	$43.9	$46.6	$49.1	$34.4	$36.5	$34.6	$36.7	$38.7
Debt alternative										
f. Outstanding debt	$40.0	$38.5	$37.0	$35.1	$33.2	$40.0	$38.5	$37.0	$35.1	$33.2
g. Unused capacity (e − f)	$ 3.6	$ 7.8	$ 6.9	$11.5	$15.9	($ 5.6)	($ 2.0)	($ 2.4)	$ 1.6	$ 5.5
Equity alternative										
h. Outstanding debt	$30.0	$29.5	$27.0	$25.5	$24.0	$30.0	$28.5	$27.0	$25.5	$24.0
i. Unused capacity (e − h)	$13.6	$17.8	$16.9	$21.1	$25.1	$ 4.4	$ 8.0	$ 7.6	$11.2	$14.7

°Same as easy money; depends on return on invested capital less fixed charges.
†Same as easy money; management decision.
‡Same as easy money, available funds ÷ target average.
§For example, 4% sinking fund + 6% interest after taxes = 4% + 6% × (1 − .55) = 4% + 2.7% = 6.7%.

considerable risk. An unexpected need for funding might force management to raise equity under depressed market conditions.

How serious is this dilemma? Although management dislikes having to depend on its ability to raise money in the equity market, it should realize that some use of equity funds is normal for a company with ambitious expansion objectives.

Here is one way of exploring the question of "bottom-side" (or equity) flexibility. Using projected EPS and historical P/E ratios, forecast market prices in each year. Adjusting the market price for the cost of issue, calculate the amount of equity capital raised by issuing a certain amount of stock—200,000 shares in Universal's case—each year. (Conversely, of course, a constant amount of equity can be used to determine the number of shares required under the varying earnings conditions.)

Then compare the annual variations. From rather conservative P/E projections and under tight-money conditions, Universal's issuance of 200,000 shares can return between about $7 million and $10 million, depending on the year of issuance—a difference of $3 million.

While the uncertainty is great whenever estimates of future market prices are attempted, nonetheless this is a useful exercise for two reasons:

1. The calculations define the range of financial return that might be expected if the company elects to remain dependent on equity financing.

2. The calculations enable the company to test the risk of being unable to cover its financing requirements if it is forced to use the equity alternative during depressed market conditions.

Universal's third- and fourth-year requirements, for example, can equal $12 million (forecast net cash outflow plus new-product contingency). Complete dependence on equity financing under restricted-credit conditions would therefore result in serious long-term dilution.

When the odds are high that the need will arise under adverse market conditions, management would be well advised to maintain covering reserves on hand, either as excess liquid assets or unused debt capacity. However, the tightening of debt capacity caused by higher interest rates increases the cost of this alternative.

Internal Maneuverability

Since management generally prefers to follow its expenditure program irrespective of the state of the money markets, the treasurer is expected to formulate a financing plan that will not cause trouble later. In most circumstances, this is a wise policy.

In Universal's case, to maintain flexibility and keep coverage ratios at satisfactory levels, a sale of stock appears desirable. As noted earlier, however, issuing equity results not only in dilution but also in a lower long-term growth rate. There is a trade-off here: accepting a degree of dilution initially to avoid the later risk of greater dilution, if not loan default. There are circumstances, however, where this choice may not make economic sense.

How can management change its expenditure commitments without reducing profitability? Usually some capital expenditures can be postponed for a year or two without adverse effects. Also, it is feasible to curtail the dividend temporarily to conserve funds, although the possible stock market reaction may be considered. How much would this conserve? Would it alleviate dependence on external capital under depressed market conditions? With Universal, for example, the partial curtailment of expenditures for only a year could eliminate this dependence.

Evaluation of the trade-offs to establish whether curtailment is advisable is extremely complex and will not be undertaken here. Suffice it to say that the cost of a financial policy necessary to avoid curtailment under *all* circumstances can exceed the benefits.

Timing of Financing

Throughout this analysis we have assumed that debt can be raised at a constant interest rate, which is of course unrealistic. The combination of higher rates and wider rate fluctuations in a time of stringent credit makes it as important to time debt issues for periods of lower rates as it is to time equity issues for periods when stock market prices are relatively high. Since the periods of low interest rates tend to be of shorter duration, timing of debt issues to maximize borrowing capacity is generally more difficult than timing of equity issues to minimize dilution.

While interest rates are often relatively low when equity financing is expensive, and vice versa, unfortunately there are long periods when neither alternative is particularly attractive. So what does management do then? We have discussed several alternatives. Additionally, some companies have turned to maverick securities like convertible debentures or convertible preferred stock as interim financing steps. But these instruments have the double disadvantage of increasing the risk in the form of larger fixed obligations while retaining the prospect of ultimate dilution.

Because of the vagaries of tight-money conditions, the most practical solution for maintaining the flexibility necessary to cover contingent capital requirements is through an appropriate increase in liquid asset reserves. Ironically, the policy of reducing liquid reserves that has prevailed since 1954 has left those corporate treasurers who were most effective in this maneuvering with the least internal flexibility at a time when it would have been most valuable.

Flexibility is now the most important consideration in developing suitable financial plans. It is also the area where uncertainties run highest and trade-offs are the most difficult. The development of financial planning models has greatly aided analysis of the variables discussed here under a range of assumptions and constraints. But, with or without formal models, sound financial policy must incorporate the implications of uncertainty for a company's priority plan and alternative plans.[1]

CONCLUSION

The changes in money-market conditions over the last decade have been profound. The higher cost of both debt and equity funding has made financing an aggressive expansion program riskier and more difficult.

The risks associated with debt financing are much greater, and the debt capacity available to a company willing to assume a certain amount of risk is sharply reduced. From the point of view of stockholders' income the benefits of debt financing now tend to be only slightly superior to equity financing. The timing of debt and equity issues is now more critical. In short, the whole process of developing a sound financial plan is much more complex than it was a decade ago.

The consequences of the recent liquidity squeeze caught a number of corporate treasurers unaware, with the result that many companies discovered in 1970 that they needed to refinance overburdened debt structures. Divestments, spinoffs, convertible issues, and other costly expedients were necessary to obtain the funds necessary to strengthen the financial structure to levels consistent with prevailing money-market conditions. But in many respects 1970 was the worst sort of a year for raising equity capital directly or indirectly. Failure to recognize the changed character of the money markets has given these companies a costly lesson in tight-money financing.

Despite evidence of the new conditions, yesterday's effective rules of thumb are still being used. "We can safely borrow 40% (or 30%) of our capital structure" can still be heard, for example.

The idea that debt should be used aggressively still appears to be gaining acceptance. Certainly, aggressive use of debt is an effective tool, but, the question is, how aggressive? Money-market conditions clearly influence the answer to this question, as do the unique circumstances of the company. Under tight-money conditions there is less room for error, and the rules of thumb—particularly those designed to fit other eras—are suspect.

---

[1]For a conception of systematic contingency planning, see Gordon Donaldson, "Strategy for Financial Emergencies," HBR November-December 1969, p. 67.

PART IV. DIVIDEND POLICY AND VALUATION

Dividend policy determines what portion of earnings will be retained in the business and what portion of earnings will be paid out to stockholders. Valuation of a firm's common stock may well be affected by the dividend policy formulated. The formulation of a dividend policy poses many problems. On the one hand, theory would seem to dictate that the firm should retain all funds which can be employed at a rate higher than the capitalization rate; on the other hand, stockholders' preference must also be considered. The articles in this section deal with both the theoretical and the practical problems of dividend policy and valuation.

Professor James E. Walter has developed a theoretical model which shows the relationship between dividend policies and common stock prices. The basic premise underlying the formulation is that stock prices reflect the present value of expected dividends in the long run. Accordingly, stock prices are influenced by retained earnings through their effect on future dividends. The model operates on the objective of maximizing common stockholders' wealth. In general, if a firm is able to earn a higher return on earnings retained than the stockholder is able to earn on a like investment, then it would appear to be beneficial to retain these earnings, all other things being equal. Professor Walter enriches the discussion with his detailed analysis of growth stocks, intermediate stocks, and creditor stocks. He presents a meaningful model for classifying common stocks.

In their article, Professors Williams and Seneca seek to establish an empirical relation between rates of growth in earnings and dividend payout policies of U.S. public utilities. Previous studies have found a negative relationship between payout policies and earnings growth rates for American and British companies, which might not be true for individual industries. Based on their study of 99 utilities in the U.S., the authors conclude that the payout ratios of utilities are significantly and negatively associated with their growth rates in earnings. The article also reviews the theoretical relation between growth rates and payout policies. In addition, Professors Williams and Seneca perform a unique empirical test of the Gordon-Shapiro model, which is generally not included in most textbooks in financial management.

Carol J. Loomis makes a case for firms to minimize cash payouts. In a period when money-capital is scarce, it would seem that there would be advantages accruing to the stockholder if the firm would employ these funds in productive investments rather than in paying cash dividends. The income tax implications are emphasized, together with the disadvantages to the firm when it must rely on the capital markets to raise the funds necessary to pay cash dividends. An actual case of a firm which proposed to substitute stock dividends for three of its quarterly cash dividends is cited. Although the advantages to the stockholders appear to be substantial, the plan was never implemented because of the adverse reactions to the proposal from individual stockholders as well as institutional holders, particularly bank trust departments. It seems that if there is to be any shift toward lower dividend payments, the stockholders will have to be reeducated. Also, if a major shift does take place, the possibility of a change in tax laws exists. The author concludes by citing actual cases in which various types of securities are used to minimize cash payments.

According to Guy J. Agrati, repurchase of their own common stock by companies is becoming more and more popular. This article emphasizes various practical considerations in common stock repurchase. The author believes that repurchase is a valid employment of excess funds which may yield greater returns in earnings per share and market price gains to the remaining stockholders as compared with other alternatives. A formula for repurchase of common stocks is presented which measures the effect of such a decision on the firm's earnings per share. The efficiency measure, which is explained through an example, gives the corporate decision maker an absolute measurement of each offer based on its EPS effect expressed as a percentage of EPS gain expected from a like amount of donated shares.

12. DIVIDEND POLICIES AND COMMON STOCK PRICES*

JAMES E. WALTER†

I

. . . Based upon the belief that stock market behavior is susceptible of rationalization, an attempt is made in this paper to fabricate a theoretical model which depicts the relationship between dividend policies and common stock prices. Attention is of necessity restricted to the common stocks of large public corporations because of the imperfect market for the securities of small companies and of the close identification of small firms with their principal shareholders. The fundamental premise upon which the formulation rests is that, over longer periods, stock prices reflect the present values of expected dividends.[1] The phrase "over long periods" is inserted to permit abstraction from the distortions caused by short-run speculative considerations.

Granted this premise, retained earnings influence stock prices principally through their effect upon future dividends. The fact that some stocks may have substantial market value even though little or no dividends are anticipated in the foreseeable future need not contradict this proposition. Undistributed earnings are immediately realizable to the shareholder, at least in part, provided prospective investors can be found who are willing to wait and to assume the required risk.

In analyzing the present worth of future dividends, the concept of capitalization rate is utilized in preference to that of multiplier, which is customarily employed by security analysts. The capitalization rate for any stock is simply the reciprocal of the multiplier. Since capitalization rates are expressed in percentage terms, their use simplifies the presentation and facilitates direct comparisons with rates of return on additional investment.

Capitalization rates are determined by the underlying yield on safe securities and by the required risk premiums. The yield on safe securities is conditioned by such factors as monetary and debt policy, income distribution, the intensity of present as opposed to future wants, and productivity. The basic risk premium, as measured by the difference between the yield on safe securities and the capitalization rate on high-grade common stocks, is dependent upon the economic climate and

°From *The Journal of Finance* (March, 1956), pp. 24-41. Reprinted by permission. This article has been shortened but no essential material has been deleted. At one point a calculation relating to interest rates was updated to reflect present interest rates.

†Professor of Finance, University of Pennsylvania.

[1]See J. B. Williams, *The Theory of Investment Value* (Cambridge, Mass.: Harvard University Press, 1938), p. 6, for a similar position.

government policy. Interindustry differences in size, capital structure, efficiency, and diversification occasion substantial variations in capitalization rates among corporations.

The level and diversity of capitalization rates influence the succeeding analysis in at least two respects. The higher the level of capitalization rates, both individually and generally, the fewer are the companies whose stocks qualify as growth stocks. The greater the diversity of capitalization rates and the more numerous their determinants, the less feasible it becomes to talk in terms of average or normal capitalization rates. The concept of market capitalization rate must, therefore, be defined arbitrarily in order to exclude irrelevant heterogeneity.

The proposition that all common stocks behave in a reasonably uniform manner does not appear to be warranted by the observed variations in stock prices. As a result, three groups, referred to respectively as growth stock, intermediate, and creditor stock categories, are isolated for consideration. A fourth possibility, the declining stock category, is ignored because of its presumed unimportance in a growing economy.

Diversity of dividend policy is often regarded as one of the principal features which differentiate among these groups. Growth stocks are customarily characterized by low dividend payout ratios; intermediate stocks, by medium to high ratios; and creditor stocks, by fixed dividend rates irrespective of short-run earnings. With the possible exception of creditor stocks, however, the dividend-earnings relationship is neither a necessary nor a sufficient condition for assigning stocks to any given category. The crucial consideration is the rate of return on additional investment. The greater the profitability, the more likely is management—in the interests of rapid expansion—to retain a substantial percentage of earnings.

II

The concept "growth stock" is familiar to investors and is understood to refer, in general terms, to common stocks which possess superior prospects for long-term appreciation. Surface characteristics of growth stocks include low dividend payout ratios, high market multipliers (i.e., low capitalization rates), and prices which increase through time with relative rapidity. Low dividend payout ratios constitute an accepted feature of growth stocks, since shareholders are presumed to benefit more from the retention of earnings than from their employment elsewhere at the going rates.

In qualifying for membership in the growth stock category, marginal profitability is the basic criterion. The rate of return on additional investment determines the magnitude of future dividends obtainable from given amounts of retained earnings or external financing. The anticipated level of future dividends, when discounted at the appropriate capitalization rate, in turn yields the present value for a given stock. If the rate of return on added investment is sufficiently great, it follows that low dividend payout ratios may add to, rather than subtract from, stock values.

For the purpose of demonstrating the potential influence of retained earnings upon stock prices, let us assume that earnings retention is the sole source of additional funds, that both the rate of return on added investment and the market capitalization rate are constants, and that all increments to earnings are immediately distributed to shareholders. The market capitalization rate for any given corporation is defined as the reciprocal of the multiplier which would prevail in the market if the dividend payout ratio were 100 percent.[2] Treating the stream of future earnings as perpetual (or at least of indefinite duration), the present value of any common stocks can then be expressed in mathematical terms as

$$V_c = \frac{D + \frac{R_a}{R_c}(E - D)}{R_c} = \frac{E}{R_c} + \frac{R_a - R_c}{R_c^2}(E - D), \tag{1}$$

where D is cash dividends, E is earnings, R_a is the rate of return on additional investment, and R_c is the market capitalization rate.[3]

Equation (1) reveals the importance of both the dividend payout ratio and the relationship between R_a and R_c. Whenever R_a exceeds R_c, the present worth of future dividends resulting from the retention of earnings is greater than the dollar magnitude of retained earnings. The lower the dividend payout ratio, under such circumstances, the higher is the value of the growth stock.

A currently high rate of return on additional investment for a given corporation need not automatically transform its stock into a growth stock. In the first place, the high rate must persist over a reasonable period of time. The market's judgment of a common stock is of necessity based primarily upon past experience. The corporation's willingness to

---

[2]This definition is introduced simply to preclude the possibility that capitalization rates will be interpreted to reflect the effect of varying dividend policies. To illustrate, let us assume that companies **A** and **B** have identical earnings per share ($10), R_a (20 percent), and R_c (10 percent), but have payout ratios of 75 percent and 50 percent respectively. Substituting in equation (1), we find that A has a V_c of $125 and B, of $150. The ratio of E to V_c, which might be called the uadjusted or composite capitalization rate, is thus 8 percent for A and $6\frac{2}{3}$ percent for B. The difference is attributable to divergent dividend policies.

[3]The second version of equation (1) is presented to show the extent to which V_c will exceed (or fall short of) the ratio of E to R_c. As in the case of most gross simplifications, equation (1) presents difficulties if used without modification. To illustrate the point and to indicate the type of modification which might be made, let us consider time as an endless succession of periods. Based upon equation (1) and its underlying assumptions, the value of the stock in question will rise in each period (without cessation) by an amount equal to $R_a(E - D)/R_c$. Since diminishing returns are an almost inevitable consequence, R_a must be viewed—for practical purposes—as a weighted average of $r_1, r_2, \ldots, r_{n-1}$, where r represents the rate of return on added investment at any given point (period) in time and $r_n = 0$. By weighted is simply meant that r_1, r_2, etc., must, because of the proximity to the present, be assigned greater importance than r_{n-1}, r_{n-2}, etc.

invest is also influenced by the anticipated permanence of R_a to the extent that increments to earnings lag behind the retention of earnings. In the second place, high rates of return on added investment must not be offset by correspondingly high market capitalization rates. In so far as new industries are characterized by small, insufficiently capitalized firms and mature industries by large, conservatively financed companies, R_a and R_c may well be directly associated.

As observed in footnote 3, modifications in equation (1), which provide added realism at the expense of simplicity, do not alter the results in any fundamental respect. Anticipated declines in the return on additional investment (R_a) affect stock values and raise serious doubts as to the propriety of permanently low dividend payout ratios. As long as R_a continues to exceed R_c, however, the substantial retention of earnings appears beneficial to shareholders.

The recognition of external sources of new financing enables growth stocks to possess low *composite* capitalization rates even in the presence of high dividend payout ratios.[4] The market in effect endeavors to forecast the willingness and ability to use external sources and discounts future dividends attributable thereto. Despite this consideration, stock prices can still be expected to vary inversely with dividend payout ratios, provided R_a exceeds R_c.

Even without reference to capital gains taxation, the market appears justified in according special treatment to growth stocks in the sense of low composite capitalization rates. The all-pervasiveness of uncertainty may of course occasion conservative interpretations of future earnings and may restrict recognized membership in the growth stock category to a relatively few outstanding corporations. For doubtful cases, retained earnings and dividends may simply be regarded as equivalents. Alternatively, the prices of marginal growth stocks may be adversely affected, provided dividend payout ratios are below what the market believes to be a reasonable compromise.

At least one further factor functions to lessen the present worth of retained earnings relative to current dividends. This consideration concerns the emphasis placed upon balanced portfolios, i.e., diversification by investors. To the extent that the market values of growth stocks appreciate through time more rapidly than those of their asset holdings, investors may be induced to redistribute the increment among all components of their portfolios.[5]

---

[4]The prevailing ratio of earnings to stock prices for a given company at any time can be thought of as a composite rate. The basic component is the market capitalization rate (R_c), as interpreted above. From R_c is deducted (if a growth stock) a percentage equivalent to the relative increase in the present worth of future dividends which is attributable to earnings retention or, as the case may be, to external financing.

[5]The line of reasoning is quite similar to that underlying the "substitution effect" in the theory of consumer choice. For the sake of simplicity, however, it is assumed that the problem of present versus future consumption does not arise.

Whenever portfolio readjustment must be achieved through the sale of shares, as opposed to the utilization of cash dividends, certain costs and risks are incurred.[6] Transfer costs, comprising commissions and taxes, have to be met. Market prices are conditioned by short-run influences and need not reflect longer run capitalized values at any given time. In addition, the augmented supply of growth shares on the market —resulting from efforts to diversify—may depress their prices below what they otherwise would have been.

The consequence is that the appropriate test for growth stocks from the viewpoint of shareholders may not be simply R_a exceeds R_c, but rather R_a exceeds R_c by an amount sufficient to cover the cost of added diversification. That is to say,

$$V_c = \frac{D + \dfrac{R_a}{R_c + p}\,(E - D)}{R_c}, \qquad (1a)$$

where p is the premium associated with the cost of diversification.

Except for outstanding cases, the isolation of growth stocks for empirical study does not appear to be a simple task. As suggested previously, changes in earnings from period to period are likely to be discontinuous and to be associated with past, rather than current, sources of funds. The reason is simply that the expansion of both facilities and markets takes time. The reported levels of historical earnings, which is the principal basis for estimating future earnings, are dependent upon arbitrary accounting techniques. In addition, price-level changes often provide a misleading illusion of growth. In some instances, these and other factors lead the market astray; in other cases, they lead the analyst to believe that the market's evaluation is incorrect when in actual fact it is not. . . .

III

A substantial majority of all *listed* industrial common stocks undoubtedly belong to the intermediate stock group. Surface characteristics of this category are dividend payout ratios in excess of 50 percent, multipliers which range in the neighborhood of the average multiplier for all listed corporations, and prices which increase slowly through time. Shareholder pressure is exerted for substantial payout ratios, since stock prices tend to vary directly with the level of dividend payout ratios. Although the retention of earnings leads to appreciation in stock values, shareholders benefit from the receipt of dividends and their investment elsewhere at the going market rate.

---

[6]As indicated subsequently, these considerations may be partially offset by the preferential tax treatment of capital gains.

In assigning stocks to this category, the underlying consideration is whether the present value of future dividends attributable to retained earnings at the margin is greater or less than the corresponding dollar amount of earnings retention. This question is essentially the same as that raised in connection with growth stocks. Its resolution hinges, in similar fashion, upon the relationship between R_a, adjusted for the preferred tax treatment of capital gains, and R_c. As shown by equation (1), if adjusted R_a exceeds R_c, the common stock in question is a growth stock; if adjusted R_a is less than R_c but greater than zero, it is an intermediate stock.

The preponderance of the intermediate stock group, particularly where large and mature public corporations are concerned, apparently leads many investment analysts to recommend high dividend payout ratios as a general rule. The best-known advocates, Graham and Dodd, state that the investment value of any industrial common stock equals

$$M\left(D + \frac{1}{3}E\right),\tag{2}$$

where M, the multiplier, is the reciprocal of the *assumed* appropriate capitalization rate, D is expected dividends, and E is expected earnings.[7] Essentially theirs must be regarded as a conservative approach which presumably emphasizes both the uncertainness of future earnings and the inevitable decline, at some point in time, in the rate of return on additional investment even for expanding enterprises.

Since equation (2) stresses the dividend factor, it is reasonably well adapted to the intermediate stock category. In the equation proper, $1 of dividends is presumed to be the equivalent of $4 of retained earnings. In terms of equation (1), the ratio of adjusted R_a to R_c is thus fixed at one fourth. Inasmuch as the numerous other possible relationships between R_a and R_c are ignored, the multiplier must be adjusted for differences between the assumed normal relationship and the actual relationship in any given circumstance. For growth stocks, the magnitudes of the adjustments required in M assume such significance that the general application of equation (2) does not appear to be feasible.

Whatever the approach employed to evaluate intermediate stocks, the presumed level of current dividends is important but not all important. Expansion may still be beneficial to shareholders even though R_a is less than R_c, provided the added investment is financed at least in part by borrowed funds.[8] The essential requirements are that the cor-

---

[7] B. Graham and D. L. Dodd, *Security Analysis* (3d ed.; New York: McGraw-Hill Book Company, 1951), p. 410.

[8] Unlike the case of capital gains taxation, benefits derived from the use of borrowed funds do not accrue automatically to shareholders. Their existence depends upon management policy. For this reason, the possibility of utilizing borrowed funds is introduced simply as a qualification to the intermediate stock category.

poration in question be conservatively financed and that the excess of R_a over the interest rate be sufficient to offset the excess of R_c over R_a. If conservatively financed, the augmented use of borrowed funds need not appreciably affect either the multiplier or its reciprocal.

For illustrative purposes, let us assume that the conventional debt-equity ratio is one half, that the market capitalization rate is un-affected as long as this relationship holds, and that added investment is financed by the same proportions of debt and retained earnings as the conventional ratio. If, under such conditions, R_a is 12 percent and the interest rate is 6 percent, the rate of return on retained earnings be-comes 15 percent. The retention of earnings is thus beneficial to share-holders, provided R_c is less than 15 percent.

Even if the use of borrowed funds is ignored, the maximum feasible dividend payout ratio is likely to be something less than 100 percent for intermediate stocks. In some instances, maintenance of relative position within the industry may be essential for profit maintenance. Whatever the relation of R_a to R_c, the affected corporation must then keep pace with the industry and with other firms. Otherwise, the company loses out, and its overall profit rate declines. In other instances, a substantial portion of reported earnings may be attributable to price-level changes. If the real position of a given company is to be maintained, a portion of reported earnings will then have to be retained. In still other instances, cash may simply be unavailable for dividends.

IV

A third group, the credit stock category, may now be isolated for examination. Creditor stocks are so named because they possess many of the attributes of debt instruments. The most important of the similari-ties is that, in determining the present worth of creditor stocks, almost exclusive emphasis is placed upon the prevailing level of dividends. Average yields on creditor stocks are somewhat higher than those on bonds, for shareholders lack legal protection and have no equity cushion upon which to rest. The limited ability of institutional investors to hold any type of equity share, due principally to legislative restrictions and to the nature of their obligations, also contributes to the yield dif-ferential between bonds and creditor stocks.[9]

As contrasted with the growth and intermediate stock categories, the retention of earnings occasions little or no appreciation in creditor stock prices over time. The low present value of retained earnings may be attributable to the fact that the rate of return on additional invest-ment approximates zero. It may be attributable to management which

---

[9]As the pressure to obtain satisfactory yields on investments increases, however, the gradual relaxation of legislative restrictions is likely to occur.

elects to retain earnings during prosperous periods and to hold them in liquid form for distribution during depressed periods. It may be attributable to public regulatory commissions which pass the benefits derived from earnings retention on to the public.

In a relevant sense the inclusion of this category modifies, as well as extends beyond, the preceding analysis. Stocks can no longer be said to qualify automatically for membership in the growth and intermediate stock groups depending upon whether adjusted R_a is greater or less than R_c. The ultimate distribution of additional earnings is not a foregone conclusion; retained earnings need not be employed in the most profitable fashion; and economic considerations are not the sole criterion.

The ability of shareholders to influence the policies of either management or regulatory commissions is frequently circumscribed. As a result, stock prices are of necessity conditioned by the expected behavior of management and government in the light of their past actions. If management and/or regulatory commissions regard shareholders as creditors and if the underlying economic conditions permit their treatment as such, it follows that the stocks which are thus affected will assume many of the characteristics of credit instruments.

Common stocks of large, well established public utilities offer excellent possibilities for inclusion in the creditor stock category.[10] Public utilities in general are characterized by an underlying element of stability and by close regulation. Rates tend to be adjusted so as to provide reasonable and stable returns to shareholders. Dividend payout ratios normally range in the neighborhood of 75 percent, and sources of additional funds are largely external.[11]

The acceptance of the idea that shareholders are creditors is reflected in the dividend policy of the largest of all public utilities. For more than three decades American Telephone and Telegraph has annually declared a $9 dividend.

Common stocks of large, mature industrial corporations whose earnings possess a reasonable degree of stability are likely to exhibit at least some features of creditor stocks. Management often elects to stabilize the dollar amount of dividends declared annually, thereby reducing dividend payout ratios during prosperous periods and raising them during depressed periods. To the extent that retained earnings are then held in liquid form, *cash* cushions are created which bear marked similarities to the equity or earning-power cushions provided for senior securities.

---

[10]It is not meant to imply that all, or even the great majority, of utility stocks are creditor stocks. Some may actually be growth stocks. The crucial considerations appear to be whether regulatory commissions permit retained earnings to augment the invested capital base and whether the allowable rate of return exceeds or falls short of R_c.

[11]Postwar payout ratios are noticeably below those for the immediate prewar period, perhaps reflecting the impact of substantial price-level changes.

Needless to say, the point of delineation between intermediate stocks and creditor stocks is difficult to ascertain.[12] Given the separation of ownership from control for large, public corporations, it may well be that shareholders are generally viewed by the managements of these companies as a form of creditor. In numerous instances, however, the nature of the corporation may be such that this attitude cannot readily be translated into policy. . . .

As a final point, the behavior of creditor stock prices can still be expected to resemble in many respects that of common stock prices in general. First, even where common stocks are creditor oriented, dividends ordinarily exhibit some relation to earnings and vary accordingly. This proposition follows from the absence of contractual agreements between management and shareholders. Second, since common stocks have no maturity dates, creditor stock prices are not conditioned by maturity values. This situation is, however, little different from that of bonds possessing remote maturities and no different from that of Consols.

Third, wherever regulatory commissions exist, rate revisions customarily operate with a lag. During the interim, higher earnings attributable to the retention of earnings may permit higher dividends. The converse is, of course, also true. Finally, the possibility is always present that, as management and commissions change, policies may also change.

V

The basic premise that stock prices, over longer periods, reflect the present values of anticipated future dividends permits derivation of a model which possesses substantial plausibility. In distinguishing between growth and intermediate stocks, the crucial question becomes whether or not the capitalized values of future dividends attributable to the retention of earnings are greater than the dollar magnitudes of retained earnings. Wherever greater, i.e., wherever rates of return on additional investment exceed market capitalization rates, the common stocks in question belong to the growth stock category. In the case of growth stocks, low dividend payout ratios can be expected to enhance stock values.

In certain instances, common stocks may assume the characteristics of growth stocks despite the fact that rates of return on added investment are less than market capitalization rates. The preferred tax treatment of capital gains augments the worth of retained earnings and enables more stocks to qualify as growth stocks. In addition, the combined use of borrowed funds and retained earnings makes it beneficial to retain earnings under special circumstances.

---

[12]In other words, R_a—in the sense of most profitable uses of funds—may be less than R_c, but greater than zero, for creditor stocks as well as intermediate stocks.

For most large industrials, rates of return on additional investment are presumed to exceed zero but to be less than the corresponding market capitalization rates. This condition leads to the commonly observed, direct relationship between dividend payout ratios and common stock prices. Although earnings retention occasions appreciation in stock prices over time, shareholders benefit from the distribution of the maximum feasible amount of earnings.

Acceptance of the fact that the control over large public corporations is often vested in management and regulatory commissions gives rise to the creditor stock category. For this group, the principal determinant of common stock prices is the prevailing level of dividends, capitalized at appropriate rates. Although retained earnings may augment dividend stability and thereby reduce capitalization rates, they contribute little to the prospects for higher dividends in the future.

Granted the inadequacies and diversity of statistical data, a model of this type has considerable utility as a foundation for empirical analysis. Most important of all, it provides a tentative basis for classifying common stocks. Even in the event that the model is not entirely valid, the heterogeneity of the statistical sample may still be reduced. Secondly, it specifies the necessary information and establishes interesting relationships for empirical verification. Finally, if, as is more than likely, the statistical data are inadequate for thoroughgoing analyses, they may nonetheless be sufficient to confirm or deny the model.

13. UTILITY DIVIDEND POLICY, GROWTH, AND RETENTION RATES*

EDWARD E. WILLIAMS†
AND J. J. SENECA††

Previous studies of English and American companies have found a surprising negative relationship between retention rates and earnings growth rates. It is questionable whether these findings are generally applicable to all industries and firms. This article seeks to examine pay-out ratios and growth rates for a single U.S. industry—the public utilities. There is a statistically significant and *negative* relationship between payout rates and earnings growth rates that is nonlinear, with the slope of the function becoming less steep as growth increases.

I. INTRODUCTION

The finance literature has generally hypothesized that an inverse relationship should exist between the dividend pay-out of firms and their rates of growth. It is suggested that firms attempting to maximize the wealth position of stockholders should retain earnings if lucrative reinvestment proposals are to be found while firms that have poor reinvestment prospects should pay out most of their earnings in dividends. It is further argued that firms which have lucrative reinvestment alternatives, and which have high retention rates, should evidence substantial earnings growth, which, in turn, should produce higher stock prices and, hence, capital gains for investors. This hypothesis has been embodied in most share-price maximization models such as the Walter formula[1] and the Gordon model.[2]

Few empirical studies have been based on these share-price maximization models, however, because they require knowledge about the marginal (or average) efficiency of investment schedule faced by the firm and the firm's cost of capital. A well-known study of 441 major English firms which ignored reinvestment and cost-of-capital considerations was conducted by I. M. D. Little. This study found a surprising negative relationship between plow-back rates and earnings growth rates.[3] A similar finding was reported by Murphy who investigated 244

---

*From *Public Utilities Fortnightly* (March, 1973), pp. 23–27. Reprinted by permission.
†Associate Professor of Finance, McGill University.
††Associate Professor of Economics, Rutgers University.
[1]"Dividend Policies and Common Stock Prices," by J. Walter, *Journal of Finance*, March, 1956.
[2]"Dividends, Earnings, and Stock Prices," by M. Gordon, *Review of Economics and Statistics*, May, 1959.
[3]"Higgledy Piggledy Growth," by I. M. D. Little, *Bulletin of the Oxford Institute of Statistics*, November, 1962.

American firms over the period 1950-65.[4] These results may indicate the Baumolian (or Galbraithian) conclusion that goals other than maximizing the wealth position of stockholders determine the dividend policy of firms and that firms which retain substantial earnings do not do appreciably better for stockholders than those firms which have high pay-outs. These findings are not inconsistent with cross-sectional regression studies of American firms which conclude that dividends are more important than retained earnings in determining the market price of a stock.[5]

This article seeks to establish an empirical relation between rates of growth in earnings and payout (or retention) policies of U.S. public utilities. Section II will briefly develop the relevant theoretical relation between these variables. Section III describes the underlying data, the method, and results of the empirical test. Emphasis is also placed on the careful interpretation of the results in terms of the theoretical implications of Section II. Finally, Section IV offers some conclusions and suggestions for further research efforts in this area.

II. GROWTH RATES AND PAY-OUT POLICIES: THE THEORETICAL RELATION

It seems appropriate that a rigorous test of the plow-back hypothesis might be made, giving explicit consideration to opportunity reinvestment rates. The public utility industry offers a unique possibility for such a test in that limits on the rates of return on real investment are prescribed by regulatory agencies. Of course, any conclusions reached regarding the plow-back hypothesis could be ascribed only to public utilities and not necessarily to all enterprise in general.

Initially, a simple plow-back growth model for U.S. public utilities will be derived. The model will be tested to determine the relationship between dividend pay-outs and the earnings growth rates. The test will be made on data for a cross section of public utility firms. Hence, the relationships in the model are portrayed at the micro level.

The following symbols will be in the derivation of this Section:

V = the firm's investment in facilities per share of common stock (i.e., the rate base).

r = the fair rate of return allowed on investment.

λ = net operating income per share after all expenses, including taxes and depreciation, but before interest and dividend payments.

B = the book value of long-term debt financing per share of common stock.

---

[4]"Return on Equity Capital, Dividend Pay-out, and Growth of Earnings Per Share," by Joseph E. Murphy, *Financial Analysts Journal*, May-June, 1967.

[5]"Dividends and Stock Prices," by Irwin Friend and Marshall Puckett, *American Economic Review*, September, 1964.

$S =$ the book value per share of equity financing.
$\theta =$ the optimal capital structure for the firm.
$i =$ the rate of interest paid on debt.
$\pi =$ net profit per share of common stock.
$d =$ dividends per share of common stock.

All values are indicated on a per share of common stock basis since the sale of additional shares could increase the total rate base while not improving the position of individual investors. Furthermore, comparisons are more easily made on a per share than an aggregate basis. Of course, all values are assumed to be adjusted for stock dividends, splits, etc.

Given the above definitions, we may specify the rate base value per share of the firm as:

$$V = B + S \tag{1}$$

For the sake of simplicity, current liabilities will be assumed to equal assets not included in the rate base. Since rates of return are based on book values, from the accounting identity that assets equal liabilities plus net worth, we may establish equation (1). If V is the rate base value, then the allowed net operating income per share is:

$$\lambda = rV \tag{2}$$

From λ, interest is paid to bondholders, leaving net profit per share of common stock:[6]

$$\pi = \lambda - iB \tag{3}$$

After dividends are paid to shareholders, the firm is left with $\pi - d$ per share to reinvest. Expressed as percentages, the dividend pay-out rate would be d/π and the retention (plow-back) rate would be $I - d/\pi$.

The relationships expressed in (1) through (3) are definitional and may be taken as the static values in any one time period. Of course, we are interested in the dynamic aspects of the model emphasizing the effect on the value of the rate base as earnings are retained. Given the accounting identity, a change in the value of the rate base per share is simply:

$$\Delta V = \Delta B + \Delta S \tag{4}$$

Furthermore, the retention of earnings will increase S such that

$$\Delta S = \pi - d \tag{5}$$

---

[6]The possibility of preferred stock financing, and hence preferred dividends, is ignored, although the model may be easily adjusted to include the existence of preferred stock.

Assuming some optimal relationship for the firm's debt-equity combination, say $\theta = B/S$, we may specify the optimal change in B, given a change in S, as:

$$\Delta B = \theta \Delta S \tag{6}$$

Now, we wish to know by how much π will grow if earnings are retained. Let g equal the growth rate in earnings per share $(\Delta \pi / \pi)$. We have established in (3) the relationship between net profits and net operating income, hence:

$$\Delta \pi = \Delta \lambda - i \Delta B \tag{7}$$

Furthermore, from (2) we can demonstrate that

$$\Delta \lambda = r \Delta V \tag{8}$$

and substituting (8) into (7), we obtain:

$$\Delta \pi = r \Delta V - i \Delta B \tag{9}$$

We know ΔV from (4) and substituting, we find:

$$\Delta \pi = r(\Delta B + \Delta S) - i \Delta B \tag{10}$$

which may be rewritten:

$$\Delta \pi = (r - i)\Delta B + r \Delta S \tag{11}$$

We know ΔB from (6) and ΔS from (5), and, by substitution,

$$\Delta \pi = (r - i)(\theta)(\pi - d) + r(\pi - d) \tag{12}$$

and factoring, we obtain:

$$\Delta \pi = (\pi - d)[\theta(r - i) + r] \tag{13}$$

The growth rate (g) is $\Delta \pi / \pi$. Thus, we may conclude that

$$g = \frac{\Delta \pi}{\pi} = \frac{\pi - d}{\pi}\,[\theta(r - i) + r)] \tag{14}$$

or,

$$g = \frac{\Delta \pi}{\pi} = \left[I - \frac{d}{\pi}\right][\theta(r - i) + r] \tag{15}$$

We see that the growth rate in earnings per share should vary positively with the rate of retention $(I - {}^d/\pi)$ and the allowed rate of return on investment and negatively with the rate of interest paid to bondholders. Specifically, the rate of growth in per share earnings should equal the retention rate times the allowed rate of return on investment plus the retention rate times the net return to shareholders on debt funds after paying interest $(r - i)$ adjusted for the capital structure ratio (θ). If all of these variables are constant over time, the growth rate would also be constant. In this case, per share earnings in period n would be given by:

$$\pi_n = \pi_0(I + g)^n \qquad (16)$$

where π_0 is earnings per share in period 0 and g is the compounded annual rate of growth. Our interest therefore settles on equations (15) and (16) and specifically on the hypothesized positive relation between the compound annual growth rate in earnings and the rate of retention. (Equivalently, this implies a negative relation with the pay-out ratio.) Section III will describe the empirical testing of this hypothesis.

III. EMPIRICAL RESULTS

The basic sample of the study was derived from Standard & Poor's per share data on 99 utilities.[7] These 99 utilities represent all major utilities in the U.S. economy and include electric and gasworks, water utilities, and communications firms. For each utility the compounded annual rate of growth in earnings per share (g) was estimated for the period 1958-67.[8] The annual dividend pay-out ratio (d/π) of each utility was then computed for each year of the ten-year time period. An average of this ratio was formed for each company. Thus, the relevant data became the compounded annual growth rate *for each* company, g_i ($i = 1, 99$), and its *average* dividend pay-out ratio, $(d/\pi)_i$, in the 1958-67 period. The relationship between these variables can yield, with some conditional caveats, a test of the theoretical result of equation (15). Thus, the general equation estimated was as follows, (17)$g_i = f[(d/\pi)_i]$ where the theoretical interest is centered on the sign and significance of the statistical association between g and (d/π). If the theoretical hypothesis developed in Section II is valid, then we can expect a negative relation between the earnings growth rate and the pay-out ratio. (Equivalently, a positive relation would exist between g and the retention rate.) However, although we can expect this negative relation, there is no a priori reasoning which would indicate the particular functional form of equation (17) and it therefore seems appropriate to use several possible specifications in an attempt to test for nonlinear relations between growth and pay-out.

Thus, equation (17) was estimated in alternative functional forms for the basic data and these results appear in Table 13-1 below. The general conclusion of the results, however, independent of the specific

---

[7]Standard & Poor's, *Stock Market Encyclopedia*, 12th ed., 1969.

[8]This involved estimating the following equation for each of the 99 utilities; Log $E^i_t = a + b$ Time where E^i_t is the earnings per share of company i ($i = 1, 99$) in time period t ($t = 1958, 1967$). The estimate of b can be used to derive the compound annual growth rate (g) of the ith firm as expressed in equation (16) in the text.

TABLE 13-1

ALL UTILITIES (1958-67) GROWTH AND PAY-OUT

	α	β	R^2
A. $g = \alpha + \beta \, ^d/\pi$	.2392	−.2543	.4301
	(12.4253)	(8.6582)	—
B. $g = \alpha + \beta \log \, ^d/\pi$	.0029	−.1611	.5005
	(.3801)	(9.9590)	—
C. $\log g = \alpha + \beta \log \, ^d/\pi$	−3.4356	−1.7003	.3838
	(34.1890)	(7.8764)	—
D. $\log g = \alpha + \beta \, ^d/\pi$	−.8301	−2.8552	.3744
	(3.4257)	(7.7227)	—

°Numbers in parenthesis below coefficients are t tests.

function used, is that a statistically *significant* and *negative* relation does not exist between growth in earnings and the observed average pay-out ratio. If we examine the results in Table 13-1, it is clear that the sign of the coefficient of the pay-out variable is consistently negative and significant over all four equations. This equation also indicates that a non-linear relation exists between growth in earnings and pay-out, with the slope of the function becoming less steep as g increases. This implies the intuitive result that continual increases in the pay-out ratio result in progressively smaller reductions in g.

The general conclusion to be drawn from Table 13-1 is that the pay-out ratios of utilities are significantly and negatively associated with their growth rates in earnings. The t tests for the average pay-out variables are all significant at the 99 percent level of confidence while the R^2's in this simple model range from .37 to a respectable .50 (for cross-section data).

However, several conditions must be stated before these results can be accepted as a confirmation of the theoretical relation of equation (15). The use of a constant compound annual growth rate to derive g for the various utilities may be somewhat restrictive. Although the fits of the 99 equations estimated to obtain gi were in general good, we have essentially assumed the constancy of this growth rate over the ten-year period.[9] More importantly we are also abstracting from the *simultaneity*

---

[9]Recall the assumption of a constant compound annual growth rate of earnings as given by equation (16) in Section II. One partial (but let us *emphasize*, far from conclusive) justification of this assumption, is that the equation fitted (see fn 2) to estimate the earnings growth rate provided a generally good graduation of the data. The distribution of R²'s for the 99 utilities is:

R^2	No. of Utilities
99 to 95	51
94 to 90	21
89 to 80	15
79 to 70	5
70 and below	7

which may exist *over* time between growth in earnings and dividend behavior. We are only examining the relationship *over* firms in a ten-year period between an estimated constant annual growth rate and the observed (average) dividend pay-out rate over this same time period. This cross-section microanalysis of the data, therefore, cannot be used to infer any expectational behavior on the part of investors or the utilities although expectational considerations are a key element in much of the underlying theoretical foundation of the relationship in question.[10]

While understanding these important constraints on the theoretical interpretations of the statistical results, it seems appropriate to explore the results of Table 13-1 in somewhat more detail. An interesting question may be to determine whether this negative relation between growth in earnings and pay-out is consistent over size classifications of the utilities. The sample of 99 utilities was divided into five subsamples based on total revenues. (These revenue size criteria are indicated in Table 13-2, page 158.) The same basic functional forms used in Table 13-1 were estimated for each of these size groups and the results appear in Table 13-2. Surveying these results indicates that the negative relation is consistently present and significant in each of the size groups. In general, the relationship holds best for the middle two size groups (where not, surprisingly, over half of the observations fall) with equation (B) again indicating a slightly but consistently better fit for the first three size groups.[11] The *t* tests for the pay-out variable are also consistently significant in all size groups although they are relatively lower in Size IV.

Again, the general conclusion is that there is a statistically significant *inverse* relation between growth rates in earnings and pay-out rates for each of the size classifications of utilities. Other methods of subsampling the basic data are possible. Perhaps a sample of firms with abnormally high and abnormally low growth rates could be used to isolate payout behavior at the extremes of growth in earnings. Utilities, however, due to regulatory constraints, do not exhibit *wide* divergencies in earnings and a sufficiently large sample of high growth rates (e.g., firms with over a 10 percent compounded annual growth rate) could not be isolated. Other studies examining this relation for more general industries may be able to perform such tests.

---

[10]"Growth of Earnings and Dividend Distribution Policy," by V. Jaaskelainen, *Swedish Journal of Economics*, September, 1967.

[11]The slopes of these functions are equal to $\frac{\beta}{\pi}(d)$ for equation (B) and $\beta \cdot g$ for equation (D). In each case, as pay-out increases (or as g decreases), with a negative β the slope of the function becomes *less* steep.

TABLE 13-2
UTILITIES BY SIZE GROUP

		α	β	R^2
Revenues under 50 $\bar{m}$ Size I				
$n = 14$ Equation A		.2040	$-$ .2092	.2642
		(3.6848)	(2.3807)	—
	B	.0108	$-$.1299	.2918
		(.41167)	(2.5211)	—
	C	-3.5577	-1.7378	.2133
		(8.6388)	(2.1270)	—
	D	$-.9541$	-2.8302	.1975
		(1.0908)	(2.0493)	—
Revenues 50-100 $\bar{m}$ Size II				
$n = 25$	A	.2240	$-.2396$	.5768
		(8.3099)	(5.8057)	—
	B	.0048	$-.1441$	.5952
		(.4280)	(6.0240)	—
	C	-3.6495	-2.0032	4684
		(18.2783)	(4.7062)	—
	D	$-.5343$	-3.4347	.4849
		(1.1567)	(4.8572)	—
Revenues 100-250 $\bar{m}$ Size III				
$n = 29$	A	.3283	$-.3825$	.5642
		(8.0285)	(6.1037)	—
	B	$-.0204$	$-.2257$	.6698
		(1.4219)	(7.6031)	—
	C	-3.4296	-1.8080	.4999
		(21.1770)	(5.3838)	—
	D	$-.5115$	-3.2577	.4794
		(1.2451)	(5.1749)	—
Revenues 250-500 $\bar{m}$ Size IV				
$n = 19$	A	.1456	$-.1105$	.2589
		(4.1627)	(2.0979)	—
	B	.0450	$-.1438$	.1321
		(3.0379)	(1.9338)	—
	C	-3.0868	-1.0306	.1575
		(14.3653)	(2.0895)	—
	D	1.5166	-1.7210	.1842
		(2.9874)	(2.2507)	—
Revenues 500 $\bar{m}$ Size V and over				
$n = 12$	A	.1719	$-.1509$	.2614
		(3.6960)	(2.2118)	—
	B	.0284	$-.1043$	.2544
		(1.4377)	(2.1804)	—
	C	-3.3657	-1.6472	.2810
		(11.3885)	(2.3021)	—
	D	-1.1065	-2.3714	.2849
		(1.5871)	(2.3200)	—

IV. CONCLUSION

This article has examined the empirical relationship between rates of growth in earnings and the payout (retention) policies of U.S. public utilities. Initially, an algebraic model was constructed to indicate the theoretical relation. It was determined that the growth in earnings per share should vary positively with the rate of earnings retention and the allowed rate of return on investment and negatively with the rate of interest paid to bondholders. The focal point of the article was the first of these relationships. Hence it was hypothesized that earnings growth and the rate of retention should be positively related, or, alternatively, that earnings growth and the rate of dividend payment should be negatively related.

The empirical results of the study must be tempered with the caveats given in Section IV above; namely, the constancy of the growth rate assumption, the lack of simultaneity in the estimated relation, and the removal of expectional considerations. However, the results do seem to be consistent and indicate that a negative and significant relation does exist between *actual* growth rate (compounded annually) and *observed* pay-out behavior of U.S. utilities in the 1958-67 period. This relationship is clearly present for the overall sample and also appears in each revenue size classification within the samples. These findings, while of a simple nature, suggest that the theoretical relations expressed in Section II do have an empirical basis. The results also indicate that a more *general* study is warranted. This study should include many *diverse* firms and industries, with particular emphasis placed on dividend behavior at the *extreme* range of high and low earnings growth rates. The development of a sample with wide variation of growth of earnings was not possible in the case of utilities. However, the use of a sample of a broader classification of firms should provide this variation.

Our conclusion that the pay-out ratios of U.S. public utilities are significantly and negatively associated with their earnings growth rates contrasts with the findings of other researchers who have examined a wider spectrum of firms in diverse industries. A possible explanation for the different findings may lie in the unique nature of the public utility industry. Whereas the expected average rate of return on assets for most industries may vary substantially, the average rate for public utilities (due to regulatory limits) is reasonably stable. Thus, it may well be that industrial firms which face uncertain returns may tend to be overly optimistic about the profitability of investments ex ante which simply do not produce the expected large profits ex post. Even without the insidious behavior toward stockholders ascribed to firms by Baumol, Galbraith et al., these concerns would tend to pay out small percentages of earnings if management *expected* to do well for stockholders. For public utilities, on the other hand, there is not the same amount of uncertainty associated with future returns. Since regulated returns preclude public utilities from being growth firms, they tend to pay-out high percentages of earnings in dividends. Unlike the case of unregulated industrial concerns, there is not the great discrepancy of ex ante illusions of potential growth. Furthermore, and perhaps more importantly, since returns for public utilities depend on the size of the rate base, any increase in total investment (i.e., the rate base) should yield approximately the regulated rate of return. This return may turn out to be, ex post, higher than the realized rates experienced by some "growth" firms.

14. A CASE FOR DROPPING DIVIDENDS*

CAROL J. LOOMIS†

Earlier this year, General Public Utilities Corp., No. 11 on *Fortune's* list of the 50 largest utilities, notified its 79,000 stockholders that it was considering adoption of a radically different dividend plan that seemed to offer some large advantages to just about everyone concerned. The company proposed to substitute stock dividends for three of its quarterly cash dividends. Simultaneously it offered to sell the shares (with minimal brokerage costs) for any stockholder who wanted to realize the same cash income he had been getting previously. The advantage to the shareholder—at least to any shareholder paying income taxes—would be a sharp reduction in his tax liability: he would be taxed on his stock dividends only if he decided to sell them and then only on that part of his proceeds that represented profit. Furthermore, any profits would be taxed at capital-gains rates (assuming the stockholder had owned his original stock for at least six months), whereas the cash dividends would, of course, be taxed at the higher rates applying to regular income. All told, it looked as if the plan might result in an immediate tax saving to the shareholders of at least $4 million annually—and probably more.

The advantages to G.P.U. itself looked equally imposing. The company is going to need enormous amounts of money for capital expenditures over the next few years—upwards of $200 million annually—and it needs to hang on to every cent it can. The elimination of three quarterly cash dividends would save the company nearly $30 million annually. Lacking that money and already burdened by a high debt ratio, the company knew it would simply have to raise an equivalent amount by selling new common stock. As it happens, G.P.U. is obligated to sell its stock through rights offerings to its present stockholders. Thus, any sale of stock would have put the company in the position of asking its stockholders, in effect, to reinvest the dollars they had received in dividends—except that those dollars would have been depleted by the payment of income taxes. Considering all that, G.P.U. President William G. Kuhns figured that it made more sense for the company just to hang on to the dividends in the first place.

Unfortunately a lot of the company's stockholders didn't see it that way. Right after G.P.U.'s plan become generally known, the company's stock, which sells in the mid-20's, dropped nearly two points. And then the letters began to come in. Some were approving, but a dismaying

number blistered the company and its officers for even considering such
a move. One stockholder called Kuhns "a hypocritical ass"; another
suggested that the president ought to see a psychiatrist. Worse yet, a
large number of institutional holders of the stock—in particular, bank
trust departments—put themselves on record as being so resolutely
against the plan that its implementation would probably impel them to
sell their stock. Some of the banks pointed out that they were committed,
in their handling of most trusts, to seek "income," and that, in their
particular states, they were barred by law from using stock dividends to
get it. Other banks had far less substantive objections. In any case, it
began to look as if up to 20 percent of G.P.U's stock might hit the market
if the company persisted with the plan. Kuhns and the board of directors
decided that neither they nor the stockholders could stand that. And so
the plan was abandoned.

HOW TO BUY EARNINGS PER SHARE

The case for cutting dividend payments at G.P.U. is of a kind that
might be made at many other companies. Under today's tax laws, any
taxpaying stockholder who gets his returns through dividends rather
than capital gains is odds on to come out second best. Furthermore,
corporate demands for capital tend to be extraordinary these days, and
for many companies, money going out in dividends is money they need
badly to finance their growth. In fact, these companies must turn to the
capital markets just to raise the funds they pay out in dividends. Some
companies, like G.P.U., end up getting their money through sales of
common stock. Others take on debt, which is now to be had only at
interest rates of around 7 percent. The interest, of course, is tax-
deductible, but, even so, the charges take a big bite out of earnings—
a bite that could have been avoided had those dividends been retained
by the company.

Some companies, it is true, are not financially strained—a few are
even cash-rich—and can easily afford to pay dividends. But even for
these fortunate few, it seems likely that dividend payments are a poor
way to benefit the stockholders. The best way would be to employ the
funds in productive investments. After all, it is generally accepted in
this era of "conglomeration" that corporate investment horizons are
virtually unlimited, that any lack of opportunities within a company's
own industry need not constrict its growth. It can go into any business
it wants; alternatively, it can buy stock in another company. And finally,
even if none of these moves seems right, there is still a better way to
reward stockholders than with dividends. The company can simply buy
in its own stock—a procedure that, by reducing the number of shares
outstanding, increases the earnings on those that remain. Any stockholder wanting to realize income would simply sell some of his stock.

He would get a price reflecting both the new, higher earnings and the presence of his own company in the market as a heavy buyer.

SKIP THE SURPRISES

The general case, then, is that dividend income received means capital-gains opportunities forgone. Most stockholders will admit the logic of this case and will declare themselves unequivocally on the side of capital gains—in general. Even in particular cases, many investors make it clear by their actions that they attach no real importance to dividends. For example, most of those who keep their stock in *Street name* allow dividends to pile up in their accounts. Ordinarily, they get around at some point to reinvesting the money in stock. About 57 percent of the dividend income received by mutual-fund shareholders is reinvested automatically—even though these shareholders include many relatively small investors whose dependence on dividends is ordinarily assumed to be great. . . .

Yet it is a peculiar fact of life that many stockholders who acknowledge that dividends generally eat into capital gains will vigorously resist any attempt by their own companies to cut their dividends. . . . A company's cash dividend, once established, becomes almost sacrosanct, and any talk of reducing it, no matter for what reasons, means that the company's stock is likely to fall. Said a trust officer at a large New York bank recently: "We're not very interested in dividends around here. We're capital-gains oriented. But I'd say this about dividends—we don't want any surprises."

Obviously, then, any sweeping move by corporations toward lower dividend payments would entail some practical difficulties. The move would surely have to be accompanied by a major reeducation program aimed at persuading stockholders that dividend cuts are bullish, not bearish. There is also some danger that any such move might lead to a change in the tax laws, possibly one imposing a higher tax on capital gains. Right now the government realizes more than $5 billion annually from taxes on dividends, and it would clearly not give up this revenue without demanding something in return. Some proponents of lower dividends have argued that greater retention of earnings by corporations would so increase their profits, and thus their tax liabilities, that any related reduction in dividend taxes could be tolerated. The Treasury does not seem to agree. . . .

Taking the 500 industrials as a whole, the number of companies that, as a matter of policy, pay no cash dividends on their common stocks is still small but growing somewhat. Ten years ago, in the list reporting on 1957, there were only 31 companies not paying a cash dividend, and of these most had been forced into that position by adversity. In all, there were only six companies on the list that seem to have had a clear policy of not paying cash dividends. But on the 1967 list there are 16 companies of that kind (there are 23 others not paying dividends, most having experienced adversity). Many of these 16 have been holdouts against cash dividends throughout their history. In addition, the 1967 list contains a handful of companies that, though they have not been so bold as to cut their dividends altogether, have frozen them at relatively low levels. One of these is Burroughs, which, though its earnings have more than tripled in the last three years (to $4.25 per share in 1967), has kept its annual payout at only $1 per share.

TWO WAYS TO A PAYOFF

The case against cash dividends is plainly supported by those 16 companies on the 1967 list. They would have made a rather interesting stock portfolio over the years. One of the companies is Seagram, which is special in that it has only one stockholder, Distillers Corp.-Seagram. . . . The other 15 companies recently had a median price-earnings ratio of 30, a number suggesting forcibly that the market regards most of them as growth situations. (The p/e prevailing on Standard & Poor's 425 industrials is 19.)

Economists, however, have long striven to make some broader points concerning the relationship between dividends and stock prices. One main question has been this: What is the relative importance of retained earnings and dividends in determining a stock's p/e? Underlying this question is the proposition that both retained earnings and dividends convey a return to the stockholder. Dividends, of course, are a direct payoff. Retained earnings, on the other hand, increase the book value of the stockholder's business and, more important in today's markets, increase the power of the business to produce additional earnings. As these are capitalized in the market, the value of the stockholder's shares increases. The question, then, is which method of payment do most investors prefer?

Considering the tax laws, one might suppose the answer was retained earnings and the capital gains resulting from them. It has been clear for many years that many shareholders, nevertheless, prefer dividends. Benjamin Graham and D. L. Dodd, in the first (1934) edition of their immensely influential *Security Analysis*, observed that a dollar's worth of dividends had about four times as much effect on market values as did a dollar's worth of retained earnings. Taxes, of course, have risen since then. However, various academicians, notably Myron Gordon of the University of Rochester, have recently done studies that seem to support Graham's and Dodd's general findings, if not their 4-to-1 relationship. Gordon says that for most companies (all but those showing "super" growth) generous dividend payouts tend to lift price-earnings ratios, and niggardly payouts, to depress them. Gordon goes on to suggest that stockholders are right in preferring dividends; he believes that it is rational to prefer the certainty of a dividend payment now to the uncertainty of a possible future return (realized through growth) flowing out of retained earnings.

Putting aside for a moment the question of what most stockholders *should* prefer, we may note that there are intense disagreements about what most of them in fact prefer. Indeed, the whole question of dividends and stock prices has produced a kind of academic sparring match, in which one authority after another has come under attack. One of Gordon's most distinguished critics is Franco Modigliani, of the Massachusetts Institute of Technology. "Gordon's mathematical models are all wrong," says Modigliani. "He builds things into them that say dividends count, and then he goes on to prove that dividends count."

ONE THIRD FOR THE FEDS

Modigliani's own findings, worked out in collaboration with Merton H. Miller of the University of Chicago, are that dividends do not count—i.e., he contends that investors are essentially indifferent to the level of dividends and that, therefore, they have virtually no effect on price-earnings ratios. (Gordon says that Modigliani's and Miller's models are poorly designed and their conclusions invalid.) Still a third view has been propounded by Irwin Friend of the University of Pennsylvania and Marshall Puckett of the Federal Reserve Bank of New York. Studying data for 1956 and 1958, they saw some indication that in nongrowth industries (they included food and steel in this category) investors tended to value dividends somewhat higher than retained earnings. But the opposite, they felt, was true for growth industries—identified as electronics, utilities, and chemicals.

As some of the formulations above suggest, the case against dividends rests very largely on the huge toll that income taxes take out of them. The toll is particularly great because so many dividends go to people in high tax brackets. As [an] illustration, consider the government's figures for 1966 (the latest available), which show that about $15.2 billion in dividend income was reported on individuals' tax returns and that about $13.3 billion of this came down to "adjusted gross income" on taxable returns—i.e., this amount remained after reported income has been reduced by the dividend exclusion (up to $100) that every taxpayer is allowed. Of the $13.3 billion, about $8.7 billion, or 65 percent, showed up on the returns of the relatively few taxpayers reporting income of $20,000 and up. Indeed, no less than $3.1 billion, or 23 percent of the taxable total, belonged to the few thousand taxpayers reporting income of $100,000 or more. Since tax rates at the $100,000 level are 62 percent (for a joint return) and at $200,000 are the maximum 70 percent, close to two thirds of this $3.1 billion can be figured to have gone to the government (the *federal* government, that is; many stockholders, of course, also have state and/or city income taxes to worry about).

Overall, the government took slightly over $5 billion, or 33 percent of that original $15.2 billion of reported dividends. By contrast, the effective rate on long-term capital gains has been estimated by the government to be 21.6 percent. This figure is derived from data showing that upwards of one third of all such gains are taxed at the maximum 25 percent rate, which applies solely to people in a tax bracket of 50 percent or higher—those reporting $52,000 of taxable income on a joint return. . . . [For 1974 the maximum tax note was 25 percent on the first $50,000 of net long-term capital gains. The maximum tax on the excess above $50,000 was 35 percent.]

Some stockholders, of course, are not "individuals" and, therefore, have different—generally very different—tax considerations to think about. Corporations, for example, receive several billion dollars in dividends annually (typically, about one third the amount going to individuals), and they have a strong reason to prefer this kind of investment payoff—i.e., most are allowed to exclude 85 percent of their dividends from taxable income, while they are taxed fully on capital gains (though only at capital-gains rates). Several more billions in dividends go annually to various kinds of institutional investors that pay no taxes at all, notably foundations, educational institutions, and corporate pension funds. The first two of these tend to want dividends, viewing them as spendable money, which they need; and though some are coming around, many still resist spending their capital gains. Most pension funds, on the other hand, have had considerably more money coming in than has been going out, and so they normally reinvest their dividends, incurring commission costs in the process. Presumably, the pension funds would just as soon have the money retained by the corporations involved.

A COST OF ZERO

But *all* investors have one good reason to forgo dividends insofar as they originate at companies having growth prospects and continuing needs for new capital. . . . New capital acquired from external sources is both expensive and hard to get; new capital acquired through retained earnings is both cheap and readily obtained, and for this reason stockholders should wish to see it used.

The word "cheap" applied to retained earnings is controversial. If you believe, with Professor Gordon, that high retention of earnings generally depresses a stock's p/e ratio and, therefore, levies a "cost" on the stockholders (and on the company as well, should it desire to sell additional stock) then retention might be viewed as expensive. This issue, as has been noted, is unresolved. But there is nothing at all debatable about the fact that retained earnings are "cheap" in the sense that their use involves neither the payment of interest (as debt does) nor the allocation of earnings to new shares (as the sale of common stock does). They, consequently, produce higher earnings per share than other kinds of capital.

Since retained earnings, in this particular sense, have a cost of zero and since their use does not involve the issuance of additional shares, *anything* made on this capital increases earnings per share. Some economists, acknowledging this general principle, have, nevertheless, argued that cost-free capital may sometimes be undesirable. . . . A management demanding a certain return from new projects to be financed with capital obtained externally will often settle for a more modest return on projects to be financed with retained earnings. Logically, the economists go on, retained earnings should not be committed to the business unless the return expected on them exceeds the stockholders' *opportunity cost*—i.e., the return they could expect to earn on these funds as individuals if they had the funds in hand and could deploy them wherever the investment opportunities seemed most promising. The difficulty with this approach is that most stockholders can get their hands on these earnings only by paying income taxes, an outlay that leaves them with considerably less capital to work with than was originally available to the company and that greatly handicaps them in any contest with the company regarding rate of return.

TAKE IT IN, PAY IT OUT

Take, for example, that odd situation at General Public Utilities. The company's retained earnings in the last few years can be assumed to have been producing an after-tax return of around 11 percent—i.e., the company earns that much on its stockholders' equity and the rate of return has actually been rising, not declining, under the thrust of new capital. Now suppose, to simplify matters drastically, that the company has $1 million in earnings and that its stockholders are all in a low, 20 percent tax bracket. . . . If G.P.U. retains the $1 million, it may expect to earn 11 percent, or $110,000, on the money. If it pays the $1 million out, its stockholders, after paying their 20 percent income taxes, will be left with $800,000. To earn $110,000 on that money (that is, to come out at least even with G.P.U.), the stockholders must find an investment yielding 13.75 percent. This higher percentage return is likely to be available only at great risk.

As this illustration suggests, a stockholder is bound to be a loser if he takes dividends out of a company, pays his taxes, and then puts the money right back into the same company. Yet that is, in effect, what many of G.P.U.'s real-life stockholders have done at one time or another. . . .

Corporations also manage to do some pretty odd things with their money, and one of these is to pay dividends out of borrowed money. Most corporations doing this don't like to think of it that way; instead, they would say that dividends are paid out of earnings and that the money they borrow goes for capital expenditures. But it is obvious that if there were no dividends, earnings could go for capital expenditures, and much of the borrowing would become unnecessary. . . . Indeed, Federal Reserve figures for the country's nonfinancial corporations, taken as a whole, show a close relationship between the amount of money raised . . . through loans and sales of securities, and the amount paid out in dividends: over the last ten years these corporations acquired $141 billion in new money from external sources, and they spent $127 billion on dividends.

Since there are some corporations that borrow but do not pay dividends and some that pay dividends but do not borrow, it is plainly not correct to think of all companies covered by the Fed's figures as having, in effect, borrowed to pay dividends. But many individual companies have been doing precisely that. In the last five years Alcoa has added $293 million to its debt and paid $156 million in common dividends, having raised its payout four times during that period. Reynolds Metals' record for the same years is $252 million in new money borrowed, $55 million paid out, and three dividend increases. . . .

If the personal income tax did not exist and if it did not take such a whack out of dividends, there would be a lot to be said for companies' borrowing and passing the proceeds along to their stockholders, for corporations can usually borrow at better terms and with greater ease than can their stockholders, and thus corporate debt theoretically represents the best way for stockholders to get leverage—assuming, of course, they're willing to have it. But the tax penalty is so great as to make most dividends uneconomic, with or without leverage.

THE PRICE OF CERTAINTY

For some companies, dividends represent an extravagance that may jeopardize their future—and that may ultimately cause the stockholders to realize that they have paid a very dear price for the "certainty" that, Professor Gordon argues, makes dividends today more attractive than earnings tomorrow. Consider, for instance, American Motors. After its formation in 1954, it recorded three years of big losses and then, in 1958, hit the jackpot with its compact car. Only a few months later it began paying dividends. Many sophisticated investors were shocked; they felt that the company should be using the money to modernize its facilities and prepare otherwise for competition with Detroit's Big Three. By the early 1960's the company was battling to stay even, and by late 1965 the losses were back—and the dividends gone. Right now the company is burdened by debt, its outlook is clouded, and it might be supposed its executives had other things to think about than dividends. But Chairman Roy D. Chapin Jr. recently said he had every intention of making American Motors a "profitable, dividend-paying" company again.

When executives are asked why their companies borrow to pay dividends or why they pay them at all, they often insist that the stockholders want it that way. Most of them seem unaware that this proposition is under fire from some economists. But even aside from the findings of Modigliani and others, it may reasonably be asked why managements, which seldom rely on stockholders for advice about corporate policy, should bend so readily to their wishes in this area.

A few managements have fought dividends in recent years. Eastern Gas & Fuel Associates, a Boston industrial company mainly producing coal, used to be known on Wall Street principally as a payer of good dividends and a substantial holder of Norfolk & Western Railway stock. In 1962 a new management, headed by Eli Goldston, a lawyer who had recently turned businessman, took control of the company and soon after proposed to do away with cash dividends.

That was quite a shock to all those stockholders who had been cherishing Eastern Gas for its reliable dividend. But Goldston had something special in mind for them. Norfolk & Western paid a nice dividend, and so Goldston offered his stockholders a chance to exchange their Eastern Gas shares for the N. & W. shares owned by the company. About 35 percent of Eastern Gas stockholders accepted the exchange offer. (This proportion might have been even lower had it not been for one circumstance unique to the Eastern Gas case: Goldston himself had only a skimpy track record in business, and any stockholders who stayed with him were obviously taking a chance.) The other 65 percent were presumably attracted by Goldston's pledge "to take the cash that went into dividends and run like hell with it."

And that's what he did. He poured money into modernization, went after long-term contracts for the sale of coal, got rid of some unprofitable divisions, and whenever he had money to spare and the price looked right, bought in his own stock. The pared-down company began to show some sparkling earnings gains, and the stock market wasted no time in acknowledging them. By last year earnings were more than four times their 1962 level, and by late last month a share of stock that in early 1963 was worth $7.50 (adjusted for splits and stock dividends) was up to $38. That's an increase of more than 400 percent. . . .

A SMALLER PIECE OF PIE

When he abandoned cash dividends, Goldston replaced them with stock dividends. Stock dividends have some limited uses, but many companies—and Eastern Gas appears to be among them—employ them less for their utility than as a sort of sop to the stockholders, many of whom tend to think they get something of value when stock dividends are handed out. Actually, about all they get is some pieces of paper and some bookkeeping problems. For, in the familiar analogy, a stock dividend does nothing but divide the pie into a greater number of pieces, leaving the stockholder with no more than he had in the first place. Some managements argue that this isn't exactly so—that small stock dividends (3 or 4 percent) enable a stockholder who wants income to realize it by selling them while still getting capital-gains treatment. This argument is invalid as far as most stockholders are concerned, since they could achieve the same end by selling shares out of their original holdings.

Stock dividends have just one real advantage. They furnish, at least in some states, a means for trusts, which normally must be managed to provide income, to hold stocks that do not pay cash dividends. For example, in New York the laws say that, unless the trust instrument specifies otherwise, all stock dividends of less than 6 percent shall be considered income. . . .

What the 500 Pay Out

Most of the companies in FORTUNE's 500 list follow a "middle course" in their dividend policy: last year about 340 of them paid out between 31 and 70 percent of their earnings per common share in cash dividends. An analysis of the same 500 companies for the previous year, 1966, shows a comparable pattern but with a slight shift to the left—i.e., percentage payouts in 1966 were somewhat lower than in 1967. Last year's higher ratios were not the result of any widespread move toward higher dividends but rather of the drop in profits. It is typical of companies to maintain existing dividends even though earnings turn down.

The 39 companies that do not pay cash dividends include some that don't believe in them (e.g., Litton, Teledyne) and some that can't afford them (American Motors, Wheeling Steel). At the other end of the spectrum are companies whose dividends exceeded earnings, either because the earnings were depressed (Ford, Allis-Chalmers) or nonexistent (Fairchild Camera, Admiral). In between these two extremes are a few companies that pay only nominal dividends—say, 5 to 10 percent of earnings—so as to qualify themselves for purchase in ten states having laws prohibiting certain institutions (insurance companies and/or banks) from buying stocks that do not pay cash dividends. The chart does not take into account any stock

FIGURE 14-4

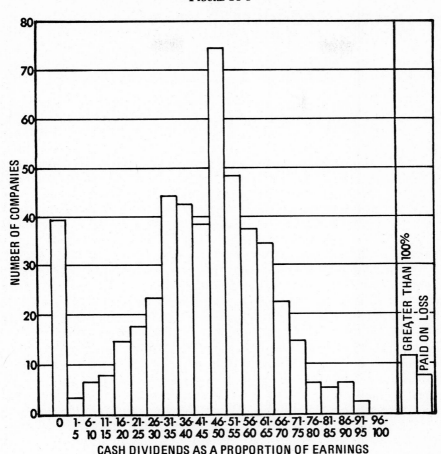

CASH DIVIDENDS AS A PROPORTION OF EARNINGS

dividends paid by companies; there were 26 that last year paid a combination of cash and stock, and ten paying stock alone.

Similar distribution charts for the various "fifty" lists in this issue would show the merchandisers spread out in a pattern similar to that of the 500: the transportation companies leaning toward lower payouts, with thirty of them below 50 percent; the banks overwhelmingly bunched in the middle; and the utilities just as overwhelmingly bunched somewhat above the middle (31 paid out between 56 and 70 percent of earnings). A similar analysis of the insurance list is not possible because of the large definitional problems in calculating their "earnings" and "dividends."

15. PRACTICAL CONSIDERATIONS IN COMMON STOCK REPURCHASE*

GUY J. AGRATI†

Although much good theoretical analysis of common stock repurchase has been published in recent years, little of practical value has filtered into the everyday world of business finance. Scholarly journals and academic texts almost invariably treat common stock repurchase as a decision in dividend policy.[1] While such an approach is logical and assists in understanding difficult questions in the financial theory surrounding capital structure, it is of nominal assistance to the corporate treasurer facing the complex problems of common share earnings and, by extension, of market price. As a consequence, senior management has no practical guidelines by which to evaluate stock repurchase, and its direct effects on earnings.

Repurchase of common stock by the corporate issuer is the converse of equity financing through distribution of new or treasury shares for cash. In the same sense that issuance of common shares results in new capital, repurchase is an "investment" in the issuer's own stock, a partial liquidation which results in a contraction of capital. Repurchase is, therefore, a valid employment of excess funds which may yield greater returns, in earnings per share and market price gains to remaining stockholders, than alternate investments, e.g., treasury bills. Whereas new equity issues (without pre-emptive rights) dilute earnings per share, repurchase by the issuer is counterdilutive, by withdrawing outstanding stock from public circulation. The knowledgeable and experienced corporate financial officer would, therefore, do well to understand the nature and practice of repurchase as the mirror strategy of equity financing. Well-rounded and effective financial management requires nothing less.

It is a basic premise of this article that common stock repurchase is a valuable financial tool which can be used to fund stock options, acquisitions for stock, and convertible obligations of the company.[2] Additionally, current and future years' earnings per share can be enhanced through repurchase, either to offset dilution from one or more of the

---

*From *Management Advisor* (May–June, 1972), pp. 35-39. Copyright 1972 by the American Institute of Certified Public Accountants, Inc. Reprinted by permission.
†Manager-Control, Chemical Bank.
[1]See for example: Harold Bierman, Jr., and Richard West, "The Acquisition of Common Stock by the Corporate Issuer," *Journal of Finance*, December, 1966, pp. 687-96; E. J. Elton and M. Gruber, "The Effect of Share Repurchase on the Value of the Firm," *Journal of Finance*, March, 1968, pp. 135-49; James C. Van Horne, *Financial Management and Policy*, Prentice-Hall, Englewood Cliffs, N.J., 1968, pp. 208-211.
[2]Recent APB opinions may discourage the issuance of repurchased stock for certain acquisitions. As a result, it would be prudent to consult a knowledgeable public accounting firm regarding repurchase prior to actually implementing the repurchase plan.

foregoing transactions; or to improve an unfavorable comparison with past period operating results. To be truly useful, however, repurchase must be measurable in terms of end result. Also helpful would be a determination of how to finance a repurchase program. Most desirable would be a method of measuring the efficiency of a given repurchase proposal—in effect relating gains resulting from an actual repurchase to potential gains from a no-cost reduction in stock outstanding, i.e., donated capital. This article addresses these questions and attempts to develop a practical method of evaluating repurchase under given, real world market conditions.

EFFECT ON EARNINGS PER SHARE

Stripped of irrelevant considerations (for the purposes of this article), earnings per share, according to generally accepted accounting principles, is simply the period income after tax divided by the average number of common shares outstanding. All other things being equal, a repurchase of common stock will affect both the numerator and denominator of the earnings per share expression by decreasing both earnings and the average number of shares outstanding. Furthermore, unless the repurchase takes place on the first day of the corporate fiscal year, effects of the repurchase on both numerator and denominator must be time adjusted, in order to correctly arrive at current year *EPS*. (*EPS* in future periods is subject to the full effect of the repurchase, barring any future distribution of shares.)

A FORMULA FOR REPURCHASE

Construction of an expression depicting the effects of repurchase is facilitated by algebraic substitution. Therefore, let:

E = period income after tax.

N = average number of shares outstanding for period given no repurchase.

n_t = number shares repurchased, adjusted for time (i.e., 10,000 shares repurchased half way through the fiscal year is 5,000 shares time adjusted).[3]

P = repurchase price per share.

D_t = dividend per share, time adjusted (for customary quarterly payment).

i = after-tax opportunity cost.

---

[3]Earnings per share gains from a given repurchase transaction may be estimated for a future year by setting n equal to the complete number of shares repurchased in the given transaction (in effect, letting $n_t = n$, the number of shares unadjusted). All other variables will, of course, be estimated for future years.

Earnings per share (*EPS*) given no repurchase is, therefore:

Equation 1:

$$EPS = E/N$$

Given the repurchase decision earnings will be affected in two ways:
• Dividends not paid on repurchased shares, i.e., treasury stock, may be invested at the opportunity rate, raising earnings. Algebraically, $E + [(i)(D_t)(n_t)]$.
• Funds used for purchase are not available for investment at the opportunity rate, lowering earnings. Again algebraically, $E - [(i)(P)(n_t)]$.

Similarly, average number of shares will decline by the time adjusted number of shares repurchased, $N - n_t$. From Equation 1 earnings per share with repurchase becomes:

Equation 2:

$$EPS_r = (E + [(i)(D_t)(n_t)] - [(i)(P)(n_t)]) \div (N - n_t)$$

EXAMPLE CALCULATION

An example may help to clarify any loose ends before proceeding further:

$$
\begin{aligned}
\text{Let:}\quad E &= \$50{,}000{,}000 \\
N &= 10{,}000{,}000 \text{ shares} \\
n_t &= 100{,}000 \text{ shares} \\
P &= \$45 \\
D_t &= \$2.00 \\
i &= 5.0\%
\end{aligned}
$$

Accordingly, Equation 1 yields:

$$EPS = \frac{50{,}000{,}000}{10{,}000{,}000} = \$5.00$$

and for Equation 2:

$$
\begin{aligned}
EPS_r &= (\$50{,}000{,}000 + [(0.05) \\
&\quad (2.00)(100{,}000)] - [(0.05) \\
&\quad (45)(100{,}000)]) \div (10{,}000{,}000 - 100{,}000) \\
&= (50{,}000{,}000 + 10{,}000 - 225{,}000) \div (9{,}900{,}000) \\
EPS_r &= \$5.029 = \$5.03
\end{aligned}
$$

Clearly in this example, as in most actual cases, the positive effect on earnings per share of the decline in the average number of shares outstanding by 100,000 overrode the negative net effect on earnings of $215,000. Consequently, $EPS_r > EPS$.

Sensitivity analysis of Equation 2 admits some interesting conclusions applicable to a wide range of plausible cases, including the example:

• Earnings per share are not appreciably increased by the non-payment of dividends on recovered treasury stock. In fact, the dividend investment effect is so small as to be relatively insignificant in almost all cases.

• Earnings per share are only slightly increased by a moderate reduction in purchase price. As a practical matter any point in the trading range of the normal stock ("base" price ± 10-15 percent) would yield essentially equivalent results in Equation 2.

• Equation 2 is moderately sensitive to changes in opportunity cost, with earnings per share upon repurchase inversely related to the opportunity rate, as expected.

• Equation 2 is quite sensitive to n_t, the time adjusted number of repurchased shares. In effect, 100,000 shares purchased in June will cause only half the gain in per share earnings as 100,000 shares purchased in January, all other factors remaining unchanged.

FINANCING REPURCHASE

The preceding equations and examples have implicitly assumed internal financing in the use of i to represent the after-tax opportunity rate. The logic hopefully apparent in Equation 2 is, of course, equally valid if the variable b, indicating the after-tax borrowing rate, replaces i in the last term of the numerator (the cost of repurchase). The cost of external funds, b, is applicable only to the cost term of the numerator because dividends not paid on treasury stock will be invested at the internal or opportunity rate, i, regardless of the financing method.

Fortunately, it is not necessary to calculate Equation 2 for both i and b. As was concluded above, the cost of repurchase dominates the dividend investment term, and, therefore, the entire numerator. Hence it follows that the lowest cost source of funds as measured by i or b will yield the highest *EPS*, e.g., if $i > b$ then $EPS_b > EPS_i$. Other reasons may exist mandating the dual calculation, i.e., company policy prohibits debt for repurchase, seasonal cash shortage, etc., therefore, alternative Equation 2 expressions are set forth below:

• Repurchase using Internal Funds

Equation 2i:

$$EPS_1 = (E + [(i)(D_t)(n_t)] - [(i)(P)(n_t)]) \div (N - n_t)$$

• Repurchase using External Funds

Equation 2b:

$$EPS_b = (E + [(i)(D_t)(n_t)] - [(b)(P)(n_t)]) \div (N - n_t)$$

AN EFFICIENCY MEASURE

Conclusions resulting from the sensitivity analysis described above indicate that the critical element in the repurchase expression is the time adjusted number of shares repurchased. The reader has noted that gains in *EPS* are directly proportional to n_t. A company with publicly traded common stock cannot always plan on a fixed number of shares being available at a given price on a particular date. Diverse market conditions and the effects of large single purchases by the corporation may temporarily influence prices. For these and other reasons it may be prudent to extend the repurchase program over a moderate period of time. Facing various offers of stock over the time frame of such a program, the corporate treasurer requires a means of relating offers to one another and to the ideal situation of a no-cost reduction in outstanding stock. (Stock price can be a guide, but may mislead over longer time periods as other underlying variables change.)

The "efficiency measure," k, described below gives the corporate decision maker an absolute measurement of each offer, based on its *EPS* effect as a percentage of *EPS* gain expected from a like amount of donated shares. The calculated k for each offer of stock is, therefore, a measure of the *EPS* "efficiency" which would result from that particular repurchase. Comparison of k, therefore, yields an ordinal measure of the optimal repurchase, as represented by the highest k.

Some may object that k cannot be used in evaluating alternative offers, that it is only useful in evaluating against a predetermined standard. We believe, however, that k is useful in evaluating offers against one another insofar as the offers differ in regard to price or financing terms. The size of various offers is automatically adjusted out by k. Evaluation of k against a predetermined standard is, of course, possible; however, each company would have to determine its own unique standard taking into account cash balances, urgency, etc.

Results of the foregoing sensitivity analysis indicate that the earnings increment from investment of unpaid dividends on donated or repurchased stock is not material. Therefore, the calculation of k is simplified by omitting the dividend effect. The three-step determination of k is as follows:

1. Calculate the gain in *EPS* which could be expected from a no-cost reduction in equivalent outstanding shares; the ratio of average shares without repurchase to average shares with repurchase:

$$k_1 = \frac{N}{N - n_t}$$

2. Calculate the gain in *EPS* which can be expected from the actual repurchase offer under consideration. In abbreviated form the value EPS_i/EPS can be expanded as follows:

$$k_2 = \left\{ \frac{E - [(i)(P)(n_t)]}{N - n_t} \right\} \Big/ (E/N)$$

3. Let k, the "efficiency measure," equal the expected actual gain in *EPS*, k_2, as a percentage of expected no-cost equivalent gain in *EPS*, k_1, (less one in both numerator and denominator to obtain gain ratio).

$$k = \frac{k_2 - 1}{k_1 - 1}$$

A FINAL EXAMPLE

At its June 15, 197x meeting the Board of Directors of ABC Corp. resolved to purchase 10 percent of outstanding ABC common stock, (500,000 shares) over a 120-day period commencing immediately, in order to fund several consummated acquisitions; thus counteracting expected dilution from these acquisitions amounting to five cents per share. Consolidated after-tax earnings for the year ending December 31, 197x are expected to reach approximately $10,000,000 or $2.00 per share indicated on an average 5,000,000 shares outstanding (without repurchase).

Offers to sell ABC stock which were accepted are listed below:

> June 30th—50,000 at 18
> July 29th—350,000 at 20
> Sept. 16th—100,000 at 17

Evaluation of the purchases should determine: (a) whether the five cents per share dilution (to $2.00 pre-repurchase) is covered; and (b) how efficient are the purchase transactions in terms of k values. See Exhibit 15-1 on page 179.

30th June Purchase

$$EPS_i = (E - [(i)(P)(n_t)]) \div (N - n_t)$$
$$EPS_i = (10,000,000 - 22,500) \div (4,975,000)$$
$$EPS_i = \underline{\$2.0055}$$

$$k_1 = \frac{N}{N - n_t}$$

$$= \frac{5,000,000}{4,975,000} = 1.0050$$

$$k_2 = EPS_i/EPS$$

$$= \frac{2.0055}{2.00} = 1.0027$$

$$k = \frac{k_2 - 1}{k_1 - 1}$$

$$= \frac{0.0027}{0.0050} = \underline{\underline{.540}}$$

29th July Purchase (base variables revised to reflect June 30th purchase)

$$EPS_b = \frac{9,977,500 - 116,648}{4,829,190}$$

$$= \$2.0419$$

$$k_1 = \frac{4,975,000}{4,829,190} = 1.0302$$

$$k_2 = \frac{2.0419}{2.0054} = 1.0182$$

$$k = \frac{0.0182}{0.0302} = \underline{\underline{.6026}}$$

16th September Purchase (base variables revised to reflect both prior purchases)

$$EPS_i = \frac{9,860,852 - 29,743}{4,800,030}$$

$$= \$2.0481$$

$$k_1 = \frac{4,829,190}{4,800,030} = 1.0060$$

$$k_2 = \frac{2.0481}{2.0419} = 1.0030$$

$$k = \frac{0.0030}{0.0060} = \underline{\underline{.500}}$$

The results of our example calculations indicate: (a) the five cent dilution *is* covered, as the cumulative gain in *EPS* is $2.0481 - $2.00 = $0.05 (rounded); and (b) that the second purchase, that of July 29th, is most efficient, yielding a value of .6013. As clearly shown by the example, price is not a sufficient guide to efficiency. Purchase at 17 is clearly less efficient than purchase at the higher price of 20 because the significant cost rate *b* of .04 in the July example has increased (as

Exhibit 15-1

Variable	Purchase Date		
	30th June	29th July	16th Sept.
P	18	20	17
N	5,000,000	4,975,000	4,829,190
n	50,000	350,000	100,000
n_t	25,000	145,810	29,160
i	.05	.05	.06
b°	—	.04	—

°Funds borrowed at 8 percent pre-tax interest for 7/29 purchase; (tax rate 50 percent).

i) to .06 in the September example, when external funds are not available.

Understood as the direct opposite of equity financing, repurchase by a corporation of portions of its own outstanding stock is a valuable addition to financial management's range of strategic alternatives. Repurchase can counter *EPS* dilution from various employee options, convertible obligations or acquisitions for stock, and additionally provides an ever present alternate investment for excess or idle corporate funds. Recognizing the unavoidable gap between financial theory and practice, the author attempted to develop a series of practical steps to determine:

• repurchase effects on *EPS*
• use of internal vs. external funds
• efficiency of a particular repurchase transaction.

Sensitivity analysis of key expressions developed in the article yields several notable conclusions:

• Dividend savings on repurchased shares are insignificant as a practical matter.

• Purchase price within broad ranges has relatively slight effect on the efficacy of repurchase.

• Opportunity cost and borrowing rates are important determinants of the repurchase decision.

• Current year *EPS* is very sensitive to repurchase timing, as a result of the "average share" accounting concept of earnings. Future year *EPS* are, of course, unaffected by timing.

PART V.   LONG-TERM FINANCING

Long-term financing decisions are a very important part of effective financial management in a free enterprise system. The readings in this section present some of the more timely subjects concerned with aspects of long-term financing. The articles provide the reader with an insight into some real-life problems which are faced by financial executives.

Professor Oswald D. Bowlin is concerned primarily with measuring the interest cost savings through refunding. He treats debt refunding as a special case in capital budgeting akin to lease financing. He recommends that when the present value method is used, ". . . future interest savings from refunding should be discounted at the cost of debt, normally the net yield on the refunding bond." A detailed description of the refunding operation is presented. Basic problems analyzed include those arising when the refunding bonds have a later maturity than the refunded bonds. The various approaches to the measurement of interest savings recommended by several noted authors are reviewed, and numerous points of disagreement are analyzed. The results of an empirical study of returns from refunding by public utilities are presented.

Mr. Joseph Van Vleck, 3rd, discusses some of the things that a corporate financial executive would want to know in order to arrange a private placement and to weigh this source of long-term capital against other sources such as publicly issued securities and term bank loans. Privately placed debt issues have amounted to about 50 percent of all corporate bond financing since World War II; however, smaller companies sold about 75 percent of their debt privately. Life insurance companies are the dominant buyers in the private placement market; they are followed by private pension funds and state and local retirement funds. After reviewing the pros and cons of a privately placed debt issue, the author discusses steps involved in making such decisions.

Mr. Robert Bullington discusses the importance of bond ratings to a firm in terms of financing cost and marketability of a debt issue. These ratings by the major agencies—Moody's Investors Service, Standard and Poor's Corporation, and Fitch Investors Service—affect all of a company's debt and equity securities. According to the author, these agencies generally investigate five aspects of the company in evaluating the relative degree of risk inherent in debt securities, namely, management, level and stability of earnings, financial resources, asset protection, and indenture provisions. Finally, the author makes several specific suggestions to corporate executives about how to deal with a rating agency.

Mr. Peter Vanderwicken presents the rationale behind the recent leasing boom in the U.S. The lessors—banks, finance companies, manufacturers and wealthy individuals—enjoy the tax-saving features of ownership, while the lessees get a rental rate that is lower than the interest they would have to pay if they borrowed money and bought the equipment themselves. According to one estimate, capital equipment with an original cost of more than $60 billion is now on lease in the U.S. The author discusses the leverage lease concept through a case study of Anaconda Company, the S.E.C.'s disclosure requirement pertaining to financial leases, and the destabilizing influence of leases on the economy.

16. THE REFUNDING DECISION: ANOTHER SPECIAL CASE IN CAPITAL BUDGETING*

OSWALD D. BOWLIN †

INTRODUCTION

Business firms may refund their outstanding debt for a number of reasons, e.g., to extend maturity or to eliminate onerous covenants in the indenture. The principal concern here, however, is with refunding for the purpose of reducing interest costs. Techniques used by business firms to measure the interest savings from refunding debt at lower coupon rates vary widely and give very different results. Teachers and researchers in business finance have made little progress in reducing the confusion surrounding this problem, despite the fact that the monetary benefits from refunding are considerably easier to estimate than those obtained from investments in operating assets. Hopefully, this paper will eliminate some of the confusion.

Refunding debt at a lower coupon rate is an anomaly among investments made by business firms, because of the degree of certainty concerning future monetary benefits. Usually most of the savings in financial expenses obtained through refunding with a lower coupon issue are assured, once the new issue is sold, whereas normally prospective earnings from assets are very uncertain at the time of purchase. This peculiar characteristic of certainty of future savings can and should be taken into account in measuring the net monetary benefits to the firm from refunding. The vehicle that can be employed to accomplish this end should be the rate used to make time adjustments of relevant cash flows.

The objective of this paper is both descriptive and normative. First, the bond refunding operation will be described. Second, some empirical evidence of methods used in measuring interest savings by public utilities that refunded bonds in the 1962-63 period will be presented. Third, several approaches to measuring interest savings in bond refunding recommended in the financial literature will be presented and compared. Next, an attempt will be made to determine the best analytical technique for use in measuring interest savings. · The most important question which will have to be answered concerns the rate that should be used in making time adjustment of cash flows resulting from the refunding operation. Last, the profitability of the 1962-63 refundings by public utilities will be determined by use of the analytical technique found to be correct. This part of the study will give some empirical evidence of the extent to which techniques generally used

*From the *Journal of Finance* (March, 1966), pp. 55-68. Reprinted by permission.
†Professor of Finance, Texas Tech University.

by business firms cause managements to make unprofitable refunding decisions. The practicality of generalizing about refunding policies of business firms also will be considered in this section.

THE REFUNDING DECISION

The decision to refund a bond issue for the purpose of reducing interest costs is an investment decision. The refunding operation requires a cash outlay which is followed by interest savings in future years. The net cash investment equals the sum of (1) the call premium on the refunded bonds, (2) duplicate interest payments, (3) issue expenses on the refunding bonds, and (4) any discount on the refunding bonds less (a) any premium on the refunding bonds and (b) any tax saving obtained because of the refunding operation.[1] The tax savings occur because the call premium, duplicate interest, and remaining issue expense and discount on the old bonds are tax deductible immediately. An unamortized premium on the old bonds would reduce immediately the tax deductible expenses.

Normally, the tax savings will not be realized at the exact time the initial investment in the refunding operation is made. Thus, the tax savings will have to be discounted back to the date of the investment. The discount rate should be the same rate used to make time adjustments of all cash flows resulting from the refunding operation. The determination of the correct discount rate is the fundamental issue with which this paper is concerned.

Future net cash benefits from the refunding operation are determined by subtracting the annual net cash outlays required on the refunding bonds from the annual net cash outlays required on the refunded bonds. The net cash outlays in both cases are the after-tax annual interest cost of the bonds less the reduction in taxes resulting from the amortization of the bond issue expenses and any bond discount. The amortization of a bond premium would increase taxes. Computation of the amount of interest charges on both bonds must be based on the total par of the refunded bonds.[2]

Usually a firm extends the maturity of the refunding bonds beyond the maturity of the refunded bonds. Thus, the new issue replaces not only the refunded bonds but also other financing that would have been required at the maturity of the refunded bonds. For example, assume that a firm refunds Bond A, maturing in 20 years, with Bond B, maturing in 25 years. Bond B is a replacement for other financing during the last five years of the life of Bond B. The cost of the other financing that would have been required to replace Bond A after 20 years, if it had not been refunded earlier,

---

[1]Duplicate interest occurs when the bonds which are to be refunded and the refunding bonds are outstanding concurrently. The duplicate interest period is frequently 30 to 60 days because the corporation usually desires to have the refunding cash on hand or assured before the old bonds are called.

[2]This statement assumes that the new bond issue is of sufficient size to refund all of the old bond issue, which is normally the case. If only part of the old bond issue is refunded with the new issue, the interest savings should be based on the total par of the bonds refunded.

will affect the net savings actually realized from refunding with Bond B. The net savings might be increased or decreased, depending upon future financing costs. Since financing costs in the future are highly uncertain, interest savings, as a practicality, are estimated generally only for the period up to the maturity of the earlier maturing bonds, normally the maturity of the refunded bonds.[3] Any error that results from this procedure would be fairly small when the maturities of both bonds are 20 years or longer in the future and the difference in maturities is only a few years, as in the above example. However, the probability of significant errors increases, the earlier the maturity of the refunded bonds and the greater the difference in the maturities.

Another problem in measuring future interest savings from refunding can arise if either the refunded or the refunding bonds, or both, are to be retired partially before maturity, e.g., through a sinking fund. The point was made above that interest charges for both bonds should be based on the total par of the refunded bonds. If the old bonds were to be retired partially before maturity, future interest savings from refunding will be reduced accordingly. If the rate of retirement of the refunding bonds is such that the amount outstanding at some date after refunding is reduced below the amount of the refunded bonds that would have been outstanding in the absence of refunding, additional financing will be required at that time unless the assets of the firm are to be reduced. The cost of the additional financing, theoretically, should be added to the interest charges on the refunding bonds outstanding in determining the net savings. Usually, however, business firms will find this procedure impractical because of the uncertainty of future financing costs and the relatively small difference in the planned rate of retirement of the two issues.

In summary, debt refunding is an investment on the part of the corporation. The cash outlay necessary to effect the refunding is followed by interest savings in future years. The measurement of the monetary benefits must relate the interest savings to the required investment.

THE MEASUREMENT OF INTEREST SAVING BY BUSINESS FIRMS

Little empirical evidence is available concerning procedures business firms actually follow in making refunding decisions. To throw some light on the subject, the author sent a questionnaire to the 33 public utilities that refunded publicly held bonds with new public bond issues carrying lower coupons during the period 1962-1963. A total of 40 bond issues was refunded by these firms during the period.

Thirty firms responded to the questionnaire. These firms included 22 companies engaged primarily in the production and distribution of electricity; five companies engaged primarily in the purchase and distribution

---

[3]This procedure usually is recommended (sometimes implicitly) in the literature. See below.

of natural gas; one large holding company whose subsidiaries are engaged primarily in the production, purchase, and distribution of natural gas; and two telephone companies.[4] Size of the firms ranged from very large companies servicing wide, heavily populated areas to small companies servicing small, sparsely populated areas. Gross revenues ranged from less than $12 million to over $1 billion.

Twenty of the responding firms indicated that the only purpose of their refunding was to reduce interest charges. The ten other respondents listed the reduction of interest charges as the most important reason for refunding. Eight of the ten indicated that the second most important reason for refunding was to lengthen the maturity of outstanding debt. The two other reasons listed as being second in importance were "to remove high interest rate issue from balance sheet" and to refund at a time when additional capital was needed. Only one firm listed as many as three reasons for refunding. The third reason indicated by this firm was to improve the appearance of the company's debt structure.

The firms were asked to state as specifically as possible how the interest savings which they had hoped to obtain by refunding were measured. An answer which could be used here required either a good record of a study of the refunding savings or a degree of technical knowledge on the part of the individual who completed the questionnaire.[5] In addition, a sufficient answer required considerable time and effort. Nineteen responses were sufficiently clear and complete to show conclusively that the firms used a wide variety of methods of measuring interest savings in bond refunding. Five firms used more than one method, and one firm used several. A tabular presentation of the responses is impractical, but a general summary will indicate the lack of certainty of the "best" method.

Seven firms used some form of payback-period calculation either exclusively or in conjunction with other procedures. Eight firms indicated the use of some form of time-adjusted calculations, but usually the procedures were not equivalent. Other methods used preclude specific classification except that they involved measuring interest savings with difference to the time of their realization.

The eight firms that used time-adjusted approaches were in general disagreement as to the rate to use in making the time adjustments. One firm used a rate which was "an indication of what overall money is worth" to the firm. Another firm used the return on equity. A total of three firms used the yield on the refunding bond. A sixth firm used all three of these rates but prefaced its specific explanation with the following statement:

---

[4]The nonresponding firms included two companies engaged primarily in the generation and distribution of electricity and one pipeline company. Gross revenues of these firms ranged from approximately $20 million to a little over $120 million.

[5]The questionnaire was sent to the individual believed to be the chief financial officer of each firm. In at least two cases the responsibility for its completion was delegated to the assistant treasurer. However, in several cases the basis for the answer to this question was a study conducted by an investment bank or a management consulting firm.

Anticipated interest savings were measured in several ways; however, the desirability of refunding was based primarily on establishing a break-even point." This break-even point was calculated by more than one method, as well . . . . Consequently, precise savings were not projected. Rather, anticipated effective cost of money below the range of break-even points indicated that real savings would be achieved. These break-even points ranged from 4.845 percent to 5.29 percent, depending upon the method used in their calculation.

The rates used by the two other firms that employed time-adjusted techniques were not defined specifically.

Break-even analysis was used frequently in evaluating refunding opportunities. Ordinarily, the net yield on the refunding bonds would have to be well below the "break-even yield" before the firm would seriously consider the possibility of refunding. There was no consistency, however, among the firms that used this type of analysis in the computation of the break-even yield.

In summary, the empirical evidence indicates that neither financial managers of business firms, investment bankers, nor management consultants are certain of the procedure that should be used to measure interest savings in bond refunding. Some form of the payback period calculation is a popular method but can be adequately defended only in cases in which the firm is more interested in liquidity or avoidance of risk than profitability. Time-adjusted techniques are used by some firms but in no consistent manner. Other approaches used by firms have little theoretical justification. Thus, the uncertainty in this area of finance can and does lead to widely differing results.

APPROACHES TO THE MEASUREMENT OF INTEREST SAVINGS RECOMMENDED IN THE LITERATURE

Academic writers have not been in agreement concerning the procedure that should be used in measuring interest savings in bond refunding. Four approaches recommended in the literature will be presented here in order to depict the major points of disagreement. The disagreement in recommended procedures has not resulted in active debate in the literature. Indeed, not one of the authors has stated why his approach is better than the others.

A few writers have recommended the use of the cost of capital in measuring interest savings.[6] Interest savings are determined for the period up to the maturity of the earlier maturing bond. Either the net present value or the rate of return technique is employed.

---

[6]See, for example, Robert W. Johnson, *Financial Management* (2d ed.; Boston: Allyn & Bacon, Inc., 1962), pp. 447-451; Pearson Hunt, Charles M. Williams, and Gordon Donaldson, *Basic Business Finance: Text and Cases* (Rev. ed.; Homewood, Ill.: Richard D. Irwin, Inc., 1961), pp. 560-564; Earl A. Spiller, Jr., "Time-Adjusted Break-Even Rate for Refunding," *Financial Executive* (July, 1963), pp. 32-35. Johnson does not distinguish between the investment opportunity rate and the average cost of future financing when discussing refunding. Hunt, Williams, and Donaldson, and Spiller use the investment opportunity rate.

Net present value is determined in the usual manner, by subtracting the net cash investment in the refunding operation from the present value of the interest savings. Future interest savings are discounted at the firm's cost of capital. If the net present value is positive, the refunding operation would be profitable for the firm. Although the literature is not always clear concerning the results of refunding when net present value is negative, the inference is that refunding would not be profitable.

If the rate of return technique is used, the present value of future interest savings and the refunding investment are equated. The discount rate required to equate the two is the rate of return. The rate of return is compared to the firm's cost of capital to determine whether or not refunding would be beneficial.

The use of the cost of capital in the measurement of interest savings in refunding will be referred to hereafter as the cost of capital approach.

Two other approaches are presented by John F. Childs in his book entitled *Long-Term Financing.*[7] Presumably, the first approach is preferred since it is presented in the text, whereas the second approach appears in a footnote.

Childs' example is a refunding decision facing a company with an issue of $10 million principal amount of bonds outstanding. The bonds carry a coupon of 5 percent, mature in 24 years, and are callable on 30-days notice at 104¾. Interest rates have declined, and the company finds that the bonds can be refunded with a new 25-year bond issue which can be sold at about 100 if the coupon rate is set at 4 percent. After underwriters' compensation and expenses of approximately 1.50, the company will net 98.50 from the sale of the new issue. Applying this information to Bond Value Tables, the cost of new money to the firm is found to be 4.10 percent.

His first approach is explained as follows:

> Now then, we have to decide what to compare the 4.10 percent cost of our new money with in order to determine the savings in terms of yield. In effect, what we are doing is selling new bonds and reinvesting the proceeds in our old bonds at their call price. Thus, we are interested in the rate to call the outstanding bonds. They have a 5 percent interest coupon, a 24-year remaining maturity, and a call price of 104¾ (call premium 4¾). The yield at the call price is 4.67 percent, as shown by referring to Bond Value Tables. On the basis of yield, we would realize a saving of 0.57 percent, which is a result of subtracting the cost rate for the new bonds of 4.10 percent from the cost to call the outstanding bonds of 4.67 percent. This is a gross saving and must be adjusted for the tax effect to get the net savings. Assuming a 50 percent tax rate, there would be a net saving of substantially one half.[8]

The second approach suggested by Childs includes the call premium on the refunded bonds in the computation of the cost of the new money. The procedure is presented as follows:

---

[7]John F. Childs, *Long-Term Financing* (Englewood Cliffs, N.J.: Prentice-Hall, Inc., 1961), pp. 239-241.

[8]*Ibid.*, pp. 239-240.

1. New bonds—4 percent coupon, maturity 25 yrs., to be sold	100.00%
2. Less compensation and expenses	1.50
3. Net proceeds	98.50%
4. Less premium to call old bonds	4.75
5. Net to company after calling old bonds	93.75%
6. Cost of old bonds: 5 percent coupon— price 100 percent	5.00%
7. Cost of new money: 4 percent coupon, maturity 25 yrs. Price 93.75 (line 5 above)	4.41
8. Savings before taxes	0.59%

This method produces a slightly greater savings because the call premium is written off at the lower interest rate over a longer period of time.[9]

Both methods suggested by Childs would base a refunding decision on the net interest savings per annum, expressed as a difference in yield, for the period up to the earlier maturity of the two bonds [10] The net cash investment in refunding, other than the call premium under the first approach, is written off on an annuity basis over the longer period of 25 years.[11] In both approaches, the write-off of the net cash investment reduces future interest savings.

The only difference in Childs' two approaches is the way in which the call premium is handled. In both approaches the write-off of the premium affects the computation of a cost, the "yield at the call price" in the first approach and the "cost of new money" in the second approach.

The significant difference in the cost of capital approach and Childs' two approaches is the rate used to adjust cash flows over time.[12] The cost of capital approach utilizes the firm's cost of capital in making time adjustments. In the example used by Childs, net refunding investment included only underwriters' compensation and expenses pertinent to the refunding bonds and the call premium on the refunded bonds. The compensation and expenses were written off on an annuity basis at the "cost of new money." The call premium was written off on an annuity basis in the first approach at the "yield at the call price," and in the second approach at the "cost of new money." In both methods used by Childs, the call premium affected the computed rate at which it was written off. In the cost of capital approach, the cost of capital is not affected by the call premium on the refunded bonds.

The net difference in the result obtained from using either of Childs' two approaches, or the cost of capital approach, depends upon the differ-

---

[9]*Ibid.*, p. 240.

[10]Note that interest is converted semiannually on both bonds.

[11]In the Childs example, the net cash investment includes only the call premium on the refunded bonds and compensation and expenses on the refunding bonds. The other components of the refunding investment are discussed in Childs' book on pages 240-241. However, the rate at which some of these components should be written off is not clear.

[12]The difference in the format used by Childs and the net present value and rate of return formats used above to explain the cost of capital approach is relatively unimportant. The (cont.)

ence in the "yield at the call price," the "cost of new money," and the firm's cost of capital. For most firms, the difference in results obtained will be substantial because of the difference in the net interest cost of new debt financing and the firm's cost of capital. This point will be further considered in the following section.

Another approach has been suggested by J. Fred Weston.[13] The essence of his approach is to reduce the future net cash benefits per year from refunding by (1) the interest cost on the additional bonds that would have to be sold to finance the net cash investment plus (2) the amount of money set aside each year which would accumulate to the par of the additional bonds.[14] The formats of the Weston and Childs approaches are similar except that Weston expresses interest savings in terms of dollars per annum whereas Childs expresses them in terms of differences in yield.

Weston's own example will be presented in order to examine his recommendations in the context in which they were made. Later, his approach will be compared with the Childs approaches.

The problem is a company which refunds a $60 million 6½ percent bond issue, callable at 106, with a new bond issue carrying a coupon of 5 percent and sold to net 96. The maturity date of neither bond is explicit in the example, but the savings are determined for a 20-year period. A total par value of $66,250,000 would have to be sold at 96 to net the firm the required $63,600,000 ($60,000,000 × 106) to refund the old bonds. The savings per annum are determined as follows:

Interest on 6.5 percent bonds $3,900,000
Interest on 5 percent bonds. 3,312,500
Savings per annum . . . .$ 587,500

He points out, however, that the savings per annum should be reduced because an additional $6,250,000 ($66,250,000 — $60,000,000) will have to be paid at the end of the 20-year period. The reduction in savings per annum according to his example is the amount of money which, set aside each year to increase at the compound rate of 5 percent per annum, will accumulate to $6,250,000 in 20 years. This amount is found to be approximately $189,000. Subtracting $189,000 from the annual savings of $587,500 gives a net savings per annum of $398,500.

The use of a 5 percent interest rate in determining the amount which would accumulate to $6,250,000 is a minor error. Perhaps the intent was to use the net yield on the bonds as the interest rate. Since the bonds carried a coupon rate of 5 percent and were sold to net 96, the net yield was approximately 5.32 percent. Using 5.32 percent in place of 5 percent to determine

---

use of different formats will be discussed in the following section.

[13]J. Fred Weston, *Managerial Finance* (New York: Holt, Rinehart & Winston, Inc., 1962), pp. 147-148.

[14]Reducing the future net cash benefits per year by (1) the interest cost of the additional bonds that would have to be sold plus (2) the amount of money set aside each year which would accumulate to the par of the additional bonds is equivalent to writing off the net investment on an annuity basis against the future benefits.

the amount of money which must be set aside each year to accumulate to $6,250,000 results in a difference in amount of about $6,250.

Incorporating the minor correction, the Weston method assumes that the net yield on the additional bonds sold to finance the net cash investment in the refunding operation is the total cost of the funds.

The significant difference in the Weston and Childs approaches is the way in which the call premium on a refunded bond affects the results. The call premium was written off against future cash benefits in Childs' first approach at the "yield at the call price," and in his second approach at the "cost of new money." In both methods the call premium affected the computation of the rate at which it was written off. In the Weston approach the call premium was written off at the net interest cost of the refunding bonds, but the write-off did not affect the computation of the net interest cost.

The difference in the Weston and Childs approaches usually will not affect the results significantly. For example, writing off the call premium in the refunding problem used as an example by Childs at the 4.10 percent interest cost of the new bonds results in savings before taxes of approximately 0.59 percent, which was the savings obtained by Childs in his second approach.

In summary, academic writers have not been in agreement concerning the measurement of interest savings in bond refunding.[15] The significant difference in the approaches that have been presented is the rate used to make time adjustments of cash flows. In the following section, an attempt will be made to determine the rate that should be used.

WHICH PROCEDURE IS BEST IN MEASURING INTEREST SAVING FROM BOND REFUNDING?

The point was made earlier that bond refunding involves an investment of funds which is followed in future time periods by savings in interest charges. If the present value of the future interest savings exceeds the present value of the investment, the refunding operation will be a profitable undertaking for the firm because a net savings has been obtained. The dis-

---

[15] The works of three other authors should be mentioned. See Arleigh P. Hess, Jr. and Willis J. Winn, *The Value of the Call Privilege* (Philadelphia: University of Pennsylvania Press 1962), particularly Chapter II and Appendix A. Appendix A is entitled "A Technical Note on the Value of the Call Privilege" and was written by Jean A. Crockett. See also Willis J. Winn and Arleigh P. Hess, Jr., "The Value of the Call Privilege," *Journal of Finance* (May, 1959), pp. 182-195.

Hess and Winn use the net present value technique in measuring interest saving in bond refunding. However, the two authors do not define the discount rate that should be used in determining the present value of future interest savings. In Appendix A of the book, Jean Crockett uses the current long-term interest rate, even when measuring interest savings from future refunding. She states on page 124, "We assume that the current long-term interest rate . . . is the proper rate for discounting . . . : but, if desired, some other rate could easily be substituted in the expressions obtained."

The present author feels that the use of the current long-term interest rate in determining the present value of interest savings from future refunding is questionable. However, this problem is beyond the scope of this paper.

count rate to apply to future interest savings should be the total cost (including both explicit and implicit costs) of the funds necessary to make the investment.

According to the net present value technique in capital budgeting theory, the cash benefits from an investment should be discounted at the firm's average cost of capital. The crucial fact here, however, is that the cash benefits from a refunding operation are not equivalent to those of the usual investment by a business firm. An investment in an operating asset involves considerable risk because the future cash benefits from its use are uncertain. Refunding a bond issue with another bond issue is entirely different, because the future cash benefits up to the earlier maturity of the two bonds are the result of contractual interest charges on the refunding bonds being less than those on the refunded bonds. Thus, once the refunding bonds are sold, the interest savings up to the earlier maturity are assured to the company.[16]

In the development of the argument that follows, interest savings will be measured up to the earlier maturity of the refunded and refunding bonds. The problem created by differences in the maturities of the two bonds will be considered later.

If a firm is able to make an investment from which earnings are certain, the financing of the investment involves no financial risk to the firm so long as the earnings are sufficient to meet all financial expenses. For example, the investment can be financed by a fixed debt without risk to the firm.[17] Since no risk is incurred, no implicit cost is associated with the debt financing; the only cost of the funds necessary to make the investment would be the net interest cost of the debt financing. The investment would be profitable to the firm if the future cash earnings discounted back to the present at the net interest cost of the debt are greater than the present value of the investment. Any part of the investment not made immediately should be discounted back to the present at the net interest cost of the debt.

Refunding a bond at a net interest savings results in a net reduction in cash outlays rather than an increase in cash inflows. Nevertheless, the refunding will cause the firm's total profits to increase or its total losses to decrease.

Since the savings are certain, the net cash investment required in the refunding can be financed by debt without necessitating an increase in equity capital to optimize the firm's capital structure. Thus, the net present value

---

[16]The refunding decision involves a risk that interest rates will rise between the date of the decision and the date the refunding bonds are sold (or if the issue is underwritten, the date the contract with the underwriters is consummated). The management of the firm may require that expected interest savings be sufficient to compensate for this risk before a decision to refund is made. The amount of expected interest savings required to compensate for the risk is a judgment problem for management.

[17]If the assumption of certainty of return on investment is extended to the lender, the net interest cost of the funds to the borrowing firm would be the pure rate of interest. However certainty of earnings on the investment by the borrowing firm does not eliminate all of the risk to the lender. The earnings could be dissipated by the borrowing firm before the lender is paid.

of the refunding operation should be determined by discounting the future net cash benefits at the after-tax cost of the source of funds used to finance the refunding investment, presumably the net yield on the refunding bonds. The net cash investment would be subtracted from the present value of the future cash benefits to determine the net present value in the usual manner. The decision to refund when the net present value is positive would be profitable for the firm. Since the interest savings are assured if the new bonds can be sold at the expected rate, the refunding operation will reduce the overall risk of the firm even though the debt to equity ratio increases. On the other hand, a negative net present value would be unprofitable.

The above procedure in measuring net interest savings will be referred to hereafter as the net yield approach. Of the four approaches discussed in the previous section, only the Weston approach, with the minor correction noted earlier, is entirely correct.

Very different results can be obtained by the use of the net yield and cost of capital approaches. As an example, assume that after a decline in interest rates a corporation finds it can refund its $20 million par 4½ percent bonds, due in 20 years, with 4 percent bonds of the same type, quality, and maturity date. Interest on both bonds is paid semiannually. Assume further that all bonds are sold at par and that the annual amortization of issue expenses amounts to $4,000 for each issue. Using a corporate income tax rate of 50 percent, the refunding operation would result in semiannual after-tax savings of $25,000 for 20 years.

If the corporation's cost of capital is 8 percent, the cost of capital approach would result in a present value of the savings stream of 19.7928 × $25,000 = $494,820. Discounting the future savings at 2 percent, the approximate after-tax cost of debt,[18] results in a present value of 32.8347 × $25,000 = $820,868. If the net cash investment required to refund is $600,000, for example, use of the cost of capital as the discount rate would lead to the rejection of the operation because a negative net present value results.

On the other hand, the bonds would be refunded if the after-tax cost of debt is the discount rate used because the net present value is $220,868. The $220,868 net present value is a net gain to the common stockholders. No additional equity capital will have to be raised to counterbalance the additional bonds; the refunding operation has reduced the financial risk of the firm.

The discussion above has been concerned primarily with the concept rather than the format of measuring the profitability of refunding. The principle of discounting future interest saving at the cost of debt can be employed in several ways. For example, either the rate of return or the Weston technique can be employed.

The use of the Childs format requires the computation of a synthetic yield on the refunding bonds. The process would be to write off the net

---

[18]The after-tax cost of the bonds is slightly higher than 2 percent because of the issue expenses.

cash investment on an annuity basis to future interest periods. The rate used to write off the investment should be the net interest cost of the refunding bonds computed in the conventional manner.[19] The write-off of the investment will serve to increase future interest costs. Then, the synthetic yield on the refunding bond is computed by discounting the future interest costs, which include the write-off of the refunding investment, back to equal the par of the refunded bonds. The yield is synthetic because it is affected by the components of the refunding investment which do not affect the conventional computation of the yield cost on bonds.[20] These components include (1) the call premium on the refunded bonds, (2) duplicate interest, and (3) any tax savings obtained because of the refunding operation.[21] If the synthetic yield on the new bonds is less than the coupon rate on the old bonds, refunding would result in a net monetary benefit to the firm.

The net yield approach recommended here can be adapted easily to a breakeven basis. For example, a firm could compute the yield on a new bond at which it would break even from refunding its debt. At lower yields, refunding would be profitable.

Another problem with which the management of a firm is confronted is whether to refund now or at some later time. If the net present value from refunding later is greater than the net present value from refunding now, the firm should delay. The difficulty in determining the net present value from a delayed refunding is in estimating future interest rates. Hess, Winn, and Crockett have proposed a solution to this problem by the use of probability analysis.[22]

This procedure might be adapted also to refunding cases in which the maturities of the refunded and refunding bonds differ. Thus, a probability estimate of the savings in financial costs between the maturities of the two bonds could be added to (or subtracted from, if the estimated savings are negative) the savings up to the earlier maturity. The development of this procedure, however, is beyond the scope of the present paper.

RETURNS FROM REFUNDING BY PUBLIC UTILITIES IN 1962-1963

The conclusion has been reached that debt refunding will be profitable to a firm when the rate of return obtained is greater than the cost of the particular funds required to finance the net cash investment. Normally, the cost of the funds would be the net yield on the refunding bonds. Thus, the

---

[19]Recall that Childs writes off the call premium on the refunded bonds at two different rates, neither of which is the net interest cost of the refunding bonds computed in the conventional manner.

[20]The significance of these components for a refunding decision is that they affect the amount of funds that must be obtained to refund the old issue. However, they should not affect the computation of the cost of the new funds, although they do affect the computation of the synthetic yield as indicated above.

[21]Components of the refunding investment that affect the conventional computation of yield include the issue expenses and any discount or premium on the refunding bonds. The refunding investment was discussed in Section II of the present paper.

[22]Arleigh P. Hess, Jr. and Willis J. Winn, *op. cit.*, Chapter II and Appendix A.

TABLE 16-1

RATES OF RETURN EARNED ON FORTY BOND REFUNDINGS BY PUBLIC UTILITIES
IN 1962 AND 1963
(Percent)

3.6°	9.1	11.5°	14.7°
5.5	9.5	11.9°	14.8
5.7	9.6°	12.3	15.3°
6.5	9.7	12.3	16.1
6.8	9.9	12.8°	16.1
7.1°	10.1	12.8	17.2
7.3	10.4°	13.0	19.7
8.0	10.4	13.1	23.8
8.2	11.2	13.8	26.7°
8.7	11.3	14.6°	43.4

Note: The 40 bonds were refunded by 34 refunding bonds. One new bond was used to refund two old bonds in four cases and three old bonds in one case.
   One utility refunded bonds at two different times.
   °Denotes that at least one other reason in addition to interest savings was indicated by the respondent to the questionnaire as a factor causing the decision to refund. In all cases, interest savings were indicated as the primary reason for refunding. Ten responding firms indicated more than one reason for refunding; the 9.6 percent and the 14.6 percent rates of return were earned from refunding two old bond issues with one new bond issue.

profitability of the refundings by the public utility firms discussed earlier can be seen by comparing the net yield on the refunding bonds with the rates of return obtained.

The yield on every refunding bond included in the study fell somewhere between 4 and 5 percent. The results of computations by the present author of the rate of return earned by the public utilities in their 1962-63 refundings are shown in Table 16-1.

The procedure followed in the computations of the rates shown in Table 16-1 was to discount net interest savings for each year to the maturity date of the refunded bonds, at a rate which would equate their present value with the net cash investment. The only data necessary for the computations which could not be obtained from Moody's *Public Utility Manual* were issue expenses on both the old and new bonds. These were estimated from the Securities and Exchange Commission's *Cost of Flotation of Corporate Securities, 1951-55*.[23]

Probably the most obvious observation that can be made from a study of the data in the table is the wide range of rates of return obtained by the refundings. Although a little more than 50 percent of the rates fell between 10 and 20 percent, there is no salient concentration.

Since the rates of return shown in the table are on an after-tax basis and the yields before taxes on all of the refunding bonds fell somewhere between 4 and 5 percent, none of the refunding operations appear unprofitable. The reader should note that the rate of return computations probably

[23]Securities and Exchange Commission, *Cost of Flotation of Corporate Securities, 1951-55* (Washington 25, D.C., June, 1957), Table 12, p. 51.

involved some errors because issue expenses for all bond issues were estimated from the Securities and Exchange Commission's *Cost of Flotation of
Corporate Securities, 1951-55.* While these probable errors would have had
a relatively small effect on the results, too much faith should not be put in
the *exact* figures obtained.

The rates of return obtained by the refundings were plotted graphically
against a long list of quantitative variables depicting financial characteristics
of the firms, e.g., sales, assets, rates of profits, rates of growth, and debt to
equity ratios. No correlations whatsoever were found. Neither were the
rates of return related to the particular type of utility. Furthermore, there
was no consistent relationship between the rates of return and the extension
of maturity dates by refunding[24] or the procurement of additional capital.[25]
Thus, no generalization can be made about the effect of any factors on the
rate of return required to entice the firms to refund.

These are several reasons why rates of return will vary considerably in
debt refunding. First, opportunities for interest savings vary among firms.
For example, firms with high-yield bonds outstanding will often be able to
refund at great savings if interest rates decline, particularly if the financial
position of the firm has improved. Second, since firms use methods of
measuring interest savings which give different results, the same refunding
opportunities will be evaluated differently. Thus, the enticement to refund
will vary. Third, management expectations of future interest rates will affect refunding decisions. If a substantial decline in interest rates is expected,
refunding will probably be deferred. Management expectations of interest
rates will vary among firms and for the same firm at different times. Fourth,
refunding often has advantages other than interest savings. Ten firms that
answered the questionnaire indicated reasons for refunding in addition to
interest savings, although the latter was always given as the primary reason.
The wide range of rates which have an asterisk beside them in Table 16-1
indicates that no relationship existed between the rates of return obtained
and the fact that factors in addition to interest savings led to the refunding
decision. Nor was any consistent relationship found between any particular
secondary reason for refunding and the rates of return obtained. Fifth,
firms differ in respect to policies and aggressiveness. Although this factor
is difficult if not impossible to measure, doubtless it was of great importance
in the case of the refundings that have been examined in this study.

SUMMARY AND CONCLUSIONS

This study has found that the investment required to refund debt
should be analyzed differently from ordinary investments in operating

---

[24]All of the maturity extensions except one fell within the range of approximately two to
six years. The one exception was an extension of a little over 17 years.
[25]A total of 34 refunding bonds was sold to refund the 40 refunded bonds. In 21 of
these 34 refunding operations, the firm obtained more capital than was required to call in
the old bonds. In 18 cases, the addition was 10 percent or more of the amount of the old
bonds outstanding. In several cases, very large amounts of additional capital were (cont.)

assets. Thus, debt refunding should join the leasing of assets as a special case in capital budgeting.

Refunding will be profitable for a business firm whenever the rate of return earned on the net cash investment in the operation is greater than the cost of debt capital to the firm. If the net present value method is used as the analytical tool, future interest savings from refunding should be discounted at the cost of debt, normally the net yield on the refunding bond. Use of this rate is better than the use of the cost of capital because debt financing of the refunding investment does not require future additions to equity capital.

Few firms use the method recommended here in measuring interest savings. The great variety of methods in use depicts the confusion and uncertainty concerning the correct procedure.

Some of the procedures used by public utilities that refunded in 1962-63 would have resulted in losses on a time-adjusted basis if the firms had not followed the practice of deferring refunding until a new bond could be sold to yield well below the computed break-even yield. Other firms employed methods of measuring interest savings which could result in passing up profitable refunding opportunities. For these reasons, it is difficult to generalize about the net effect of the widespread use of theoretically incorrect procedures in measuring interest savings. The effect probably has not been great, because most firms that refund primarily to take advantage of lower interest rates do not base their decisions on precise estimates of profits, although these are generally made. The reasonable assurance of considerable profits seems to be much more important.

---

obtained. Recall, however, that only one firm that answered the questionnaire discussed earlier indicated that the need for additional capital had any effect on the decision to refund.

17. ARRANGING A PRIVATE PLACEMENT*

JOSEPH VAN VLECK, 3rd†

The paucity of information on private placements can be attributed to the structure of the market itself, in which new issues are distributed with little, if any, publicity, and to the fact that this market has been, for the most part, the private preserve of a limited number of investment bankers.

A private placement may be defined as an offering of securities by an issuing company to a single or limited number of sophisticated investors, the offering being handled by the company itself or by an agent, such as an investment banker. The birth of the private placement came with the enactment of the SEC Act of 1933, which sought to protect the uninformed investor by requiring registration of all publicly offered securities with the SEC.

The concept took off immediately following passage of the Act, as approximately 25% of all corporate debt issues sold during 1934-40 were privately placed. Since World War II, privately placed debt issues have amounted to over $100 billion, equal to about 50% of all corporate bond financing.

During 1953-70, *Fortune* 500 companies sold 37% of their debt privately, whereas smaller companies sold 75% of their debt privately. In 1970-71 the average public debt issue was $43.0 million, whereas the average private placement was $6.0 million. These statistics, of course, indicate the historical preference of the larger, financially stronger companies to sell debt publicly.

On the supply side, life insurance companies have always been the dominant buyers in the private placement market. They tend to concentrate their investment activity in lower quality, higher return issues, including off-the-balance sheet financings with financially secure companies. During periods when the demand for long-term monies by BAA-BA companies is down in comparison to supply of funds available, life insurance companies have purchased large amounts of private paper from AA-AAA borrowers. This is particularly true when demand for mortgage monies from life insurance companies is also down.

Private pension funds and state and local retirement funds have also been important buyers of private placements from time to time. These buyers tend to differ from the average insurance company buyer because they concentrate in higher quality issues, such as those normally available in the public bond market.

°From The Conference Board Record (August, 1974), pp. 35-38. Reprinted by permission.

†Vice President, The Travelers Insurance Companies.

THE PROS AND CONS

Since the private placement market has been and will continue to be, in my opinion, a major and relatively stable source of long-term debt monies for corporations, a financial vice president should be asking himself about the advantages and disadvantages of such placement over a public debt issue. Disadvantages of a private placement from my, the borrower's, standpoint include:

• An interest rate $\frac{1}{4}$ of 1% to $\frac{1}{2}$ of 1% higher than in going public to compensate the lender for the fact that his investment will be substantially nonmarketable.

• More restrictive legal covenants.

• The bond issue would have no market.

• There would be little or no publicity on the issue.

• And I would have to tell my lender everything I know about my company—its past, present and future, my industry, my organization and my management—and I would have to keep the lenders completely informed for as long as the debt issue was outstanding.

But there would also be advantages to the company by issuing a private placement:

• The cost of issuance would be less; SEC registration fees and underwriting costs would be eliminated.

• The sale could be handled in a shorter period of time.

• The information on the company's operations, which it regards as confidential, would be in the hands of a very few rather than divulged to the public.

• Though the restrictive covenants in the loan agreement would be tighter, they would be tailored closely to the company's organizational structure and financial statements, and any renegotiation necessary as the company grew and/or changed could be handled with relative ease.

• A delayed takedown of funds as they were required could be arranged and interest costs saved.

• Negotiations would be with highly qualified financial people from a few lenders rather than on an impersonal basis with the public.

• And if I cooperated with the lender and gave him all the formation [sic] he required to analyze and evaluate my company, we would have a good working relationship and he would be able to respond quickly to questions, ideas and requests for additional funds.

MAKING A DECISION

Now, again wearing the hat of a financial vice president, let's assume I want to move ahead and arrange a private placement for debt. How do I go about it, and whom can I call on to help me?

The first things I would ask myself would be: What are my present visible outside long-term capital requirements? What are the chances I will need additional private debt monies in a couple of years? What do I want and need from a relationship with a lender other than his funds? How much time are my associates in top management and I willing to give to this project?

If my company was large and financially very strong, and if my management did not want to spend much time on the project and I saw no need for a continuing direct relationship with the lenders, I would definitely hire an investment banking firm to place the issue for me. However I felt about the above areas, I would also hire an outside agent if my contemplated financing was so large that more than three or four lenders would have to be involved.

On the other hand, any of the following factors, or a combination thereof, would lead me to believe that the contemplated financing might be difficult to carry out without top management becoming involved in the project:

• My company is BAA-BA in quality, privately owned or small and relatively unknown.

• My company would be difficult to analyze and evaluate.

• My company is in the middle of an earnings turnaround; thus, any ability to repay the contemplated debt is based more on future earning power than historical earnings.

• My company is a leader in an industry currently out of favor with investors.

• My company participates in an industry which is relatively new and not yet known or accepted by Wall Street.

• My pro forma balance sheet is very highly leveraged, and I will be forced to make an in-depth presentation on how we plan to handle this leverage.

• I want a close relationship with my lenders because I will be in need of additional private money.

• My company lacks financial expertise at the operating and board levels, and I have need for a good outsider who is knowledgeable in this area.

• My company has energy, pollution, parts-supply, or other problems which will make it mandatory for us to substantiate our financial projections on a face-to-face basis with the lender.

If, after considering the above factors, I decided that it would be impossible to raise private debt monies without the complete involvement of my top management, whether or not an investment banker was involved, I would consider placing the issue myself.

Before coming to a decision, I would have to ascertain the level of expertise and capabilities of my management and my company's close outside business associates, such as our outside board members, our legal counsel, our accounting firm and our commercial banker, in three areas: (1) the current status of the bond market and the outlook for long-term interest rates, (2) the type of restrictive covenants in private loan agreements and the ability to negotiate favorable terms, and (3) established contacts with investment personnel in the insurance industry.

With or without the assistance of an investment banker or other agent, my next step would be to start gathering all the information that a new outside investor would require.

POINTS TO REMEMBER

I realize that the average private placement loan is unsecured and has a final maturity of 15-25 years. I understand that the insurance company financial analyst will spend 15-30 man-days analyzing my company and the industry in which it participates. He will attempt to make judgments concerning my company's ability to pay interest and principal on scheduled dates under varying economic and industry conditions over a long period of years into the future.

I know the analyst will attempt to ascertain the major factors which determine my company's earnings power and financial position and try to project these into the future. I realize his analysis will be no better than the quality and quantity of information which I give to him.

I realize that my associates and I must organize an objective and well-quantified presentation on all aspects of our company's activities and operations. We must be willing to discuss or respond to questions with open candor on problem areas, weakness in management, points of vulnerability, and our plans and projections for the future. I realize that we will have to give the analyst more information than we have ever given to any outsider before.

I also know the analyst may make a number of outside checks with people who know us, such as our customers, suppliers, banks, accounting firm, etc.

I must plan to have all members of top management at the office on the day the analyst plans to visit so that those he wants to meet with are accessible to him. I know, too, that the analyst will wish to visit some, or perhaps all, of our principal plant facilities.

In summary, I realize I will save time for everybody concerned if my investment proposal is well done and backed up by detailed quantification. Gaps in the information provided, inconsistencies and errors can only lead to delays in obtaining the financing, and, even worse, may adversely affect the credibility of my management in the eyes of the outsider, to the extent that the lender ultimately decides to reject the deal.

FINDING A LENDER

After I had gathered together the necessary information package and had prepared myself and my associates as best I could to withstand an in-depth interview by experienced and well-trained financial personnel in the various areas above, I would start to make visits to insurance companies, either by myself or with an associate or two and/or an investment banker or other outside agent. My objective is to find a lender who knows my industry and, perhaps, knows something about my company and who is competitive with the market in terms and rate. I can ascertain whether he has experience in my industry or in related industries by quickly scanning his loan portfolio. Since a private placement relationship is long-term, I would like to work with individuals who are "my kind of people," individuals with whom I can quickly establish "chemistry" and rapport and with whom I find it easy to communicate. I would also like my lender or lenders to be large enough to not only provide the capital I am seeking at present, but also provide incremental monies my company might require in future years.

The lead lender I have selected will want to negotiate the principal terms and covenants of the proposed financing before spending 15-25 man-days analyzing or evaluating my company. Thus, prior to my meeting with the selected lenders, it would be wise for me to discuss this matter with my agent, if any, president and board, so that I will have a fairly well-structured package of principal terms to offer, and so that I will know the areas where I have freedom to negotiate and areas where I have no room to negotiate.

CLOSING THE DEAL

After the insurance company completes its analysis and approves the loan, it would be wise for me to obtain a written commitment letter from the lender, especially if I think long-term interest rates are going to move upward. At this point, the lawyers enter the picture and the final complete set of terms is negotiated. I realize that the lender selects his own counsel, but my company must pay his fee. I also realize that the drafting of all documents is handled by the lender's counsel.

My principal concern at this point is that once deals get into the hands of the lawyers, they tend to drag; and it is up to my counsel and myself to keep the deal moving along. I might consider requesting the new lender to select a law firm which is known for its expertise in the "green goods" area and which has a man free to start work immediately on documents relating to my deal.

I must not forget that private loan agreements are far more heterogenous than public loan agreements, and that the covenants will appear somewhat tight but will be tailored specifically to my company. But because my new lender has a thorough understanding of my company and because I have established a good working relationship with him, I am confident that the terms in the loan agreement will be well-tailored at the outset and changed with relative ease as my company develops.

Last, after the deal is closed, I must take every effort to hold up my end of the bargain. I must send the lender all the quarterly and annual financial information as well as the other data called for by our agreement. I must be careful not to break any of the negative covenants, so that, out of ignorance, I throw the loan into default. Among other things, I have to maintain working capital at a certain level, clean up bank borrowings 30 days a year, and keep dividends on my common below a percentage of my earnings.

I will drop by and visit my lender once or twice a year. If I see that my company will need a liberalization of a specific restrictive covenant, I will contact my lender well before I go into default with a well-quantified proposal as to why the covenant should be liberalized. If I have kept the lender completely up-to-date on the activities and operations of my company, he will be able to react quickly with an affirmative response to my request. If my lender tends to be noncooperative, I will try to ascertain what his problem is. If I am unsuccessful, I will move quickly to find a new sole or lead lender and refund my present debt.

18. HOW CORPORATE DEBT ISSUES ARE RATED*

ROBERT A. BULLINGTON†

Security ratings have a direct and often dramatic effect on the debt market. In assessing risk to determine security quality, many investors rely heavily on ratings. Consequently, the cost to the company and even the marketability of a debt issue is, in large part, determined by the rating assigned. In addition, the investment community generally regards the most recent bond rating as an indication of a company's investment quality overall; thus, ratings affect all company securities, whether debt or equity.

There are three major rating agencies—Moody's Investors Service, Standard and Poor's Corporation, and Fitch Investors Service. All three agencies have been publishing security ratings in one form or another for at least 50 years.

METHODS FOR DETERMINING RATINGS

There is no magic formula for determining ratings. This point is stressed by the rating agencies. Each case is different. The final rating decision results from an analysis of many quantitative and qualitative factors and is highly judgmental in nature. However, while it is not possible to pinpoint any precise formula, it is possible to outline certain general areas of investigation. In assessing the relative degree of risk inherent in debt securities, the agencies generally investigate five aspects of the company and the particular issue in question:

1. *Management*—What are management's objectives and how do they plan to achieve them? What are management's financial and operating policies? If the present management team has been in control for a few years, has it been effective in implementing these policies? Has management provided for unforeseen events? The agencies' overall assessment of management's prudence and capability is extremely important in determining the final rating.

2. *Level and stability of earnings*—Companies must demonstrate an ability to earn good returns consistently and to maintain adequate coverages (the number of times the company is able to earn its interest charges) and margins before their securities will be considered of investment quality. Stability of earnings is generally more important than the earnings level. A company with modest but relatively predictable future earnings will probably be viewed more favorably by the agencies than

---

*From *Financial Executive* (September, 1974), pp. 28-30. Reprinted by permission.
†Assistant Secretary, Irving Trust Company.

a company with high but volatile returns. The agencies normally consider: (a) nature of and trends within the industry and economy, (b) the company's position within its industry, (c) past performance, (d) age and size of the company, (e) breadth of product line, and (f) forecast earnings.

3. *Financial resources*—A company's current liquidity and its ability to obtain additional funds from external sources is examined. The agencies calculate various cash flow relationships and examine current assets from the standpoint both of relative size (e.g., current ratio, net current assets) and of quality (e.g., inventory turnover, receivables turnover, accounting procedures used to value inventories and receivables). This provides a good indication of the company's internal resources. A company's unused credit lines, as verified by calling the respective banks, and its ability to borrow additional long-term funds, as suggested by its capital structure, are used to determine external resources.

4. *Asset protection*—Specific indices (e.g., total long-term debt/net plant, net tangible assets/total long-term debt) are calculated to determine the degree of protection afforded by the company's assets. In most instances, this is a relatively mechanical process; however, prior to making these calculations, the agencies do attempt to determine whether stated values correspond to "real" values (e.g., book versus market value of tangible properties, impact of long-term leases and goodwill). The emphasis placed on asset protection varies with the nature of the industry or operation. For example, asset protection is not very important in the publishing industry, but quite important in rating public utilities.

5. *Indenture provisions*—Initially, the agencies review existing and proposed indenture provisions (not available with commercial paper issues), to determine the repayment schedule in the event of liquidation. When specific guarantees (e.g., parental guarantees, bank letters of credit) exist or the issue is secured by a lien on tangible assets, further analysis is done to determine the value of these guarantees or liens. The repayment schedule makes a difference in the final rating since, all other things being equal, a subordinated issue, such as a convertible subordinated debenture, entails more risk than a senior issue. (The investment community assumes that a subordinated issue will normally be rated one rating below its senior counterpart.) The agencies also look to see whether (a) the terms of issue require a sinking fund, (b) there are suitable safeguards against default, (c) management is restricted in the amount of additional debt it can raise, and (d) management retains sufficient freedom of action to react to changes in the competitive environment without violating the terms of issue.

The emphasis placed on each of these five factors varies according to the type of debt issue being rated. When rating long-term debt, the agencies are particularly interested in assessing the relationship between the level and stability of future earnings and the total amount of long-term debt outstanding (existing debt + new issue + estimate of subsequent debt financing). This, coupled with an appraisal of management's capabilities and an analysis of the other factors—financial resources, asset protection, indenture provisions—provides the basis for the rating decision. In rating commercial paper the ability to obtain cash is paramount, since both interest and principal must be repaid within a relatively short period of time (commercial paper maturities do not exceed 270 days). In general, the other factors are important only as they affect the company's cash position (e.g., earnings affect cash flow and asset protection can affect the company's ability to borrow long term). This is extremely important in rating public utilities since commercial paper is generally used to fund long-term needs temporarily.

The most important factors in any given rating depend to some extent on the type of company. For example, in rating consumer goods companies, the company's marketing strategy is very important. On the other hand, marketing strategy is less important in rating public utilities than are the regulatory environment, the geographic area served, and the company's construction program. Bank holding companies pose a slightly different problem. Here, the agencies examine not only the applicable regulations and the geographic area served, but also plans for diversification, the type of loans (investments) management considers acceptable, and the controls used to insure compliance with sound lending practices. In rating finance companies and REITs, the type of loans deemed acceptable, the control mechanism employed, and accounting procedures are of prime importance.

To determine a rating, each agency compares its view of the company's quality characteristics with norms for each rating level. If other companies in the same industry have rated debt, these companies become benchmarks in determining the rating. Although industry averages are examined to position a company within its industry and to highlight substantial differences, far greater emphasis is placed on fundamental standards of good quality.

In the event of a specific parental guarantee or bank letter of credit, the agencies also examine the credit worthiness of the parent company or bank involved. However, the issue does not automatically receive a rating comparable to that of the guarantor. For example, if the issuing company would receive a rating of BBB (Baa) and the parent an AA (Aa) rating, the issue could well be rated A. In rating issues not specifically guaranteed by the parent company, the agencies do not assume that the parent will meet the subsidiary's obligations unless the subsidiary plays a major role in supporting the parent's basic operations (e.g., a captive finance company).

DEALING WITH RATING AGENCIES

Throughout the rating process management should endeavor to provide all pertinent data and to cooperate fully with agency personnel. Management should display a willingness to discuss the company's strengths and weaknesses and to outline plans for correcting existing problems. Three specific benefits result: first, providing all pertinent data insures that the agencies have access to sufficient accurate and timely information with which to make an informed judgment; second, by discussing the company's strengths and weaknesses, management adds credibility to all of the information submitted; and third, by co-operating fully, the company establishes a good working relationship with the agencies—a relationship that could prove valuable when dis-cussing a proposed rating or a rating change.

Here are several specific suggestions on how to deal with a rating agency. Each contributes to a company's ability to secure and maintain a rating that accurately reflects the quality of its securities.

1. With the exception of the prospectus, all written material sub-mitted to the agencies for the purpose of obtaining a rating should be consolidated into one document. This helps the agency to evaluate the company and may expedite the rating process. Back-up material, such as annual reports, prior prospectuses, copies of loan/lease agreements, etc., should be in an appendix.

2. The president or some other policymaker should begin the initial meeting with agency personnel with a summary of the key points in the written material, a brief description of the new issue, and a statement of the company's general policies. The chief financial officer should dis-cuss the company's present and projected financial condition. Addi-tionally, some comments by a sales/marketing representative are in order.

3. Management should always ask the agencies, either directly or through its investment banker, to outline the agencies' reasons for assigning the proposed rating. In particular, borderline cases (those in which the agencies admit difficulty in deciding between the proposed rating and the next highest rating) and split ratings (e.g., S&P assigns a BBB rating and Moody's rates the issue A) should be questioned. In the event management feels the rating was based in large part on factual errors, it should request reconsideration. In general, proposed ratings are changed only if a major factual error is discovered.

4. Management should take the initiative in establishing and main-taining a good working relationship with the agencies by (a) forwarding the required data (quarterly and annual reports, etc.) on a timely basis, (b) notifying the rating agencies of any change in policy or planned temporary deviations from established policy by meeting with agency personnel prior to any such changes, and (c) displaying a willingness to answer questions as they arise. Whenever material is forwarded to the agencies, it should include the name and telephone number of some-one who can answer any questions about it. In addition, management should establish a policy of contacting the agencies, either by phone or letter, at least once a year to determine whether a meeting should be arranged.

19. THE POWERFUL LOGIC OF THE LEASING BOOM*

PETER VANDERWICKEN†

[An aluminum-reduction mill near Sebree, Kentucky, is operated by Anaconda Co. It is relatively new and efficient, but its technology is essentially a familiar one: it takes in alumina and turns out aluminum ingots. The mill represents about 3 percent of U.S. aluminum capacity these days. What *is* unique about the mill is its ownership. There are quite a few owners, as the diagram on page 208 suggests—and Anaconda is not among them.—Editor.]

Anaconda has leased the mill, for twenty years. The lessors put up $110.7 million of the $138-million cost, which makes the lease the largest ever for an industrial plant. The deal has some astonishing benefits for Anaconda. It also involves some sizable perils; still, the calculations Anaconda made when it signed the lease do a lot to explain why equipment leasing is now growing so explosively.

Anaconda began building the mill early in 1971 and originally assumed that it would be the owner. The company's investment banker, First Boston Corp., arranged for most of the financing when it lined up three insurance companies that agreed to buy $100 million of twenty-year notes bearing interest of 8⅞ percent. While the financing was being arranged, however, two events sharply altered Anaconda's perspective on the deal.

First, the Allende government in Chile expropriated the company's copper mines there. This misfortune was reflected in a whopping $356.3 million write-off—a loss that could be carried forward for ten years. The second event was Congress's reinstatement of the 7 percent investment tax credit in December, 1971. The credit could, of course, be applied to the new mill; but since Anaconda's tax liabilities were plainly going to be low for ten years, the credit would be only marginally useful to it. So, for that matter, would depreciation and interest charges related to the new mill.

HOW TO CONCENTRATE TAX BENEFITS

And so, late in 1971, Anaconda's executives began to question whether they were financing the mill in the most economic way. Charles Kraft, the company's treasurer, had formerly worked at U.S. Steel, where he helped to start its leasing subsidiary. Kraft immediately perceived that by leasing rather than owning the mill, Anaconda would be able to pass on the tax benefits it could not use. A lessor who *could* use them

---

*Preprinted from the November, 1973, issue of *Fortune Magazine* by special permission; © 1973 by Time Inc.
†Associate Editor, *Fortune*.

FIGURE 19-1

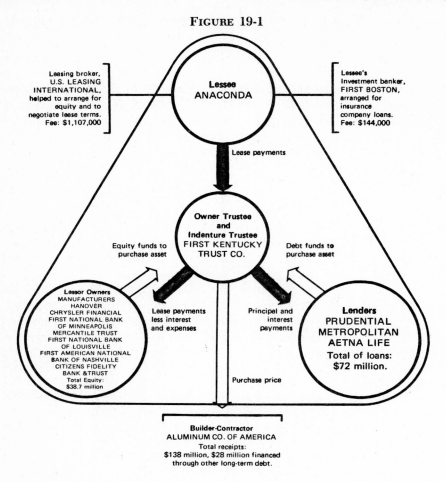

Lessee
ANACONDA

Leasing broker,
U.S. LEASING
INTERNATIONAL,
helped to arrange for
equity and to
negotiate lease terms.
Fee: $1,107,000

Lessee's
Investment banker,
FIRST BOSTON,
arranged for
insurance
company loans.
Fee: $144,000

Lease payments

Owner Trustee
and
Indenture Trustee
FIRST KENTUCKY
TRUST CO.

Equity funds to
purchase asset

Debt funds to
purchase asset

Lessor Owners
MANUFACTURERS
HANOVER
CHRYSLER FINANCIAL
FIRST NATIONAL BANK
OF MINNEAPOLIS
MERCANTILE TRUST
FIRST NATIONAL BANK
OF LOUISVILLE
FIRST AMERICAN NATIONAL
BANK OF NASHVILLE
CITIZENS FIDELITY
BANK &TRUST
Total Equity:
$38.7 million

Lease payments
less interest
and expenses

Principal and
interest
payments

Lenders
PRUDENTIAL
METROPOLITAN
AETNA LIFE
Total of loans:
$72 million.

Purchase price

Builder-Contractor
ALUMINUM CO. OF AMERICA
Total receipts:
$138 million, $28 million financed
through other long-term debt.

HOW TO SAVE $74 MILLION, MAYBE

Leasing deals tend to be complicated. . . . Fourteen other companies were involved in the deal that raised $110.7 million and brought the [Anaconda] plant into being (Anaconda itself financed another $28 million not involved in the lease.)

Two of the companies did a lot of consulting and arranging for Anaconda. U.S. Leasing (upper left of the diagram), a company that specializes in "packaging" leasing deals, helped to design this one after it outbid another packager and several banks.

First Boston (upper right), which has served for many years as Anaconda's investment banker, arranged for 65 percent of the financing by lining up three insurance companies, Prudential, Metropolitan, and Aetna Life (lower right), which together agreed to lend $72 million. The insurance companies will earn $9\frac{1}{8}$ percent on this investment, with interest and principal coming out of Anaconda's annual lease payments.

The other 35 percent is "equity capital," put up by those six banks and Chrysler (lower left). In return for putting up $38.7 million, the seven get the rest of the lease payments. They also get to own the plant itself, which means that they receive the tax benefits from depreciation and the federal investment tax credit on the plant.

The property is held in the banks' name by First Kentucky Trust Co. (center of the diagram), which took in both the debt and equity capital needed for construction and paid it out to the builder-contractor, the Aluminum Co. of America. In addition, First Kentucky will funnel the lease payments from Anaconda to the insurance companies and banks. (The banks, as owners of the property, pay the trustee's expenses, which will be deducted from those lease payments.)

The point of this involved exercise, from Anaconda's point of view, is to reduce the cost of financing the plant. The company has calculated that over the twenty-year term of the lease, its lease payments will total some $74 million less than would the cost of interest payments on bonded debt. This calculation assumes, however, that Anaconda's effective tax rate, which has been extremely low recently (because of heavy losses in 1971), will stay low. If the company's tax rate should rise sharply, then it will miss the tax shelter it has given up by forgoing ownership of the plant.

---

would reciprocate by giving Anaconda a break on the lease-rental rate, which should, Kraft calculated, be well below the interest rate on the company's long-term debt.

Calculations like these are at the heart of most big leasing deals these days—deals involving machinery, oil tankers, computers, aircraft, and a lot of other capital equipment. The tax-saving features of the investment credit and accelerated depreciation are passed on, through leasing, to an owner who can make the most use of them. And the owner's economies are reflected in lease rates that cost less than interest payments on conventional debt.

The benefits can be concentrated, furthermore, by "leveraging" a large lease—i.e., splitting it into debt and equity portions. The debt holders, typically such institutional lenders as insurance companies, put up most of the cost; in return they receive most of the lease payments, representing interest and reduction of principal. The equity holders, commonly banks, are the lessors—and legal owners—of the equipment. They put up the remainder of the cost and receive the rest of the rental income. But they receive *all* of the tax benefits associated with ownership. And at the end of the lease term, of course, the lessors have the equipment to use in any manner they please.

BIDS BASED ON GUESSES

Leasing is a sharp-pencil operation, and some high-powered arithmetic is usually needed to find that optimal point at which the lessee has the lowest cost and the lessors the highest yield. Scores of variables are involved. For example, the lessors must make a judgment about the economic life of the asset at the end of the lease. The Anaconda lease assumes, conservatively, that the Sebree plant will have no economic value (apart from scrap) at the end of twenty years. The lessors need a higher return from Anaconda—a higher lease rate—than they would if they assumed that the plant would have some residual value.

Another cluster of variables has to do with the tax bracket, desired cash flow, and yield goal of each lessor. Cash flow can be varied by the depreciation schedule on the leased equipment. In the Anaconda deal, depreciation is being taken on a relatively rapid sum-of-the-digits basis. Rapid depreciation generates heavy tax savings and cash flow in the early years of a lease, but it creates a tax liability later, and a sinking fund must be created to pay those taxes.

The rate of interest that the sinking fund can be expected to earn becomes still another variable. In addition, the ratio of equity to debt in the financing has an important effect on the terms: a high proportion of equity requires the lessors to make a larger investment and can create lower yields (and higher costs for the lessee).

Still another variable concerns casualty insurance, whose costs are reflected in the lease rate. A casualty schedule must be devised for each lessor. In the event that a plant, say, is damaged or destroyed after some years of use, a lessor in a lower tax bracket would require a higher insurance settlement to recover his investment because he would have had a smaller return over the years.

One major practical complication about lease financing derives from the sequence in which deals are typically put together. Many leveraged deals are arranged by the commercial banks and other investors that put up the equity capital. Some deals are assembled by investment bankers, some by companies whose main business is "packaging" leveraged leases.

A lease deal generally begins with these companies submitting bids to prospective lessees, specifying the lease rate that would be paid if they agreed to a deal. But the companies submitting the bids may not know at this point who the lessors and lenders will eventually be or what yields they will accept; hence their bids are based heavily on assumptions and guesses. When the lessee has accepted a bid and the winner has gathered a group of investors for the equity and lenders for the debt, intensive negotiations among all the parties frequently result in an upward adjustment of the lease payment.

ARE POTLINES PERSONAL?

In early 1972, Anaconda's Kraft went to two lease packagers and several banks and requested bids on the Sebree plant. The total cost of

FIGURE 19-2

Several different kinds of companies are in the business of leasing equipment, and the companies here—ranked by the acquisition cost of equipment they have put on lease—are not all competing with one another. The ranking refers to leases in effect or fully committed at the end of August; the two columns at the right show how recently the business has been arranged.

The totals include only true leases financed in the U.S. (several companies do a large foreign business). Figures for investment bankers and lease packagers primarily represent equipment that is on leases they have arranged but in which they have invested no money. Other companies listed are primarily lessor-owners.

RANK	COMPANY	Kind of Company	Cumulative Cost of Equipment on Lease and Committed for Lease ($000)	Equipment Leased and Committed for Lease, 8 months 1973 ($000)	Equipment Leased 1972 ($000)
1	U.S. Leasing International	(A)	1,752,400	481,300	293,100
2	Salomon Brothers	(C)	1,687,610	290,000	641,507
3	Citicorp Leasing	(B)	1,650,000*	n.a.	n.a.
4	General American Transp.	(D)	1,640,672	342,460	348,640
5	ITEL Leasing	(A)	1,445,619	380,525	449,098
6	Commercial Credit	(E)	1,413,293	183,251	281,697
7	Dillon, Read	(C)	1,225,800	206,600	103,000
8	Kidder, Peabody	(C)	1,136,514	791,591	72,903
9	Morgan Stanley	(C)	1,007,547	326,271	213,475
10	Lehman Corp.	(C)	961,000	196,600	388,900
11	C.I.T. Financial	(E)	910,000	n.a.	n.a.
12	Greyhound Leasing & Financial	(D)	793,250	144,705	74,950
13	First Chicago Leasing	(B)	783,176	469,102	221,613
14	Manufacturers Hanover Leasing	(B)	733,900	255,000	153,200
15	Trans Union	(D)	655,435	83,875	75,603
16	Bankers Leasing	(E)	650,000	20,000	40,000
17	Peterson, Howell, & Heather	(F)	570,000	207,000	211,000
18	Union Bank	(B)	525,912	57,003	296,772
19	Goldman, Sachs	(C)	507,000	192,000	88,200
20	Ford Motor Credit	(D)	500,000	n.a.	n.a.
21	Halsey, Stuart	(C)	450,000	140,000	195,000
22	Chrysler Financial	(D)	427,000	427,000	324,000
23	Leasco	(E)	408,448	45,108	57,537
24	First Boston	(C)	406,076	210,350	143,576
25	Security Pacific	(B)	400,000*	301,000	n.a.

LEASE PACKAGER (A)
COMMERCIAL BANK (B)
INVESTMENT BANK (C)
INDUSTRIAL COMPANY (D)
FINANCE COMPANY (E)
AUTOMOTIVE LESSOR (F)

*Estimated.

the equipment to be leased was now put at $110.7 million. The lowest bidder, who was one of the packagers, proposed a lease rate of $4\frac{7}{8}$ percent—i.e., Anaconda's annual payments would average $5.4 million ($4\frac{7}{8}$ percent of the $110.7-million lease). But Kraft and his advisers rejected the bid as unrealistic; they believed that no lessor could be found to accept the low return implied in such a rate. The next-lowest bid, by United States Leasing International of San Francisco, which is the largest lease packager in the world, proposed a rate of $5\frac{1}{8}$ percent. Several bids from banks clustered around $5\frac{3}{4}$ percent.

Anaconda accepted the U.S. Leasing bid and gave that company two months to form a syndicate of investors to buy the equity portion of the lease and become the plant's legal owners. At the same time, First Boston went back to the insurance companies to tell them that Anaconda was now planning to lease the plant, rather than own and finance it through long-term debt. Of the $110.7 million, equity investors would be putting up 35 percent—i.e., $38.7 million—and the insurance companies' investment would thus be reduced to $72 million, assuming, of course, that they still wanted to be in the deal.

The insurance companies agreed to remain in the restructured deal. But their situation was now different from what it had earlier been, and that $8\frac{7}{8}$ percent return had to be renegotiated. A lease obligation is a less senior—and therefore slightly more risky—form of debt than the direct obligation earlier envisaged.

Moreover, there was a question about the extent to which the Sebree plant could be considered real estate. The federal bankruptcy law permits a lessor of real estate to recover only three years' lease payments if the lessee goes into reorganization. In addition, there are legal difficulties in the way of banks' leasing real estate to others. For these reasons, most big leasing deals exclude real property (and, at Sebree, Anaconda financed $28 million of real property through a separate placement of debt).

On the other hand, lessors of what is generally called "personal property," i.e., everything but land and permanent buildings, have a claim on its full value if the lessee defaults (although they must prove damages).

The central question at Sebree was whether elevated conveyor belts, aluminum potlines dug fifty feet below ground level, and some mill buildings were special-purpose structures—and therefore personal property. U.S. Leasing got two out of three major Kentucky law firms to opine that they were. The lenders agreed to accept the legal opinions but, because of the slight additional risk of the lease form, they demanded and got a higher interest rate—$9\frac{1}{8}$ percent.

LOOKING FOR 12 PERCENT

Meantime, U.S. Leasing had been unable to come up with any equity investors. Banks wanted a higher yield than the 5⅛ percent lease rate would allow them. In general, the banks were looking for a deal in which their share of the lease payments, combined with their lessor tax benefits, would provide yields of something over 12 percent on their investment. With the lenders, too, getting a higher return, the lease charge clearly had to be raised.

Kraft asked one of Anaconda's banks, Manufacturers Hanover Trust Co., to propose a new lease rate. The bank proposed 5⅝ percent, and agreed to take half the equity. U.S. Leasing was then able to line up seven other banks to buy the remaining equity.

Before the deal was completed, the rate changed again—this time moving down. The lessors had assumed that the Internal Revenue Service would permit only 95 percent of the equipment included in the lease to qualify for the investment tax credit. But when the IRS reviewed the lease, it ruled that all of the equipment would qualify. Since that ruling increased the lessors' tax benefits (and yields), they reduced the charge to its final rate of 5.542 percent.

Shortly before the lease became effective last April, two of those seven banks, Chemical Bank New York Trust Co. and Valley National Bank of Arizona, found that the deal did not make sense for them after all. Both banks had a similar problem: their taxable income was now heavily sheltered by other deals. They dropped out, leaving 20 percent of the equity untaken. Manufacturers quickly brought in Chrysler Financial Corp. to replace them.

Under the terms of the final lease, Anaconda will pay an annual average of a bit more than $6 million (5.542 percent of the principal amount) to lease the plant for twenty years. At the end of the lease period, Anaconda can either buy the plant at a determined "fair market value" or re-lease it at a fair market rental. If Anaconda does neither, the lessors can lease it to another company or sell it for scrap. Meanwhile, they have leased the land under the plant (from Anaconda, which owns it) for forty years, so that if the plant is scrapped they can receive an additional return by leasing the land for another twenty years.

By leasing rather than buying, Anaconda should save an enormous amount of money. When the lease rate was set a year ago, Kraft calculated that, over the twenty years, the lease payments would cost Anaconda $74 million less than it would have paid in interest on long-term debt at the original rate of 8⅞ percent. That sum is, says Kraft matter of factly, "a good piece."

THE TROUBLE WITH PROFITS

Some recent news has suddenly raised a question about the size of that piece, however. Since January, the price of copper has jumped from 50 to 60 cents a pound, and Anaconda's profits—and tax rate—have soared. This process has, of course, raised the value to Anaconda of the tax benefits it is passing on to the lessors. Moreover, it is at least conceivable—though still unlikely—that the new military regime in Chile will return Anaconda's mines, canceling its write-offs and pushing its tax rate up steeply.

Any such combination of events would make the lease appear much less attractive. Kraft believes that it will still turn out to be right for Anaconda. "Say it reduced our savings to $30 million," he argues. "The lease would still be a good deal. It still seems the cheaper way."

But the case seems not to be ironclad. First Boston has calculated that if the company's profits continue to improve, its lease could become more expensive than borrowing in as little as four years. This implies that Anaconda would then be locked into an uneconomic deal for quite a while.

Some such risks are visible in quite a few leasing deals, but they haven't prevented the deals from flourishing. There are so many forms of leasing, and so many different kinds of lessors, that nobody can know for sure how big the business is or how fast it is growing. An obviously increasing, but unknown, number of manufacturers now offer their products on a lease as well as a purchase basis. Some 1,800 financial institutions and subsidiaries of industrial companies are engaged in general-equipment leasing.

NUCLEAR FUEL ON BROAD STREET

In addition, an uncertain number of wealthy *individuals* own millions of dollars of leased assets. Just by way of indicating the possibilities open to individuals with money and imagination, take the case of several partners of Goldman, Sachs & Co., the investment banker. They have formed a private company, Broad Street Contract Services, Inc., which has leased $199 million worth of nuclear fuel to several electric utilities. (Under Atomic Energy Commission regulations, only its licensees may use nuclear materials—but individuals may *own* them.)

Though statistics on total leasing are nonexistent, there are several indications of the strength of the boom. The Comptroller of the Currency, who chronicles the activities of national banks in detail, reports that in 1972 the book value of equipment on lease by such banks rose 23 percent, to $1.1 billion; the same report indicated that the number of national banks engaged in leasing rose from 446 to 510. And these figures exclude the leasing business of many banks that operate through subsidiaries of bank holding companies.

FORTUNE has estimated the volume of equipment leasing on the basis of an extensive sampling of lessors, of surveys and estimates by others, and of the available statistics. The estimate excludes conditional sales and installment sales, even though these are sometimes labeled leases. It excludes short-term rentals but includes leases of equipment by manufacturers and others for six months or longer where the lease has a fixed term and the lessor retains title to the equipment after the lease has expired.

On this basis, then, FORTUNE estimates that capital equipment with an original cost of somewhat more than $60 billion is now on lease in the U.S. to corporations, institutions, and governments. New equipment worth over $11 billion was leased last year, and it accounted for about 14 percent of all business investment in capital equipment. Over-all, the volume of leasing is expanding by around 20 percent a year. If leasing continues to grow at its recent rate, by 1977 about one-fifth of all new capital equipment put in use by business will be leased.

THE COMPTROLLER OPENS THE DOOR

Equipment leasing, which can be traced back to the ancient practice of ship chartering, was briefly in vogue after World War II and again in the mid-Fifties. But it had an aura of illegitimacy about it, and was widely—and correctly—associated with businessmen who simply lacked the conventional means of obtaining financing.

The recent explosion in leasing dates back to 1963. The Comptroller of the Currency ruled in that year that banks could lease personal property. It took a while for bankers to exploit the new opportunities; but by the late Sixties many of them had established separate leasing departments or subsidiaries that could offer the special analytical and marketing techniques the business demands.

Then, as banks began to give leasing a new respectability, the corporate liquidity squeeze of 1969-70 got many corporate treasurers interested in new financing methods. As the business expanded, many small packaging firms sprang up to offer specialized leasing services. The investment tax credit has also done a lot for leasing.

Leases have some practical benefits that seem important to many companies—especially small companies. Unlike many bank loans, leases involve fixed monthly payments that permit accurate predictions of cash needs. A lease typically requires no down payment and, unlike a bank loan, requires no compensating balances; hence it conserves cash. A lease transaction does not give the lessor power to restrict other financing by the company; the lessor's financial interest is presumed to be secured by the equipment itself.

And leasing is often more flexible than borrowing. Since leases are treated as operating, rather than capital, expenses, plant managers with some discretion about expenses can make lease deals rapidly, without needing the approval of corporate headquarters. (Many corporate treasurers are, in fact, unaware of the extent of leasing in their company.)

The flexibility is useful even in large companies. Brooks Walker Jr., chairman of U. S. Leasing, says, "In many big companies and in government, the capital appropriations process is so complex that any change, especially in the middle of a year, is very difficult. Leasing is a way to get around that."

It has often been said that a major reason for the leasing boom is the desire of companies to keep additional debt off their balance sheets—to avoid raising debt ratios that may already be uncomfortably high. Most corporate treasurers insist that debt ratios really have little to do with leasing deals nowadays. In any case, some recent regulations of the Securities and Exchange Commission will severely inhibit deals developed on any such basis.

THE CHAIRMAN CAN SAY NO

However, companies may have other reasons for not wanting to be owners of some equipment. Virtually every major lessor has leased executive aircraft to companies. Which means that, when a stockholder asks at the annual meeting, "Do you own any executive airplanes?" the chairman can truthfully, if disingenuously, say no.

The vast majority of leases made are for equipment worth less than $50,000—for trucks, office machines, a single machine tool, a farm irrigation system—and involve no real savings for the lessee. The main point of these deals is their presumed convenience. Most such leases probably don't make economic sense in the last analysis. Even though the lease payments are deductible, the loss of the tax benefits of ownership, the forgoing of any residual value to the equipment, and the payment of the lessor's profit, normally involve more total cost than the convenience is worth. Joseph M. Nachbin, executive vice president of Continental Illinois Corp.'s leasing subsidiary, says, "If you have the cash in your pocket and you can use all the tax advantages of ownership, then there's no advantage to leasing."

EQUIPMENT AT NEGATIVE COST

Big lease deals, however, are typically oriented to tax savings rather than convenience. A company can often obtain the use of equipment under a tax-oriented lease for a lease rate that is three to four percentage points below its usual long-term borrowing rate. Not infrequently a lessee's net cost is only 1 or 2 percent; occasionally, equipment can be leased at a *negative* interest rate. That is, the lessee's total payments to the lessor over the term of the lease add up to less than the original cost of the equipment. The lessor would presumably be able to offer such magnanimous terms only if he expected the equipment to have a high residual value.

Just about every large tax-oriented lease is submitted to the Internal Revenue Service for approval before it becomes effective. In general, the point that IRS wants to be clear about before approving a deal is the ownership of the property: is the party getting the tax benefits really the owner? The agency's principal test has to do with the residual value of the equipment after the lease expires.

Generally, a lease will receive IRS approval if it provides that the equipment will have at least two years of its life expectancy remaining at the end of the lease; if the lessor assumes for financial-reporting purposes that it will have a residual value of at least 15 percent of its cost; and if the owner-lessor puts up at least 20 percent of the cost in equity funds.

If these tests are not met, IRS is apt to view the transaction as a "disguised conditional sale"—which would mean that the lessee was the real owner (and therefore the lessor was not entitled to the tax benefits). Obviously, any such ruling would torpedo the deal.

In computing the yields and lease rates they require to justify a deal, lessors usually make much more conservative assumptions than those required for financial-reporting purposes. Lessors usually assume that leased equipment will in fact have no residual value, or at most a nominal 5 percent scrap value, at the end of a lease. By assuming no further value, they protect themselves against both obsolescence and the user's failure to maintain the equipment.

This conservative posture doesn't always last when several lessors are bidding for a deal, however. They sometimes inflate the imputed residual value so that they can reduce the proposed lease rate and thereby get the deal. In doing so, of course, they are increasing the risk of a write-off if it proves impossible to re-lease or sell the equipment at its inflated value.

THE QUESTION ABOUT VLCC'S

Estimating the market value and useful life of complex equipment many years in the future is obviously a tricky business, and both lessors and lessees can find themselves taking heavy losses if the estimates prove wrong. Standard Oil Co. of California, for example, now leases several "very large cargo carrier" ships for twenty-five years. But some engineers believe that such VLCC ships will in fact have a useful life of only about sixteen years.

Many more companies are able to take advantage of tax-oriented leases than one might think. Companies that report sizable profits to stockholders may still be able to show losses on tax returns. In any case, a company does not need losses to justify tax-oriented lease deals.

Many profitable companies, notably oil and mining companies, can often make use of leasing simply because depletion allowances hold their effective tax rates below those of lessors—the difference being used to reduce the lessee's net cost. The rule of thumb is that a tax-oriented lease can make sense for a lessee if his effective tax rate is below 35 percent.

Some limits to leasing are becoming apparent, however. Bank of America, the nation's largest bank, plays only a modest role in leasing because its new headquarters building in San Francisco provides so much tax-sheltering depreciation that competitive bids on large leases are hard to make. Other large banks, including Morgan Guaranty, have sheltered so many taxes in previous lease deals and other banking operations that they cannot participate in many new deals.

GREYHOUND TAKES TO THE AIR

Some industrial corporations and their subsidiaries are meanwhile becoming substantial lessors. U.S. Steel, Eltra, Chrysler Financial, General Electric Credit, and PepsiCo are committing large sums to leasing. General American Transportation, which has leased railroad tank cars for seventy-five years, has diversified into general-equipment leasing. Greyhound's leasing subsidiary markets a fair volume of aircraft leases to regional airlines and a variety of capital equipment to medium-sized industrial companies—customers that the big banks tend to bypass.

On the other hand, there are problems confronting industrial companies that get into equipment leasing. "To prosper," says W. Carroll Bumpers, the president of Greyhound Leasing, "a leasing company must be highly leveraged. Many industrial companies get scared at being so highly leveraged." Beyond this difficulty, industrial companies getting into leasing often find it bothersome to be in a nonliquid, passive position in which their assets are under the control of other managements.

The cost of leasing may be rising in the future. In general, lease rates have not risen nearly as much as most lending rates during the past year —in part because so many banks have been entering the business and seeking market shares that rate competition has been intense. As more banks use up their tax shelters, however, the banks still making lease investments will demand higher yields.

Bankers may become less enthusiastic about leasing, moreover, when they realize the uncertainties of some of those future commitments they are making. The profitability of a lease for a lessor is heavily dependent upon his tax rate. Should it decline, even marginally, he can quickly begin losing money. Just as Anaconda's rising tax rate might reduce its savings and make that lease uneconomic, a bank's declining tax rate could eliminate its profit.

Even more important, however, are all the uncertainties about residual values. Technological change, the decline of an industry, misuse by the lessee—all these can destroy an asset's value before the lease term expires. Lessees in such cases might decide to cancel leases— as many did with their computer leases—with rather expensive consequences for lessors.

FINDING OUT FOR REAL

When leases expire, furthermore, banks could find themselves the owners of enormous quantities of used and unsalable equipment that they have not fully depreciated. So far, only computers have come off lease in significant numbers. But in 1975 the first large group of leases for DC-8 jets expire and then, says Brian Livsey, managing director of Citicorp Leasing, "we shall find out for real" what risks the banks have taken.

Another major deterrent to leasing might be the mounting pressure to capitalize leases—i.e., to show the entire commitment on the lessee's balance sheet. Many businessmen and accountants concede that capitalization is perhaps reasonable in principle, since leasing and borrowing have the same purpose and usually the same consequences, but they believe it would create enormous problems in practice.

Overriding these concerns, the SEC last month took a long step in the direction of capitalization. The SEC order, effective next month, pertains to finance leases that cover 75 percent or more of an asset's anticipated life, or where lease payments guarantee the lessor recovery of his cost. In either case, the lessee must disclose, in a footnote to his financial statements, the present value of his future commitments to make payments and the interest rate implicit in the lease cost. He must also disclose what the effect on net income would have been had the assets been purchased.

The SEC order could have a severe impact on some lessees. Most bond indentures limit or prohibit the debtor's right to incur future debt. The definitions of debt vary, but the SEC ruling places leases within the definition under broadly worded indentures. The companies with such restrictive indentures—nobody knows how many there are— are now technically in default on their bonds if they have entered into lease agreements. Accountants and attorneys have not yet decided what to do about this sticky detail; but conceivably, these companies will have to take on the nuisance and expense of redeeming their old bonds and selling new ones with less restrictive indentures.

Beyond all these particular corporate problems, it seems likely that the rapid growth of leasing may have some powerful indirect effects on public policy about the economy. By permitting tax benefits to be used more efficiently, leasing enhances the function of the investment tax credit and depreciation allowances, enables industry to modernize its plant at a lower cost than would otherwise be possible, and so presumably benefits the economy.

HOW TO EVADE MONETARY POLICY

But leasing also reduces the importance of interest rates in corporate investment decisions, and thereby reduces the effectiveness of monetary policy in regulating the economy. To the extent that corporations can evade a tight monetary policy by leasing rather than borrowing, leasing may be a destabilizing influence in the economy. Meanwhile, corporations that become direct lessors also become unregulated financial intermediaries.

Perhaps, in the end, none of these trends will create troublesome policy problems. But economists, businessmen, and governmental regulators should be thinking about them as those leasing totals continue to soar.

PART VI. WORKING CAPITAL MANAGEMENT

Working capital management absorbs a substantial part of the time of financial managers and their staffs. The working capital or current assets of all U.S. nonfinancial corporations is approaching one trillion dollars. The three largest current asset accounts are in descending order: notes and accounts receivable, inventories, and cash and government securities. Inventory, accounts receivable, and cash and government securities are about 40, 40, and 12 percent of the total respectively.

During the past ten years increasing attention has been given to both the theory and the practice of working capital management. The use of the computer and electronic communications is changing one extremely important part of background within which firms must manage their current assets and liabilities. The three articles reprinted provide a view of some of the major analytical, theoretical, and underlying procedural changes in working capital management.

Professors Merton H. Miller and Daniel Orr demonstrate how operations research or management science may be applied to an area of finance. They describe and demonstrate the use of a control-limits model in the management of a firm's cash position. The objective of the model is to balance the amount held in cash and in short-term marketable securities in such a way as to optimize the net earnings on the securities while not violating the lower or upper limits established for the cash balance. The net earnings are the difference between the interest earned from holding marketable securities and transactions costs.

The authors were fortunate to secure the cooperation of the assistant treasurer of Union Tank Car Company (UTX). He provided them with his real information and they applied their model to these data. The model out-performed the assistant treasurer. An important advantage of such a model is that it structures a problem with careful logic. Even when such a model is not utilized directly, it may help others redesign their analysis and improve their performance.

Mr. F. Edward Lake, Treasurer of The Greyhound Corporation, candidly describes how corporate cash management has evolved in one large, conglomerate company that has experienced somewhat specialized problems in response to high interest rates and improving technology. Greyhound utilizes over 1,300 banks around the world. Banking activities are concentrated in 100 banks and funds are borrowed from about 80 banks. Fund transfers and borrowing are centralized from their Phoenix home office but disbursements are decentralized.

Among the technological and procedural developments that have affected Greyhound's cash management system are the reduction in clearing time for checks, utilization of lock boxes, wire transfers of funds, and electronic funds transfers. Regional check processing centers being established by the Federal Reserve System will speed check clearing still more. Computers assist in the analysis of fund levels, compensating balances, and service charges.

Banking relationships are carefully maintained. Compensating balances are analyzed in terms of their adequacy to support transfer activities and loans. In many cases service charges are preferred to compensating balances. The creditworthiness of banks that are small relative to Greyhound's balances are monitored. Bankers' attitudes have changed toward furnishing information needed for analysis by corporate treasurers. Further changes can be anticipated as electronic equipment and procedures come into greater use.

Professor Michael Schiff has made several studies of the financial aspects of the marketing function. He makes the obvious point that inventory management and accounts receivable management are studied separately and operated separately in business. The historical record suggests that control methods and models have maintained efficiency in inventory management but that receivables management probably has decreased somewhat in efficiency.

Inventory control may be more efficient than accounts receivable control because the former uses inventory models and other analytical tools, is closely related to efficient methods of production management, and because more appropriate measures are used. Well-developed models for coordination of inventory and accounts receivable management do not exist.

As accounting records are now kept, both customer service from existing inventories and credit extension are "free" services for increasing sales. However, there is a trade-off function between inventory and accounts receivable costs. If these costs were made explicit, improved management might develop. However, the organizational structure would have to be changed in order to move toward the coordination and optimal efficiency of accounts receivable and inventory management viewed as a whole.

20. MATHEMATICAL MODELS FOR FINANCIAL MANAGEMENT*

MERTON H. MILLER †
and DANIEL ORR ††

One stream of current research in finance involves the extension to the field of finance of the methods and approaches that have come to be called "operations research" or "management science." Researchers working along these lines try to develop mathematical representations or "models" of typical decision-making problems in finance and, where they are given the opportunity to do so, to test and apply these models in actual decision settings. At the moment, this stream of research is still a relatively small one—really only a trickle as compared to the flood of material pouring out on the subjects of capital budgeting or valuation. But it is a stream that can be expected to grow rapidly in the years ahead with the improvement in mathematical and computer technology and especially with the increase in the number of people who are being taught to use the tools effectively and creatively.

Rather than attempting any broad survey of work to date, this paper will present a single example of this type of research, describing both the development of the mathematical model and its application in a specific firm. Such an example can convey more graphically and more convincingly than any amount of preaching many of the important implications for management of this kind of research.

THE CASH BALANCE AS AN INVENTORY

The particular financial problem involved in our example is that of managing a cash balance in conjunction with a portfolio of short-term securities. And the particular mathematical model that will be used is a type of *inventory* model that might be called a "control-limit" model.

It may be a little startling at first to think of your firm's cash balance as just another inventory—an inventory of dollars, so to speak—but is it

*From Selected Paper No. 23 (Chicago: University of Chicago Graduate School of Business, 1966). This paper was originally presented at the Conference of Financial Research and its Implications for Management, Stanford University, June, 1966.
†Edward Eagle Brown Professor of Finance and Economics, University of Chicago.
††Professor of Economics, the University of California—La Jolla.

really so farfetched? Consider, for example, some raw material item that your company stocks, and ask yourself why you keep so much of it around or why you don't simply order each day's or each hour's requirement on a hand-to-mouth basis. The answer is, of course, that this would be a very wasteful policy. The clerical and other costs involved in placing orders for the material are not trivial; and there would be further costs incurred in the form of production delays or interruptions if materials were slow in arriving or if requirements on any day should happen to be higher than had been anticipated. Why, then, not eliminate these costs once and for all by placing one big order for a mountain of the stuff? Here, of course, the answer would be that there are also costs connected with *holding* inventory. These would include not just the physical costs connected with the storage space and handling but also the cost of deterioration, or of obsolescence, or of adverse price fluctuations, and especially of the earnings foregone on the capital tied up in the inventory. The inventory management problem for any physical commodity is thus one of striking a balance between these different kinds of costs; and the goal is to develop a policy in which orders will be placed on the average at just the right frequency and in just the right amounts so as to produce the smallest *combined* costs of ordering, of holding inventory, and of running out of stock.

Similarly with cash. If you want to add to or subtract from your inventory of cash by making a transfer to or from your portfolio of securities, there is an order cost involved, partly in the form of internal clerical and decision-making costs and partly in the form of brokerage fees, wire transfer costs, and the like. In the other direction, if you try to cut down these in-and-out costs by holding large cash balances, there is a substantial holding cost in the form of the interest loss on the funds tied up in the balance. As for the costs connected with running out of cash, these are perhaps too obvious to require discussion before a group of this kind.

THE CONTROL-LIMIT APPROACH TO CASH MANAGEMENT

Accepting the inventory analogy as valid, what form of inventory management policy would be suitable for cash balances? Here, since the typical cash balance fluctuates up and down and, in part, unpredictably, it seemed to us that the most natural approach for a wide variety of cases might be a control-limit policy.

How one particular kind of control-limit policy might work when applied to a cash balance is illustrated in Figure 20-1. We say "one particular kind" since the control-limit approach is quite flexible and many different variations can be used depending on the circumstances. The one illustrated happens to be an especially simple one and one that can be shown to be appropriate whenever the internal clerical and decision-making costs are the main costs involved in making portfolio transactions. It is also the form of policy actually used in the specific application to be described later.

The wiggly line that starts at the left at m_0 traces out the hypothetical

FIGURE 20-1

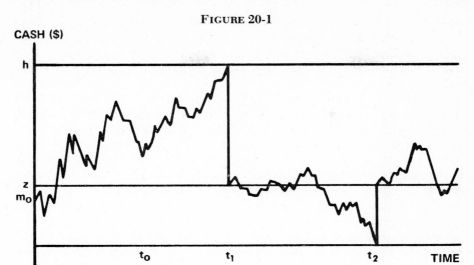

path of a cash balance over time. As drawn, it first seems to fluctuate aimlessly until about day t_0, at which point a rising trend appears to set in. During this interval receipts are exceeding expenditures and the cash balance is building up. The buildup is allowed to continue until the day on which the cash balance first reaches or breaks through the *upper control limit* of h dollars. At this point in time—day t_1 on the graph—a portfolio purchase is made in an amount large enough to restore the cash balance to the *return point* z. Once back at z, the cash balance is allowed to wander again. No further purchases or sales are made until the balance either breaks through the upper bound at h again or until it breaks through the *lower control limit* as at day t_2. When the lower control limit is reached, a sale of securities from the portfolio is signalled in an amount such that the balance is once again restored to the return point z.

AN OPTIMAL SOLUTION FOR A SIMPLE SPECIAL CASE

Given that this kind of control policy seems reasonable—and we would argue that it is reasonable not only in dealing with some types of cash management problems but in many other kinds of settings where there is a substantial cost in managerial intervention to restore a "wandering" system to some desired state—the task of the researcher then becomes that of applying mathematical or numerical methods to determine the *optimal* values of the limits. By optimal we mean values that provide the most advantageous trade-off between interest loss on idle cash and the costs involved in transfers of cash to and from the portfolio. As it turns out, there happen to be some simple but important special cases in which these optimal values can be derived in relatively straightforward fashion and where the results can be expressed in the form of a simple, compact formula. In particular, we have been able to obtain such a formula for the optimal values of the limits for cases which meet the following conditions: (1) where it is meaningful to talk about both the cash balance and the portfolio as if they were each single homogeneous assets;[1] (2) where transfers between cash and the portfolio may take place at any time but only at a given "fixed" cost, i.e., a cost that is the same regardless of the amount transferred, the direction of the transfer, or of the time since the previous transfer;[2] (3) where such transfers may be regarded as taking place instantaneously, that is, where the "lead time" involved in portfolio transfers is short enough to be ignored; (4) where the lower limit on the cash balance is determined outside the model, presumably as the result of negotiations between the bank and the firm as to what the firm's required minimum balance is to be; and (5) where the fluctuations in the cash balance are entirely random. There may perhaps be a trend or "drift" as it is called in this kind of analysis; but aside from this kind of simple systematic component, the day-to-day changes in the cash balance are completely unpredictable.

As for the specific formula that constitutes the solution under these assumptions, there is little point in discussing it any length here. The complete derivations and other details can be found in a recently published article.[3] It might, perhaps, just be worth noting here that the solution defines the limits in terms of the fixed transfer cost, the daily rate of interest on the portfolio, and the variability of daily changes in the cash balance (exclusive of changes related to the portfolio). As would be expected, the higher the transfer cost and greater the variability, the wider the spread between the upper and the lower limits; and the higher the rate of interest, the lower the spread. There are, however, some surprises. In particular, for the "no-drift" case, it turns out that despite the fact that the cash balance is equally likely to go up or down and that it's equally costly to buy or to sell securities, the optimal return point z—the point at which the average long-run costs of operating the system are lowest—does not lie midway between the upper and lower limits. Instead, it lies substantially below the midpoint. To be precise, it lies at one third of the way between the lower and upper bounds, and it stays at the one third point regardless of the numerical values that are assigned to the transfer costs or to the daily rate of interest that can be earned on the portfolio. As these values are changed, the whole system expands or contracts, but the relation between the parts remains the same.

---

[1]We have also recently been able to develop approximately optimal solutions for certain special kinds of "three-asset" models, i.e., models in which there are two kinds of securities (e.g., a line of credit and commercial paper) in addition to cash.

[2]Simple solutions also have been developed for the case in which the cost is not fixed but proportional to the amount transferred. More complicated, mixed cases involving both a fixed and a proportional component have been analyzed by our colleagues G. Eppen and E. Fama who have developed a very flexible method of obtaining numerical values for the limits under a wide variety of circumstances.

[3]M. H. Miller and D. Orr, "Model of the Demand for Money by Firms," *Quarterly Journal of Economics*, LXXX (August, 1966), pp. 413-435.

A TEST APPLICATION OF THE SIMPLE MODEL

Your initial reaction is likely to be that this model and the assumptions on which it was based are much too special and restrictive to have any important applicability to real-world problems. In management science, however, as in science generally, it is rash to pass judgment on the range of applicability of a model solely on the basis of assumptions that underlie it. Mathematical models often turn out to be surprisingly robust and insensitive to errors in the assumptions. The only safe way to determine how well or how poorly a model works is to try it out and see.

In obtaining the basis for this kind of test of the model, we were extremely fortunate in having the active collaboration of Mr. D. B. Romans, Assistant Treasurer of the Union Tank Car Company.[4] Mr. Romans had seen an earlier version of our original paper and was struck by the similarity between the model and his own policies in putting his firm's idle cash to work. The systematic investment of idle cash in short term, money market securities was a relatively new program for his company—one that he had instituted only about a year previously. The interest earnings for that year were quite large not only in relation to the costs involved but to the total budget of the treasurer's department. Now that the year's experience had been accumulated, he wanted to go back over the record, to study it in detail and to see whether any changes in practice might be suggested that would make the operation even more profitable. He felt, and we agreed, that the model might be extremely helpful in this kind of evaluation. If the model did seem to behave sensibly when applied to the company's past cash flow, then it might be used to provide an objective standard or "bogey" against which past performance could be measured.

Since mathematical modeling of business decisions is still quite new, and since few people outside the production area have had much direct connection with it, it is perhaps worth emphasizing that at no time was it intended or contemplated that a model should be developed to do the actual on-line decision making. The purpose of the study was to be *evaluation* by the treasurer of his own operation. This is a valuable but unglamorous use of models that tends to be overlooked amidst all the hoopla of the Sunday supplement variety surrounding the subject of automated management. An important point that must be kept in mind about mathematical models is that they are not intended to *replace* management—though, like any other technological improvement, they sometimes have that effect—but that they provide managers with new tools or techniques to be used *in conjunction with* other managerial techniques (including good judgment) for improving overall performance.

---

[4]We have also benefited greatly from discussions of cash management problems and practices with several officers of the Harris Trust and Savings Bank of Chicago. We hope that they will benefit too from this chance to see how the problem looks from the other side of the account.

THE SETTING OF THE OPERATION

Since our objective was to compare the model's decisions over some trial period with those of the Assistant Treasurer, the first step was to examine carefully the setting in which he actually operated and to see how closely or how poorly the circumstances matched the assumptions of the model. As would be expected, the results were mixed. On the one hand, there were some respects in which the assumptions fit quite well. The Assistant Treasurer did behave, for example, as if he were in fact controlling only a single-central cash balance. Note the phrase "as if," because as a matter of fact the firm does have many separate balances in many banks. For purposes of cash management, however, the Assistant Treasurer works with one single balance representing the free funds that he can marshal throughout the system without regard to the particular banks they happen to be in at the moment (or where the funds derived from a portfolio liquidation must ultimately be routed).

It was also clear that there were substantial order costs involved in making portfolio transfers. In the case of a portfolio purchase, for example, some of the main cost components include: (a) making two or more long-distance phone calls plus 15 minutes to a half hour of the Assistant Treasurer's time; (b) typing up and carefully checking an authorization letter with four copies; (c) carrying the original of the letter to be signed by the Treasurer; and (d) carrying the copies to the controller's office where special accounts are opened, the entries are posted, and further checks of the arithmetic made. It is hard to establish a precise dollar figure for these costs, but at least the approximate order of magnitude for a complete round trip is probably somewhere between $20 and $50. That this is not a trivial amount of money in the present context becomes clear when you remember that interest earnings at the then prevailing level of interest rates were running at about $10 per day per $100,000 in the portfolio and that his average size of portfolio purchase during the test period was about $400,000.

Not surprisingly, we also found that there was a considerable amount of randomness or unpredictability in the daily cash flow. In fact, the Assistant Treasurer did not even attempt to forecast or project flows more than a day or two ahead except for certain large recurring outflows such as tax payments, dividend payments, sinking fund deposits, transfers to subsidiaries and the like; and even here the forecasts were made more with a view to deciding the appropriate maturities to hold in the portfolio than as part of the cash balance control *per se*. As for the drift or trend, analysis of the cash flow over the 9-month test period showed no evidence of any significant drift in either direction.

As opposed to these similarities between the assumptions of the model and the reality of the firm's operation, there were very definitely a number of respects in which the fit was much less comfortable. The model assumes, for example, that when the lower bound on cash is hit or breached, there will

FIGURE 20-2

DAILY CASH CHANGES

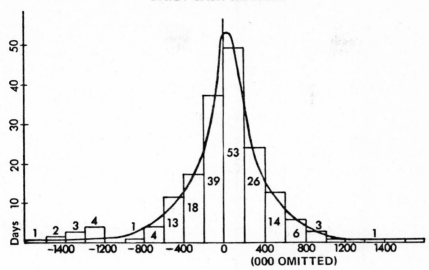

(000 OMITTED)

be an immediate sale of securities out of the portfolio to make up the cash deficiency. The Assistant Treasurer, however, followed a policy of buying only nonmarketable securities and holding them to maturity primarily because he wanted to try his new cash management program without requiring any change in the company's standard accounting procedures. Hence, if a large net cash drain occurred unexpectedly on a day on which he had no maturing security, he simply let his cash balance drop below his normal minimum which he and his banks regarded as an average minimum rather than as the strict minimum contemplated by the model.

A discrepancy between the model and reality that was more disturbing appeared when we constructed the frequency distribution of daily cash changes by size of change over the 9-month sample period of 189 working days. The distribution of these daily changes is shown in graphic form in Figure 20-2. The logic of the model requires that this distribution be at least approximately of a form that statisticians refer to as "normal" or "Gaussian." A hasty glance at the figure might lead one to conclude that this requirement is met. Closer study reveals, however, that not only is the distribution not normal, but it almost seems to be a member of a particularly ill-behaved class of *fat-tailed* distributions that have come to be called *Paretian distributions.*[5] In these distributions—which may be familiar to

---

[5]We say "almost seems to be" because despite the conspicuously fat tails, the distributions as computed cumulatively month by month remain roughly similar with no tendency for the tails to get fatter and fatter over time as in a true Paretian process. The Paretian-like tails are mainly the reflection of such large but relatively controllable and definitely size-limited items as dividends, taxes, transfers to and from subsidiaries, and the like.

those of you who have been following the debate about random walks in the stock market[6]—large changes occur much more frequently than in the case of the normal distribution. In fact, the frequency of large changes is so much greater that we were quite uncertain as to whether the model would behave in even roughly sensible fashion or whether it would simply find itself being whipsawed to death by the violent swings through the control range. As indicated earlier, however, there is only one way to tell; and that's by trying it out and seeing what happens.

THE TEST OF THE MODEL AGAINST THE DATA

To get a close basis for comparison with the Assistant Treasurer's actual decisions, it was decided to run the model under various alternative assumptions about the true value of the transfer cost. That is, we would start with a conservatively high value of say $90 per transfer, compute the optimal upper limit h and return point z, run the model against the actual data, and tabulate its portfolio purchases and sales. If, as expected, the model made fewer transfers than the Assistant Treasurer, then we would go back, use a lower value for the costs, recompute the new optimal limits, and so on until we had finally forced the model to make approximately the same number of transfers over the sample interval as the Assistant Treasurer himself. Then, assuming the model was behaving sensibly, we could compare and contrast their patterns of portfolio decisions over the interval as well as get at least some rough idea of what figure for the cost of a transfer the Assistant Treasurer was implicitly using in his own operation.

The only difficulty encountered in implementing this straightforward kind of test was in the matter of deciding precisely how many transfers the Assistant Treasurer should be regarded as having made. Because of his policy of holding only nonmarketable issues, his portfolio tended to be of quite short average duration. Hence, there were inevitably days on which he had a maturity that proved to be too early. If he had merely rolled these issues over, there would have been no problem; we would simply have washed that transaction out and not counted either the maturity or the reinvestment as a transfer. But it is clearly not always efficient just to roll over the maturing issue. Given that a purchase must be made anyway on that day, it would be wise to pick up any additional cash that also happened to be lying around, even if the amount involved would not have been large enough by itself to have justified incurring a transfer cost. Accordingly, we decided not to count any transfers on roll-over days unless the Assistant Treasurer indicated that the balance was so large even without the maturing issue that he would almost certainly have bought anyway (in which case he would be charged with the purchase but not the sale). Similarly with the case of net sale days. If there was a larger maturity on a given day than was

---

[6]*Random Walks in Stock-Market Prices,* Selected Paper No. 16 (Chicago: Graduate School of Business, University of Chicago).

actually needed to meet the cash drain and if some small part of the excess proceeds were rolled over, then he was charged with a sale but not a purchase. By this criterion we were able to agree on a figure of 112 total transactions by the Assistant Treasurer during the 189 test days of which 58 were purchases and 54 were sales (maturities).

THE RESULTS OF THE TEST

When we commenced the trial-and-error process of matching the total number of transactions by the model with those of the Assistant Treasurer, our hope was that the model might be able to achieve an average daily cash balance no more than say 20 to 30 percent above the Assistant Treasurer's average. We felt that if we could get that close and if the model did behave sensibly, then there was a very real prospect of being able to use the model as a bogey against which to measure and evaluate actual performance. As it turned out, however, we found that, at 112 transactions, the model not only came close but actually did better—producing an average daily cash balance about 40 percent *lower* than that of the Assistant Treasurer ($160,000 for the model as compared with about $275,000). Or, looking at it from the other side, if we matched the average daily cash holdings at $275,000, the model was able to reach this level with only about 80 transactions or about one third less than the 112 actually required.

It can be argued, of course, that this sort of comparison is unfairly loaded in favor of the model not only because it was applied on a hindsight basis but because the transfer costs would actually have been higher for the model than the simple matching of total numbers of transfers would seem to suggest. The Assistant Treasurer, it will be recalled, never really sold a security; he merely let it run off. Hence, the model would have had to incur additional costs on at least those sales that did not occur on the easily forecastable, large outflow days. Check of the numbers involved showed, however, that the model would still have dominated in terms of net interest minus transfer costs over the sample period even if these extra costs of liquidation were included on every sale. And, of course, that is much too extreme an adjustment. Many of the actual sale days of the model coincided with the large outflow days, and appropriately maturing securities could have been purchased to hit these dates. In fact, the postmortem showed that about half the model's sales took place on days when the Assistant Treasurer also sold, and nearly 80 percent occurred either on the same day or within one day either way of a day on which he scheduled a maturity.

Furthermore, the model too is operating under some handicaps in the comparison. At no time, for example, did the model ever violate the minimum cash balance marked on the Assistant Treasurer's work sheets, whereas no less than 10 percent of his total dollar days invested were represented by the cash deficiencies on the days in which he let his balance dip temporarily below the minimum. In addition, the model did not receive instructions to

FIGURE 20-3a

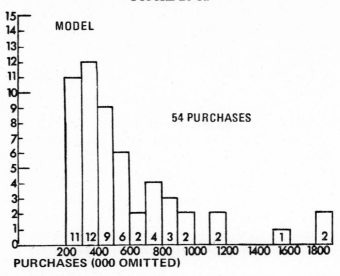

change its policies before weekends and holidays. The Assistant Treasurer, on the other hand, always knew when it was Friday and was thus able to sock away additional amounts on which he could get two extra days' interest.

All in all then the comparison would seem to be basically a fair one; and it is a tribute to the Assistant Treasurer's personal and professional character that he never became ego-involved in the comparison or wasted time alibiing.

FIGURE 20-3b

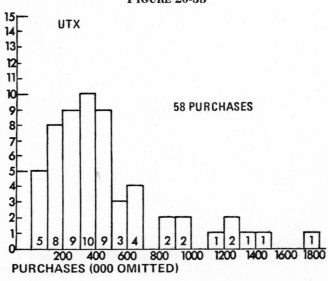

He was concerned about one thing and one thing only: how to do an even better job.

THE COMPARISON OF OPERATING POLICIES

With this question in mind, we then went on to make a detailed comparison of the actual decisions with those called for by the model. The complete record of these comparisons is, of course, too long and too specialized to be spelled out at length here, but there are at least a few simple contrasts that can be presented to illustrate the sorts of things that turned up.

Figures 20-3a and 20-3b, for example, show the frequency distributions of portfolio purchases by size of purchase for the model and for the Assistant Treasurer. Notice that even though we have forced the total number of transfers to match, the model makes somewhat fewer purchases (54 as against 58) and does so in considerably larger average size (about $600,000 as compared with only $440,000). The difference in operating policy is particularly striking at the lower end of the size scale because of the rigid rule built into the model that keeps it from ever buying in units smaller than h—z, which was about $250,000 when the model was set to produce 112 transfers. The Assistant Treasurer, by contrast, made about 13 purchases (or nearly 25 percent of his total purchases) in amounts smaller than that size including five in amounts of $100,000 or less. Even allowing for the fact that some of these small transactions were for weekends, the total impression conveyed is one of an excessive amount of small-lot purchasing activity. This impression was further reinforced both by the very low implicit transfer cost that was necessary to force the model to make 112 transfers as well as by the fact that more than 90 percent of the total interest earnings achieved by the model with 112 transfers could have been attained with only about 50 total transfers. Of these 50, moreover, only some 20 were purchases, and all were of fairly large size.

Even more revealing are Figures 20-4a and 20-4b which show the distribution of the closing cash balance by size on days when no portfolio action was taken in either direction. Notice again that, because of its rigid upper limit, the model never lets the cash balance go above h which in this case is about $400,000. The Assistant Treasurer, however, seems to be much less consistent in this respect, having foregone no less than 23 buying opportunities of this amount or larger including three of over $1 million. When and why so many opportunities were missed is still not entirely clear. Part of the trouble undoubtedly stems from the fact that the Assistant Treasurer has many other responsibilities and cannot always count on being at his desk at the time of day when the decision has to be made. And without actually interrupting to construct his worksheet, there is no way for him to determine whether an interruption of his other work would really be profitable. Hopefully, however, by making his limits more explicit (in the spirit of the model) and by delegating to others much of the purely mechanical task of monitoring these limits, he will be able to achieve in the future a significant reduction in the size and frequency of these lost opportunities.

CONCLUSION

We have tried here to present a concrete example of how mathematical methods can be and are being applied to management problems in the

FIGURE 20-4a

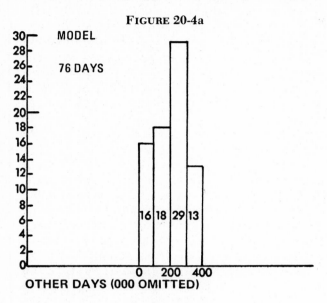

FIGURE 20-4b

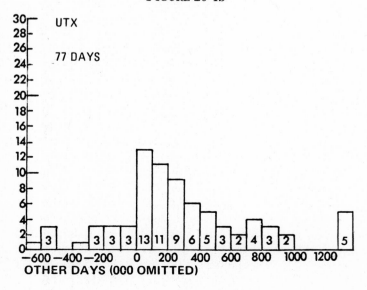

field of finance. The example happens to be a particularly simple one. But it does at least serve to illustrate very neatly a number of points about this kind of research that senior financial managers would do well to keep in mind.

First, it is important for financial managers to disabuse themselves of the notion that there is something special or unique about financial problems. In particular, we have seen that what is commonly regarded as a peculiarly financial problem—to wit, managing the cash balance and a portfolio of liquid securities—turns out to be nothing more than an inventory problem.

Second, mathematical models of decision or control problems should not be thought of as something fundamentally different from ordinary management principles or techniques. They are merely more disciplined and systematic ways of exploiting these principles. In particular, control-limit models of the kind we have seen here—and remember that many additional variations are possible—are essentially extensions of the fundamental notion of *management by exception.*

Third, be careful not to prejudge mathematical models solely on the basis of the lack of literal realism in the assumptions underlying them. To develop a workable model, simplifications—sometimes, extreme simplifications—must be made. But if it has been properly conceived, a simple model may still perform extremely well. It is not a matter of getting something for nothing; rather that the gains made by doing a good job on the really essential parts of the problem are often more than large enough to offset the errors introduced by the simplications (errors, incidentally, that often cancel out).

Finally, remember that there is a trade-off between improving decision procedures and improving the information and forecasts used in arriving at the decisions. In the present instance, for example, we saw a case in which a model that assumed the cash flow to be completely random was still able to do a very successful job of decision making. Nor is this result unique or exceptional. The slogan everywhere today is "more, better, and faster information for management." We suspect, however, that thanks to the computer, many firms may already be in the position of having more, better, and faster information than they can use effectively with present management techniques. There is likely to be as much or more real pay-off in the years ahead in rationalizing and improving decision procedures than there is in simply trying to get an even bigger bang from the information explosion.

21. CASH MANAGEMENT IN THE 70'S—THOSE DANCING DOLLAR BILLS*

As I look back over my 14 years of involvement in corporate cash management, I am amazed to see the changes in philosophy and methods of operation that have taken place. This evolution I believe can be traced principally to two factors: high interest rates and improved technology. During my early years in corporate finance the bank prime rate of interest was very stable at 4½%. And while Treasury securities, certificates of deposit and commercial paper were available to the corporate treasurer as an alternative to bank deposits, the 2½% to 3½% yield on such securities caused many treasurers to be rather complacent about maintaining an aggressive temporary cash investment portfolio. As a result of this, bankers were under no great pressure to attract deposits from their corporate customers or to justify the deposits maintained with them in terms of banking services rendered. Rather, banks were essentially able to present themselves as institutions available to store these deposits as a by-product of providing the normal, routine banking services. Most cash management activities in those days were performed manually, requiring several days in some cases to conclude a transaction. There was very little recognition given to the time value of money, and the corporate treasurer gave very little thought to the clearing time of his checks and the collection time on his deposits.

RECENT CHANGES AND THEIR EFFECTS

All of this has now changed. What we see in the cash management of the 1970s is quite different from what we saw in the early 1960s. Cash management today finds the treasurer facing a fluctuating prime rate, which has reached a high of 12% during a period when he has needed more working capital to finance his operations. He now looks at his deposits more fondly and realizes that he has a valuable asset from a time-value standpoint. He now looks to his bankers to justify the deposits he maintains. The bankers have responded by developing new services to justify these balances, which services either reduce the treasurer's administrative burden or accelerate his cash flow or usually a combination of both. Tne technological improvements in the 1970s have mechanized cash management, and the corporate treasurer today

*From *The Journal of Commercial Bank Lending,* published by The Robert Morris Associates (October, 1974), pp. 47-59. Reprinted by permission. This article is based on an address which Mr. Lake presented before a meeting of the Arizona Chapter of Robert Morris Associates.
†Treasurer, The Greyhound Corporation.

is very much aware of the collection time on his deposits, which affects the fund availability being awarded him by his banks and the clearing time of his checks.

While all of this has been going on, our economy has experienced several credit crunches which have given the corporate treasurer some nightmares on occasion, making him wonder where he was going to finance the shortfalls in his cash flow. These tight money periods have tempered the treasurer from converting all of his demand deposits to investable funds since he realizes he must maintain good banking relationships as well. During the same period, however, banks have expanded their scope of lending, providing the corporate treasurer with intermediate-term financing as well as short-term, thereby increasing his flexibility and ability of working with the banks. And if these aren't enough cash management variables for the treasurer to consume, he has also had to face a deteriorating mail service upon which he has previously depended very heavily for much of his cash management program and, in addition, an aggressive program on the part of the Federal Reserve System and the banks to reduce the clearing time of his outstanding checks. All in all, with these changes, there is very little similarity between the philosophies and systems of today with those of the early 1960s, with the treasurer finding it essential that he be aggressive with his cash management activities. In fact, as I look at our situation today, I am often reminded of some joshing we used to do back in Chicago several years ago. One of my associates there would always needle me a little whenever we would meet in the hall or by the elevator by asking, "And how are the little dollar bills doing today?" My retort quite often was, "They're really dancing," which, as I think about it today, really describes the cash management of the 1970s—dancing dollar bills.

THE GREYHOUND CASH MANAGEMENT SYSTEM

In expressing my views on cash management, I would like to do it within the framework of the Greyhound cash management system. I should probably start off by telling you a little about Greyhound and our cash management requirements, so that my remarks will be in perspective. We are an organization of more than 130 active companies involved in a wide variety of businesses virtually worldwide. Our 1973 earnings approximated $76.4 million on gross revenues of $3.4 billion, which in both categories makes 1973 our best year ever. Greyhound ranks 31st in Fortune's Five Hundred largest industrial corporations and has in excess of 200,000 stockholders and 54,000 employees.

From Phoenix we control the largest inter-city bus service in the world. Greyhound is the nation's only national transportation company, serving all 48 contiguous states, Alaska and Canada through 148 company-owned bus stations and over 3,900 agents. We operate more than 60% of the nation's inter-city bus service, and last year we carried 90 million passengers for a total of 9.7 billion passenger miles.

From Phoenix we also run Armour and Company and Armour-Dial, acquired by Greyhound in 1969 and 1970, which operate approximately 120 meat slaughtering plants, manufacturing and processing plants and distribution centers throughout the United States. Armour is the largest processor of pork in the United States, ranks fifth in the processing of beef and is a large processor of turkeys. Armour bacon is first in sales and Armour hot dogs rank second in volume in the United States.

Armour-Dial manufactures and sells a wide variety of products, including Dial soap, which is by far the most popular bar soap, with about 19% of the U.S. market. Among its other products are Dial deodorants, anti-perspirants and shampoos, Chiffon liquid detergent, Bruce floor waxes, Parson's ammonia, Magic Spray sizing, Appian Way pizza mixes and Treet and Armour Star canned meat products, which are the country's largest selling lines of canned meat products.

In addition, we control or run directly from Phoenix companies involved in the following businesses: Industrial leasing, money orders, aircraft servicing and fueling, fire and casualty insurance, rental cars, tour service arrangements, sightseeing operations, airport ground transportation, a pharmaceutical company, custom brokerage, duty-free stores, convention and trade show servicing, temporary help service, industrial and institutional food operations, cattle feeding and inter-city bus manufacturing.

As I am sure you can appreciate, each of these business operations has its own cash management requirements, making it necessary for our cash management system to be tailor-made to each company's needs, while at the same time meshing harmoniously with all the others. In addition, a number of these companies, including the parent company and our leasing companies, are heavy users of bank credit throughout the world. To give you an idea of the size of our banking system, our active bank accounts total 2,500, which are maintained in approximately 1,300 banks around the world. Our credit facilities through some 80 U.S. banks approach $600 million, and in addition we have approximately $85 million in credit facilities provided us by Canadian and foreign banks.

I don't mean to be bragging in mentioning the scope of our operations and banking system, nor am I trying to give you a commercial message. Rather, I feel it is important that you understand the magnitude of our operations so that you will appreciate the magnitude of our cash management requirements. From these requirements, I think you can see that the scope of our banking system requires that we maintain sound banking relationships, not only to provide us with our active banking services but also to provide us with the credit we require for our various operations. It should follow, then, that the maintenance of a dependable banking network, which includes sound banking relationships, is an integral part of any cash management system. I would like to spend a few minutes talking about these relationships and then move on to what I consider the second major part of a cash management program—the systems and procedures that make the network function on a day-to-day basis.

OUR BANKING RELATIONSHIPS

First of all, in discussing the maintenance of a banking network, I think I should talk about our basic banking philosophies, which of course are an important part of maintaining adequate banking relationships. While Greyhound's operations are largely decentralized, we do centralize the financial function within the corporate headquarters in Phoenix. Through this centralization, we believe that we are better able to coordinate the financial and banking activities for all of our companies and utilize our cash resources more effectively. Most of our subsidiaries are tied into the parent company for cash flow purposes, and we tailor each company's cash management system to its own particular characteristics and requirements. By the same token, we ask our banks to view our relationships on a consolidated basis, enabling us to utilize the banking dollars generated by our active companies to assist us in supporting our compensating balance requirements for both banking activity and credit. In Phoenix, we designate the banking activity and the balance levels that each of our subsidiaries maintains with our banks in order to attain the desired balance and activity level on a consolidated basis. And while you may not believe it from hearing about the 1,300 banks we do business with, we do attempt to consolidate our banking within the fewest number of banks possible. In most cases, we attempt to consolidate our primary activity within a given city in one bank, although there are certainly exceptions to this. These are the banks that we really concentrate on and probably there are no more than 100 in number. Most of the remaining 1,200 banks have very modest relationships and primarily serve as depositories for local offices and agents that are outside of our primary banking network. Consistent with our policy of consolidating our activity, we also consolidate our credit with the same banks so that our relationships are built on both credit and banking activity.

I might also restate our bank compensation philosophy, as covered by the Chairman of the Board of The Greyhound Corporation, Mr. Gerald H. Trautman, in a speech before the Robert Morris Associates Fall Conference in Phoenix last October. In his remarks, he said:

> We have an obligation to our stockholders to obtain the highest return possible on company assets, including cash. A very important

return in the form of good banking relations is derived from cash on deposit with our banks. And sound bank relationships are vital and necessary to the future health of any business. It therefore follows that it is to our stockholders' best interest, and consequently our objective, to maintain balances at a level that will foster good relations and to invest every dollar over this amount.

THE USE OF ANALYSIS REPORTS

We supervise and control the balance levels in our larger banks through the evaluation of analysis reports which are forwarded us periodically by some 200 banks throughout the country. The modest balances and activity in the remainder of our banks do not warrant our requesting this information. I know that many of you are familiar with these analysis reports, which basically provide the corporate treasurer with a picture of the operation of each of his accounts, usually for a period of a month. These reports show the average ledger and collected balances that were maintained during the month and the banking services that were performed during the period, such as the number of checks deposited, lock box items, checks drawn against the account and reconciliation services. An earnings credit is awarded, on paper, based on the average loanable balances maintained during the month; loanable balances being the collected balances after a deduction for bank reserves. From that earnings credit, there is a deduction for activity charges, based on the monthly volume of services, priced out at a per-item activity charge. In essence, the report is similar to a personal checking account service charge statement, with the resulting profit or loss on the analysis being an indication of the adequacy of collected balances maintained in the account, or through the consolidated relationship, to pay for the services rendered. We receive these analysis reports on a quarterly basis from most of our banks, although we do feel important in some situations where there are significant balances and activity to obtain this information more frequently.

The analysis reports also serve as an effective internal policing mechanism of our banking system. Often a noticeable change in banking activity and balance levels in one of our accounts points out a problem that has developed in the cash management system of one of our subsidiaries. This centralized policing is essential if we are to have an effective cash management system with most of our operations decentralized.

The analysis report has gone through quite an evolution over the past 10 to 15 years. Originally it was looked at as more of an internal bank management tool for evaluating the corporate relationship and really not for the perusal of the corporate treasurer. I will never forget my first experience in asking for such a report, which would have been shortly after I joined the treasurer's staff of an insurance company in the early 1960s. The treasurer asked me to call one of our major banks to get an analysis of our account. I have to admit that I was a neophyte at the time and not really sure what I was requesting. Anyway, I called our contact officer and told him what I wanted. There was a brief silence at the other end of the telephone. About the only thing he could come up with was, "Let me check it out and I'll call you back." About half an hour later he returned my call and said, "How about getting together today for lunch?" I said, "Fine" and walked over to the bank at lunchtime, only to be surprised and somewhat overwhelmed when I was ushered into a private dining room with five or six vice presidents sitting around the table. During the lunch it was explained that this information was really considered confidential within the bank since to release it would require the bank to divulge its operating costs. In the end, they did provide the report and I have often thought there should have been a pretty large miscellaneous charge on that analysis report to reflect all of the lunches it cost the bank to lay the groundwork.

I mention this incident not to ridicule the bank, but to illustrate the reluctance of banks at that time to provide corporate treasurers with this type of information, a situation which is very much different today. I also use this story to emphasize a point regarding activity charges which is contrary to the approach taken by the bank in my story. When I ask a bank for an analysis report on our relationship, I am certainly not asking them to tell me their cost of performing each of their services any more than I would expect you to ask me the cost of providing passenger service between Phoenix and Tucson. Rather, I am really asking the bank to tell me the price of its services, and my underlying assumption is that there is an element of profit built into these charges. Consequently, if I feel a bank's activity charges are out of line, I reserve the right to challenge them and to take my business elsewhere if I am unhappy about them.

Because of the volume of analysis reports we receive from banks all over the country, we see a wide variety of presentations, varying all the way from the very sophisticated computer analysis report to mere photocopies of bank statements. The basic, and probably original, analysis report shows ledger, collected and loanable balances and an earnings credit offset by activity charges, with the resulting profit or loss on the account indicating the adequacy of the collected balances maintained during the period. While this is the basic format, there are wide variations among banks as to the per item activity charges, such as for deposits and checks cleared against the account, and also wide variations in the earnings allowance rate used to calculate the earnings credit on the balances. Some banks have a very low earnings allowance rate along with very low activity charges. Other banks have higher earnings allowances with higher activity charges, although the resulting balance requirement in both situations could be fairly similar because of variations in both the income and expense sides of the equation. The ones that really concern me obviously are those with a low earnings allowance and high charges which require high balances, and I frequently complain about them.

COMPENSATING BALANCES VERSUS SERVICE CHARGES

I think it is safe to say that banks prefer that corporations maintain balances as compensation for banking services rather than have them pay service charges. From the corporate side, balances are obviously more expensive than fees in that the earnings allowance rate on the analysis report is, in most cases, less than money market rates and is awarded on loanable balances after the deduction for reserves. The treasurer really has to decide how important his banking relationships are to his cash management program. In our case, we maintain balances to compensate our major banks, but we withdraw our funds as fast as possible from our less important banks and pay the resulting service charges.

We are also seeing some analysis reports now with fluctuating earnings allowance rates which are tied to some current money market rates. I am not sure that I agree with this approach since short-term fluctuations in money market rates can potentially result in a significant change in the deposits required to support a given amount of banking activity. While the earnings allowance is a measure of the worth of the balances to the bank, short-term fluctuations in this rate have very little or no relationship to the bank's short run ability to perform its services for its corporate customers. It is, therefore, my view that the balances maintained to support banking activity should be looked at over a reasonably long period of time and should not be subject to short-term changes in the earnings allowance rate.

Because of the wide variety of earnings allowances and activity charges we encounter, we end up converting all of our bank analysis charges to a balance equivalent basis for each type of service in order to put all our banks on an equivalent basis and to enable us to compare these charges. That is, we calculate the dollar amount of deposits we would have to maintain on a monthly basis in order to compensate each bank for its services, such as for making a deposit, clearing a check or making a wire transfer. In fact, many of our banks are now providing this type of account analysis report, stating all activity charges in terms of the balances required to compensate the bank for its services. I frankly prefer this approach in that it eliminates all the variables and makes our calculations easier in developing our comparative activity charge information. With the number of analyses we receive, we still find some rather wide pricing variations between banks, even within the same city, and frequently challenge them when we feel they are out of line.

The analysis report takes on added meaning when a credit is involved since this report is used to evaluate whether the corporation has maintained adequate deposits to support compensating balance requirements for credit as well as for banking activity. In compensating his banks for these services, the corporate treasurer quite frequently requests the bank to look at a portion of his balances on a double duty basis, that is to support both credit and activity. This saves him from providing separate balances for each type of service. While the bank would obviously prefer separate balances for each, such double counting arrangements are nevertheless negotiated. My justification for such an arrangement is that, as a corporate treasurer, I look at the overall profitability of the relationship to the bank. There is certainly an element of profit in the interest charged on the borrowings and the maintenance of, say, 10% to 20% compensating balances certainly adds to the lending profitability. And, as I have already mentioned, I assume there is profit built into the activity charges. Taking all these elements together, when the relationship is significant, I may not feel that the bank should receive 100% of the profitability in all areas and look to the partial double counting of balances to temper this profitability somewhat. Obviously, the degree of double counting must depend on the size, scope and potential of the relationship, and be subject to negotiation between the bank and the corporation.

I believe the bank also benefits from this double counting in that it encourages the treasurer to establish active banking with his credit-line banks, which activity will probably stay with them long after the need for credit has dissipated. Without this incentive, treasurers would undoubtedly put most of their activity with the bank that offers the best service for the lowest possible price. In addition, without double counting, compensating balances for credit have to be looked at as purely a pricing mechanism, adding to the cost of bank borrowing. This could potentially make such financing less competitive as compared with other sources of credit, discouraging bank borrowing.

This brings up the question of credit compensating balances in general and their role as a pricing mechanism in bank financing. I frankly think we will see the day when the treasurer has the alternative of providing balances or paying the entire financing charge through the interest rate. We have occasionally seen situations already where we could have had that option. My view is that once the corporation has reached the point where it no longer requires balances for cash management transaction purposes, I would prefer to pay the rate and avoid the necessity of borrowing additional funds in order to maintain these compensating balances.

By now you probably think that I am out to eliminate most of the balances that corporations maintain with their banks. Such is not the case. Rather, my purpose is to define the balance levels that will develop and maintain satisfactory banking relationships. It really boils down to a judgmental decision where the treasurer must evaluate the services provided him by his banks, some of which may not be reflected in the analysis report. He must then reduce the complexities of his relationships to overall balance level figures for each of his banks.

BANK CREDIT WORTHINESS

Before leaving the banking network side of cash management, there is one more important consideration that I wish to comment upon—the credit worthiness of all the banks within that network. Banks of course have sophisticated credit departments to analyze their corporate borrowers, but in my view the corporate treasurer does not do enough to analyze the financial strength of the banking institutions to which he has entrusted his funds. Since we have acquired Armour, I have become more interested in this area since Armour generates big ledger balances in small banks in many outlying cities and towns. We pay very close attention to the maximum level of our balances in these banks relative to the banks' total capital and surplus. However, I don't feel that this is enough. We are currently embarking on a program of analyzing our banks, with particular emphasis on the smaller ones where we likely have our greater exposure. On the other hand, the problems experienced in San Diego should point out the fallacy of assuming that larger banks are immune to financial problems.

THE SYSTEMS AND PROCEDURAL ASPECTS OF CASH MANAGEMENT

I would now like to turn to the second major part of a cash management program, the systems and procedural aspects. We have seen many new innovations developed over the past few years to accelerate cash flow and to improve the treasurer's control over his cash flow, primarily as a result of the tight money periods and the high level of interest rates. The banks are certainly to be credited with developing many of these new techniques. In Greyhound, with the complexity of our banking network, we tend to be exposed to all of these innovations, and we use them in varying degrees in the cash management systems of our subsidiary companies. Because of the decentralized nature of our operations, we must develop cash management programs for our subsidiaries that provide them with the necessary operating cash, while at the same time ensuring that all funds over these operating requirements are transferred to the parent company for use elsewhere in the system. The Greyhound Corporation really acts as a bank for its companies by receiving excess funds as generated from its subsidiaries and advancing these funds to other companies that are in need of working capital. From Phoenix, we borrow from our banks and sell commercial paper through several of our companies to finance our operations and to smooth out fluctuations in our cash flow. We generally do not allow our decentralized companies to do any external borrowing. Rather, they look to the parent company for all of their borrowing requirements. We have an intercompany mechanism whereby we charge our subsidiary companies interest on their borrowings from the parent company and award interest to companies that are in a creditor position. As I know you can appreciate, it does not make sense for some subsidiaries to be investing excess cash on the open market while other subsidiaries are borrowing to meet their current operating requirements.

Cash Receipts

Our cash flow systems vary from company to company. However, we do follow one cardinal principle throughout—we take all decision-making control away from our local personnel related to balance levels and the movement of funds, substituting in its place standing instructions which must be followed on a daily basis for all phases of the cash management program. By reducing cash management activities to a routine pattern, we are better able to control our balance levels throughout the country without having to be aware of each subsidiary's day-to-day receipt and disbursement activity. In moving our funds from our local accounts, we use depository transfer checks drawn on these accounts and payable to a regional concentration bank and also wire transfer systems. At present, we depend on our local personnel to initiate and mail the depository transfer checks to the regional concentration banks in order to transfer their daily deposits out of their local accounts.

We are not as yet using the new system which has been promoted by the National Data Corporation of Atlanta. This new system eliminates the mail delay, in that the local personnel call a National Data office, toll free, and advise them of the total daily deposit amount. This deposit information for all reporting units is stored in a computer and once daily is sent by wire to the regional concentration banks where depository transfer checks are produced and deposited to the company accounts there, moving the funds in from the local accounts with no dependency on the U.S. mails. We do not see the benefit of this system in moving funds out of many of our major banks, or where the daily deposit is small, when considering the greater cost of this system over the present one. Also, the accelerated withdrawal of funds from a major bank necessitates that we put additional balances back in that bank in order to maintain our required balance levels. However, we do see some benefits from a cost and fund availability standpoint in a number of our banks where we have large deposits and are currently using a wire transfer system which is more expensive than National Data. We anticipate we will be converting these accounts to this new system in the near future.

Our wire transfer procedures are generally handled by standing instructions filed with our banks, requiring daily transfers of all funds over a certain amount to a central account for that company of the parent company. Where such an account handles disbursements as well as receipts, we further ask the bank to call us if the balance level goes below a certain lower level as a result of check clearings so that we can transfer funds back to the bank to bring the balance back to the desired level. In essence, we establish a balance bracket for these receipt and disbursement accounts, with the average level being somewhere between the two transfer levels. This system enables us to obtain the benefit of excess funds as generated, while at the same time alerting us of the need to replenish the account if disbursement activity is abnormally heavy.

We also utilize lock boxes quite extensively. We have recently been expanding them in Armour where the check amounts are large and check presentation is important not only for the accelerated availability of our funds but also for more timely notice of credit problems where NSF checks are involved. Because of the nature of Armour's business, receivables must be carried on the local office books. The lock box enables us to channel these receipts into regional cities, without passing the checks through the local offices, accelerating the deposit of these checks by some 2 or 3 days in many cases. In expanding our use of lock boxes, particularly in Armour, we have the added benefit of transferring banking activity and balance generation out of the small city banks and into regional banks where we have major relationships and can utilize the funds for compensating balance purposes. This also reduces our financial exposure in these small banks and cuts down the number of banks we must analyze from a financial soundness basis.

In conjunction with our lock box operations, we hope to utilize the capabilities of some of our banks in the near future to receive information on our daily remittances over telephone lines that can be fed directly into our computers. With mail delays, this will overcome one objection our credit people currently have with lock box use—they feel they presently experience delays in receiving customer payment information mailed from our banks. And I must admit that the mail delays have been a significant problem for us in managing our cash flow system from Phoenix. However, we have compensated for these problems by using telephone and telegraph systems, and in some areas, our banks can even transmit information directly to the computer that maintains our banking records. We are enthusiastic about these capabilities where transmitted information can be inserted right into our accounting system because it reduces our handling of this information and enables us to update our records on a more timely basis. The only shortfall to the system revolves around a problem we all have—the availability of well trained personnel who will process this information on a regular basis with a minimum number of errors.

Cash Disbursements

On the disbursement side, while practically all of our checks are drawn on the subsidiary and field offices, a large percentage of these items are cleared against centralized disbursement accounts under the control of the Phoenix office. We utilize a good number of zero-balance account arrangements. This involves a group of accounts at a certain bank that have no balances, but that are reimbursed daily from a major account within the same bank for the checks that have cleared through these so-called sub-accounts. The advantage of these zero-balance accounts is that the disbursements of decentralized operations can be centralized, eliminating the need for maintaining balances all over the country to pay for these clearing checks. In addition, the use of zero-balance accounts allows each unit to maintain its own identifiability of disbursements and to receive a bank statement and cancelled checks as a by-product of a centralized disbursement system.

Our disbursing accounts are maintained in a number of cities throughout the country, principally tied in with our major banking relationships where we have a substantial pool of balances available to absorb fluctuations in day-to-day clearings. I would be less than honest if I didn't admit that we recognize and take advantage of the delayed clearing benefits from the geographic distance between the issuing point and the clearing point, although I do feel that this can be carried to extremes. Most of these disbursing cities are Federal Reserve cities, although we do a significant amount of disbursing through Phoenix, which is a notable exception. I am frequently asked why we don't draw all of our disbursements on banks in a number of non-Federal Reserve cities around the country in order to benefit from the greater clearing times afforded checks drawn on these cities. As many of you undoubtedly are aware, there have been some rather aggressive programs developed under this concept; in some cases, the banks can even provide you the amount of clearings to enable you to pay for them on a same-day basis, eliminating the need for the maintenance of large local deposits. We have given the benefits of this system a great deal of thought and do take advantage of this concept where it meshes compatibly with our overall banking relationship considerations. However, with the size of Greyhound's banking system, we have developed banking relationships throughout the country to handle both our banking activity and credit requirements. Frankly, we are not convinced that the Federal Reserve System will allow these delayed clearing advantages to continue, especially when they are widely advertised in individual banks' business development programs. Rather, we think the Fed will take fast action as check clearings increase in some of the cities by establishing additional Regional Check Processing Centers to speed up their processing operations. These centers will effectively eliminate any delayed check clearing benefits that are currently available in these cities. Therefore, on the assumption that these advantages will be temporary, we are reluctant to disturb our current banking system and relationships and incur the substantial expense required to implement these changes, only to find out at a later date that it was all for naught.

There is one other area in the systems and procedures of cash management that bears mentioning—the tool of cash forecasting. I don't think that it is necessary to dwell on this subject for any length of time other than to say that it should not be overlooked. Cash forecasting must be done on a regular basis to enable the corporate treasurer to plan accordingly, manage his cash properly and keep top management informed of cash requirements. Each company's requirements will govern the amount of detail required in the forecast and the time span involved, although I heartily endorse both a long range and a short range forecast. It is of utmost importance however that the actual results be compared with the forecast on a regular basis, with the goal toward improving the model.

SUMMARY

In summary, corporate cash management has gone through quite an evolution over the last decade or so, and I am sure we will continue to see further changes taking place throughout the remainder of the 70s. The banking industry plays a vital role in the treasurer's cash management program and, as I have already indicated, it is essential that he maintain sound banking relationships in order to make his system function. With our current interest rate levels and tight money periods, the treasurer recognizes more and more the worth of the asset that falls within his responsibility and must aggressively run his cash management program to keep his dollar bills dancing.

22. CREDIT AND INVENTORY MANAGEMENT: SEPARATE OR TOGETHER?*

MICHAEL SCHIFF†

The management of working capital has received considerable attention in recent years. Each of the elements of working capital—cash, receivables, and inventory—has been studied separately, and modern quantitative analysis has been applied in the search for better planning and control.

The interface between credit management and inventory management is essential in effecting the trade-off in costs between the two and in achieving more effective planning and control for these elements of working capital.

The need for this interface was underscored by my recent experience in connection with a study of cost control in physical distribution management.[1] After the study was released to some 200 large corporate sponsors, a series of 11 seminars were conducted in New York, Chicago, and San Francisco attended by key marketing, distribution, and financial executives from the sponsoring organizations. Even though the interaction between the management of receivables and inventory was not covered in the study, it was presented as a topic for discussion. At these meetings we learned that not one of the participant companies had recognized the need for the joint management of these functions. And everyone agreed that there is a real need to consider credit and customer service jointly in the marketing decision process.

CURRENT STATUS

How well have financial managers performed in dealing with receivables and inventory? Exhibit 22-1 shows index numbers for receivables, sales, profits before income taxes, inventories, and accounts receivable for manufacturing corporations, using 1956 experience as a base. From 1956-1970 sales increased 2.3 times, inventories 2.4 times, while accounts receivable increased 3.3 times. These increases were accompanied by a before-tax profit increase of only 1.6 times. Inventories as a percentage of sales show a range of 17.1 to 18.7 percent over the period studied, while receivables show a steady rise going from 10.1 percent to 14.1 percent of sales. (Exhibit 22-2).

---

*From *Financial Executive* (November, 1972), pp. 29-33. Reprinted by permission.
†Ross Professor of Accounting, Graduate School of Business, New York University.
[1]Michael Schiff, *Accounting and Control in Physical Distribution Management*, National Council of Physical Distribution Management, 1971.

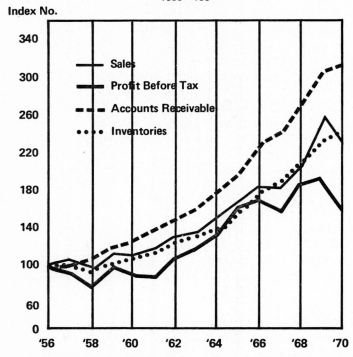

EXHIBIT 22-1

INDEX NUMBERS
SALES, PROFITS BEFORE TAX, ACCOUNTS RECEIVABLE,
AND INVENTORIES ALL MANUFACTURING CORPORATIONS
1956–1970
1956 = 100

SOURCE: Derived from Quarterly Financial Report for Manufacturing Corporations.
U.S. Federal Trade Commission and SEC.

For all manufacturing companies, control of inventories was significantly better than the control of receivables. The fact that the rate of profit growth was slower than sales while receivables increased at a much greater pace than sales suggests a decreasing return on an increased investment in receivables.

One can attribute the trends to external forces such as changes in monetary policy affecting interest rates, varying degrees of uncertainty, changes in customers mix (direct sales vs. sales through wholesalers and distributors), changes in selling price levels and costs, and many other factors. Indeed, business decisions are made under conditions of change and are affected by a host of external factors. The business manager considers these changes as he develops policies and strategies. The strategies must include cost trade-offs. If he fails to recognize available

EXHIBIT 22-2

**PROFIT BEFORE TAX, ACCOUNTS RECEIVABLE, AND
INVENTORIES AS PERCENTAGE OF SALES
ALL MANUFACTURING CORPORATIONS
1956–1970**

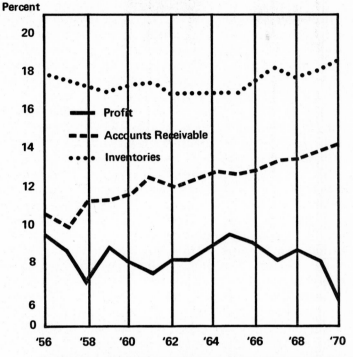

SOURCE: Derived from Quarterly Financial Report for Manufacturing Corporations.
U.S. Federal Trade Commission and SEC.

trade-offs, substitutions such as advertising vs. price reduction, packaging vs. advertising, promotion vs. advertising, technical service vs. personal selling, etc., he will not respond in an optimal fashion. Likewise, if he does not consider cost trade-offs in inventory and credit management he will not produce the best possible results.

The data in Exhibits 22-1 and 22-2 suggest the existence of a problem; what follows is an attempt to identify the causes and possible solutions.

Companies may have been able to maintain better control on inventories as reflected by their close correlation with sales than they have on receivables because executives are more concerned with inventory control and have achieved it by shipping goods on especially attractive terms. The result has been an increased amount of receivables accompanied by a declining rate of turnover.

Why should this be so? Surely, costs are attributable to carrying accounts receivable just as costs are associated with holding inventories. Why should one set of costs appear to be ignored while the other is carefully controlled?

There are three answers to these questions. First, inventory control, with its utilization of inventory models, has received much attention and modern analytical tools generally have been accepted in the field. Not so with accounts receivable. Some attempts have been made to develop mathematical models for studying the effect of changes in credit terms on sales, but no models which integrate receivables and inventories have been reported.

Second, the functions of inventory management and receivables management are separated in the typical business organization. Credit management, which includes granting credit and the collection of accounts receivable, is viewed as a fund management problem and is generally assigned to the treasurer or controller. Inventory management, on the other hand, is viewed as a function of developing and controlling optimum inventory levels by relating production costs, losses due to stock-outs, inventory carrying costs, and customer service costs to seek the optimum inventory levels.

In addition, the position of this function in the organization has undergone some change. Traditionally, it was part of the manufacturing activity, where it remains in many organizations. It was shifted to marketing management in some companies as part of the adoption of the "marketing concept" and, in recent years, some companies have placed it in a separate function called physical distribution. By keeping the two functions of inventory management and receivables management in separate areas of responsibility, limited integration has been achieved.

A third factor accounting for the growth of receivables and inventory is the difference in approach in measuring the effectiveness of each. While inventory management stresses the optimum balance of manufacturing capabilities with marketing needs (a positive approach to profit improvement), credit management still retains bad debt loss minimization (a negative approach). The phrase "bad debt losses" conveys a notion of a cost to be avoided, a form of cost aversion. Realistically, bad debt losses are a cost of marketing goods on credit and should be viewed as part of the marketing mix along with costs such as advertising, promotion, field selling, etc.—costs incurred with a positive purpose to achieve sales and profits. One does not identify advertising or promotion as *bad* advertising or *bad* promotion—costs to be avoided if one is careful. Costs are incurred to achieve benefits ultimately reflected in sales revenue and profits. Credit extension, along with advertising, promotion, customer service, and other elements of the marketing mix, have these attributes and should be viewed constructively.

The failure to integrate receivable and inventory management can, therefore, be attributed to lack of well-developed integrated planning models for receivables and inventory, to the separation of these inventories in the organization, and to differences in the evaluative criteria for judging performance in these functions.

It is interesting to note that during the 1956-1970 period smaller companies ($1-$5 million of assets) displayed a more effective control of receivables. Over the years studied, receivables as a percentage of sales increased at the rate of only 2 percent, while large corporations (assets over $1 billion) showed an increase of 5 percent. Indeed, for smaller companies the relationship of both inventory and receivables to sales has been consistent. The likelihood of companies of this size utilizing sophisticated inventory management techniques is remote. Perhaps their relative success is a result of the closeness of management to decision making and the greater likelihood of the interaction of marketing, production, and credit resulting from better communication and supervision. The larger corporation must rely on more indirect controls.

MARKETING

The importance of the problem can be viewed from another practical operational side. Marketing activities create the demand for accumulating inventories and for credit extension. Since the functions of credit management and inventory management are separate organizational units with minimum communication between them, marketing has two separate sources for bargaining for services which will result in increased sales. It can make its plea for maximum customer service with minimal lag between order placement and shipment and then seek extended terms or more liberalized credit.

The point is frequently made that inventory management and customer service áre controlled within the organization, while credit terms are set externally, determined by the marketplace and standardized by industry. One need only examine credit terms in an industry and then calculate actual average credit terms extended as reflected by receivable turnover ratios to observe the variations in extension of credit terms. Similarly, the level of customer service extended by a firm reflects market conditions. In short, the credit extension and customer service policy of a firm reflects its reaction to market demands as much as it reflects reactions to competitive price, advertising, promotion, etc.

Where marketing performance is evaluated on an actual-to-planned-sales measure, the benefits from improved customer service and more liberal credit terms are viewed as free services, and marketing executives increasingly are abusing them. Indeed, it is fair to say that marketing management could be criticized if it does not use free services if the goal is increased sales! The statistics previously cited suggest that where demands for service are thwarted by well-managed inventory activity, marketing has had greater success in its demand for greater credit extension because credit extension is not profit oriented. The frequent result of this kind of arrangement is increased bonuses for marketing managers and declining profits for the company.

Even where marketing is evaluated and rewarded on contribution to profit, the full cost of extended credit terms is rarely considered in calculating the profit and, as a result, the pressure on credit management for greater extension persists.

The failure to consider the impact of a marketing decision on accounts receivable and inventories can be highlighted in still another way. Consider a proposal to spend $30,000 for a machine or other capital asset in a company today. A capital budget proposal is required with extensive detail on the nature of the expenditure and a projection of cash flows over the life of the project. The proposal, which requires top management approval, is very carefully reviewed relating investment to cash flows.

By contrast, consider a salesman working out of a district office, who after much effort has landed a customer who will purchase on the average $100,000 worth of relatively profitable goods a year. All he needs to do is to get this order through the credit department. One does not usually stop to consider how much additional inventory will have to be kept to service this customer nor does anyone relate to this amount the additional investment in new accounts receivable generated by this sale. If we assume $30,000 as the sum of the average annual investment for both receivables and inventory to sustain the sales volume, then we have made an investment of $30,000 without any evaluation of the return. As a matter of fact, should the customer continue to buy over a long period of time, as expected, the investment in receivables and inventories is far more fixed than was the earlier commitment of $30,000 for the fixed asset.

In the latter situation, the return on investment provided by depreciation is cash flow, which is available for alternative investment from the moment of use (in an asset with a 10-year life the first year would return $6,000—20 percent of $30,000 using double declining balance depreciation). The investment in so-called current assets, accounts receivable, and inventory will not be released for alternative investment until the firm stops selling goods to this customer. Small wonder that these assets have increased while profits have declined.

POSITIVE APPROACH

Credit-inventory management is an integrated approach in the management of these functions, an integration which recognizes jointly the costs involved in these functions and measures trade-off in a logical way. Inventory models consider manufacturing costs, annual usage, order handling costs, cost of carrying inventory (physical handling, storage, obsolescence, taxes, insurance, and imputed interest), stockout costs, etc. The costs of credit include credit extension, collection, losses from uncollected accounts, and the imputed interest in carrying accounts receivable. One need not wait for the development of integrated models to achieve the interface between credit and inventory management.

The idea of cost trade-offs has been explored and implemented in inventory management. These relate the costs of physical movement of goods, holding costs, service, production, and sales costs, and are considered on an intrafirm (two or more operations within a firm) and on an interfirm (seller vs. customer) basis. The interfirm trade-offs consider relative costs of seller and customer and aim at that combination of services and service level which is economical to both. Yet these carefully considered trade-offs will be illusory if credit costs are not included. The statistics previously cited suggest that intrafirm trade-offs are deceiving when credit costs are not considered.

An initial step can be taken immediately by examining inventory and credit policies as they relate to individual customers and channels of distribution. Exhibit 22-3 illustrates an income statement wherein inventory and receivables carrying costs are considered. For the assumed carrying costs (inventories 30 percent and receivables 15 percent), it would appear that longer credit terms involving a reduction in inventory (poorer customer service) and its associated costs would be desirable (Alternative B). The more frequently encountered case is Alternative A, where the customer service is not charged and pressure is exerted on the credit department to permit the customer to pay in 60 days. Were this to happen, the company would incur an extra $1,200 in credit carrying costs, thus reducing the contribution income by $1,200.

Inventory carrying costs and receivables carrying costs vary for different firms depending on their physical facilities, financial resources, and investment alternatives. The point should be stressed that the opportunity cost of money identified as interest is common to the tie-up of capital in both inventory and accounts receivable. This interest is automatically incorporated in inventory models and should be included in evaluating alternatives in credit extension. The approach suggested in the illustration will lead to a better matching of the seller's capabilities and costs in customer service and credit extension to the needs and

EXHIBIT 22-3

ILLUSTRATION OF CONTRIBUTION INCOME INCLUDING INVENTORY
AND RECEIVABLES CARRYING COSTS

	Alternative A	Alternative B
Annual sales 96,000 units @ $1	$96,000	$96,000
Cost of goods sold 96,000 units @ $.75	72,000	72,000
Gross margin	$24,000	$24,000
Direct marketing costs	$ 5,000	$ 5,000
Inventory carrying costs		
8,000 × $.75 × 30%	1,800	—
Receivables carrying costs		
8,000 × 15%	1,200	
16,000 × 15%		2,400
	8,000	7,400
Contribution income	16,000	16,600

ASSUMPTIONS

1. Alternative A. Sell 8,000 units per month (one shipment a month), credit terms—30 days net.
2. Alternative B. Sell 16,000 units (one shipment every two months), credit terms—60 days net.
3. Production run: 16,000 units every 2 months shipped directly for Alternative B.
4. Inventory carrying costs equal 30% of factory cost. (Includes 10% for imputed interest.)
5. Receivables carrying cost includes credit checking, collection, expected bad debts, and 10% for imputed interest.
6. Customer pays delivery charges.

capabilities of the customer. Inventory and credit policies would be co-ordinated to achieve maximum profits.

To assure the administration of this interactive policy, corporate management should review the current corporate structure for inventory and credit management. I suggest combining the credit function and the inventory management function into a new independent organizational unit. This new combined function would be responsible for credit activities, inventory management, and physical distribution. It would be the source for providing marketing management with the inventory and credit costs necessary in developing alternative strategies incorporating the costs of credit and customer service with other elements of the marketing mix—personal selling, promotion, advertising, packaging, etc. The profit plan arrived at with this approach would be comprehensive because it includes the costs of all services available to marketing. It provides for a positive use of credit as an income-generating expense rather than as the negative cost aversion approach typically practiced in credit extension.

Altering traditional organizational structure and responsibilities is not easy. As an alternative, a closer interaction between the two functions recognizing the cost trade-offs between the services of credit and inventory management could achieve desirable results within the current organizational framework.

The statistics cited in Exhibits 22-1 and 22-2 suggest that control of credit extension is not effective, as is evidenced by the far more rapid increase in investment in receivables as contrasted to the increase in profits. It indicates increasing investment in receivables at decreasing rates of return. This trend can and should be reversed by including costs of credit in the planning process.

CONCLUSION

What is recommended is a coordination of control of inventory and credit management to achieve a maximum return on investment in receivables and inventories. It has been established that inventory control has been achieved in part at the expense of receivables control, the result of dealing with these two interrelated activities as if they were separated and unrelated.

Inventory and receivables policies should and can be developed jointly with a recognition that there are cost trade-offs between them. Combinations of tighter inventory policy and relaxed credit, looser inventory policy, and tighter credit policy in varying mixes can be evaluated together in facing the market to arrive at policies which will generate the maximum return on investment, specifically, the return on the firm's investment in receivables and inventories.

PART VII. MERGERS AND ACQUISITIONS

The third and greatest wave of mergers gathered strength in the early 1960s, reached frenzied activity after 1965, and peaked in 1969 and 1970. In 1968 about 2,500 large manufacturing and mining firms that had an asset value of over $15 billion were acquired. The giant conglomerates such as Gulf and Western, Litton Industries, and International Telephone and Telegraph (ITT) erupted upon the United States and the world; they have permanently changed the corporate landscape. The merger forces have subsided temporarily but they will burst forth again when the stock market pushes into new high ground, when the mood of the country is buoyant, and when new accounting and legal devices are found to outflank the new bulwarks against major mergers. Changes in accounting rules to reduce the use of pooling of interests, increased vigilance against fraud and stricter—or new and novel—enforcement of antitrust laws have been a part of the reaction to the great merger wave. In 1974 the number of mergers was about 42 percent below its high point according to *Mergers & Acquisitions* and the dollar value of acquired corporations has fallen much more than that.

The article by Donald J. Smalter and Roderic C. Lancey shows the importance of P/E (price-earnings ratio) analysis in acquisition strategy. Most successful growth companies can link their achievements with a mixture of three types of strategies—internal programs for new products and market development, joint ventures, and acquisitions. One aspect of the growth by acquisition strategy is maintaining and improving the acquiring company's P/E ratio. A high P/E ratio, which is essential to an acquisition strategy, depends upon a steady, high, long-term growth rate for earnings per share. Well selected acquisitions acquired on favorable terms contribute to a favorable growth rate.

Major questions covered in the article include: (1) What factors appear to control the level of the P/E ratio? (2) How can a company raise its P/E ratio? (3) How can an acquisition upgrade the company's per-share earnings results? (4) How does a candidate company's P/E ratio affect the acquiring firm's acquisition strategy? (5) Under what circumstances can both parties experience marginal gains?

Smalter and Lancey use a hypothetical case to show how the P/E ratio relates to immediate dilution of or additions to per-share earnings. They demonstrate how quickly acquired earnings must grow to wash out immediate dilution during the post-merger years.

Mr. John Heath, Jr., a vice president of a prominent appraisal firm, discusses valuation factors and techniques in mergers and acquisitions.

Fair market value appraisals have been required for corporate tax returns since 1954 and have become important in more mergers and acquisitions because of changes in accounting rules.

The Accounting Principles Board Opinion Number 16, Business Combinations, issued in August 1970 contains guidelines that have reduced the number of mergers that may be accounted for on a pooling-of-interests basis and correspondingly increased the number that must be accounted for on a purchase basis. When the purchase method of accounting is used, acquired assets must be revalued to reflect their fair market value. Furthermore, purchase acquisitions are much more likely to be taxable for federal income tax purposes.

Pre-merger and post-merger appraisals are recommended for the sake of both parties. In the post-merger phase when purchase accounting is used, appraisals are essential to distribute the purchase price to each item of value purchased for recordkeeping, income tax, and insurance purposes. The two basic approaches to business valuation are discussed: item-by-item appraisals and capitalization of the estimated future earnings. Determination of the appropriate capitalization rate is described. These two approaches to valuation are illustrated in a simplified case study.

Tender offers for stock are a financial device for acquiring other companies. Reference to the financial press shows that such activity is continuing and very likely increasing from its low point in 1971. Professor Douglas Austin has been a student of tender offers, purchases of stock for treasury purposes, and of proxy contests. In the present article he reviews the history of tender offers, and compares tender offers in the period 1956-1967 with those of 1968-1972. The rise and fall in the number of tender offers coincided with the third merger wave and may be considered to be a part of the same general movement. The analytical procedures of Smalter and Lancey would help to explain why the tender offers discussed were made at all. The analysis and data presented by Professor Austin help in furthering the understanding of the basis, importance, and degree of success of tender offers.

The Austin article discusses the reasons for the changing relative number of cash and exchange tender offers, and the conditions that are more likely to be associated with a successful tender. After 1967 there was an increase in the proportion of tenders that were only partly successful or totally unsuccessful. Corporations may have learned how to guard themselves from such attacks. Professor Austin documents such important aspects of tender offers as bidding premiums, industrial classifications of attacking and target firms, and the profitability of target firms. The asset size, liquidity, and market-value-to-book-value ratios of the target firms are examined.

23. P/E ANALYSIS IN ACQUISITION STRATEGY*

DONALD J. SMALTER †
and RODERIC C. LANCEY ††

The achievements of most successful growth companies have been based on a mixture of three types of strategies: internal programs for new products and market development, joint ventures, and acquisitions. Each of these routes provides top management with a means to implement overall corporate objectives and goals.

Use of the mergers and acquisitions route has been increasing sharply during the past several years. Continued growth in its popularity is likely because it serves numerous corporate needs and growth motivations. An acquisition can strengthen a weakness; for instance, it can help to fill a raw material need or improve a vulnerable patent position. It can buy valuable time for a company. It can help management capitalize on the strengths of each partner and utilize the synergistic possibilities which may arise in terms of geographic and product line expansion. It can provide diversification opportunities. And it can enable a company to enter growth markets and reduce its dependence on existing activities for earnings growth.

One aspect of growth by acquisition which deserves particular attention is that of maintaining and improving the acquiring company's price-earnings (P/E) ratio. The importance of this ratio in any acquisition strategy may not always be fully appreciated; yet the ratio has a decided impact on the range of purchasable companies. The relationship between the P/E ratio of the candidate and that of the prospective parent determines whether there is earnings dilution and hence whether the survivor can afford to swap stock. Also, the stock market's valuation of the negotiating companies, as reflected in their P/E ratios, is by far the most important financial factor in the negotiation of agreeable exchange terms.[1]

In this discussion we shall summarize the factors which most directly influence and control a company stock's P/E ratio. We shall attempt to develop a useful perspective on the ratio's controlling effect in stock-for-stock and stock-for-assets acquisition strategy. More specifically, these

---

*Reprinted from *Harvard Business Review* (November-December, 1966), pp. 85-95: © 1966 by the President and Fellows of Harvard College; all rights reserved.
†Corporate Director of Strategic Planning, International Minerals and Chemical Corporation, Skokie, Illinois.
††Corporate Planner, International Minerals and Chemical Corporation, Skokie, Illinois.
[1]See F. K. Reilly, "What Determines the Ratio of Exchange in Corporate Mergers?" *Financial Analysts Journal* (November-December, 1962), p. 47.

questions will be addressed:

What factors appear to control the level of the P/E ratio?
How can a company raise its P/E ratio?
How can an acquisition upgrade the company's per-share earnings results?
How does a candidate company's P/E ratio affect the acquiring firm's acquisition strategy?
Under what circumstances (if any) can both parties experience "magical gains"?

A high P/E ratio brings a number of values to any company. It enables a more advantageous exchange of shares; that is, it enables "cheaper" acquisitions of other companies, a point to be developed later in this discussion. Also, it generates capital gains for shareholders and provides additional incentive for executive stock-option compensation. It enhances the possible use of stock as a substitute for dividends, thereby preserving cash for internal expansion, and provides greater net proceeds to the company for any new equity offering.

Of course, good decision rules for selecting candidates for acquisition are not by themselves the answer to management's need. As we know well from the experience of our own company, International Minerals & Chemical Corporation, and other organizations, much work must also go into making contacts with the heads of other companies, negotiating prices, revising the post-merger organization structure, and related activities. These tasks will *not* be discussed in this article, but their omission here takes nothing away from their importance.

INFLUENCES ON P/E LEVEL

The range of P/E ratios for companies varies widely. Within the process industries, for example, the ratios range from a low in the vicinity of 8 to a high of over 40. Exhibit 23-1 shows average ratios during the past three years for several components of the process industries.

Generally, a few companies in each category enjoy a P/E ratio considerably higher than the group average. To illustrate:

1. Pennsalt, a specialty chemical manufacturer, has consistently commanded a P/E ratio of at least 20 during the past several years. Two points seem to stand out: first, the company has maintained an aggressive R & D program, with emphasis on "glamour" chemicals; and second, it has *frequently* introduced new chemical specialty products which apparently impress investors.
2. In the diversified chemical category, Du Pont has enjoyed a ratio typically 20 percent to 25 percent above the group average. This highly diversified corporation has supported an innovative research program for years and regularly introduces new products which seem to convey promises of great commercial potential, such as Corfam, its new substitute for leather.

EXHIBIT 23-1
AVERAGE PRICE-EARNINGS RATIOS IN SELECTED PROCESS INDUSTRIES

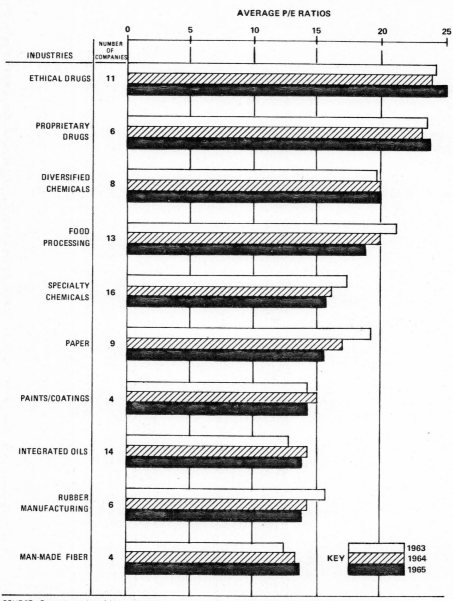

SOURCE: Quarterly service of Value Line Investment Survey, Part III (New York, Arnold Bernhard & Co., Inc.).

We have conducted an extensive study of the literature to learn more about the factors affecting the P/E ratio. No great agreement was found among investment analysts on how to rate the price of a stock. In fact, the consensus of experienced investment analysts seems to be that much of the rating process is based on psychological reactions to future prospects and on subjective judgments rather than on detailed, soundly conceived quantitative analysis. Only recently have there been any serious attempts to develop formulas for determining the future market value of a stock in a systematic mathematical manner. The editorial box following this article includes some of the more revealing passages from articles which deal with aspects of P/E ratios germane to this article.

Controlling Factors

On the basis of our study, we have selected six factors controlling P/E ratios. Ranked in order of importance, they are as follows:

1. The prospect of *future per-share earnings growth* is the obvious primary influence affecting the P/E ratio.
2. Investors want *minimum fluctuation* from the anticipated earnings trend line. In other words, lower risks are associated with stocks which appear to promise lower per-share earnings volatility.
3. Investors favor companies which promise earnings growth for *long term*. They develop confidence, based on a company's historical performance, that the company's earnings growth will continue steadily for many years' duration.
4. Heavy emphasis on *research and development* is often a major component of a company's growth image. Investors are willing to pay high prices for Polaroid, Corning Glass, 3M, and IBM because they expect these firms to identify and successfully commercialize new products.
5. *Frequent introduction of new products* reinforces investors' confidence that R & D expenditures are productive. Thus, R & D results and investors' expectations become closely associated and help to sustain superior P/E ratios.
6. Companies which participate in *recognized* growth markets are apt to have bright futures. This point follows from the previous two and means that companies which expend resources in growth markets will receive recognition from investors, provided earnings benefits appear achievable.

When judging the price they are willing to pay, many investors, especially the more speculative types looking for capital gains appreciation, tend to place relatively low marks on such well known factors as:

A high rate of return on equity.
A high rate of earnings retention or plowback.
A high rate of dividend payout.
A high rate of dividend yield.
A low level of debt utilization in the capital structure.

The last point—de-emphasis of the level of debt utilization—appears significant. It can be shown that many companies with high P/E ratios possess long-term debt in excess of 30 percent of capital structure. This illustrates, perhaps, that such companies have *generated* numerous opportunities which warrant extension of their debt burden, with the benefits accruing to the stockholders through the effects of leveraging.

RAISING THE RATIO

From the previous discussion we may conclude that management must continuously strive to produce a *steady* upward trend in per-share earnings over the long term. First of all, internally generated growth opportunities should be carefully considered. Projects should be appraised both for overall profitability and for the incremental risks which would be incurred if additional debt financing were used to lever the anticipated profits for the common shareholder. Secondly, earnings growth can benefit directly from a deliberate acquisition strategy. A company can acquire other firms that (a) expand its market position in fields of high growth potential, (b) improve its technological capability and image, or (c) improve its per-share earnings because of a favorable trading position. Let us consider each of these three possibilities.

Picking Growth Prospects

In attempting to develop a rational approach for planning its growth, management should first examine growth opportunities and rates in the industries and/or business missions which it serves.[2] As illustrated in Exhibit 23-2, these rates can vary considerably, typically from 8 percent or 9 percent down to 2 percent per year. Spectacular growth in excess of 20 percent will be found in some of the newer, usually technically oriented and specialized markets until they begin to approach supply-and-demand equilibrium.

It is much more difficult to grow profitably in mature industries which demonstrate a decaying growth rate or a rate below that of the gross national product. So it is desirable to identify those businesses which have good or even outstanding growth rate potentials. This objective should dominate any searching process unless it is possible to pinpoint *bargain* candidates, i.e., sick or poorly performing companies that can be converted into healthy, contributing assets if marketing, merchandising, or other types of know-how are applied.

Buying Technology

In considering the acquisition of companies with desired technological strengths, management should ask if the *time* is right for buying. In a

---

[2]For an exposition of corporate missions, see Donald J. Smalter and Rudy L. Ruggles, Jr., "Six Business Lessons From the Pentagon," *Harvard Business Review* (March-April, 1966), pp. 65-68.

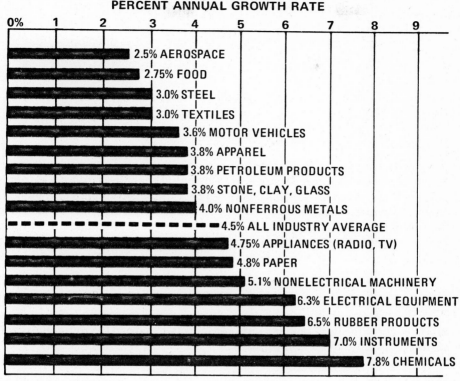

EXHIBIT 23-2
INDUSTRY GROWTH RATE PROJECTIONS THROUGH 1980

PERCENT ANNUAL GROWTH RATE

2.5% AEROSPACE
2.75% FOOD
3.0% STEEL
3.0% TEXTILES
3.6% MOTOR VEHICLES
3.8% APPAREL
3.8% PETROLEUM PRODUCTS
3.8% STONE, CLAY, GLASS
4.0% NONFERROUS METALS
4.5% ALL INDUSTRY AVERAGE
4.75% APPLIANCES (RADIO, TV)
4.8% PAPER
5.1% NONELECTRICAL MACHINERY
6.3% ELECTRICAL EQUIPMENT
6.5% RUBBER PRODUCTS
7.0% INSTRUMENTS
7.8% CHEMICALS

SOURCE: "ECONOMISTS PAINT A BRIGHT PICTURE FOR 1980," *CHEMICAL ENGINEERING*, JANUARY 31, 1966, p. 34.

business where technology is critical, there is a well known time lag before it is possible to capitalize on scientific findings. For instance, over the years Textron has demonstrated awareness of this fact; it has acquired companies that already have expended substantial efforts in developing new technology. At the appropriate time, but not before, these companies were acquired, and additional financial resources were applied to capitalize on their know-how.

Naturally, it is preferable to acquire firms whose products are in early growth phases of the life cycle, rather than declining phases, and that possess exceptional potential for creating new products from their R & D programs. But simply to look at an industry segment and find that it is growing is not enough. Inspection must take place in depth, and analyses must be conducted which determine *where* the profits are to be made. In devising a growth strategy, questions like these must be addressed:

Should horizontal moves be undertaken for the purpose of broadening the product line?

What products, when combined with present products, could be sold profitably through common distribution channels?
Should vertical integration be pursued?
What percentage of the market will be a captive market in the future?
What are the possibilities for technical innovation?
Could any shortcuts in distribution channels be developed that would increase profits and bring a unique competitive advantage?
Are there companies available which might fulfill these needs and desires?

The answers to these questions do not come easily. They require inquisitive, perceptive, and time-consuming analysis.

Favorable Trading Position

In any acquisition involving the use of common stock or other securities exchangeable into common stock, it is essential that the acquired earnings be evaluated for their per-share contribution to the surviving company. If the increase in the number of shares is proportionally greater than the increase in annual earnings, then *dilution* is incurred. However, *the opposite can also occur*. Whether or not dilution results depends on:

1. The ratio of the buying price to the earnings of the acquired company.
2. The value assigned to the securities to be exchanged by the surviving company.

This brings us to the next major question in our discussion—determining whether an acquisition will upgrade earnings per share in the merged organization and improve its P/E ratio.

IMPACT ON EARNINGS

Here we want to propose a way of analyzing anticipated earnings. For the sake of specificity, let us consider the hypothetical case outlined in Exhibit 23-3.

The management of a growing corporation, Company A, is considering the purchase of either of two smaller companies, B and C. Both B and C are believed to offer A some attractive opportunities to serve A's needs and growth objectives. Although B and C have the same assumed sales, earnings, and shares outstanding (an extremely unlikely occurrence, in reality, but convenient for purposes of illustration), B has a considerably greater P/E ratio. This advantage substantially differentiates the bargaining positions of B and C in merger negotiations. As a result, B negotiates a selling price of 22.5 times earnings, well above A's multiplier of 18. A's shareholders would then incur some minor and immediate dilution in their per-share earnings if B were bought.

This would not be true, however, if Company C were bought. Here shareholders of Company A would benefit by obtaining an immediate boost in per-share earnings in the current year. In this case, A would utilize its higher P/E ratio to escalate per-share earnings. (Looking at the problem from the standpoint of stockholders of B and C, per-share earnings for B would rise from $5 to $5.82, and per-share earnings for C would drop from $5 to $4.37.)

Exhibit 23-3

COMPARATIVE EFFECT ON EARNINGS OF TWO PROSPECTIVE ACQUISITIONS

(PURCHASE BY EXCHANGE OF STOCK)

Financial Data Prior To Acquisition

	Company A	Candidate B	Candidate C
Sales ($ millions)	$300	$100	$100
Earnings ($ millions)	$ 25	$ 10	$ 10
Shares (millions)	10	2	2
Earnings per share	$ 2.50	$ 5	$ 5
Stock price	$ 45	$100	$ 75
P/E multiple	18	20	15

Acquisition of B by A

Negotiated price is $225 million, or 22.5 times current estimated earnings. This is equivalent to a 12.5% premium over the current P/E ratio for B's stock. To make the purchase, therefore, A must issue 5 million shares of its common stock ($225 million divided by $45).

Earnings-per-share computations are as follows:

(a) COMPANY B—$2.00 per share ($10 million earnings divided by 5 million shares).

(b) COMPOSITE OPERATIONS—$2.33 per share (composite earnings of $25 million plus $10 million, or $35 million, divided by 10 million shares of A's stock outstanding plus 5 million shares issued to B).

(c) EFFECT ON SHAREHOLDERS OF A—6.8% dilution ($2.50 minus $2.33, or $0.17, divided by $2.50).

Acquisition of C by A

Negotiated price is $150 million, or 15 times current estimated earnings. This is the same ratio as the current one on the market for C's stock. To make the purchase, therefore, A must issue 3.333 million shares of its common stock ($150 million divided by $45).

Earnings-per-share computations are as follows:

(a) COMPANY C—$3.00 per share ($10 million divided by 3.333 million shares).

(b) COMPOSITE OPERATIONS—$2.62 per share (composite earnings of $25 million plus $10 million, or $35 million, divided by 10 million shares of A's stock outstanding plus 3.333 million shares issued to C).

(c) EFFECT ON SHAREHOLDERS OF A—4.8% gain ($2.62 minus $2.50, or $0.12, divided by $2.50).

But these numerical comparisons do not provide the answer. It is axiomatic that A carefully identify its motivations and needs in acquiring C instead of, or in addition to, B. Immediate per-share benefits may well prove illusory unless the composite company can exploit some available strengths and capabilities which will boost the acquired earnings over the longer term, at a rate *at least* equivalent to what A expects to achieve without acquiring C. Otherwise, C would gradually exert a "sea anchor" effect on Company A's overall earnings growth; i.e., C would gradually increase *future* dilution.

Company A should also attempt to estimate how investors will react to an acquisition of B or C. Exhibit 23-4 shows composite stock prices which could result from a range of P/E multiples for each merger, as well as the

EXHIBIT 23-4
RANGE OF STOCK PRICES DUE TO MERGER OF COMPANY A
WITH COMPANY B OR COMPANY C

P/E ratio	Composite stock price of A and B	Value of extinguished B stock	Composite stock price of A and C	Value of extinguished C stock
15	—	—	$39.30	$65.50
16	—	—	41.87	69.87
17	—	—	44.50	74.25
18	$42.00	$104.75	47.25	78.62
19	44.25	110.62	49.75	83.00
20	46.62	116.37	—	—
21	49.00	122.25	—	—
22	51.25	128.00	—	—

values associated with the "extinguished" shares of B or C. We see that:

1. If A acquires B, investors would have to upgrade A's multiplier to at least 19.3 to sustain its current $45 stock price; otherwise, the dilutional effect of acquiring B will immediately lower A's stock value, and B's original shareholders would not obtain the value originally anticipated.

2. If A acquires C, the multiplier could relax to 17 without reducing A's current stock price, and *any higher value would benefit both A's and C's shareholders.*

These are only the immediate effects on A's existing shareholders. Of equal, if not greater, importance are the price effects over the longer term. Management should, therefore, focus major attention on the likely P/E multipliers which investors will apply to future composite earnings.

Testing for Dilution

The reader may already have noted in these straight common-for-common swap examples that there is a sample method to test for dilution: divide the acquiring company's stock value by the negotiated P/E multiple being applied to the acquired earnings. (For instance, if A acquires B, divide $45 by 22.5 to get $2; if A acquires C, divide $45 by 15 to get $3.) The quotient should equal or exceed the acquiring company's current per-share earnings; if it does not, immediate dilution will result, as illustrated in Exhibit 23-3.

In more complicated swap arrangements involving use of securities convertible into common stock at some future date, the same technique can be used. Here the conversion price is divided by a multiplier based on the level of acquired earnings at the probable date of conversion. The quotient is then compared with per-share earnings anticipated at that future date *without* the proposed acquisition.

STRATEGIC CONSIDERATIONS

Exhibit 23-3 was designed to illustrate how the P/E ratio relates to imme-

EXHIBIT 23-5
IMMEDIATE PER-SHARE EFFECTS OF PROSPECTIVE ACQUISITIONS BY COMPANY A

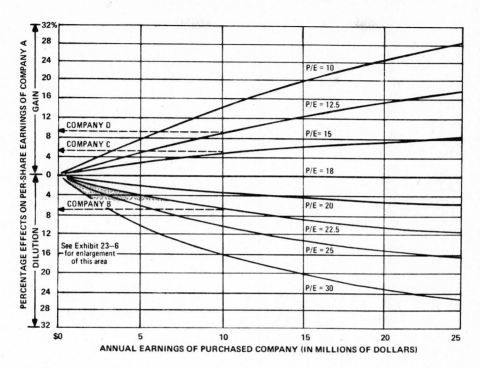

diate dilution or additions to per-share earnings. However, these two simple examples fail to provide adequate perspective on how the P/E ratio can influence selection and implementation of an acquisition strategy. To do this, the *amount* of earnings being acquired must be considered simultaneously along with the negotiated P/E multiplier being applied to them, as illustrated in Exhibit 23-5. This diagram is constructed with Company A data (10 million shares, earnings of $25 million, a stock value of $45, and a P/E of 18). It measures per-share effects on Company A's current earnings ($2.50 per share) for any combination of negotiated P/E ratios over the range of 10 to 30 for a given amount of acquired earning power.

A similar diagram could be readily constructed for any company whose management desires a tool for quick, visual reading of the effects on earnings of prospective acquisitions.

Exhibit 23-5 obviously divides into two fields of interest, with an 18 multiplier representing the boundary line between dilution of and additions to per-share earnings. Consider the field of prospective acquisitions with earnings at negotiated P/E ratios below 18:

1. Company C, which earns $10 million, would bring an immediate beneficial boost of 12 cents, or 4.8 percent, to Company

A's per-share earnings. But perhaps another candidate—call it
Company D—with the same approximate earning power and
attributes for A's particular needs is available at a P/E of 12.5.
The benefits to A would be over 9 percent, or double those of
Company C.

2. Alternatively, perhaps A should be considering a larger candidate with a somewhat lower P/E than 15, and reach for substantially greater benefits than C can offer. A candidate with $15
million in earnings and a P/E of 12.5 would generate an addition
of about 32 cents (approximately 13 percent) to A's immediate
per-share results.

ACCOUNTING FOR GROWTH

To refer back to the example previously described, acquisition of Company B by Company A would immediately reduce A's current per-share
earnings by 17 cents, or nearly 7 percent (see Exhibit 23-3). Before proceeding
to absorb this impact, A's management should consider the following kinds
of questions:

Should there be a guideline or decision rule which sets a limit on
dilution due to acquisitions?
If so, should this statement apply uniformly to all candidates, or
should a range of limits be selected in recognition of the purpose
or motive that may be served by selected types of candidates?
Even after adjusting for anticipated synergisms and savings, will
the acquired earnings grow fast enough to eliminate per-share
dilution over the next several years?
Is it likely that some permanent drawbacks will result which are
justifiable in terms of overall corporate needs and objectives?

One area likely to be of special interest to growth-oriented companies is
the acquisition of new technology. Company A, for example, may have
inadequacies or even voids in its R & D skills, manufacturing technologies,
or patent position in an attractive growth market. By identifying its technical needs, A could set some specific acquisition decision rules for this area,
such as:

1. Up to 5 percent immediate dilution is acceptable even though
there are no direct assurances that acquired earnings will grow
as fast as A's projected rate.
2. The acquired company's P/E ratio should exceed 22.5.

The shaded area in Exhibit 23-6 blocks out the resulting "field of interest"
for A's searching process. This delineation restricts A's candidate list to small
companies—those with earnings ranging from $1 million to $7.5 million.
(The lower limit of $1 million is selected arbitrarily for this discussion, since,
in Company's A's case, dilution resulting from buying a company with earnings below this level would be minor.) A prime motivation would be to
exploit substantially greater P/E ratios of *qualified* candidates which have
already obtained recognition of technical competence from investors. Note
that a candidate earning slightly over $2 million would be acceptable, even
with a negotiated P/E of 30! Company A would, therefore, deliberately

EXHIBIT 23-6
FIELD OF INTEREST IN SEARCHING FOR ACQUISITIONS

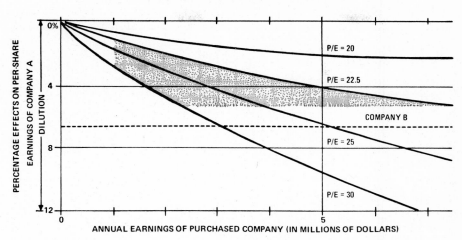

search for technology sources whose P/E ratio would "rub off" onto A's overall image to investors and either reduce or eliminate adverse stock-price effects.

Company B does not strictly satisfy these guidelines; it falls outside the colored area. Perhaps B is attractive, however, because it could save A several years in building a position in a desirable growth market. If so, this means that A is looking to B primarily for direct contributions to A's earnings growth. This in turn raises a more serious issue: How fast must acquired earnings grow to wash out immediate dilution during the next several years? Exhibit 23-7 has been prepared to illustrate the answer to this problem:

> The exhibit assumes that Company A is planning on a 10 percent per year growth in its per-share earnings for current operations. To learn how fast acquired earnings must grow to eliminate dilution completely within three or four years for a range of negotiated P/E ratios, run a line horizontally from the acquisition's P/E ratio to the time period curves; the growth rate figure directly beneath the point of intersection is the answer.

The results are somewhat unsettling, as Company B's earnings, including synergistic contributions and savings, would have to grow at 18 percent per year to eliminate dilution within three years and 16 percent per year to wash out dilution in four years. A higher priced candidate—say, Company E, priced at 25 times earnings—would demand acquired earnings growth in excess of 20 percent per year to eliminate dilution. Since these levels of earnings growth are so high, A's management is challenged to define (at least to itself) the reasons which would justify some *permanent* dilution in its per-share earnings.

It is difficult to generalize on these issues, since each company encounters a unique set of circumstances, including its own anticipated rate of earnings growth, its P/E ratio, and the P/E ratio of desirable acquisition candidates.

EXHIBIT 23-7
EARNINGS GROWTH OF ACQUIRED COMPANY REQUIRED TO ELIMINATE DILUTION

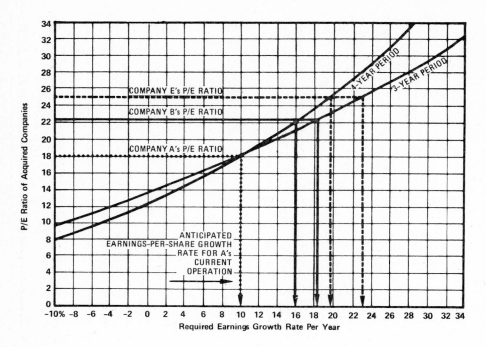

It seems clear, however, that management should deliberately define its acquisition decision rules and clearly perceive the per-share effects of each acquisition candidate. Preparation of charts similar to Exhibits 23-5 and 23-7 is particularly helpful in developing this perspective and in formulating an overall acquisition strategy.

CONCLUSION

Growth companies have been sharply increasing their use of acquisitions as a major component of their overall corporate growth strategy. At the same time, they apparently recognize that an acquisition program can be meaningful and truly successful only if it is closely keyed to corporate motives, needs, and objectives, and contributes to the company's longer term growth goals for its per-share earnings.

Per-share earnings are directly affected by any acquisition based on the exchange of common stock or securities convertible into common stock. When this is the case, management's acquisition strategy should be formulated to link earnings growth goals to the company's P/E ratio. This ratio, when compared with the most likely negotiated P/E ratio of qualified acquisition candidates, directly determines whether per-share earnings will be diluted or beneficially boosted, both immediately and during the longer term future.

In this article we have suggested that acquisition strategy can be more clearly perceived and communicated if management defines the firm's fields of interest—that is, identifies preferred zones in a diagram like Exhibit 23-5, which correlates the amount of acquired earning power, the related P/E ratios, and the resulting per-share effects. Such a diagram forces management to think through the role being assigned to acquisitions and to ascertain whether or not candidates which serve business needs and motives are also compatible with the company's basic financial goal—*sustained* growth in per-share earnings.

WHAT EXPERTS SAY ABOUT P/E RATIOS

"High price-earnings multiples typically reflect investor satisfaction with companies of high quality or with those which have experienced several years of expansion and rising earnings. In such cases, prices have often risen faster than earnings. A resultant increase in price-earnings ratios may be justified in individual instances, but under the impact of public approval or even glamour, it often runs to extremes." —S. Francis Nicholson, "Price-Earnings Ratios," *Financial Analysts Journal* (July-August, 1960), p. 45.

"Although prospective earnings frequently enter into theoretical analyses, any attempt at empirical measurement of earnings ordinarily requires heavy reliance on past data. Since stock prices are determined primarily by how people feel about the future, considerable instability has resulted in computed price-earnings ratios." —Oswald D. Bowlin, "The Price-Earnings Ratio: A Whimsical Variable," *Commercial Financial Chronicle* (September 7, 1961), p. 4.

"The extent to which he [the investor] will be willing to pay more depends upon the outlook for the earnings and dividends of the two companies and the investor's best guess as to how other investors will view the two firms sometime in the future." —Sanford L. Margoshes, "Price-Earnings Ratio in Financial Analysis," *Financial Analysts Journal* (November-December, 1960), p. 126.

"The price-earnings concept is relevant principally in analyses of growth stocks. It is fairly obvious that IBM's notoriously high P/E (currently around 50) reflects an expectation that its earnings will grow considerably. A corporation whose earnings are stable, on the other hand, is valued by investors principally for its net-asset value and/or its yield. . . . How *should* stock prices be related to earnings? Scarcely any two analysts will answer this question quite the same way; but most would probably agree that, in gauging the answer for any particular stock, there are two basic judgments the investor must make at the outset: one about the company's expected growth rate; another about the return the public will demand from stock investments in general." —"Personal Investing," *Fortune* (January, 1963), pp. 184 and 186.

24. VALUATION FACTORS AND TECHNIQUES IN MERGERS AND ACQUISITIONS*

JOHN HEATH, JR.†

Corporate mergers and acquisitions have been on the increase in recent years; in 1969, mergers reached an all-time high of approximately 6,100. The rate continued high in the first part of 1970, but the subsequent sharp decline in the stock market and the high interest rates caused a dramatic decrease in merger activity in the balance of 1970 and through 1971.

Even while the number of mergers and acquisitions was growing steadily, there was—and still is—an alarming increase in the corporate divorce rate. A number of causes are responsible for the failure of so many mergers, but one of the most basic is the lack of understanding of fundamental valuation theory by those involved in negotiating mergers and acquisitions. Too often the principal valuation consideration is limited to some price/earnings ratio developed from minimal basic data.

While all the facets of valuation theory cannot be covered in one relatively short article, we can touch on the principal concepts and definitions pertinent to valuation of a corporate entity as a going concern.

FAIR MARKET VALUE

Since 1954, federal tax regulations have specified the use of fair market value in corporate tax returns. This term has become the basis of value used in mergers and acquisitions.

What is fair market value and how is it determined? The generally accepted definition is this: fair market value is the price at which property would change hands between a willing buyer and a willing seller, each having reasonable knowledge of all pertinent facts and neither being under compulsion to buy or sell.

Fair market value is without a doubt the best-defined of valuation terms; appraisers and others involved in valuation work generally agree on this definition. However, since appraising is not an exact science, most valuation processes contain an element of opinion.

To express an opinion of the fair market value of a business entity involves consideration of many factors including but not limited to past

---

*From *Financial Executive* (April, 1972), pp. 34-36, 38, 40, 42, 44. Reprinted by permission.
†Vice President, Marshall and Stevens Incorporated.

earning performance, future earning potential, economic climate of the industry, and, in any particular business, a study of the health, ability, vitality, and the age of management. Further, in expressing such an opinion, one must consider to whom it is expressed, for what purpose, and at what time.

Some persons have gone so far as to state that fair market value is a fictitious number when valuing a business entity or even a significant segment of a business because subjective factors are always present and affect the opinion to a great degree.

Let's consider an example to illustrate this point. An aerospace company wished to acquire the government-furnished equipment in its plant. The government was willing to sell the equipment at a fair market value. Here we had a willing buyer and a willing seller. But what was the fair market value of the equipment? The original cost to the government of some 1,600 pieces of equipment of all kinds installed in the contractor's plant between 1950 and 1969 amounted to $22 million. An appraiser expressed the opinion that, if the company wished to keep it, the equipment assembled in place for continued use had a fair market value of $15 million. It was also his opinion that, if the company did not want it and the government had to remove the equipment and sell it in an orderly manner on the open market, the equipment would bring only about $4.5 million. Either transaction would involve a willing buyer and a willing seller; but the terms and conditions radically affected the opinion of value.

PRE-MERGER VALUATION APPLICATIONS

After the basic hurdle of determining what constitutes fair market value has been overcome, we can move on to discover how the technique of determining value enters into the acquisition process. Most businessmen think of determining the fair market value by bringing in an appraiser to allocate the purchase price after the acquisition has been consummated. Although this typically has been the way in which this problem has been handled, I believe it is important to include the value determination in pre-merger planning and negotiations.

One of the first areas to be studied in any merger or acquisition is the existing assets of the selling company. Buying companies often are surprised after the acquisition to learn about assets they didn't know existed, and, in many cases, to learn sadly of the non-existence of assets carried in the seller's financial statements. A checklist of capital assets can be helpful in preventing these kinds of errors. By following the checklist, a potential buyer will have a better understanding of what is or is not being acquired. The list should contain the following principal classes of assets:

Working Capital and Non-Operating Investments
Cash
Receivables
Inventories
  Raw materials
  Work in progress
  Finished goods
Non-operating investments

Tangible Assets	**Intangible Assets**
Land	Patents
Buildings	Patent applications
Leasehold improvements	Franchise agreements
Leasehold interests in real estate	License agreements
Machinery and equipment	Commercial contracts
Automotive	Research and development
Dies, jigs, fixtures	Technical know-how
Molds, patterns, special tooling	Special staff
Drawings	Product line
Prototypes	Goodwill

This is, of course, a generalized list, and it can be expanded greatly as circumstances dictate.

While many of these assets may exist, some may have a negative value. For instance, old buildings or machinery may have a value lower than the cost to remove them. Many times machinery appears in the accounting records when in reality it is long gone. There are also situations when long-term contracts to supply finished goods at a fixed price could result in a substantial loss.

An awareness of the existence of each of the assets included in the checklist is of significant importance to a potential buyer. Very often, however, a buyer is not in a position to have his staff make an investigation at the seller's premises. In such a situation an outsider may be called upon to investigate tangible assets using the cover of an insurance appraisal in order not to divulge negotiations going on in confidence.

The second area to be studied in an acquisition or merger is the age, condition, and capability of the assets to meet anticipated production requirements. With this information, the buyer can estimate the capital expenditures necessary to replace obsolete or wornout assets.

Quite often an appraiser is called upon to make a "broad brush" study to determine the value of the tangible assets within broad limits. Such a study gives the prospective buyer an idea of the magnitude of his expected acquisition, thus providing a basis for a go or no-go decision.

When a buyer and a seller come together, a number of other considerations are involved in establishing a price at which the transaction should take place. Does the transaction coincide with the over-all business strategy of the buyer and the seller? Are the products involved complementary and are they in an expanding—or a retracting—market? Can marketing costs be reduced by a partial or full consolidation of sales staffs? Of considerable interest to the buyer might be a study of the cost of developing a competing product compared with the cost of the acquisition, including a present-worth study of earnings or losses during the development period.

Studies also can be made from an engineering standpoint. Are the facilities of optimum size? Is there room for expansion? Are they laid out properly? What types of material handling equipment are available? What is the relationship of manufacturing space to warehouse space? How is the site situated with regard to rail and truck transportation? Is the topography suitable and practical for expansion of the facility?

Let us suppose that the buyer and seller have agreed in principle that a merger or an acquisition is mutually beneficial, and the negotiations start in earnest. How is the transaction to be structured and what is to be the purchase price? Certainly many criteria have to be considered, and in any given situation one factor may predominate. For example, one buyer may prefer to make the acquisition through the use of his stock, another to pay cash for assets, a third to pay cash for stock. One seller may accept only cash, while another, wanting to defer his tax consequences, will accept only the buyer's stock for his stock.

Another element to be considered is the tax position of the buyer and seller. In my opinion, the decision to consummate a business combination should not be determined by federal taxes. However, both the buyer and seller should know the tax consequences of a given transaction.

A significant rise in the number of taxable transactions may be anticipated because of the restrictions placed on pooling and the required amortization of goodwill in an accounting purchase as a result of Opinions No. 16 and No. 17 (effective November 1, 1970) of the Accounting Principles Board of the American Institute of Certified Public Accountants. These opinions set down the guidelines to be used in determining whether an acquisition is to be accounted for as a pooling of interests or as a purchase.

A prudent investor needs to know the benefits, liabilities, and the possible tax consequences of structuring a transaction as taxable or non-taxable. In a non-taxable transaction, the basis for depreciation of the acquired property "flows through" to the acquiring concern for tax purposes. Any premium paid by the company in excess of book value is not recoverable through depreciation, and, in some instances, is not amortizable.

On the other hand, in a taxable transaction where assets are acquired or where at least 80 percent of the stock of a corporation is acquired followed by a liquidation into the acquiring company (a Section 334 (b) 2 liquidation), the price paid must be allocated on the basis of fair market value to all the assets acquired, tangible or intangible, depreciable or non-depreciable. Allocation requires an estimate of the value of the various classes of property and their relationship to the total purchase price paid. These values provide the basis for the calculation of the amount of potential future depreciation and the exposure to depreciation recapture.

A valuation study made prior to the culmination of the deal can be of great assistance to both buyer and seller. A seller is interested in knowing the value of the enterprise and the value of each class of assets in order that he may calculate capital gains and recapture taxes should he sell the assets.

A buyer is interested in the same information, but for different reasons. If he plans a stock-for-stock transaction to be treated as a pooling, he needs to determine the value of the enterprise. If he plans a stock-for-stock acquisition to be treated as a purchase, he needs to determine values for each class of assets in order to calculate accounting depreciation and possible goodwill amortization. The buyer would also be interested in ascertaining asset class values to weigh the pros and cons of acquiring assets for cash and the resulting depreciation he will recover versus buying the stock of the company for cash and liquidating under Internal Revenue Code Section 334 (b) 2. The latter procedure allows a write-up of the assets, but also triggers recapture taxes. In this situation, the buyer will need to ascertain values in order to calculate and weigh the present worth of future depreciation and amortization (of intangibles) resulting from the write-up of the assets versus the amount of recapture tax liability.

POST-MERGER VALUATION APPLICATIONS

Following a merger or acquisition, an acquiring company needs to (1) distribute the purchase cost to each element of the enterprise in conformance with federal tax requirements and generally accepted accounting practice; (2) provide, if not already available, an accurate inventory of property, plant, and equipment, and a system for its control either manually or electronically; (3) establish a means of estimating proper insurable values and provide a record of the property in sufficient detail to meet the "proof of loss" requirements of the insurance policy.

If a selling company sells assets for a lump sum, it will need to allocate the proceeds to the various assets in order to calculate its tax liabilities.

Space permits a discussion of only the first requirement. However, meeting the other requirements follows logically and easily from the work done to allocate the purchase price.

Federal tax law and regulations state that when a taxable acquisition occurs, the price paid must be distributed to all of the assets acquired, tangible or intangible, depreciable and nondepreciable, in accordance with their fair market value. Only cash and its equivalent are excluded from the apportionment. Interpretative decisions from the tax courts and other tax review agencies indicate that inventory and accounts receivable are considered non-cash items, although many taxpayers continue to exclude accounts receivable from the allocation.

At present, federal tax regulations do not require an allocation of the purchase price in a nontaxable transaction. Rather, the acquired company's tax basis for all assets and liabilities must be carried forward.

Under what situations, then, is an allocation of purchase price to be made? They are as follows: accounting "purchase," cash for assets, and cash for stock and liquidation.

An accounting purchase is a transaction in which the basis of the assets does not necessarily change for tax purposes, and which cannot qualify as a pooling for accounting purposes under APB Opinion No. 16.

A cash for assets transaction must be treated as a purchase and is considered taxable to the seller (a Code Section No. 167 transaction).

A cash for stock (at least 80 percent acquired within 12 months) transaction followed within two years by filing a plan of liquidation (a Code Section 334 (b) 2 transaction) also provides for allocation of the price paid to all assets acquired. This usually results in a step-up in basis of the assets for depreciation purposes, but it also triggers depreciation recapture liabilities to the buyer.

In order to illustrate the valuation problems subsequent to an acquisition, let us assume that Corporation A acquires Corporation B, and that we must allocate the purchase cost to the various elements that made up Corporation B. The requirement of the allocation is to establish the fair market value of the whole enterprise and each of its principal elements, including intangibles in proper relationship to each other and to the whole. This value, together with the proper life assignment to each asset, results in an acceptable basis for depreciation and amortization charges.

Before illustrating the valuation process with a case study, I would like to simplify the discussion with a formula:

$$E = WC + (PP + I)$$

or

$$E - WC = (PP + I)$$

in which E represents the enterprise value, WC represents working capital, PP represents plant/property, and I represents intangibles.

Some taxpayers, some accountants, and some taxing agencies attempt to measure the value of intangibles by the "residual" or "dropout" method. In this approach, the value of all tangible assets, working capital, and plant/property is established by appraisal, and the excess of the purchase price over the sum of these values is considered to be a measure of the value of intangibles. When the purchase price is in excess of the tangible assets and the amount of the excess is considered good-will, the tax authorities are sometimes willing to accept this method. However, when the purchase price is equal to or less than the sum of the tangible assets, they usually are not willing to concede that there is no element of goodwill or intangible value in the transaction.

A better approach is to value the enterprise as a whole, giving consideration to the present worth of future benefits, a key indicator of value. This is true whether or not intangibles such as patents and good-will in fact exist. The concept of present worth of future benefits is equally valid in valuing tangibles and intangibles. Consequently, the use of a residual technique to indicate value of intangibles will not re-sult in a reasonable valuation of the present worth of future benefits.

The importance of establishing the value of the total business enter-prise should be recognized. The purchase price of a business will rarely be precisely the same as the fair market value, as previously defined. For example, many business transactions are influenced by the tax position of the buyer and the seller; the tax consequences of the acquisition affect both the mutually acceptable price and the form of the transaction. Other factors, such as the motivations of the principals and the ability of the negotiators, also will affect the price.

Since the purchase price usually will differ from the appraised value, an allocation of the purchase price must be made. The inclusion of all assets of the business in this appraisal, including intangibles, provides an acceptable basis of allocation, and the actual allocation becomes a matter of simple mathematics.

There is no one approach to determining value. An appraiser must use all of the tools available to perform his two jobs—to establish the value of the corporation or business entity acquired, and then to define its several elements, to which a proper and reasonable distribution of the purchase cost must be made on the basis of fair market value.

To establish the value of the corporation, the appraiser must have full access to the people, property, and records that will bear on his conclusions.

The following information, together with appropriate study, analy-sis, and normalization of the company's financial statements, provides a basis for developing a reasonable estimate of projected earnings for the business operation as it is presently conducted with the facilities, talent, and assets currently available to it.

The exact form the data will take depends on the data available. Data is often normalized to a pre-tax cash flow, debt-free basis for ease of comparison. This normalization is necessary because of the myriad of reporting methods allowed under generally accepted accounting prin-ciples, and because of differences such as debt structure and loss carry-forward.

The following must be made available and analyzed:

■ All year-end balance sheets and income statements, preferably audited, for a period of five years and the stub [*sic*] period to the valuation date.

■ All accounting control information relating to inventory, sales, cost, and profit contribution by product line or other segment; property cost and depreciation records; executive compensation; and corporate structure.

■ All records of patents, trademarks, contracts, or other agreements.

■ A history of the company, including all subsidiaries.

Analysis of these items provides data upon which forecasts of earnings, cash flow, etc., can be predicated.

VALUATION PROCESS

Up to this point, the appraiser has been compiling and studying the data needed to begin the valuation process. He is concerned with the same basic considerations as would be any prudent investor—security of principal and prospective income from the investment. From this point on, the appraiser follows a theoretically simple but technically complex procedure. In valuing the whole enterprise, he must seek out financial data on comparable companies in order to determine definitive ratios that can be used to give an indication of the value of the company he is analyzing. The data is analyzed to estimate reasonable future earnings for the subject company.

Capitalizing estimated future earnings requires determination of a capitalization rate consistent with the risk involved. A good indication of capitalization rates may be found in the prices at which the stocks of comparable companies sell on a stock exchange or in the over-the-counter market in relation to their earnings, dividends, and book net worth. The companies used in the comparisons must be carefully scrutinized to be sure that they are truly comparable and that their capital structure, long-term debt, and other elements are similar to those of the company being evaluated.

From the assembled data on the comparative companies, price times earnings, price times dividends, and price-to-net-worth ratios can be computed and applied to the appropriate earnings, dividends, and net worth of the company being valued, which provides an indicated value for the stock of the company. The reliability accorded to the value will vary depending upon the circumstances and, in the final analysis, will be determined by judgment and experience.

In recent years, data has been published on prices paid in reported corporate acquisitions, usually stated in terms of price paid in relation to current earnings and in relation to book net worth.

The fair market value developed as I have described constitutes the fair market value of the stock of the company being valued, assuming it has a market similar to that of the stock to which it is being compared. It also represents, by the very nature of stock transactions on an exchange or in the over-the-counter market, a fair market value to minority stockholders. However, since we are concerned with the value of a total enterprise, a premium factor must be considered to recognize the control aspects of the enterprise. A common premium factor is 25 percent of the market price, although each situation requires separate consideration.

One of the steps in determining the valuation of the various parts of the enterprise requires a review of the working capital of the subject company and a comparison with its normal requirements. This is accomplished by making an analysis of the subject company's historical working capital tradition as related to its historical sales volume. A comparison must then be made with companies in the same industry and with similar sales levels to determine what working capital is normally carried by such companies.

CASE STUDY

Our case study uses a corporate entity with a history of earnings which permits a forecast of reasonable future income. (Consideration of corporations with a history of losses, tax loss carry-forwards, and similar situations is beyond the scope of this study.)

For purposes of illustration, we have a simplified case study, which assumes a business enterprise whose past history results in a forecast of future earnings on a pre-tax cash flow basis of $3,100,000 per year. From a study of the earnings of selected comparable companies converted to a similar basis, let us assume a cash flow multiplier of 6.0, which represents prices paid in the market for minority shares. To establish the value of the whole, we must add a premium for control of a prospective acquisition, say of 25 percent, giving an adjusted multiplier of 7.5. Using the projected cash flow of $3,100,000 and the multiplier of 7.5, we generate an indicator of total enterprise value of $23,250,000.

This conclusion will be verified with similar calculations related to after-tax earnings and net worth. For simplicity in this case study, we have developed a tentative conclusion using cash flow only.

Let us also assume that a study of the company leads us to a projection of average sales at $24,000,000. Our study of other companies, adjusted for comparability, indicates that companies in this industry and of this size have a working capital turnover of, say, five, thus indicating a normal working capital for the subject company of $4,800,000.

Returning to our formula—

$$E = WC + (PP + I)$$

now looks like—

$$E - WC = (PP + I)$$
$$23,250,000 - 4,800,000 = (PP + I)$$
$$18,450,000 = (PP + I)$$

While the total value of the business enterprise based on earnings is of critical importance, the distribution of this total value to the component parts is equally important. Consequently, it is essential that, concurrent with establishing the enterprise value, an investigation must be made on the plant, property, and intangibles. A variety of appraisal principles and approaches is available for this purpose, and careful consideration must be given to choosing the appropriate method. The methods used must result in a coordinated and supportable premise. Fragmented appraisals, such as using a separate real estate appraiser for the land, a building contractor for the buildings, and a used machinery dealer for the equipment, will not produce a coordinated or proper result. The sum of the values of independent parts is not necessarily equal to the value of the whole.

For the property, plant, and equipment, the initial approach is to determine the cost to acquire these assets new, less physical deterioration and functional obsolescence for each class of assets. This approach is based upon a physical inventory of the assets acquired, not upon the book inventory of assets of the acquired company; seldom do the books accurately reflect the property in existence.

Before an initial opinion may be expressed about the value of plant facilities, reference must be made to a general operating and engineering study. This study will consider the ability of the production facilities to produce in sufficient quantity and quality to meet forecasted sales. If production needs cannot be met, the best financial analysis and study is without meaning. A general operating and engineering study provides the insight necessary to determine factors of functional and economic obsolescence affecting the plant/property of the company being appraised.

There is a popular misconception that the value of a business cannot be less than the sum of the reproduction cost, less observed depreciation of tangible assets plus other assets. This is not true. In many cases such a value would simply indicate that, based on earnings, it would be impossible to replace the property, plant, and equipment at current cost and to operate the business entity. If value is determined in a period following consistent and perhaps serious operating losses, value might be represented by liquidation value for the tangible assets. Book value in an accounting form and replacement or reproduction cost less depreciation does not necessarily represent *value*.

The proper valuation of intangibles may utilize numerous techniques. The variety of intangible assets is as great as that of fixed assets. Some have determinable physical life, some determinable economic life, and others have an indeterminate life. Some generate a predictable income stream, while others generate income that can only be estimated. Generally, each intangible asset is valued based upon the capitalization, over its life expectancy, of its relative contribution to profit of the enterprise.

For our case study, the analysis of values results in the following:

Land	$ 1,500,000
Buildings	4,800,000
Machinery and equipment	8,200,000
Office machinery furniture and fixtures	1,200,000
Autos and trucks	300,000
Total plant property	$16,000,000
Patent	1,500,000
License agreements	300,000
Trademarks	600,000
Corporate name	600,000
Goodwill	600,000
Total intangibles	$ 3,600,000
Normal working capital	4,800,000
Grand total	$24,400,000

In the case study, two different procedures have been used to estimate value, resulting in tentative conclusions for the value of the enterprise of $23,250,000 and $24,400,000. At this point, the appraiser must make a final judgment of the company's value after weighing all the facts and circumstances. In this instance, it was felt the financial study was more conclusive. Consequently it was decided, after considering many factors—including the fact that less than the determined amount of normal working capital would be acquired with the business—that the fair market value of the enterprise was $23 million.

Some readers may consider the amount of $600,000 for goodwill excessive. Experience indicates, however, that the IRS believes that every going business has an element of goodwill. Thus, it is better, I believe, to admit to a supportable value to goodwill than to let the IRS determine a value for goodwill or other intangibles.

Solving our equation for the values in this case study:

$$E - WC = (PP + I)$$
$$23,000,000 - 4,800,000 = (PP + I)$$
$$18,200,000 = (PP + I)$$

Since, however, the two valuation procedures resulted in not too dissimilar answers, it can be concluded that the procedures are reason-

EXHIBIT 24-1

	Tentative Conclusion	Prorated Fair Market Value
Land	$ 1,500	$ 1,393
Buildings	4,800	4,457
Machinery and Equipment	8,200	7,614
Office Equipment	1,200	1,114
Autos and Trucks	300	278
Patent	1,500	1,393
License Agreements	300	279
Trademark	600	557
Corporate Name	600	557
Goodwill	600	600
	$19,600	$18,200

able and that they provide a basis for pro-rating the total enterprise value to each of the parts.

Such pro-ration provides the values shown in Exhibit 24-1.

As we have stated, the estimated fair market value of the enterprise, based on conventional valuation procedures as interpreted by an experienced appraiser, is rarely the same as the purchase price. The theory of allocating purchase price is very simple: after removing cash at 100 percent, the allocation becomes merely an exercise of arithmetic. The new basis of the assets is equal to the prorated fair market value times the ratio of the purchase price to the enterprise value after the cash has been removed from both.

$$\text{New basis of assets} = \text{Prorated FMV of assets} \times \frac{\text{Purchase Price—Cash}}{\text{Enterprise Value—Cash}}$$

This formula is simple in theory, but sometimes difficult in practice. The difficulty occurs in determining the real purchase price, which is not just the amount that changes hands. The real purchase price is the price to be paid, including contingency payouts, plus liabilities assumed. In addition to the assumed liabilities, a purchase of stock followed by a liquidation (a Section 334 (b) 2 transaction) triggers depreciation recapture. The problem that arises in this situation is that one must first allocate the purchase price to each depreciable asset in order to determine the amount of depreciation recapture (recapture resulting from Sections 38, 1245, and 1250 of the Internal Revenue Code), yet it is this depreciation recapture that becomes one of the liabilities which must be included to determine the purchase price. Thus, it becomes a case of which comes first, the chicken or the egg—allocation or liability?

SUMMARY

In summary, the number of merger and acquisition marriages over the years has increased and probably will continue to increase, even in the face of a temporary decline from time to time. The number of divorces, however, climbs at a greater rate, due in part to a lack of understanding of valuation concepts.

Since 1954, the basic value to be used in mergers and acquisitions is fair market value. This value is well defined in the theoretical sense, but in actual practice the circumstances affecting the transaction must be considered before arriving at an opinion of value.

After the acquisition or merger is finalized, the buyer or seller, under varying circumstances, faces the problem of allocating the real purchase price on the basis of fair market value. Allocation is required when there is 1) an accounting purchase under the requirements of APB Opinion No. 16, 2) a purchase of assets for cash, or 3) a purchase of stock for cash followed by a liquidation within two years.

The results of the allocation of the real purchase price provides the new basis for tax and accounting depreciation and amortization calculations and upon which possible tax liabilities may be determined.

Another area of importance to a buyer is to establish an accurate and usable property record and assets value for insurance placement and proof of loss purposes.

25. TENDER OFFERS REVISITED: 1968-1972 COMPARISONS WITH THE PAST AND FUTURE TRENDS*

DOUGLAS V. AUSTIN†

The tender offer, as a corporate takeover device, matured during the latter half of the 1960s as many major corporations (and some not so major) succeeded in taking over other corporations, some very much larger than the attacker. What startled the American businessman and intrigued the American financial press was the high success rate.

But less is heard today of the tender offer. Why? Because the major acquisition-by-tender-offer companies either have continuing liquidity crises; have operating problems; or have a management that doesn't care for the new Rules of the SEC, which govern the manner in which tender offers are made. The purpose of this article is to compare the tender offers from the period 1957-1967 to the period 1968-1972. Comparisons of size, type, success, premiums, outcomes and subsequent behavior of attacked corporations are analyzed in a manner similar to that in which the author prepared a previous study.[1]

HISTORICAL DEVELOPMENT

The tender offer as a means of takeover is not a new technique. Offers to purchase securities by tender occurred as far back as the 1920s. However, prior to the 1950s, tender offers were utilized primarily for stock reacquisitions—corporations offered to repurchase preferred or common stock from shareholders in the open market. This was, and is today, so long as substantial amounts of stock remain in "street name," the only way to effect a substantial reacquisition. But as a means of corporate takeover, the tender offer did not become a viable financial weapon until the 1960s. It wasn't until 1963 that the number of tender offers reached 23. By 1967, the number climbed to 86. For the period of 1956-1967 there were 235 tender offers.

By examination of Table 25-1[2] entitled "Growth of Tender Offers," it can be seen that the tender offer trend continued strong through 1968 although the number started to decline. In 1968, there was a total of 62

*From *Mergers & Acquisitions*, The Journal of Corporate Venture, McLean, Virginia 22101 (Spring, 1973), pp. 16-29. Reprinted by permission.
†Chairman, Department of Finance, College of Business Administration, University of Toledo.
[1]See Douglas V. Austin and J. A. Fishman, *Corporations in Conflict: The Tender Offer*, Masterco Press, 1970.
[2]All tables are from the "Austin Data Bank" maintained by the author over many years. For his previous efforts in MERGERS & ACQUISITIONS, please see Vol. 3 No. 5 (pages 4-13) and Vol. 4 No. 3 (pages 4-23).

TABLE 25-1

GROWTH OF TENDER OFFERS—1956-1972

Year	Cash	Exchange	Combination
1956	1	1	—
1957	0	0	—
1958	3	0	—
1959	4	0	—
1960	5	2	—
1961	6	1	—
1962	8	3	—
1963	21	2	—
1964	9	3	—
1965	31	4	—
1966	29	16	—
1967	76	10	—
Sub-Total	193	42	—
1968	33	27	2
1969	19	29	1
1970	7	7	1
1971	1	5	0
1972	6	3	0
Sub-Total	66	71	4
1956-72 TOTAL	259	113	4

Friendly Offers—1956-1972

	1956-1967	0
	1968	6
	1969	3
	1970	2
	1971	3
	1972	1

tender offers versus 86 in 1967, and in 1969 it declined to 49. In 1970, the number declined still further to 15, and a low was reached in 1971 with only 6 tender offers being recorded. In 1972, the number of tender offers increased, but only to 9. For the five-year period there was a total of 141 tender offers most of which occurred during the period 1968-1970. It can be seen plainly from Table 25-1 that the tender offer declined as a significant means of corporate takeover after 1969 and has not yet recovered.[3,4]

---

[3]It should be noted that a new category arises in the computation of tender offers during the 1968-1972 period. In the prior collection of information the tender offers were categorized either as cash or exchange tender offers and only the unfriendly or corporate takeover offers were tabulated. During the 1968-1972 period there were 15 so-called "friendly" tender offers which should be considered as continued acquisitions of stock formerly tendered successfully for by a corporation desirous of increasing the amount of shares held.

[4]There is no one single tabulation of tender offers available to the student of corporate conflict. There are several less-than-definitive sources to be scrutinized. Prior to (cont.)

Table 25-1, in addition to indicating a decline in the popularity of the tender offer as a method of financial takeover, also reveals another trend. During the period 1956-1967, the number of cash tender offers exceeded exchange tender offers almost 5 to 1. During the period 1968-1972 the number of cash tender offers, 66, was actually 5 less than the number of exchange tender offers, 71. An examination of the period, year by year, shows that the trend changed in 1969. In 1968, there were 33 cash tender offers and 27 exchange tender offers. However, in 1969, there were only 19 cash offers and there were 29 exchange offers. In 1970, there were 7 of each type and in 1971 there were 1 cash offer and 5 exchange offers. However, by 1972 the number of cash offers had again increased to double that of exchange offers, 6 to 3.

What is the reason for this change and the significance of cash versus exchange tender offers? If one analyzes money market conditions, one marvels at the high correlations of the number of cash tender offers with the periods of easy money and above-average corporate liquidity, and the use of exchange offers during periods of low liquidity and high rates in the money market. For example, 1972 was the first time in three years that corporations found liquidity ample enough to utilize the cash tender offer over the exchange offer. When cash is plentiful it's simply easier and quicker to make a cash tender than to formulate an exchange offer.

It should also be noted that during the period 1968-1972 for the first time, combinations of cash and exchange offers were utilized. During the entire period of 1956-1967 exhaustive research reveals not one single incident utilizing a combination cash-exchange offer! Research did reveal, however, two instances in 1968 and one instance each in 1969 and in 1970. The lack of popularity of the combination tender offer technique is not surprising. It is hard enough for the shareholders to understand the terms in *any* exchange tender offer (especially in his haste to find the premium he is being offered) and to place a tender offer utilizing a combination of exchange and cash further compounds his ignorance.

1968, when the SEC Act was modified by the Williams Bill, thus forcing formal pre-tender registration, there was no need for any corporation to tell anyone in government or in the press about it. It just happened. Therefore, the Austin Data Bank for the period of 1956-1967 utilized the New York Stock Exchange's Catalog of Tender Offers. Other tender offers were discovered through research in the financial press: *The Wall Street Journal*, *Barron's* and other such sources. For the period 1968-1972 the SEC listing of all firms filing 13D and 14D registration statements with the SEC was used as a base list and added to this list of tender offer registrations were all such announcements of tender offers which were made available in the public press through any source possible. In addition, and for a limited period of time, *Finance* printed tender offer lists which were partially correct. Therefore, the compilation of tender offer material in this article is the result of thousands of man hours of searching through financial publications and is considered by the author to be an excellent proxy for the total number of tender offers during that period of time. It is conceivable that a tender offer here and there could have been missed but it is the author's contention that the trends and results outlined in this article are an accurate reflection of the real state of affairs.

What has caused the major decline in the number of takeover tenders? There are two reasons. The first is the enactment of the Williams Bill in 1968 which forced registration of corporate bidders in tender offer wars. In the 1970 amendments, further restrictions were placed upon the bidders and further information was required of the bidder for the purpose of "disclosing the true facts to the shareholders." The second major reason for the decline in the number of tender offers during the 1968-72 period, and especially since 1970. is the previously-referred-to change in money market conditions.

A third reason should be mentioned. During the period of the mid-1960s, especially from 1963-1967, corporate takeovers via the tender offer mechanism were, in general, highly successful. However, by 1968-1970, the number of successful tender offers declined through more astute defenses by the attacked corporations, especially through utilization of New York-based proxy and tender offer solicitation firms who knew how to organize massive resistance to offers. These same firms, through astute forward planning, took away much of the advantage usually gained by the surprise aspects of the tender.

SUCCESS, PARTIAL SUCCESS, OR FAILURE

The first thing that anyone asks about the tender offer technique is how often and under what conditions is it successful. Table 25-2 shows the success and failure of the tender offer as a technique of corporate takeover for the period 1956-1972. For the period 1956-1967, 157 tender offers were successful, 27 were partially successful and 48 were unsuccessful. Therefore, of the 232 total tender offers during that period of time. approximately 80 percent were either successful or partially successful. This is in comparison to a much lower rate of success realized formerly by corporations attempting to take over others via the proxy contest technique. By success, the author means the fulfillment of the goal requested by the bidder at the time the initial or extended tender offer was made. Partially successful tender offers can be defined as those tender offers which resulted in the bidding corporation accepting partial settlements for shares extended or, over a period of time. successfully completing the tender offer, or gaining control of the firm in another manner. Failure of the tender offer is assumed when the attacking firm withdraws and fails to pick up the tendered shares.

During the 1968-1972 period, the success rate of the tender offers decreased significantly. Of the total of 141, 96 were successful, 4 were partially successful, and 41 were failures. In 1968, 37 offers were successful, 2 partially successful and 23 unsuccessful, or approximately $\frac{2}{3}$ were successful during that year. In 1969, 35 of 49 offers were successful or partially successful, or approximately 70 percent. During the past three years, and though the number of unsuccessful tender offers were

TABLE 25-2

TENDER OFFER SUCCESS, PARTIAL SUCCESS, FAILURE—
1956-1972

Year	Successful	Partially Successful	Unsuccessful	Total
1956	2	0	0	2
1957	0	0	0	0
1958	1	1	1	3
1959	3	1	0	4
1960	5	0	2	7
1961	4	1	2	7
1962	6	2	2	10
1963	18	1	2	21
1964	6	1	5	12
1965	30	0	5	35
1966	29	9	7	45
1967	53	11	22	86
Total	157	27	48	232
1968	37	2	23	62
1969	33	2	14	49
1970	13	0	2	15
1971	6	0	0	6
1972	7	0	2	9
Total	96	4	41	141

less, in spite of the increased ability of a corporation to ward off attacks by tender offer, the success *rate* has increased. In 1970, for example, 13 of 15 tender offers were successful, in 1971 all 6 tender offers attempted resulted in success for the bidder and in 1972, 7 of 9 tender offers were successful. Thus the last three year period has shown a marked increase in the success of tender offers, although the *number* has declined significantly. Based upon this table and other material researched, it is believed that more careful preparation of the offer, including utilization of larger premiums to intrigue the capital-gains-oriented shareholder, were the major contributing reasons for the increased success rates.

It has often been said by this author (and others) that cash tender offers are usually more successful than are exchange tender offers because they are more easily understood by the shareholder. An examination of the total of 191 cash tender offers during the period 1956-1967, shows that 125 were successful, 24 were partially successful, and a total of 42 were unsuccessful. This is a success rate of about 78 percent. During the same period of time, 35 of 41 exchange tender offers were successful or an 85 percent success ratio.

The conflict is further compounded by the results of the period 1968-1972. During that period, the success of cash tender offers continued to fall short of that of the exchange tender offer. Of the total of

66 cash tender offers during the 1968-1972 period, 36 were successful, 4 were partially successful and 26 resulted in failure or a success rate of 66⅔ percent—slightly less than the overall 70 percent rate. On the other hand, the total number of exchange tender offers during the same period of time was 71, and of the 71 tender offers, 57 were successful, none were partially successful, and 14 resulted in failure. This 80 percent success rate was significantly higher than the 70 percent success rate of the 1956-67 period.

Finally, a minor but interesting statistic, shows that in the case of the 4 "combined" cash and exchange tender offers during the 1968-1972 period, 3 of the 4 were successful and 1 was a failure. Overall, the total success rate of tender offers declined from approximately 80 percent to 70 percent during the 1968-1972 period and during the same period of time, the success rate of exchange tender offers continued to outstrip the success of cash tender offers in terms of achieving goals or partial goals.

THE BIDDING PREMIUMS

What does it cost to take over a corporation by the tender offer method? The answer has always been a premium. Hayes and Taussig[5] in their early study of tender offer premiums stated that the average tender offer premium was approximately 16 percent. (See Table 25-3 for a description of these bidding premiums.) It is noticeable from Table 25-4 that the premiums were no higher than 40-44 percent (which occurred only 4 times or 8 percent of the total number of premiums studied), and that only about 12 percent of the tender offers were offered at a premium less than 10 percent above the market price. In the 1956-67 study, premiums were analyzed by determination of stock prices one day prior to the announcement of the tender offer. But subsequent research has led the author to believe that the amount of pre-tender stock market activity was significant and is significant enough to materially cut the tender offer premium calculations if a date approximate to the tender offer announcement is utilized. Therefore, in the calculations of premiums for the 1968-1972 period, a date two weeks prior to the tender offer announcement was utilized for the calculation of premiums and the resulting premium range is quite different.

Examination of Table 25-4 shows that a premium in excess of 100 percent was paid in 4 cases, or 3 percent of the tender offers, during the 1968-1972 period. All told, 16 tender offers of the 133 (out of the total of 141 tender offers), in which premiums could be calculated, were higher than 50 percent over the market value of the stock two weeks

---

[5]Hayes and Taussig, "Tactics of Cash Takeover Bids," *Harvard Business Review*, (March-April, 1967).

TABLE 25-3
BIDDING PREMIUMS—1956-67

Premium	Number Offered	Percent of Total
40-44	4	8%
35-39	0	0
30-34	2	4
25-29	5	10
20-24	8	16
15-11	11	22
10-14	14	29
5-9	4	8
0-4	2	4
Total	50	100%

TABLE 25-4
BIDDING PREMIUMS—1968-1972

Premium	Number Offered	Percent of Total
100 +	4	3.00
95-99	—	—
90-94	1	.75
85-89	1	.75
80-84	2	1.50
75-79	—	—
70-74	—	—
65-69	2	1.60
60-64	1	.75
55-59	1	.75
50-54	4	3.00
45-49	3	2.25
40-44	3	2.25
35-39	6	4.51
30-34	16	12.03
25-29	9	6.77
20-24	17	12.78
15-19	10	7.52
10-14	13	9.77
05-09	11	8.23
00-04	29	21.80
Total	133	100.00%

prior to the tender offer announcement. In 8 cases the market price was not available due to circumstances such as closely held non-tradable securities or transactions so small in number that market prices could not be determined. Table 25-4 shows that the amount of premiums paid during the 1968-72 period ranged below 50 percent but was fairly evenly spread from almost 0 percent to 50 percent. The largest sub-group of premium payers was in the 0-4.9 percent range where 21.8 percent of

TABLE 25-5

SIZE OF PREMIUMS VERSUS OUTCOMES—1956-1967

Size of Premium	Successful	Failure	Total
Under 16%	13	12	25
Over 16%	7	18	25
Total	20	30	50

all tender offer premiums were calculated. All told, the analysis of the tender offer premiums during the 1968-72 period reveals that the average tender offer premium did not change materially from that of the early study although the largest premiums paid were far in excess of what they were in the previous period. During the 1956-67 period, 50 premiums were analyzed in terms of success versus failure and the percent of premium (See Table 25-5). Of a total of 25 premiums above 16 percent, 13 were successful and 12 were unsuccessful. Of 25 premiums under 16 percent only 7 were successful and 18 were unsuccessful.

During the 1968-72 period, all premiums analyzed above were correlated to the degree of success or failure of the outcome of the tender offer. Table 25-5 shows the correlation of the size of premium with that of success or failure of the bid.

PREMIUM SIZE AND OUTCOME, 1968-1972

One would expect that the outcome of tender offers would correlate positively and directly with the size of premiums. The author compared the success of the tender offer with the size of premiums for the period 1968-1972. As can be seen from Table 25-6, the expectations are rewarded in that the higher the premium the more successful the tender offer. But it is not a verity. For example, the first unsuccessful tender offer of the cash variety had a premium in the range of 80-84 percent. The second unsuccessful offer had a premium in the range of 65-69 percent. This also was a cash tender offer as revealed by Table 25-6. In the range of 45-49 percent, there was an additional cash tender offer which was unsuccessful and in the range of 35-39 percent there were 2 more. In the range of 35-39 percent, and for the first time, an exchange tender offer became unsuccessful. All exchange offers above the range of 40 percent have been successful, whereas 5 of the cash offers have not been. This is not quite the form that most people would consider to be a pattern, primarily due to the increased complexity of exchange offers over cash offers.

It would be expected that the lower the premium on the tender offer the increased probability of failure. This is borne out by Table 25-6. Starting in the range of 30-34 percent, we can see a notable change in the amount of success correlated to the size of premium. For example,

TABLE 25-6

OUTCOME CORRELATED TO PREMIUM SIZE—1968-1972

Premium	CASH Success	CASH Partial Success	CASH Unsuccess	EXCHANGE Success	EXCHANGE Partial Success	EXCHANGE Unsuccess
100 +	2			1		
95-99						
90-94	1					
85-89	1					
80-84			1	1		
75-79						
70-74						
65-69			1	1		
60-64				1		
55-59			1			
50-54	1		1	2		
45-49			1	2		
40-44	1			2		
35-39	1		2	2		1
30-34	6		3	5		2
25-29	4		1	4		
20-24	7	2	4	2		2
15-19	5		1	2		2
10-14	2	2	3	4		1
05-09	4		2	4		1
00-04	6		4	13		5

in the 30-34 percent range, 6 cash offers were successful, none partially successful and 3 unsuccessful. At the lower premium range, the overall total number of tender offers was more successful than unsuccessful. In the same range there were 5 exchange tender offers successful and 2 unsuccessful.

One would expect a perfect correlation between lack of success and premium dimunition [*sic*]. But the fit is not that good. In the range of 25-29 percent for example, there were 4 cash offers successful and only 1 unsuccessful, and 4 exchange offers successful and none unsuccessful, whereas in the 30-34 percent range noted above, the lack of success was much greater. Again note that in the 20-24 percent range the number of failures increases again. There were 7 cash offers successful, 2 partially successful and 4 unsuccessful and there were 2 exchange offers successful and 2 failures. This increased failure rate is carried down all the way to a 0 percent premium on either a cash or exchange tender offer. The number of exchange offers is not necessarily any lower in terms of success at low premium levels than that of the cash offers. In fact, an examination of Table 25-6 shows that the number of cash exchange offers, percentage-wise, was much greater in terms of failure at low premium levels than that of exchange offers. The answer for this might be that the people did not realize the true amount of premium in exchange offers and therefore voted on qualitative rather than quantitative factors.

INDUSTRIAL CLASSIFICATION OF BIDDERS

Tables 25-7 and 25-8 present the industrial classifications of both the bidders and target corporations. First let us examine the bidders.

TABLE 25-7

INDUSTRIAL CLASSIFICATION OF TENDER OFFER
BIDDERS—1956-1967 and 1968-1972

Industries	1956-67 Percent	1968-72 Percent
Financial Services	13.30%	9.64%
Stores	8.88	1.20
Chemical	8.23	2.42
Electrical Machines	7.59	1.20
Transportation	7.59	2.42
Non-Electric	5.05	0.00
Communications	0.63	2.42
Construction	0.63	0.00
Furniture	0.63	0.00
Instruments	0.63	0.00
Rubber	0.63	0.00
Miscellaneous	0.63	1.20
Textiles	6.33	0.00
Food Products	1.90	1.20
Mining	1.90	1.20
Paper	1.90	0.00
Printing	1.90	1.20
Agriculture	1.26	0.00
Apparel	1.26	0.00
Business Services	0.63	0.00
Fabricated Metal	3.80	0.00
Tobacco	3.80	0.00
Petroleum	3.80	12.04
Primary Metal	3.17	0.00
Private Groups	3.17	0.00
Utilities	2.53	0.00
Clay, Gravel, Stone	1.90	0.00
Transportation Equipment	6.33	0.00
Conglomerates	0.00	21.68
Insurance	0.00	14.46
Manufacturing	0.00	13.25
Railroads	0.00	7.23
Holding Companies	0.00	4.84
Motor Vehicles	0.00	1.20
Computer	0.00	1.20
Total	100.00%	100.00%

TABLE 25-8

INDUSTRIAL CLASSIFICATION OF TENDER OFFER
TARGETS—1956-1967 and 1968-1972

Industries	1956-67 Percent	1968-72 Percent
Wholesale	11.29	1.32
Financial Services	9.31	3.95
Non-Electric	9.31	0.00
Fabricated Metal	7.85	0.00
Transportation	7.35	2.63
Primary Metal	6.38	0.00
Chemicals	5.88	3.95
Electrical Machinery	4.90	5.26
Food Products	5.88	1.32
Business Services	4.41	0.00
Utilities	3.92	2.63
Transportation	2.94	0.00
Mining	2.45	1.32
Paper	2.45	0.00
Textiles	2.45	0.00
Instruments	1.96	1.32
Petroleum	1.96	10.52
Printing	1.96	0.00
Apparel	0.98	0.00
Clay, Gravel and Stone	0.98	0.00
Communications	0.98	5.26
Construction	0.49	1.32
Furniture	0.49	0.00
Leather	0.49	0.00
Rubber	0.49	0.00
Tobacco	0.49	0.00
Miscellaneous	2.00	0.00
Insurance	0.00	21.04
Manufacturing	0.00	17.10
Railroads	0.00	9.21
Department Stores	0.00	2.63
Agriculture	0.00	2.63
Motor Vehicles	0.00	2.63
Stockyard	0.00	1.32
Conglomerates	0.00	1.32
Broadcasting	0.00	1.32
Total	100.00%	100.00%

During the 1956-67 period, the major industrial classifications for the corporations according to S.I.C. codes were: Financial Services, Stores, Chemicals, Electrical Machines, Transportation, Non-electric, Textile and Transportation Equipment. On the other hand, during the 1968-72 period, the predominant industrial classification of bidders were Conglomerates, Insurance, Manufacturing, Petroleum, Financial Services and Railroads. In only one case, that of Financial Services were these industrial groups the same as in the 1956-67 period. Note also the increased role of conglomerates, a classification which did not exist prior to the 1968-1972 period, which accounted for over 21 percent of all tender offers.

From 1956-67, the major firms targeted for takeover via the tender offer method were industrially classified as: Wholesale, Financial Services, Non-electrical, Fabricated Metals, Transportation, Primary Metals and Chemicals. On the other hand, during the 1968-1972 period, insurance corporations were the major target accounting for 21 percent of all tender offers; Manufacturing corporations were the target in 17 percent of the cases; and railroads were 9 percent. The balance ranged widely over the entire gamut of industrial activity as can be seen in Table 25-8.

RATES OF RETURN VERSUS TENDER OFFER OUTCOME

The rates of return on the total capital of target firms correlated poorly with the success of the tender offers. Table 25-9 shows the correlation of the rates of return of the target companies to the success of the tender offer for both of the periods 1956-67 and 1968-72. During the 1956-67 period, there was less success when firms with a rate of return on invested capital less than the industry average were attacked than there were in the cases where the rates of return were equal to or above the industry average. Note that in the case of the firms with above-industry-average performance, 10 of 11 tender offers studied showed that the tender offers were successful even though the firm was operating above the industry average. During the 1968-72 period, the firms which operated below the industry average were successfully or partially successfully tendered for in 55 of 71 total attempts, whereas those firms which operated equal to or above the industry average had a higher

TABLE 25-9

RATES OF RETURN ON CAPITAL OF TARGET FIRMS CORRELATED TO OUTCOME OF TENDER OFFERS — 1956-1972

1956-1967	Successful	Partially Successful	Unsuccessful
Above Industry	10	0	1
Same as Industry	7	1	1
Below Industry	43	5	11
1968-1972			
Above Industry	25	3	18
Same as Industry	2	1	1
Below Industry	52	3	16

success rate, although at a lower percent than the 1956-1967 period. The increasing rate of failure of attacks against target firms operating at or above the industry average during the latter period would have to be directly attributable to the improved defenses by the corporation attacked. Furthermore, the complexity of tender offer exchange proposals also enabled the companies under attack to achieve greater defense success.

PERFORMANCE OF TARGET COMPANIES INVOLVED IN TENDER OFFERS 1956-1972

The past performance of target corporations involved in tender offers has often been the subject of scrutiny. In proxy contests, corporations attacked were almost exclusively operating below industry averages. In tender offers, however, the motivations for attack are more varied since the ultimate weapon, the amount of premium that captures the attention of the stockholders, is more significant than the previous performance of the corporation. Table 25-10 shows the comparison of the performance of target corporations involved in tender offers for the period 1967-1972 and is broken into two sub-periods. It is interesting to note that during the 1968-72 period the number of firms above the industry average was a higher proportion of the total in terms of both rates of return on capital and profit margin, thus showing that the firms under attack were often attacked for many different reasons rather than simply assuming successful takeover would be insured by shareholder disenchantment with profit performance. (It should be noted that in the examination of the 1968-72 period, not all 141 firms were analyzed because of a lack of data. But 120-124 out of a universe of 141 firms is a statistically reliable sample. In terms of relating to specific outcomes to both profit margins and rates of return on capital, the following two sections of the paper show the correlation between past performance of attacked firms and the outcome of the tender offer. . . .

TABLE 25-10
PERFORMANCE OF TARGET FIRMS — 1956-1972

1956-1967	Total	Below Industry	Same as Industry	Above Industry
Profit Margin	74	45	17	12
Return on Equity Capital	79	59	9	11
1967-1972				
Profit Margin	124	78	4	42
Return on Equity Capital	120	71	3	46

BOOK VALUES, MARKET VALUES AND OUTCOMES

When the market price of a corporate stock falls below its book value most entrepreneurs would utilize the tender offer device to gain control as a precondition to liquidation. This can be attained by continued purchases in the open market, since it can be assumed that shareholders will be disenchanted with the market performance of the stock. Table 25-11, "Book Values, Market Values and Tender Offer Outcome, 1956-1972" compares the book value/market value relationships with the outcome of the tender offers. During the 1956-67 period, 33 of 44 firms whose book value exceeded market value were either successfully or partially successfully tendered for—a percentage of 75 whereas during the same period of time, 66 firms out of 81 firms whose book value was less than market value were successfully tendered for—a percentage of 82. During the 1968-72 period, 21 of 31 companies whose market value was less than book value were successfully tendered, or a percentage of 67, a decline of approximately 8 percent over the earlier period whereas 63 of the 93 firms which operated with market values exceeding book values were successfully tendered for.

TABLE 25-11

BOOK VALUES, MARKET VALUES AND TENDER OFFER OUTCOME—1956-1972

1956-1967	Successful	Partially Successful	Unsuccessful
Book Values Greater than Market Value	31	2	11
Book Values Less than Market Value	30	3	4
Total	61	5	15
1968-1972			
Book Values Greater than Market Value	20	1	10
Book Values Less than Market Value	58	5	28
Total	78	6	38

ASSET SIZE OF TARGET CORPORATIONS

During the 1956-67 period, almost 40 percent of the corporations under attack were larger than $50 million in total assets. Table 25-12, "Asset Size of Target Corporations, 1967-72," shows that almost two-thirds of all corporations under attack during the 1968-1972 period had assets of over $50 million. Discounting inflation as a factor in this analysis, it can be assumed that the targets, during this latter period,

TABLE 25-12

ASSET SIZE OF CORPORATE CORPORATIONS—1956-1972

Asset Size	Percent	Number of Corp.
1956-1967		
Less than $5 million	8.49	20
$5-$10 million	11.51	26
$10-$25 million	24.80	57
$25-$50 million	15.75	36
Greater than $50 million	39.45	91
Total	100.00%	230
1968-1972		
Less than $5 million	.72	1
$5-$10 million	5.76	8
$10-$25 million	10.79	15
$25-$50 million	14.39	20
$50-$75 million	10.07	14
$75-$100 million	5.76	8
$100-$200 million	16.55	23
$200-$300 million	10.07	14
$300 and above	25.89	36
Total	100.00%	139

were chosen not on the basis of size but on the basis of industrial classification, or the need criteria of the bidder; and that the size criterion most likely approached random. Not only did larger corporations attack larger targets, but in many cases small corporations attacked firms many times their size.

LIQUIDITY OF TARGET FIRMS

Corporations have often been attacked in the past based upon their liquidity. In fact, many a corporation has been taken over by utilization of its own cash! During the 1956-67 period, almost 65 percent of the corporations had high-to-excessively-high liquidity. However, during the 1968-72 period, the number of corporations whose liquidity was high-to-excessive in terms of Table 25-13 had fallen to approximately 44 percent or less than half of the number of firms being attacked. (It should be noted that excessive liquidity means a current ratio greater than— 5 to 1—very high 3 to 1 to 5 to 1; high 2.25 to 3.0; average 1.75 to 2.25.)

WHERE HAVE THEY GONE?

It is always interesting to examine corporate conflict situations in terms of where the companies have gone that were attacked. During the 1956-67 period, as can be seen from Table 25-14, some 83 percent of the firms attacked were either merged or acquired. For example, 42 firms

TABLE 25-13

LIQUIDITY OF TARGET CORPORATIONS—
—1956-1972

Liquidity	Number	Percentage
1956-1967		
Excessive	9	10.8
Very High	26	31.3
High	19	22.9
Normal	18	21.7
Low	11	13.3
Total	83	100.0
1968-1972		
Excessive	7	6.19
Very High	21	18.58
High	22	19.48
Normal	36	31.86
Low	27	23.89
Total	113	100.00

TABLE 25-14

FIRMS ATTACKED VIA TENDER OFFER MERGED OR ACQUIRED—1956-1972

	Time Period	Successful	Partially Successful	Unsuccessful
1956-67	Less than 3 months	8	0	4
	3-8 months	16	0	2
	9-12 months	12	0	2
	13-18 months	5	0	0
	18 months and over	1	2	1
	Total Mergers	42	2	7
	Percent Total	79.25%	3.77%	16.98%
1968-72	Less than 3 months	42	0	6
	3-8 months	25	0	5
	9-12 months	7	0	1
	13-18 months	2	0	4
	18 months and over	9	2	3
	Total Mergers	85	2	19
	Percent Total	80.2%	1.9%	17.9%

that were successfully tendered for during this period of time, were merged or became subsidiaries of bidding corporations or were controlled ("controlled" means more than 50 percent of the firm was acquired) less than three years after the attack, and 6 firms were so controlled after the attack in less than three months. All told, 80 percent of the firms became merged subsidiaries or were controlled by the firms doing the attacking within a three year period.

During the 1956-67 period, 79.3 percent of the firms that were successfully tendered for, became merged subsidiaries or were controlled within a three-year period. Of those partially tendered for, 3.77 percent became so involved. On the other hand, 16.98 percent of the firms that successfully weathered a tender offer were merged, controlled, or became subsidiaries of corporations which had attacked it. During the 1968-72 period, (and in this particular case, all corporations were examined) 85 firms that were successfully tendered for became subsidiaries, were controlled or were merged with attacking corporations during the first three years after the attack. This was 80.2 percent of the total that were successfully tendered for. On the other hand, 19 firms which were successful in warding off takeovers during this period of time were merged during the first three years of post-tender activity equal to 17.9 percent of the total. (These are slightly higher figures than during the 1956-67 period but this change is probably due to more sophisticated resistance tactics and accelerated accounting and legal procedures by bidding corporations in quickly converting controlled subsidiaries into family units.)

Of the 141 companies involved in tender offers during the 1968-72 period, 106 were merged, became wholly-owned subsidiaries, or were controlled by an attacking corporation during the first three years after operations. Of these 106 firms, 23 or 21.69 percent became wholly-owned or controlled by a second firm, not involved directly in the original tender offer. Furthermore, Table 25-15 shows the number and percentage of firms involved in each category that were merged, controlled, or became wholly-owned subsidiaries of the corporation in the period of time in which acquisition or changes in control took place.

CONCLUSIONS AND IMPLICATIONS

What does our comparative research into tender offers reveal? First, it shows that the number of tender offers has declined materially during the past five years, probably due to: more sophisticated resistance techniques utilized by target firms; decreasing liquidity of potential bidding corporations; and finally, the SEC's new antitakeover legislation, which imposes formidable and costly legal and accounting restraints and conditions on the old laissez faire takeover processes.

Second, we have noted that corporations under attack have been larger; that their liquidity has been less during the period under attack; and that the amount of merger or absorption by other methods has been continuing to run strong.

Third, the premiums as a percentage of market price paid by some bidding corporations has increased substantially compared to the 1956-67 period, but the *average* premium has not changed much over that

TABLE 25-15

WHERE DID THEY GO? MERGERS,
WHOLLY-OWNED SUBSIDIARIES,
CONTROLLED

Length of Time	Number
Merger	
Less than 3 months	9
3-8 months	10
9-12 months	3
13-18 months	4
18 and over	0
Total	26
Percent	24.53%
Wholly-owned Subsidiaries	
Less than 3 months	11
3-8 months	9
9-12 months	3
13-18 months	1
18 and over	5
Total	29
Percent	27.36%
Controlled	
Less than 3 months	28
3-8 months	11
9-12 months	2
13-18 months	1
18 and over	9
Total	51
Percent	48.11%

former period. In fact, by the utilization of increased numbers of exchange offers in relation to the earlier period, premiums have been less while success has been at least as high as before.

Fourth, the number of cash tender offers has declined dramatically during the 1968-72 period, probably due to decreased corporate liquidity, while the number of exchange offers has increased. For the first time (although it has not been noted for the last several years) combination offers of cash and debt were offered in exchange. With current liquidity binds at a near historical level, it can be assumed that the exchange offer will continue to be the major form of tender offer during the next year or two or until the economy returns to a measurable period of easier money and high corporate liquidity.

Fifth, industrial classification of both bidders and targets changed dramatically from the 1956-67 period to the 1968-72 period. During the later period, conglomerates were the major bidders and insurance companies were the major targets.

Sixth, even though inflation and growth increased the size of most corporations in the United States, it was still seen that the asset size of targets increased something more than the average of the inflationary factors between the two periods. And size itself seemed no barrier to any form of tender offer.

Seventh, in terms of profit margins and rates of return on capital there seemed to be no significant differences between the two periods. The tender offers during 1968-72 still showed that corporations were not exempt from attack even though they operated far above industry averages. It can be concluded that these firms became targets for tender offers *because of* their profitability.

Eighth, finally the relationship between market value and book value for attacked companies was little different during the 1968-72 period from the earlier 1956-67 period. Although some firms attacked had book value exceeding market value per share which promised faster returns on attackers' investments, the majority of firms had market values exceeding book value per share.

This article should not be concluded without remarking on the growing significance of the activities of proxy solicitation firms in generating standby plans for most large public corporations to bring instant and massive resistance to any takeover attempt by any method including the tender offer. The energy and expense presently being diverted from profits to maintain these contingency plans is considerable. This author hopes to explore the back offices of the proxy solicitation firms to discover the economics of the standby and the effectiveness of plans when actually called into use.

PART VIII. APPROACHES TO FINANCIAL PLANNING

Regardless of the firm's size and business, financial planning activities are important for its success as well as survival. The degree of sophistication in carrying out these activities varies from one firm to another. The articles in this section present several approaches and tools related to financial planning.

A description of financial modeling from a practical businessman's point of view is presented by Donald R. Smith. The article raises the important question: "Will financial modeling withstand the test of exposure to real life problems and the executives who must deal with these problems as decision-makers?" According to the author, financial modeling is in its gestation period at present. Two breakthroughs in financial modeling—the advent of computer time-sharing terminals, and the development of packaged programs and of specialized programming languages—are discussed. The author evaluates reasons why the modeling technique has not been successful in a number of firms. Finally, the article presents benefits of financial models.

In his paper, Joel M. Stern suggests that financial planning should set reasonable goals that result in attainable market values for the common shareholders. However, conventional accounting measures can easily distort desirable corporate strategy, thereby rendering financial planning useless and misleading. The author presents an analytical framework for financial planning which measures attainable management goals, while separating investment decision-making from financial policy and simulating the impact of financial plans on the market value of the firm. The analytical framework deals with the firm's cost of capital, its investment opportunities, and its valuation in the market. Finally, the author shows applications of his analytical framework for setting corporate objectives, dividend policy, financial reporting, and acquisition analysis.

In his article, Surendra S. Singhvi argues that corporate growth can and should be planned. To help in such planning, the author describes an earnings-growth model that can be used for determining the expected rate of return on new investments or for testing the validity of projected earnings. Dr. Singhvi believes that planned growth—internal or external—is necessary for business firms, and that to achieve planned growth management must make policy decisions on such matters as its dividend-payout target, debt-ratio target, and allocation of resources.

26. WHAT A CHIEF EXECUTIVE SHOULD KNOW ABOUT FINANCIAL MODELING*

DONALD R. SMITH†

What is financial modeling? Is it another fancy buzz word that will spawn many articles in professional journals and then fade away quietly? Or is it a meaningful concept that will gradually, over time, be absorbed into our body of business knowledge and become an integral part of the financial planning and control function?

Most new techniques are initially oversold to create interest and to overcome the natural forces that resist change. Financial modeling has not been an exception. However, the important question is: Will it withstand the test of exposure to real life problems and the executives who must deal with these problems as decision-makers?

Any new technique must have a gestation period during which it will be critically evaluated by business and the profession in terms of meaningful results. If results are forthcoming within a reasonable time, the technique becomes part of standard business practice.

At present, financial modeling is in its gestation period. There have been many well publicized success stories concerning its benefits; there are also a number of disappointments and failures that have received little or no public comment. The jury is still out at this time.

WHAT IS A FINANCIAL MODEL?

The term, financial modeling, has been defined in many different ways. All too frequently these definitions have created an atmosphere of pseudo-sophistication, an image more appropriately associated with the Wizard of Oz.

Actually, financial modeling is not a complex concept. It is simply the process of developing financial statements and ratios which deal typically with future projections based upon a defined set of assumptions and logical relationships.

When an accountant develops a set of assumptions and historical ratios, and then applies normal accounting logic in the preparation and summarization of spread sheets, we refer to the end product as financial projections or pro forma statements. If the same process is followed— except that, instead of pencil, paper and a 10 key adding machine—a computer time-sharing terminal is utilized, the process becomes financial modeling.

*From *Price Waterhouse & Co. Review*, 1973, Volume 18, No. 1, pp. 31-41. Reprinted by permission.
†Partner, Price Waterhouse & Co.

As the term is frequently used today, a financial model is a mechanized way of preparing financial projections. The advantages of mechanization in this case are basically threefold: the time required to prepare and revise the projections, the cost of preparation, and the accuracy of the projections.

In terms of mathematical-statistical sophistication, most financial models use the same algebra found in accounting: add, multiply, divide and, of course, debits equal credits. In addition, logic routines normally found in the models relate to depreciation calculations, interest rates, discounting of cash flow, return-on-investment calculations, and growth rates. The output of a financial model is typically a financial statement such as an income statement, a balance sheet or a source of funds statement. In many cases, while evaluating alternate assumptions, only selected lines of different statements will be printed so as to reduce printing time.

Until a few years ago, mechanization of projections was not particularly attractive because the programs required for an in-house computer were expensive to write. Once the programs were completed, the computer could prepare the projections in a matter of minutes with a very high degree of accuracy. However, there frequently were substantial delays, often in terms of days, in keypunching the data and then scheduling the program on the computer.

RECENT BREAKTHROUGHS IN FINANCIAL MODELING

Approximately three years ago, two major technical developments materially affected the limitation just mentioned, thus providing the opportunity to greatly expand the use of financial models.

The first development was the advent of computer time-sharing terminals. This eliminated the problem of turn-around time in a typical company computer center. Assumptions could be changed and new reports or selected line items could be prepared in a matter of minutes instead of days. Portable terminals, which are connected to time-sharing computer facilities via ordinary telephone lines, moved the processing out of the frequently over-scheduled computer center and back to the financial analyst's desk.

The second breakthrough was the development of packages and specialized programming languages that reduce tremendously the time and cost of programming a financial modeling system. To date, the impact of the specialized programming languages has not been fully realized. However, to point out the significance of this change, a model in the past that might have taken 20 man-weeks to write and test can be completed in as little as two man-weeks by an analyst skilled in use of the new packages or languages. Because of this increased efficiency, it is now practical to have the systems analyst program the models he has designed—rather than going through the normal cycle of having the analyst turn over the system specifications to a programmer to complete the job. By eliminating the programmer in the cycle, the problem of communications between the systems analyst and the programmer is eliminated.

While it is always desirable to accomplish something for less cost, the real value of increased efficiency in programming a financial model is in the end product. The new languages have permitted the development of models that are more comprehensive in nature and more adaptable to the needs of the executives and planners who use the models. Revisions in the models can be made easily and quickly. The models are no longer cast in stone but are adaptable to revisions and refinements.

FINANCIAL MODELS AS A BUSINESS TOOL

The description of a new technique, such as financial modeling, is frequently of intellectual interest. But, for the technique to be of value, it must serve a function. The complexity and sophistication of a technique may intrigue the mind and imagination (as space flight has)—but in the end it must be evaluated in a practical sense. This seems to have been the problem with many of the earlier attempts at financial modeling. In effect, the models tended to become ends unto themselves rather than useful tools for others to use. They did not meet the critical test in terms of contributing to the achievement of corporate goals.

Financial modeling should be viewed in a functional sense rather than as a technical achievement. How and where can it be used? Some proponents of the technique envision huge corporate models with video-tube displays whereby a captain of industry could plot future courses of action—like a Napoleon evaluating tactical military decisions using a model of the battlefield in a sandbox. Eventually such modeling systems may exist. They do not appear to be practical today.

What approaches can you follow in gaining initial exposure to the actual operations of a financial model? There are several: through special analysis problems, financial planning models and corporate models.

SPECIAL ANALYSIS

Recent experience indicates financial modeling is very successful when it is initially used in a limited area to solve specific problems. Some examples of such areas are real estate projections, foreign exchange rates, income tax planning, merger and acquisition analysis, capital equipment evaluation, and analysis of capital structure and bank financing. Real benefits have resulted from financial models applied in these areas. This route also enables executives to test the water before deciding whether to jump in—or how deep they should get into it.

FINANCIAL MODELING AND PLANNING

Another approach to financial modeling is to view it as a part of the planning function in an organization. While this approach has been successful in a number of cases, the chances of success are highly dependent on how well the planning function is organized and accepted by executive management. You cannot use financial modeling as a substitute for planning, but you can use financial modeling to improve planning in an organization.

It is difficult to generalize about how financial modeling may be used in planning activities because these activities vary so much from company to company and industry to industry. When the emphasis is primarily on the annual plan, the model is usually set up in monthly increments and may be adjusted to reflect monthly operating results and budget revisions. This capability has been particularly useful in industries where prices vary substantially for raw materials (such as livestock and grains). Another important use is in multi-division companies where the clerical-mechanical problems of consolidation limit the use of revised budgets and current outlooks. With a model, consolidations of the budgets of the individual divisions can be accomplished within minutes. With current pressures from investors for earnings projections, a financial model related to the budget may be of considerable value in preparing press releases and comments to security dealers.

In addition to the annual planning cycle, most companies today are preparing long-range plans extending over a number of years. In this connection, financial models are useful in evaluating alternate plans and strategies. The "what if" capability of a model is of particular value in this regard.

An example of such a question is: What would be the annual earnings per share if Division Alpha's sales grew at 5% instead of 3% and Division Omega's sales at 1% instead of 7%? Of course, such a question could be answered without a model. But, because of short response time and low cost of analysis with a model, more questions are asked and management tends to get a more comprehensive understanding of the financial implications of different strategies and economic conditions.

CORPORATE MODELS

Financial modeling has also been used in operating management systems. In these situations, the financial model becomes a part (often referred to as a module) of a corporate model which encompasses a number of modules. The nonfinancially oriented modules in a corporate model typically relate to the physical characteristics of production and marketing. For example, the production modules may relate to raw material requirements in tons, production capacities in units, and manpower requirements in man-hours. The marketing modules typically deal with factors such as market segments, advertising and promotion programs, market penetration, price-volume relationships, discounts and allowances, and channels of distribution.

Just as accounting systems eventually tie together the results of the many operating segments of a company in developing financial statements, the financial portion of a corporate model integrates the various modules relating to operations.

COMMUNICATION AND UNDERSTANDING GAP

It is much easier to identify application areas where modeling should be beneficial than to explain why it is not being more widely used today in business decision-making. If you read the technical literature on the subject, you will find there is obviously a broad gap between how the technician thinks modeling should be used and how executives actually use it.

This communication or understanding gap is not new or unique to financial modeling. Executives have always received an abundance of advice from critics who are anxious to tell them how to run their business. While technicians criticize management for being backward and resistant to change, they themselves are usually at fault for not communicating more effectively. They persist in using their unique jargon in such a way as to turn off individuals outside their own circle. Jargon also is an excellent screen to hide behind when you don't have an intelligent answer to a good question.

Another reason for the limited use of modeling is the lack of success of early modeling projects. Many of these projects did not succeed because they were oversold to executive management. Others failed because the models became unnecessarily complex. Some technicians wanted executive management to surrender its decision-making responsibility to the assumed logic of the "black box." When executive management asked what was in the "black box," the answer too often was "that is a technical matter that you won't understand because of your limited background in this area—but I assure you that it will work." The typical executive reaction to such a comment was that the model builder didn't understand the business because of his limited background in executive management—therefore, why pursue the subject any further?

There are ways, however, of narrowing this communication-understanding gap, and they do not involve replacing executive management.

The first step is the selection of a person to be responsible for the financial modeling effort. The selection should not be based on technical expertise or years of experience. The right individual will typically be a comer in the organization who relates primarily to executive management and communicates effectively at this level. He must also be a problem solver with a capability to work with financial data and quantitative analysis. He must be oriented toward making things happen on an orderly and timely basis.

The second step in closing the communication-understanding gap relates to executive management. As a group and as individuals, they must define more precisely how the planning function should operate and what role projections and quantitative analysis will play in the decision-making process. Executive management must also analyze its own management style and the management style of the company. A company with an autocratic president who makes seat of the pants decisions will have little need for a financial model. On the other hand, a corporation which emphasizes planning and uses financial analysis as a primary means of control will find that financial modeling is a meaningful asset.

ABUSES OF FINANCIAL MODELING

Rather than extol the limitless benefits of financial modeling (as a number of learned articles have), I think it would be more useful to evaluate some reasons why the technique has not been successful in a number of practical business situations.

1. Don't meander into financial modeling.

A number of companies have launched financial modeling projects without adequate knowledge or a sense of direction. When this happens, the bureaucratic elements inherent in all organizations slowly grab hold of the project. Before you know it, "ad hoc" committees have blurred the objectives of the project and extended the completion dates indefinitely.

2. Problems of excessive evaluation of computer software.

While it is important to learn about computer software used in financial modeling, this can be overdone. Because of the number of competing software systems available and the rapid technological change in this area, it is easy to lose sight of the forest (the use of the models) because of the trees (the software systems).

3. Beware of sophisticated statistical models.

As I mentioned earlier, a financial model typically is built upon the logic of accounting statements. Some people outside the accounting profession may not be impressed with the complexity of accounting logic. But they usually find it is considerably more difficult to understand than they expect when they are charged with developing financial models. Statistical probability distributions are technically interesting and potentially useful. However, they should not be incorporated into the financial models until the models have been in operation for some time. Generally speaking, these techniques are like candles on a birthday cake. They improve the looks of the cake but not its ultimate use.

4. *Recognize the "future shock" syndrome.*

A number of well conceived financial models have failed because of the reactions of the people who run and use them. The "future shock," or rate at which an organization can change, must be carefully evaluated and considered in both the design of the models and in the way they are introduced into the organization. The spread sheet approach to projections may be laborious and ineffective. However, it is a known element to the assistant controller who has been working with it during his whole career. The financial model may be a superior technique. But, to many, it may seem to be a threat both to their technical knowledge and their relationship to the organization.

5. *Financial models are not for everyone.*

There are many situations where financial modeling would be of very limited use. Before a model can be applied, some form of logical structure must exist and be accepted by the decision-making group. In addition to structure, there must be a means of developing input data and assumptions. The structure of the model may take into account both fixed and variable elements of cost. However, the model will be of little value if there is not a similar breakdown of cost data available for input into the model.

6. *Financial models, budgets and general ledgers are different.*

Some articles have stressed the potential use of computerized general ledger systems as a financial model. While the theory is good, the approach usually is not practical. The level of detail required in a general ledger and the volume of data in the files make it a complex data processing system—even on a monthly closing cycle. Typically, budget data is included in a computer-based general ledger system. However, this is normally at a summary level above the lowest level transaction code. A financial model normally is at a summary level above the budget, but it should be integrated to the budget level. The financial model must operate at an aggregate level in order to keep the number of input elements within reason and to keep the processing time under control.

THE USES AND BENEFITS OF FINANCIAL MODELS

The advent of cost-benefit analysis, which is another new and only partially proven financial tool, means that management must evaluate new systems in a rational manner that compares related costs and benefits. Applying this to financial modeling is difficult because the most important benefits are those that improve the quality of executive decisions. The problem is to determine how much the quality of executive decisions has been improved and how much of this improvement is due to the financial model and how much to the executives themselves. There are a number of explicit benefits related to financial modeling, but the really important benefits are implicit and imbedded within the executive decision-making process. Most of these benefits can only be evaluated by an executive through first-hand experience. Yet, it can be useful to explore some of them. Here are five particularly pertinent ones.

1. Increase the breadth of analysis leading to decision-making.

In evaluating capital expenditure decisions or a profit plan, it has been fairly common to consider only a few alternate strategies or economic assumptions before reaching a decision. Cost has been one factor limiting the number of contingency plans reviewed, but time to prepare the alternatives has usually been the primary limiting factor.

With a financial model, both the cost and time limitations are greatly reduced. As a result, a decision that might have been based on three or four cycles of analysis might now be predicated on 30 or 40 cycles of analysis. In a similar manner, budget outlooks can be adjusted more frequently to reflect new data and changes in assumptions and forecasts. In effect, the financial model shifts the effort of the financial analyst away from pencil pushing and toward the evaluation of alternate conditions and decisions.

2. Provide a framework for long-range planning.

The primary problem of long-range planning in industry is that everybody talks about it but few people do anything about it. One reason for this is the lack of structure within the planning process. A financial model may provide a focal point for structuring the planning process. In some cases the financial model and its implications for planning have been used as a vehicle for improving communications between individuals of varied backgrounds within the organization.

3. Evaluating new forms and uses of financial information.

In some companies financial modeling has been used to evaluate alternate forms and uses of financial information. Because of the flexibility inherent in modeling and the ability to evaluate the impact of various financial factors on profits, the financial model is used as an experimental lab for testing and evaluating new accounting approaches.

4. Tool for special problems.

More and more attention is being devoted by management to one-time or temporary problem situations. Because they are not of a continuing nature, it is not practical to develop typical data-processing systems for these problems. Financial models can frequently fill this gap. Some recent applications in this area relate to wage-price controls,

changes in tax law, international monetary rates, and mergers and acquisitions.

5. *Understanding the inherent logic of the financial system.*

As a by-product of financial modeling, some executives have found
that the experience of defining the logic and interaction of the financial
system in developing the model was, in itself, a very important and
revealing activity. In effect, it forces a soul-searching in terms of "why
do we do it that way?" For the first time, many relationships are recognized on a more explicit basis.

SUMMARY

Experience indicates financial modeling techniques can be applied
effectively in a number of business situations, especially those in which
there is a logical structure and where a degree of uncertainty is inherent
in the assumptions involved.

With business facing the conflicting forces of the energy crisis,
environmental constraints, etc., executive management must look for
new ways to evaluate alternate courses of action and their impact on
profitability. Financial modeling may provide management with important tools for dealing with the increasing complexities and uncertainties facing industry today and tomorrow.

27. THE DYNAMICS OF FINANCIAL PLANNING*

JOEL M. STERN†

Financial planning should set reasonable goals that result in attainable market values for the ordinary shareholders. That is, goals should be defined in terms that relate directly to the concepts and parameters that investors believe are systematically important in evaluating management's performance. Hence, if management achieves its goals, a predictable market value for the firm's equity should result.

How effective is this corporate performance-market reaction link when conventional accounting tools are employed to formulate corporate objectives? Unfortunately, popular accounting measures, such as earnings per share (eps), return on stockholders' equity (r_e) and the price/earnings multiple for the ordinary shares (PE), can easily distort desirable corporate strategy, thereby rendering financial planning useless and misleading and, very often, costly to the shareholders.

The major problem with conventional measures is that they fail to separate investment decision-making from financing policy. Consequently, poor investment opportunities (i.e. opportunities with low expected rates of return) may appear to be beneficial for the shareholders because a particular financing vehicle is employed to gear up the eps and r_e. Proper planning tools should evaluate investments on their own merits. The financing device should be relatively passive, because it is impossible to identify specific sources of funds with specific uses of funds.

The purposes of this paper are to investigate the shortcomings of the aforementioned tools—eps, r_e and PE—highlighting the problems with disguised examples that pinpoint the issues; present an alternative analytical framework that overcomes the problems; and, examine the implications for real-world decision-making. In particular, establishing corporate objectives, acquisition analysis, dividend policy and financial reporting are discussed in detail. Finally, the shortcomings of our approach are identified and areas for future research are suggested.

An underlying theme is that the high degree of association of conventional tools with stock prices is partly the cause of the steady state of misunderstanding in financial planning. Because this high degree of correlation is absent when the tools are employed in financial planning accounts for management's frequent rejection of desirable opportunities.

---

*From *Analytical Methods in Financial Planning* (New York: The Chase Manhattan Bank, N.A., 1974), pp. 5-17. Reprinted by permission.
†Vice President, Corporate Financial Research Division, Chase Manhattan Bank.

CONVENTIONAL ACCOUNTING TOOLS

The shortcomings of *eps*, r_e and PE can be identified if we examine their current use in setting corporate objectives and acquisition analysis.

Setting Corporate Objectives

Corporate goals should be formulated in a quantitative framework that relates directly to the price of the firm's ordinary shares. Therefore, fulfilling the objectives should result in a predictable market value.

Not long ago, we were asked to evaluate a company's goals which summarised the management's five-year plan. Briefly, the plan called for a 6% annual increase in *eps*, r_e of 12% and a target PE of fifteen.

To our amazement, we found that each of the first two goals could be achieved while shortchanging the ordinary shareholders. That is, the *eps* and r_e goals were attainable if the firm's expected rate of return on fixed capital (all interest-bearing debt and equity), r, was less than the return the stockholders could earn by investing their money elsewhere in portfolios of similar risk. Second, the PE goal of fifteen was inconsistent with other stated objectives. Even if the market's confidence about managerial capability and the future of the company's technology were as glamorous as IBM, its PE would not exceed thirteen! And, finally, we found that specific underlying assumptions were omitted from these quantitative measures and, hence, the operating officers in the company could easily be confused or misled in attempting to carry them out.

A closer look at the basis for our conclusions pinpoints the problems with *eps* and r_e. If a firm earned £1,000 all of which was reinvested earning a return of say, 12%, next year's earnings would be £1,120, the second year's earnings would be £1,254, and so on. That is, the earnings would grow at the same 12% as the rate of return on investment. The curious result was that the firm's management called for a rate of growth in earnings per share of 6% when the desirable rate of return was 12%. In other words, the implication must have been that the management was planning to pay out 50% of the company's earnings in the form of dividends to the shareholders. Only then would the earnings grow at a mere 6%. When we asked the management about the expected dividend payout, we were told that the dividend payout would be far less than 50%! And, of course, the implication of this answer was that the first two goals were inconsistent with each other.

Furthermore, having specified the goals in terms of the shareholder's equity meant that they were attainable if only the debt ratio were manoeuvred and the rate of return on total investment—the debt *and* equity—exceeded the cost of the company's borrowed funds. For example, if the after-tax cost of debt were 4% and the after-tax return on total investment were 5% (which is probably far less than the return shareholders could hope to earn by investing elsewhere in alternative opportunities of similar risk), the earnings per share would rise and the rate of return on shareholders' equity could be altered simply by changing the capital structure—the proportion of debt as a source of funds. If a given capital structure were too low to achieve the 12% return on equity, management need only increase the degree of gearing by increasing the level of debt until 12% is attained. In other words, an underlying assumption must be made about the firm's target capital structure.

Without some specification of the firm's dividend policy and its target capital structure, the operating personnel could be confused in their attempt to achieve the firm's goals. As we shall see shortly, the use of an analytical framework for planning that is related closely to the market value of the firm would prohibit both the inevitable confusion and the costly mistakes of intuition and arbitrary goal setting.

Conventional acquisition analysis is a noteworthy example of the shortcomings of *eps* and PE as workable tools for managerial decision-making and setting corporate goals.

Acquisition Analysis

Often we are told in business publications about the desirability of improving the firm's *eps* when the impact of an acquisition on the buyer's *eps* is entirely irrelevant. For example, company *A* may be about to acquire company *B*. *A* sells at a higher PE than the PE *A* is to offer *B*'s shareholders. *A* may sell at, say, twenty times earnings and offer *B*'s shareholders a PE of fifteen when *B* is selling at ten times earnings. If *A* buys *B* with an equity swap to form the new company *AB*, *AB*'s (the pro forma) *eps* will always exceed *A*'s *eps*. This is because *A* (i.e., the firm selling at the higher PE) is issuing fewer shares per pence of earnings acquired. Hence, we are told that *AB* is good for *A*'s shareholders.

The problem with this result is that we are told that *AB* is good for *A*'s shareholders because *AB*'s *eps* exceeds *A*'s *eps*. And, of course, this occurs even if there are no operating savings. This logic is erroneous. *B* appears to be a desirable acquisition not because of its value to *A*, but because of *A*'s higher PE before the acquisition. The business writer fails to realise that were *A* to acquire any firm for which it paid full value (i.e. there is no added benefit to the buyer's shareholders), its PE would fall to offset the gain in *eps*.

Let us turn the example around. If *B* buys *A* to form *BA*, the firm selling at the lower PE (ten) is buying a company at a price greater than its own PE. *B* will pay at least *A*'s PE of twenty. But now *BA*'s (pro forma) *eps* will be less than *B*'s, because the firm with the lower PE must offer more shares per pence of acquired earnings. The same people who tell us that *AB* is good for *A's* shareholders tell us that *BA* is bad for *B's* shareholders even though *AB* and *BA* are the same company, most often with the same assets and earnings expectations and, even, the same management.

"The *AB-BA* fallacy" is that the analyst believes the pro forma *eps* is a proximate determinant of the pro forma share price, when the pro forma *eps* is in no way related to the pro forma share price. It is emphasising *eps* when *eps* is irrelevant and misleading, and usually results in costly decisions by management. Failing to evaluate the acquisition with a tool that is systematically related to the firm's market value is the cause of the confusion. For example, the president of a company recently mentioned to us that in 1955 his company was a small machine tool manufacturer selling at about ten times earnings. Therefore, he concluded that he could only acquire companies selling at PE's of ten or less. Otherwise he would dilute the *eps* and stockholders' equity' of his firm (whatever that might mean). In the earlier example, this was company *B* and any firm selling above a PE of ten was company *A*. Since the president of the small machine tool company did not want to "dilute" his *eps*, he chose to acquire companies whose PE did not exceed his PE of ten: mostly other machine tool companies. These acquisitions did nothing to reduce the amplitudes of the cyclical swings in sales and profits. And, as we might expect, his company continues to sell at about 10 times earnings.

Another example extends "the *AB-BA* fallacy" to capital structure planning. The president of a well diversified manufacturer selling at sixteen times earnings wanted to acquire a small, but exceptionally profitable, engineering consulting firm selling for a PE of twenty-five. An equity swap would "dilute" the pro forma *eps*. Facetiously, we suggested that he sell his company to the engineering firm, even though the latter was only about 10% as large as the manufacturer. Company *A* would be acquiring *B*, rather than the reverse, and the pro forma *eps* would rise. He suggested an alternative: finance the acquisition with a vehicle that would gear up the pro forma *eps*. The anticipated profits from the acquisition would more than cover the out-of-pocket cost of interest on debt, or dividends on preference shares. He was right; the pro forma *eps* would rise.

However there is a conceptual problem with this solution. The pro forma *eps* (and r_e) can be enhanced simply by gearing the firm with debt or preference shares. Thus, employing an *eps* criterion, bad investments can appear to be good investments because the management can gear the firm and increase the *eps* at the time the investment is undertaken. Furthermore, in the United States, for example, the management can increase the *eps* without making any investment by borrowing to retire ordinary shares.

ANALYTICAL FRAMEWORK

It is because of the shortcomings of conventional measures employed in financial planning that we suggest an alternative approach: an analytical framework which (*a*) measures attainable management goals, while (*b*) separating investment decision-making from financing policy, that (*c*) permits management to test the sensitivity of input assumptions and, perhaps most important, (*d*) simulates the impact of financial plans on the market value of the firm's ordinary shares.

The procedure is to (*a*) introduce a diagram that describes the market's mechanism for valuation, (*b*) present the basic model for a taxless world in which there is no "growth potential" (strictly defined), (*c*) relax these tax and growth assumptions and (*d*) apply the resulting model to financial planning—setting corporate goals, acquisition analysis, capital structure planning and dividend policy and financial reporting.

Diagrammatic Description of the Market Mechanism

On the horizontal axis in Figure 27-1, *I* is incremental investment in the current year. It is net fixed capital additions: capital expenditures minus depreciation and other non-cash charges plus additions to working capital (net current assets) and other long-term assets, or, what amounts to the same thing, additions to total assets minus additions to current liabilities. (As we will demonstrate later, current liabilities are only non-interest-bearing items, such as accrued expenses and accounts payable. In the analytical framework, short-term interest-bearing debt, such as bank debt and the current portion of long-term debt, is considered to be part of the company's fixed capital.)

On the vertical axis, we measure the expected rates of return on *I* and denote them with the symbol *r*. If the best investment is selected first and it has, say, an anticipated return of 25% for a £100,000 outlay, the point *A* represents the project. If the next best investment of £150,000 has an anticipated return of 20%, it may be represented by point *B*. Note that the horizontal axis measures total investment and, hence, project *B* is matched up with the total projects *A* and *B*, £250,000.

The schedule may continue all the way down to 0% and cross the horizontal axis at the point Z. Projects with expected negative rates of return, cannot be relevant. The question we must ask is how far down the schedule can management proceed before they begin to shortchange their shareholders? The answer is that there is some hurdle or cut-off rate below which the management cannot, or should not, undertake investment because the shareholders can take their money and invest it in alternative securities of similar risk earning this hurdle rate.

FIGURE 27-1

INVESTMENT AND RETURN

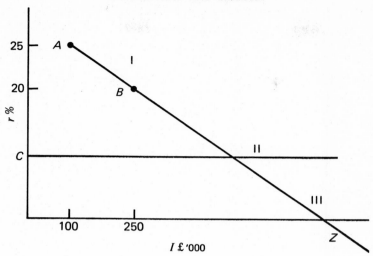

This cut-off rate is popularly known as the cost of capital (c) because it represents the cost to the ordinary shareholders of foregoing alternative available opportunities for investment. It is the rate of return that could be expected elsewhere on identically-risky investments. Although there may not be a perfect substitute for the shareholders' investment in the firm, there is some combination of other investments that will offer the same expected risk-return trade-off.

Hence, *the cost of capital is the minimum rate of return (c) that must be expected by management on new investments in order to compensate the shareholders for the business or asset risk they undertake by investing in the firm's ordinary shares, because the shareholders have alternative, identically-risky opportunities elsewhere.*

The diagram can be especially valuable in specifying the reasons why some firms sell at higher prices than others. If the expected rate of return (r) on new investment exceeds the rate of return the shareholders can otherwise expect by investing elsewhere (c), management can outperform the market (group I projects in the diagram). Consequently, the market will pay a premium for an ability it cannot duplicate: the market value will exceed the economic book value. And the wider the spread between r and c, the greater the price and PE will be. Group I is the case of "growth potential."

When the management cannot outperform the market, r and c will be identical. These are the group II projects, the absence of growth potential: the market value and economic book value will be the same because management possesses no unusual ability to outperform the market. Of course, if r is less than c, management will be shortchanging the shareholders. These are the group III projects. The greater the investments in this area, the greater will be the discount of the firm's market value from its economic book value.

Analytical Framework in a Taxless World with No Growth

We can describe a firm's market value for the simple case, in which there are no corporate income taxes and no growth potential—group II for which $r = c$.

The procedure for developing the simple model is to examine a single investment opportunity, an outlay (I) of £10,000 that is expected to generate net operating profit (NOP) of £1,000 annually, an anticipated rate of return (r) of 10% equal to c:[1,2]

$$r = \frac{\text{NOP}}{I} \tag{1}$$

We can substitute the symbol V for I, where V is the market value of the interest-bearing debt and/or ordinary shares issued to finance I, and since $r = c$ for this group II investment, Expression (1) becomes:

$$c = \frac{\text{NOP}}{V} \tag{2}$$

which implies that c is the rate that discounts or capitalises the expected stream of net operating profit back to the current market value of the firm. Rearranging the terms, the firm's market value is described in terms of two parameters, NOP and c, in the simplified taxless world in which there is no growth:

$$V \equiv D + E = \frac{\text{NOP}}{c} \tag{3}$$

where D is the value of all interest-bearing debt and E is the value of all the ordinary shares.

Expression (3) is the *fundamental principle of valuation: the market value of the firm's debt and equity is equal to the anticipated net operating profit discounted at the rate c that is a measure of business risk inherent in the assets generating the profits (NOP).*

---

[1]The numerator should be expressed in terms of cash flows, but, for simplicity, we assume that the annual depreciation is reinvested to maintain the level of investment at £10,000 and NOP at £1,000.

[2]Note that the numerator is NOP, not net profit (NP) which is reported to ordinary shareholders. The difference between NOP and NP is the interest expense on borrowed capital. Since I is additions to fixed capital (i.e. interest-bearing debt *and* shareholders' equity), the numerator of the fraction must be expressed in comparable terms—the returns to bondholders as well as shareholders.

Analytical Framework in a Taxable World with No Growth

In the world of corporate income taxes, there are two components: (*a*) the anticipated net operating profit after taxes capitalised at an after-tax rate of discount and (*b*) the capitalised tax saving that arises from the deductibility of interest expense in calculating the firm's taxable income.

The capitalised profits component is $NOPAT/c_t$, where NOPAT is the expected net operating profit after taxes, and c_t is the hurdle rate for business risk in a taxable world. NOPAT is expected profits before financing costs but after taxes. Since NOP was defined in an accounting sense as net profit NP plus interest expense, NOPAT is the expected net profit after taxes, NPAT, plus interest expense after taxes. If b is the cost of borrowed capital and D is the amount of borrowed capital, bD is the interest expense and $(1 - t)\,bD$ is the after-tax interest expense, where t is the marginal corporate income tax rate. Hence, $NOP = NP + bD$ and $NOPAT = NPAT + (1 - t)\,bD$.

Since interest expense is tax deductible, it pays to employ borrowed capital. If $(1 - t)\,bD$ is the after-tax cost of debt, the annual expected government tax saving is the marginal corporate income tax multiplied by the pre-tax interest expense: tbD.

If the firm has a target, or long run expected, capital structure,[3] the market will capitalise the annual government tax saving as if it were available in perpetuity because the shareholders will expect outstanding debt to be refinanced as it comes due. Therefore, the firm's market value will include not only the capitalised anticipated profits, $NOPAT/c_t$, but the capitalised tax saving as well, which is tbD divided by a rate that measures the risk inherent in the source of tbD.

NOPAT is capitalised at the rate c_t because c_t measures the risk in I that generates NOPAT. The annual tax saving, tbD, is more certain than NOPAT; that is, the expected rate of return before corporate income taxes on the firm's total fixed capital need only be equal to the rate of interest on borrowed capital for the firm to obtain the tax saving. On new investment, r need only be equal to b to obtain the tax saving, which is much less than c_t and, hence, tbD is a more certain stream than NOPAT. The discount rate that measures the uncertainty in receiving the annual expected tax saving is identical with the discount rate bondholders employ to measure the uncertainty attached to receiving their interest income (bD): the rate of interest on debt itself, b.

Therefore, the total market value of the firm in the real world of taxes (but retaining the assumption about the absence of growth potential) becomes:

---

[3] The firm's capital structure is the relative sources of its fixed capital. Its fixed capital is all interest-bearing debt, reserves, preference capital and ordinary shareholders' capital. Thus, the target capital structure is the fraction of fixed capital that management expects to finance with interest-bearing debt on average and over time.

$$V \equiv D + E = \frac{\text{NOPAT}}{c_t} + \frac{tbD}{b} \tag{4}$$

$$= \frac{\text{NOPAT}}{c_t} + tD$$

Three observations are especially useful for financial planning:

1. Within "prudent limits," incremental debt financing will add to the firm's market value: If the marginal corporate income tax rate is 40%, the total market value (V) and the market value of the ordinary shares (E) will increase 40 pence for each pound's increase in the target capital structure's level of debt.
2. Preference shares never "add value" to the firm's market value, because the dividends are not tax deductible and, hence, provide no tax saving.
3. Maximising the firm's market value and its PE are incompatible. Debt will add to the firm's market value, but it will also drive down the PE. Therefore, corporate goals should never be stated in terms of maximising PE for non-growth firms.

If we introduce an arithmetic example, each of these observations will become clear. Consider the following values for each of the parameters:

$$\text{NOPAT} = \pounds 1,000$$
$$c_t = 10\%$$
$$t = 40\%$$

Hence, V is £10,000 if the firm is debt-free:

$$V \equiv D + E = \frac{\text{NOPAT}}{c_t} + tD$$

$$= \frac{1,000}{0.10} + 0.40(0) = 10,000$$

If the firm issues £5,000 of debt to retire £5,000 of equity,[4] we might expect the total market value to remain unchanged, since holding the asset size and, hence, NOPAT unchanged means that only the sources of financing are altered. But in the real-world of taxes, the capitalised tax saving adds $tD = \pounds 2,000$ to the market value. The new total market

---

[4]An expansion of a firm's assets financed with debt is equivalent in concept and result to financing the expansion with equity followed by an issue of debt to retire the equity. In the example in the paper, we employ debt to retire existing equity only because we wish to hold the level of the firm's assets and NOPAT constant, examining the implications of changes in the firm's capital structure on its market value. Although share repurchase is technically not permitted in the United Kingdom, its equivalence to financing expansion with debt (with $r = c$) means that the example in the paper *is* 'relevant' for financial planning in the UK.

value is £12,000 and the equity's market value increases to £7,000 (= $V - D$) on half as many outstanding shares.

In the absence of the tax saving, the equity market value would have been £5,000. The conclusion is that it pays to borrow because of the deductibility of interest expense in calculating the firm's taxable income. The market value of the firm's equity will increase 40 pence for each £1 increase in debt. But debt ratios will be limited, in part, by lender's risk preferences. Additions to the debt ratio beyond the lenders' expectation of "prudent limits" will result in cumbersome restrictions in loan agreements and bond indentures on management's operating flexibility. Hence, in the real-world, the apparently unlimited benefits of increasing debt ratios will be modified by management's desire to remain "bankable" or "institutionable."

Although the value of the ordinary shares rises with increases in the debt ratio, the PE falls; that is, the price per share increases but the *eps* rises even faster.[5] First, we will examine this effect in our example by calculating the PE before and after gearing. Second, we will explain its intuitive support.

The PE is the price per share divided by the *eps* or, what amounts to the same thing, the total market value of the ordinary shares divided by the net profit after taxes (NPAT): PE = E/NPAT.

In the debt-free situation, E was £10,000, which was the total market value of the firm, V, as well. Since debt was absent, NOPAT and NPAT were identical, £1,000. Hence, the PE was 10:

$$PE = \frac{E}{NPAT} = \frac{10,000}{1,000} = 10$$

When gearing was introduced, E was £7,000 on half as many shares. NPAT was NOPAT (£1,000) minus the after-tax interest expense, $(1 - t)\, bD$, which was $(1 - 0.40)\,(0.06)\,(5,000)$, or £180. Therefore, NPAT was $1,000 - 180$, or £820, and the PE was approximately $8\frac{1}{2}$:

$$PE = \frac{E}{NPAT} = \frac{7,000}{820} = 8\frac{1}{2}$$

The intuitive support for the decline in the PE is also straightforward. In the absence of debt, the ordinary shareholder need be concerned only with the business risk of the firm's assets that generate NOPAT. When debt is introduced as a source of funds, financial risk is added in the form of an additional fixed cost, the interest expense. Hence, the additional return in *eps* that accrues to the shareholders is not as valuable as in the debt-free case. Gearing from financing has been

---

[5]Since $r_t = c_t$ in this case and $c_t \geqq b_t$, the firm's *eps* will rise from gearing. The question is: will the *eps* rise faster than (the same as) (slower than) the price per share or, what amounts to the same thing, will the PE fall (remain the same) (rise) as the firm's debt ratio increases?

added to operating leverage (i.e. employing assets with fixed operating costs). In the absence of the government subsidy for debt, there would be no reason for the price of the equity to increase. The larger return on net worth and *eps* would be offset completely by the greater financial risk, the price of the shares remaining unchanged. The meaning of the government subsidy for debt is that the government bears a portion of the financial risk (i.e. *tbD*), the benefit of which accrues directly to the ordinary shareholders.

If we extend this reasoning to preference shares, it is clear that a firm's PE is lower when preference shares are employed instead of debt. Since preference shares' cash dividends are not tax deductible for corporations, there is no tax saving. That is, the ordinary shareholders bear the complete financial risk of the incremental fixed expense of the dividends. Even though preference shares provide gearing and, hence, greater *eps*, the price of the ordinary shares remains the same. Since employing debt increases the price of the ordinary shares, the PE will not fall as much as when preference shares are used as a source of funds.

Share price maximisation, which is always a desirable goal, is incompatible with PE maximisation. Although gearing always reduces the PE, within prudent limits, debt always increases the ordinary share price. Thus, we can conclude that PE maximisation should never be a corporate goal in this taxable but non-growth world.

The tax subsidy for debt appears to have been a major factor in the conglomerate movement in the United States. In most cases, their managements sought over-capitalised companies for takeover. Even without improved profitability (i.e. return on fixed capital), premiums above the sellers' market values could be justified. For example, a well-known debt-free company with 10 million shares outstanding and a market value of $50 for a total value of $500 million could have sufficient profitability to service, say, $300 million of interest-bearing debt. Thus, the conglomerate could offer a premium above the current market value at least equal to the tax saving, *tD*, which is about $150 million in the US where the marginal corporate income tax rate is close to 50%. This is $15 a share. That is, the buyer could offer up to $65 a share simply by altering the expected debt ratio. Since the buyer probably would not have to offer a 30% premium ($15 on the current price of $50), its return, *r*, would exceed *c*—the difference between the offering price and the maximum offering price—and this difference would accrue to the conglomerate's share price and shareholders.

Analytical Framework in a Taxable World with Growth

The final development of the analytical framework is the relaxation of the assumption that growth is absent. This is the case of group I projects in Figure 27-1 in which r_t (the expected rate of return after taxes) exceeds c_t. However, it is insufficient to describe growth as the difference, $r_t - c_t$, because r_t and c_t are expressed as percentages such as 20 and 10%, respectively, whereas V, D, and E are expressed in pounds. The important considerations are not only $r_t - c_t$, but the amount of net fixed capital additions, I, that is expected to earn r_t and the length of time in years for which r_t is expected to exceed c_t.

For example, consider the simple case in which the firm reinvests all of its earnings (i.e. $I = $ NOPAT). If NOPAT $= I = £1,000$, $r_t = 0.20$, and $c_t = 0.10$, investors will expect next year's NOPAT to be 20% greater than the current £1,000, or £1,200. Two years hence NOPAT will be expected to be £1,440, three years hence £1,728, and so on.[6]

If investors were given each year's earnings which they invested elsewhere with the expectation that they would earn 10% annually, their wealth would be expected to grow at the annual rate of 10% to £1,100 next year, £1,210 two years hence, £1,331 three years hence, and so on.

If we compare these two expected streams the concept of growth becomes clear.

Expected Rates of Return	Amount Invested Today	Year 1	Year 2	Year 3
By Management: $r_t = 0.20$	£1,000	£1,200	£1,440	£1,728
By Investors: $c_t = 0.10$	£1,000	£1,100	£1,210	£1,331
Difference Between Management's and Investors' Expected Returns		£100	£230	£397

From the table we can see that growth is the difference between the investors' expected future corporate profits and their expected future wealth for as long as the market's investors have confidence that the unusual opportunities will continue, namely, r_t will exceed c_t.

$I(r_t - c_t)$, the discounted value of which would be $I(r_t - c_t)/c_t$ beginning today and continuing forever, is somewhat analogous to the nongrowth component, NOPAT/c_t. However, r_t cannot exceed c_t forever because the discounted value of the growth potential would be infinite. Considering the likelihood of only a finite time horizon presents an extremely complex expression that can be simplified if the fraction $[1 + (Ir_t/\text{NOPAT})]/(1 + c_t)$ is close to 1 and if the finite time horizon for which r_t is expected to exceed c_t is not too large.[7] This simplified expression is $(r_t - c_t)IT/[c_t(1 + c_t)]$, where $c_t(1 + c_t)$ is a discounting mechanism

---

[6] If $I = $ NOPAT, the expected rate of growth in profits is the same as the expected rate of return on new investment, r_t, because the expected rate of growth in profits is the reinvestment rate, $I/$NOPAT (in our example, this is 1.00), multiplied by r_t.

[7] $Ir_t/$NOPAT is the expected rate of growth in NOPAT and n is the finite time horizon for which r_t is expected to exceed c_t.

for the unusual opportunities (i.e. r_t exceeding c_t) for their expected life, T years.

The analytical framework in its entirety contains three components of capitalised values—group II projects, NOPAT/c_t, the tax saving, tD; and, group I projects, $(r_t - c_t)IT/[c_t(1 + c_t)]$.

$$V = D + E = \frac{\text{NOPAT}}{c_t} + tD + \frac{r_t - c_t}{c_t(1 + c_t)}\, IT \qquad (5)$$

Subsequent to a correction in this model that was omitted in order to simplify the exposition, we will examine the implications for setting corporate goals, dividend policy, financial reporting and acquisition analysis.

Alternatively, the expression may be shown with the tax saving impounded into c_t; that is, the less expensive nature of debt need not be shown separately as tD. Synthesised with c_t, the tax saving would appear to disappear in favour of an after-tax weighted average cost of capital, $c_t^{\,\circ}$, the costs of debt and equity weighted by the proportions of debt and equity in the firm's target or long-run expected capital structure:

$$V \equiv D + E = \frac{\text{NOPAT}}{c_t^{\,\circ}} \qquad (6)$$

Returning briefly to our earlier arithmetic example, expression (4) yielded $V = 12,000$.

Employing expression (6), we can calculate the weighted average cost of capital by "solving" for $c_t^{\,\circ}$ to obtain $c_t^{\,\circ} = 0.0833$.[8]

-----

[8]To calculate a firm's hurdle rate, $c_t^{\,\circ}$, we substitute $c_t^{\,\circ}V$ in expression (6) for NOPAT in expression (4) to obtain

$$V = \frac{c_t^{\,\circ}V}{c_t} + tD$$

Simplifying and solving for $c_t^{\,\circ}$ in terms of c_t,

$$c_t V = c_t^{\,\circ}V + c_t D$$

$$\frac{c_t V - c_t tD}{V} = c_t^{\,\circ}$$

$$c_t\left(1 - \frac{tD}{V}\right) = c_t^{\,\circ}$$

This is the taxable, but non-growth case. In the case of growth, A_F is substituted for V, where A_F is the economic book value of the firm's fixed capital. (Fixed capital is total assets minus non-interest-bearing current liabilities.)

$$c_t^{\,\circ} = c_t\left(1 - \frac{tD}{A_F}\right)$$

Since the analytical framework is based on expectations, D/A_F is the fraction of the original cash cost of fixed capital that the market expects will be financed with interest-bearing debt on average and over time. The implications for financial reporting, which are considerable, are discussed in detail in APPLICATIONS OF THE ANALYTICAL FRAMEWORK FOR DECISION-MAKING on this page.

If we were to rewrite the entire analytical framework in terms of c_t^*, the omission in the development of the growth term should become clear:

$$V \equiv D + E = \frac{\text{NOPAT}}{c_t^*} + IT \cdot \frac{r_t - c_t^*}{c_t^*(1 + c_t^*)} \tag{7}$$

Note that the tax saving component, tD, is absent because it is impounded into the first term. Including it as the second term as we did in the earlier version, expression (5), would be double counting. More significant is the substitution of c_t^* for c_t in the growth term. Earlier, we had failed to note that the non-growth component was not NOPAT/c_t alone, but $\text{NOPAT}/c_t + tD$ or, what amounts to the same thing, NOPAT/c_t^*. Furthermore, it is clear that the presence of growth does not necessarily alter the market's discount rate, c_t^*. To demonstrate both the use of c_t and c_t^*, we can describe the analytical framework as

$$V \equiv D + E = \frac{\text{NOPAT}}{c_t} + tD + IT \frac{r_t - c_t^*}{c_t^*(1 + c_t^*)} \tag{8}$$

The importance of this "correction" for financial planning can be seen when we examine the implications of the analytical framework for setting proper corporate objectives in the next section.

APPLICATIONS OF THE ANALYTICAL FRAMEWORK FOR DECISION-MAKING

Virtually all important issues in financial planning can (and should be) evaluated within the analytical framework—issues that involve:

1. Setting corporate objectives
2. Investment decisions, including capital equipment analysis and acquisition pricing
3. Financing policy (i.e. capital structure planning), including selecting an appropriate dividend policy, refunding existing debt, lease financing, captive finance companies, convertible securities
4. Financial reporting

Space limitations permit investigating the implications of the methodology for only four issues in this section: setting corporate objectives and dividend policy, financial reporting and acquisition analysis.

Setting Corporate Objectives

The analytical framework is a description of the interrelationships of parameters that systematically determine the market prices of firms.

Consequently, achievable corporate goals expressed in terms contained in the model should result in attainable market values.

Given the empirically measurable hurdle rate for asset risk, c_t, and the confidence (T years) market investors have in management's ability to outperform the weighted average cost of capital c_t^*, management's overriding objective should be to undertake investment opportunities on which they expect to earn a return that is at least sufficient to cover the risk: r_t must be at least as large as c_t^*. Therefore, corporate objectives should be stated in terms of r_t and c_t^*. That is, management should first evaluate alternative investment opportunities as probabilistic cash flows to determine both r_t and c_t and, given management's and lenders' risk preferences and, hence, the target debt ratio, calculate c_t^*. Thus, management's goals should describe the latitude of acceptable projects, including product mix, size, location, and expected and acceptable profitability. Calculations of profitability should be in terms of expected future cash flows—NOPAT minus I. Finally, the firm's over-all desired capital structure must be determined in order to calculate c_t^*.[9,10]

Therefore, financial planning should concentrate on the parameters in the framework that management can influence or control—NOPAT, tD, I and r_t.

It is noteworthy that a target PE is *not* included as a goal. Not only does the firm's expected market value and, thus, the PE result from the aforementioned statement of goals, but it is not entirely clear that share price and PE move in the same direction if management's policies are attained. Earlier, we illustrated the relationship of share price and PE maximisation for the taxable, but non-growth case: within prudent limits, increases in the firm's debt ratio increase its share price but decrease its PE, as financial risk is added to the business risk borne by the ordinary shareholders.[11] An examination of the taxable world with growth con-

---

[9]Selecting a desirable capital structure is not an easy task. And it is not as simple as many texts in finance would have us believe. Management must first determine the degree of total risk—asset *and* financial risk—they wish the ordinary shareholders to bear. This would be expressed in probabilistic NPAT that accrues to the ordinary shareholders, rather than in terms of NOPAT. Given an assessment of the firm's expected future asset composition and a probabilistic estimate of future NOPAT and, hence, a value for c_t, the amount of financial risk would be determined by subtraction: financial risk, a function of gearing, is equal to desired expected total risk minus desired expected asset risk. Both theory and empirical study have progressed sufficiently for managers to employ this method of capital structure determination.

[10]Although c_t is a partial equilibrium concept in the model (i.e. given the asset structure, c_t is determinable), it is dynamic in the real world. That is, c_t is codetermined with changes in the firm's asset composition. Increasing (decreasing) liquidity, decreasing (increasing) cash flow cyclicality and/or increasing (decreasing) government regulation of the public utility variety would be expected to decrease (increase) c_t if investors are risk averse. For example, ceteris paribus, a bank reducing its fraction of government bonds in favour of mortgages should expect to increase its c_t. An implication is that a baby food manufactuer would reduce its c_t by acquiring a "pill" manufacturer. This is an example of reducing the asset risk that results from cash flow cyclicality.

[11]Quantitatively, the required rate of return on ordinary equity, Y_t, is the reciprocal of the PE. It can be described as the hurdle rate for asset or business risk, c_t, plus a required return for financial risk: $Y_t = c_t + (1 - t)(c_t - b)D/E$ where $(1 - t)(c_t - b)D/E$ is the (cont.)

cludes that share price and PE maximisation may, and very often will, be compatible goals. But since they are not always compatible, it can be dangerous for management to have its objectives include maximising the PE, which is a price-relative, rather than maximising share price, which is a price-absolute.

In the case of growth, adding to the target debt ratio decreases c_t^* in the growth term as well as in the nongrowth term (the latter being tD). Consequently, the numerator of the growth term increases as the spread between r_t and c_t^* increases, recalling that r_t is independent of financing: it is the expected rate of return before financing charges as a fraction of the incremental fixed capital (interest-bearing debt and equity) employed. Furthermore, the denominator declines in magnitude as the debt ratio increases because c_t^* is less than c_t. Thus, $(r_t - c_t^*)/c_t^*(1 + c_t^*)$ is always greater than $(r_t - c_t)/c_t(1 + c_t)$, if debt is employed and if the debt ratio is not excessive.

If I and T are large enough, the increase in the size of the growth term, arising from an increase in the target debt ratio, will overcome the added financial risk of gearing.[12] Thus, both the share price and PE will rise as the expected debt ratio increases.

Dividend Policy

The only financing policy that alters a firm's market value is a change in the target debt ratio, because the expected tax subsidy changes. Expression (8) is completely independent of dividend policy, because the firm's investment decision-making is not dependent on its dividend policy. Earnings retained for reinvestment are essentially a compulsory, pre-emptive rights offering. As long as management acts in the share-

---

required return for financial risk. This is described in greater detail in Joel M. Stern, *Valuation and Cost of Capital Theory*, 1967.

In our arithmetic example, c_t was 0.10, t was 0.40, b was 0.06 and D and E were £5,000 and £7,000, respectively. Thus, Y_t was 0.117:

$$Y_t = 0.10 + (1 - 0.40)(0.10 - 0.06)\frac{5000}{7000}$$

$$= 0.10 + (0.06)(0.04)\frac{5}{7}$$

$$= 0.10 + 0.017 = 0.117$$

Since the after-tax cost of debt is $(1 - t)\,b$ (or b_t), $(1 - 0.40)\,0.06$, or 0.036, the weighted average cost of capital can be calculated to be $8\frac{1}{3}\%$ by weighting Y_t and b_t by the proportions of debt and equity, 5,000/12,000 ($0.41\frac{2}{3}$) and 7,000/12,000 ($0.58\frac{1}{3}$). Alternatively, the expression for c_t° in Footnote 8 can be employed:

$$c_t^\circ = c_t\left(1 - \frac{tD}{A_F}\right) = 0.10\left(1 - \frac{0.40(5000)}{12000}\right)$$

$$= 0.10\left(1 - \frac{1}{6}\right) = 0.10(0.83\frac{1}{3}) = 0.08\frac{1}{3}$$

[12]This point is so important, the Appendix to this chapter develops the issue completely. [The Appendix is not included in this book.]

holders' best interest by undertaking projects with expected rates of return at least as large as the hurdle rate ($r_t \geqq c_t^*$), the dividend policy determines only the form that the shareholders' expected return will take —dividends and/or capital appreciation. This conclusion should be modified for tax considerations.

If there were no income taxes and no costs of buying and selling securities, the proper dividend policy would be to pay out nothing to the ordinary shareholders, provided management has ample group I projects ($r_t \geqq c_t^*$) in which to invest the earnings. In this hypothetical world, investors could sell shares to obtain cash for other purposes. If group II projects ($r_t = c_t^*$) are expected, management can be indifferent between reinvestment and dividend payout, whereas group III projects ($r_t \leqq c_t^*$) imply liquidation.

In the real world of both taxes and transaction costs, a large number of investors prefer cash dividends because they pay little or no taxes on ordinary income. For others in high income tax brackets, little or no cash dividends are preferable because the costs of capital gains taxes and selling securities are far less than the tax on ordinary income. Consequently, an interesting and nontrivial phenomenon occurs when a firm sells ordinary shares to the public for the first time. A clientele effect builds up as investors with particular needs are attracted to the company for, among other reasons, the tax consequences of the dividend policy.

Therefore, if management's objective is to act in the best interest of its shareholders, it should never alter the fraction of expected earnings to be paid out as cash dividends. The dividend payout ratio (i.e. dividend as a percentage of earnings) should be maintained in order that the return expected by the shareholders from dividends remains a fixed percentage of the total return they expect on average and over time from dividends and capital appreciation. This will occur as long as the average PE does not change significantly over time. Changing the payout ratio would compel the ordinary shareholders to alter their investment portfolios in order to maintain their greatest after-tax return. Even unexpectedly large group I opportunities do not alter our conclusion. Shareholders would prefer the dividend payout and periodic issues of equity.

Financial Reporting

The analytical framework underlying expression (8) implies that financial reporting should be an integral part of corporate planning. Expression (8) presents six parameters that should account for systematic market valuation. If management can influence the parameters significantly, changes in policy that affect these parameters should be reported because markets pay a discount for uncertainty, not a premium.

Two parameters are exogenous to the firm (c_t and T) in that they are determined subjectively and almost exclusively by market investors. Thus, c_t, which is the market's required rate of return for business risk, is a function of the firm's expected asset composition, but it is the market's risk evaluation that matters. Consequently, management influences c_t only by selecting the nature of the firm's assets. T is a measure of the market's confidence that r_t will exceed c_t^*. T is a function of product cyclicality, the state of monetary policy, and the degree of government regulation and product technology. Again, given the firm's expected asset composition, the market determines T. Therefore, planned changes by management of the asset composition should be reported to the market. This includes industry and geographical distribution.

The remaining four parameters can be influenced significantly by the management: "normalised" net operating profits, the target capital structure, capital spending forecasts, and the historical annual rate of internal growth in NOPAT.

"Normalised" Net Operating Profits.   Reported profits include the impact of non-recurring factors, such as strikes, other interruptions in operations and windfall gains. The chief executive officer in his letter to the shareholders should elaborate on the nature and extent of abnormal episodes that affected reported net operating profits.

We select net operating profits (profits before interest expense and income taxes) because it is a measure of management's investment performance. It is independent of financing policy (which is discussed below) and changes in the firm's required tax burden. Interest rate fluctuations and tax statutes are not influenced significantly (if at all) by individual managers and, hence, should not be included in a measure of management's performance.

Target Capital Structure.   Within wide bounds, management controls the firm's capital structure. Within prudent limits set by lenders' and management's risk preferences, the proportions of debt and equity can be established by the management. The debt limitations depend on the degree of protection the assets afford lenders and the amount of earnings anticipated to be available to repay interest and principal.

The sources of funds are important to investors only as a result of the corporate tax structure. The second component of expression (8), tD, and the decline of c_t to c_t^* in the third component means that debt financing can increase both the share price and the PE. But communication of the target capital structure can be an important prerequisite.

At a minimum, the aggregate market values of the ordinary shares increases 40 pence for each £1 of incremental interest-bearing debt when the marginal corporate income tax rate is 40%. This is the impact of the second component. Thus, two non-growth firms, say companies X and Y, with identical assets and earnings expectations that differ only in their expected sources of financing can have considerably different market values. If X borrows £10 million but Y is debt-free, the market value of X's ordinary shares will be at least £4 million greater than the market value of Y's ordinary shares. The significance of expression (8), especially the importance of investor expectations rather than current amounts, is that Y can become X immediately simply by announcing a change in its financing policy. The market will not delay in bestowing the benefit of the expected tax saving on the company's ordinary shares.

Thus, management should convey its target debt ratio to the market: the fraction of fixed capital (total assets minus non-interest-bearing current liabilities) that it expects to finance with interest-bearing debt on average and over time, especially if (1) the target capital structure differs from the current capital structure and/or (2) the company's debt ratio has fluctuated widely in the past.

Capital Spending Forecasts. Capital spending is defined as additions to fixed capital (i.e. incremental total assets minus additions to non-interest-bearing current liabilities). This incremental investment (I) is important to investors because it conveys management's forecast of future profits better than almost any other information. Since rates of return on fixed capital do not change much on average and over time, and since the rate of return multiplied by the amount of fixed capital is equal to the level of net operating profit, a forecast of anticipated incremental investment tells investors half of what they need to know in order to calculate future profits. Investors will then be able to spend their time estimating the remaining unknown: the expected rate of return on fixed capital.

Rate of Internal Growth. Although rates of return on fixed capital (i.e. $NOPAT/A_F$) do not change much on average and over time, considerable confusion can occur in its calculation when employing published financial data. It is caused by the effects of acquisitions. Unfortunately, current accounting conventions can be extremely misleading. Because of this problem, we suggest that all companies include a statement about, and even the calculation of, the rate of internal growth in net operating profits in their annual reports and in presentations to investment analysts. This rate of growth is a measure of management's investment performance from the time they have had control of the firm's assets.

The measure can facilitate the market's estimate of the expected rate of return on new investment, r_t. The product of the actual rate of return on fixed capital and historical additions to fixed capital (historical I) is equal to the historical rate of internal growth in NOPAT. Historical financial reports tell us about the historical I. Hence, reporting the rate of internal growth in net operating profits will convey the historical rate of return on fixed capital. And since rates of return on fixed capital do not change much over time, the market will know much about r_t.

An examination of the effects of acquisitions on reporting describes the potential confusion of existing reporting techniques. When acquisitions have a significant impact on a company's financial reporting, announced (explicit) growth can differ substantially from internal (real) growth. Pooling of interests accounting rules permit a seller's historical performance to be added to the buyer's profitability, even though the buyer was in no way responsible for it. Thus, for a company on a calendar year basis, an acquisition made on, say, 1 November 1970 can be reported as if it occurred on 1 January 1970. "Purchase" accounting would include only the profits of the acquired company for November and December in 1970's combined report and thereafter profits for the entire year. This seems to be fair, but 1971's reporting will, in effect, compare the acquired company's twelve months' performance with 1970's last two months. This could cause quite an economic distortion of the buying management's ability.

A clearer method of reporting calculates the rate of growth in profits from the time the buyer's management has control of the acquired assets. This is the rate of internal growth. Under this method, the 1969 report of the buyer would have been restated to include the earnings of the acquired company for November and December 1969. This would place the 1969 and 1970 figures on a comparable basis. Then in 1971's report, when earnings of the acquired company are automatically included for the entire year, the 1970 figures would be restated to include the profits of the acquired company for the entire year of 1970. This suggestion eliminates distortions created by "adding profits" for which the buyer's management is hardly responsible.

Acquisition Analysis[13]

Evaluating prospective acquisitions can be accomplished within the framework of expression (8). Employing our analytical framework offers three important advantages that are absent in the aforementioned traditional tools. First, our methodology *separates investment decision-making from financing policy*, which prevents analysts from falling into "the *AB-BA* fallacy" as well as believing that specific sources of funds

---

[13]This paper has been a lengthy development of an analytical framework and its implications for financial planning. This discussion of acquisition analysis should contain a complete development of a simple model that can be understood and employed by senior managers. However, we shall leave this extensive exposition to a later paper, presenting only a brief statement here based on the analytical framework in expression (8). The later paper considers the similarity of capital equipment analysis and acquisitions: acquisitions are multi-plant decisions.

can be identified with specific uses of funds. Second, we can test the sensitivity of assumptions by varying estimates of the parameters. Third, management can simulate the impact of its assumptions on the pro forma price of its firm's ordinary shares.

Pricing an acquisition requires the buyer to substitute his estimates of the parameters contained in expression (8). The result is the value he attaches to the seller or, what amounts to the same thing, it is the maximum price he can afford to pay for the seller. At this price, $r_t = c_t^\circ$. Thus, if he can negotiate a lower price, r_t will exceed c_t°. The difference between the price he pays and the maximum permissible price he can offer is the added market value for the buyer's firm.

There are only three bases for a buyer to offer a greater price than the seller's current market value: (*a*) operating savings, which improve NOPAT and r_t; (*b*) financial savings that result from buying an over-capitalised firm and increasing the pro forma target debt ratio (increasing tD and reducing c_t°); and (*c*) portfolio or risk savings, which means that the pro forma asset risk is reduced, for example, by combining contra-cyclical products (e.g. a baby foods company and a "pill" manufacturer) or changing the pro forma liquidity (reducing c_t).[14]

CONCLUSIONS

The analytical framework can be applied to conceptual problems as well as to answer specific questions. Conceptually, we have shown that management can employ the methodology to set realistic corporate objectives, to formulate an "optimal" dividend policy, to select issues for emphasis in financial reporting and to evaluate prospective acquisitions.

The conceptual advantage of the analytical framework is that investment decisions are examined independently of financing policy. Consequently, management avoids the problems of identifying specific

---

[14]Applying footnote 8's measure of c_t°, the proper discount rate to be used by a buyer for an acquisition should be considered in two stages. First, it might be appealing to describe it as

$$c_t^\circ = c_{ts}\left(1 - \frac{tD}{A_F}b\right)$$

where c_{ts} is the hurdle rate for the seller's assets and $(D/A_F)b$ is the debt ratio the buyer is expected to employ as the *pro forma* debt ratio. However, this formulation is insufficient. First, c_{ts} is likely to change if there are risk savings (i.e. the *pro forma* covariance is reduced). Second, a seller with small asset size and, hence, a relatively large value for c_t will probably experience a decline in the risk of its assets if it becomes part of a larger buyer, because c_t is inversely related to asset size.

Thus, optimal acquisition pricing values the *pro forma* firm using parameter estimates for the *pro forma* firm, including $c_t^\circ = c_{tp}(1 - tD/A_F)$ where c_{tp} is the *pro forma* hurdle rate for asset risk. Given the current market value of the buyer, the maximum price to be paid for the seller is determined by subtraction: the *pro forma* market value minus the buyer's market value is equal to the maximum permissible price for the seller.

sources of funds with specific uses of funds. Employing our methodology, management can never fall into "the *AB-BA* fallacy."

Specifically, management can test the sensitivity of inputs to the
decision-making process and simulate the impact of its plans on the
price of the company's ordinary shares. A timely implication is that
earnings per share need not (and should not) be required reporting for
companies in spite of recent interest in the concept by accountants in
the United Kingdom.

The most important limitations of our approach are not conceptual
in nature. Rather it is in specifying measures for c_t and T for various
industry groups and for predicting the impact of diversification on these
parameters. However, this problem is greater for investment analysts
than for management. Although techniques are available for analysts
to approximate c_t—by utilising the tools of portfolio theory to estimate
beta-values—management can employ the same techniques to examine
the economic profitability of alternative courses of action, thereby being
a step ahead of the analysts. That is, management can analyse the implications of achieving various plans by simulating the firm's resulting
market value.

28. A CONCEPTUAL FRAMEWORK FOR PLANNED GROWTH*

SURENDRA S. SINGHVI†

The investing public places a premium on common stocks of corporations that show a more rapid rate of growth than the economy in general and than other companies in the same industry. The common stocks of these corporations command a high price/earnings ratio, important if management is to raise risk capital at an attractive cost. In addition, growth corporations are more capable of responding effectively to change instead of becoming its victims.

Corporate growth can be measured in terms of net sales or revenues; net earnings or earnings per share; dividend per share; total assets; shareholders' equity; number of employees; or market price per share.

Which variable is the right one for measuring a given firm's growth depends on the firm's goals. If its goal is to provide cash return to stockholders each year, the growth in dividends would be used. If the objective is to create more jobs, the growth in the number of employees would be more appropriate. Hindustan Steel Company, a government-controlled organization in India, has done a good job in terms of growth in the number of employees. The company, however, has never been in the black since its creation in the mid-1950s.

In a free enterprise system, one of the important goals for management is to increase the wealth of the firm and consequently increase its market value. Once it has created the wealth, the next question involves how to distribute it among such interests as stockholders, creditors, employees, consumers, governments, and the community.

In most ordinary circumstances, the market value of a firm is determined by its past and expected future earning power. In a recession period like 1970-71, numerous firms experienced growth in sales but substantial declines in earnings. Consequently, the market value of these firms declined in the same period. (During the 1973-74 period, however, because of unusual monetary and economic conditions and despite high sales and earnings, the market value of most firms declined.) Growth or decline in dividends is also dependent upon earnings performance. It seems, therefore, that under most circumstances earnings, rather than sales, are the proper measure of growth.

Growth in shareholders' equity and total assets is not as relevant in modern times as it used to be in the 1920s and 1930s, when the emphasis

*From *S.A.M. Advanced Management Journal* (October, 1974), pp. 43-52. © 1974 by S.A.M., a division of American Management Associations. Reprinted by permission.

†Manager of Financial Planning and Analysis, Armco Steel Corporation, and Adjunct Professor of Finance, Miami University.

by the Wall Street analysts was placed on the firm's balance sheet rather than on the income statement. However, growth in sales, shareholders' equity, and total assets could be established as secondary goals.

SOURCES OF CORPORATE GROWTH

To illustrate how earnings growth can be maintained, let's assume that a group of people forms an investment club with an initial equity investment of $1,000. The club invests $1,000 in Alpha Company's preferred stocks yielding 7 percent return after taxes. If all earnings of the club are distributed to the owners, the club's annual earnings of $70 will not grow unless the club decides to divest Alpha's preferred stocks (assuming no liquidation loss) and reinvests $1,000 in another security that yields, say, 8 percent. By changing its assets, the club has increased its profits by 14.3 percent. The earnings will continue to grow if the club can invest its resources to earn a higher rate of return than in the previous year. However, this process of growth without new capital will stop once the opportunities to earn a higher rate of return with a specified degree of risk are no longer available to the club. In addition, it will be difficult to divest present assets and reinvest in new assets without any loss of time and money.

Assuming the club members have decided to invest only in Alpha's preferred, yielding 7 percent per year, the growth in the club's profits will depend upon the percent of its profits reinvested to buy more preferred stocks. The rate of growth in the club's profits will be the rate of return on investment multiplied by the percentage of profits reinvested within the club. This can be expressed in terms of a model as shown in Exhibit 28-1.

EXHIBIT 28-1

SOURCES OF CORPORATE GROWTH

$$G = (R \times P) \cdot 100$$

Where

G = Maximum Growth Rate in Earnings
R = Return on Investments
P = Percentage Earnings Reinvested

If the investment club decides to reinvest 60 percent of its profits, the annual rate of growth in earnings would be 4.2 percent compounded (Exhibit 28-2).

The maximum rate of growth by reinvesting earnings is limited to the rate of return on investment. If the club decides to reinvest 100 percent of its profits, the annual rate of growth in earnings would amount to 7 percent per annum ($.07 \times 1.00 \times 100$).

EXHIBIT 28-2

THE INVESTMENT CLUB'S GROWTH

Period	Investment	Earnings @ 7%	Reinvest @ 60%	Growth Rate
1	$1,000.00	$70.00	$42.00	—
2	1,042.00	72.94	43.76	4.2%
3	1,085.76	76.00	45.60	4.2%
4	1,131.36	79.20	47.52	4.2%

$$G = (.07 \times .60) \cdot 100$$
$$= 4.2\%$$

The club can further improve its rate of growth in profits by using *financial leverage*. For example, the club decides to borrow 20 percent of its total capitalization, and it is estimated that the after tax borrowing cost would be 4 percent per annum. (In no case should the club borrow money to expand its investment activities if it has to pay 7 percent or more after-tax interest, since this would lead to a reduction in earnings.) With the introduction of financial leverage, the maximum rate of growth in earnings could be derived using the model presented in Exhibit 28-3.

EXHIBIT 28-3

EARNINGS GROWTH MODEL

$$G = [P(R - I)\frac{D}{E} + (P \cdot R)] \times 100$$

Where

G = Growth Rate in Earnings
R = Return on Investments
P = Percentage Earnings Reinvested
D = Debt Capital (long-term)
E = Equity Capital
I = Interest Rate After Tax

Substituting the data for the club in the growth model, the rate of growth is shown in Exhibit 28-4. The process of earnings growth for the club is shown in Exhibit 28-5.

EXHIBIT 28-4

EARNINGS GROWTH MODEL: THE INVESTMENT CLUB EXAMPLE

$$G = [(P(R - I)\frac{D}{E} + (P \cdot R)] \times 100$$

$$= [.60(.07 - .04)\frac{.20}{.80} + (.60 \times .07)] \times 100$$

$$= [.0045 + .042] \times 100$$

$$= 4.65\%$$

EXHIBIT 28-5

PROCESS OF EARNINGS GROWTH

Period	Equity	Debt	Gross Earnings @ 7%	Interest Expense @ 4%	Net Earnings	Growth in Earnings
1	$1,000.0	$250.0	$ 87.50	$10.00	$77.50	—
2	1,046.5	261.6	91.57	10.47	81.10	4.65%
3	1,095.2	273.8	95.83	10.95	84.88	4.65%
4	1,146.1	286.5	100.28	11.46	88.82	4.65%

It can be seen that the introduction of financial leverage improves the rate of growth for the club from 4.2 percent to 4.65 percent. In addition, the return on equity improves from 7 percent to 7.75 percent. In this illustration, approximately 90 percent of the growth in earnings comes from the retention of earnings and the remaining growth comes from the use of financial leverage.

The key variables in the growth model are the return on investments (R) and the percentage of earnings retained (P). If the difference between the return on investments and the after-tax interest rate on borrowed funds is substantial, financial leverage would also affect the growth rate even more than shown in the above illustration.

The rate of growth in earnings is also influenced by the excess of depreciation over obsolescence and maintenance requirements. The growth model discussed here can be modified for depreciation as shown in Exhibit 28-6.

EXHIBIT 28-6

GROWTH MODEL ADJUSTED FOR DEPRECIATION

$$G = [P(R - I)\frac{D}{E} + (P \cdot R)] + \frac{XR}{E} \times 100$$

Where

X = Excess depreciation over obsolescence and maintenance requirements

The growth model described here can be very useful in two major areas:

1. *To undertake sensitivity analysis:* The model can be used to determine the return on new investments if management desires a given level of earnings growth, debt ratio, and payout ratio. Similarly, the model can be used to determine the target payout ratio if management desires a given level of earnings growth, debt ratio, and return on new investments.

2. *To test the validity of earnings projected by profit centers:* In a profit-center oriented firm, long-range plans are prepared by each profit center within the strategic framework outlined by top management.

These plans are consolidated at the corporate level and then reviewed by top management. Some firms have found that the individual profit center plans look reasonable, but the consolidated plan looks very optimistic or pessimistic. To check the validity of consolidated earnings over the next few years, the growth model can be used at the corporate level. If the projected earnings based on the growth model seem different from those projected by individual profit centers, some modifications in the latter forecast can be made by management. To use the growth model, the planner must select a base year that is not abnormal.

TRUE GROWTH VERSUS EXPANSION

According to Professor Ezra Solomon of Stanford University, it is necessary to distinguish between two separate types of growth: true growth and expansion. *True growth* is based on the existence of opportunities to use capital at yields that are above normal rates of return. In terms of our growth model, true growth would require that the return on investments (R) be greater than the cost of capital. This means that true growth depends on specific but finite opportunities that stem from a company's special position in technology, manpower, or markets.

On the other hand, regular reinvestment out of earnings brings about an expansion in assets, earnings, and dividends, but the firm does not anticipate specific opportunities to invest funds at higher than normal rates of return. In terms of the growth model, the return on investments (R) is the same as the cost of capital for expansion.

In addition, a planner must recognize the existence of temporary growth or expansion resulting from short-lived situations. For example, a firm's profit might increase due to the investment tax credit allowed by the government, which would last only for 12 months.

PLANNED GROWTH

Corporate growth can be planned. To do so, management must make some policy decisions such as:

1. *Dividend payout target:* What proportion of the firm's earnings should be paid out in dividends during the planning horizon? This will determine how much is available for reinvestment in the firm for future expansion and growth.

2. *Debt ratio target:* What rating must the firm's debt securities maintain in the marketplace? In other words, how much long-term debt should it maintain on an average without accepting unreasonable interest rates and terms? This decision will influence the firm's ability to grow.

These two policy decisions by the management will determine the availability of total funds for growth and expansion.

3. *Allocation of resources:* The next question before management is how to allocate these additional funds to increase earnings at a target rate of growth. As shown in the growth model, the rate of growth in earnings depends to a great extent on the rate of return on investments a firm can earn. Therefore, the objective of management is to invest these funds in those activities that will improve the rate of return.

The opportunities to improve the rate of return can be classified into two categories: *internal growth opportunities,* derived from research and development and capital expenditures, and *external growth opportunities,* derived from acquisition and divestment.

INTERNAL GROWTH

a. *Research and development planning:* Corporate growth can be planned through the planning of the firm's R&D activities. According to a recent McGraw-Hill survey, American business expects 13 percent of its 1976 sales will be in new products that were not in production in 1972. The main purposes of the current R&D programs underway in these companies are the improvement of existing products (44 percent of the surveyed companies), the development of new products (38 percent), and the development of new processes (18 percent). It was also revealed in the survey that 27 percent of the participating manufacturers expect a technological breakthrough in their respective fields by 1976.

b. *Capital expenditures planning:* Internal growth depends on the rational allocation of resources within the firm. Additional funds made available from retained earnings and borrowings should be expended on those facilities that will enable the firm to maintain its market share in a growing industry or to increase its market share in a stable industry. Capital expenditures, generating benefits over a long period, must be based on sound economic justification. Management must not accept any project that yields less than the cut-off or hurdle rate established unless non-financial considerations, such as pollution control, are crucial. The hurdle rates for capital expenditures must be determined, based on the cost of capital and the degree of risk perceived in a given project. As indicated previously, the earnings will grow if the rate of return (R) is in excess of the cost of capital.

Let us review the investment club illustration. Its financial position at the end of the first period is presented in Exhibit 28-7.

The calculation of the cost of equity capital is based on the assumption that the club owners expect only 7 percent return on their equity investment. Since the weighted average cost of capital is 6.4 percent after tax as shown in Exhibit 28-8, and the club has invested its resources in the asset that produces 7 percent after-tax yield, the earnings of the club will grow every year at the rate of 4.65 percent, as shown previously. The rate of growth could be improved if the club invests its funds in those projects or assets that yield more than 7 percent after taxes.

EXHIBIT 28-7

INVESTMENT CLUB BALANCE SHEET AS OF DECEMBER 31

Assets		Liabilities & Equity	
Current assets	50	Current liab.	50
Investments in Alpha's		Debt	250
preferred stock	1,250	Equity	1,000
Total	1,300	Total	1,300

EXHIBIT 28-8

WEIGHTED AVERAGE COST OF CAPITAL

	Amounts	Weights	After Tax Cost	Weighted Cost
Debt	$ 250	.20	.04	.008
Equity	1,000	.80	.07	.056
	$1,250	1.00		.064
		6.4%		

EXTERNAL GROWTH

c. *Acquisition planning:* Many firms in the past decade have grown by acquiring other businesses in the same industry or in unrelated industries. External growth through acquisition is preferred by some company executives for several reasons, such as:

• *Speed*—New facilities, products, processes, and plants in a fully operative condition may be acquired quickly through mergers.

• *Cost*—The desired assets may be obtained less expensively by purchasing the common stock of the companies to be acquired than by purchasing the assets themselves.

• *Personnel*—The services of desired personnel could be obtained quickly at a lower cost.

• *Financing*—Many times it is possible to finance an acquisition when it is not possible to finance internal growth. For example, a large steel plant involves a huge investment. However, a firm might obtain steel capacity by acquiring another firm through an exchange of stock less expensively than it could by constructing the facilities themselves, provided the Justice Department has no objection.

• *Risk*—The acquired facility may already have demonstrated its earning power and hence has a lower degree of risk.

• *Competitive advantage*—A share of the market may be obtained more rapidly with less risk through acquisition than by internal expansion.

It should be remembered that unless acquisitions are properly evaluated financially and otherwise, such actions could be a deterrent to corporate growth. In recent years, miscarried acquisitions have proven costly to many acquiring firms. One must analyze thoroughly the hoped-for "synergy" benefits, the effect on reported earnings, the price/earnings ratio, and the overall rate of return. The acquisitions of other firms will provide a company with growth or expansion in sales and assets but may not provide any growth in earnings per share. The acquisition strategy should consider the rate of growth in earnings and strike a balance between the near-term and long-term earnings potential.

d. *Divestment planning:* Since an increasing number of businesses view themselves as a portfolio of businesses, it is desirable to have a balanced portfolio to achieve a pre-determined growth without assuming unreasonable risk. Divestment of low-return businesses is necessary to maintain this balance.

The divestment decision is the reverse of the acquisition decision. Divesting is simply closing rather than opening plants or selling rather than acquiring assets or divisions. The objective in either case is to maximize profits within a given time period. For example, a division that is independent of the other activities of the firm is losing $1 million per annum and is expected to lose similar amounts for five years with only break-even results thereafter. If the firm's investment opportunity rate is 15 percent, the division's projected losses represent a negative present value of $3.8 million. The present value of the entire firm would be increased by divesting the division even with substantial abandonment costs, as long as these costs do not exceed $3.8 million.

I believe there is going to be a significant increase in divestment activities in the next decade. There are a number of reasons for this prediction. The federal government is going to take an increasingly anti-merger stand as the size of conglomerates increase. The number of "good buys" are likely to decrease when compared to the fantastic rush to merge and consolidate experienced in the last half of the 1960s. Companies are going to find that some of their acquisitions are not working out as planned, and those companies that did not plan their acquisitions are going to discover their errors. All this will lead businesses to consider divestment of one sort or another as a way out of problems and as a means of increasing the growth and value of their organization.

IS PLANNED GROWTH NECESSARY?

Planned growth is vital to the well-being of an organization. Unplanned growth on the other hand, could pose several problems, such as a dearth of competent people, a paucity of required financial resources, and operating bottlenecks. The American economy moved from scarcity to affluence as a result of planned growth, and it can be said that such growth will still be the best vehicle for overall socio-economic progress in coming decades.

Planned growth, whether external or internal, is necessary because:

(a) The growth firm is able to attract and retain the very competent individuals it needs to solve increasingly complex business problems.

(b) The growth firm is able to finance large-scale research on a centralized basis, which may benefit a number of its diverse operations.

(c) Corporations in the process of growth tend to become large and could therefore enjoy operating economies of scale if properly planned. These economies result by consolidating certain activities, such as advertising, taxes, legal work, systems, and the like.

(d) The securities of growth firms enjoy relatively high marketability. These firms are able to diversify and thus reduce overall risks. These factors, among others, lead to higher price/earnings ratios. Consequently, it is possible to acquire firms and have the resulting market value greater than the sum of their individual values.

Even if a firm decides that further growth is not a goal, planning for growth might still be necessary. With the changing technologies and buyer behavior that characterize the 1970s, firms cannot rely on traditional acceptance of their products and services. New products and markets must be developed continuously to replace the old or obsolete. Just to maintain the present position in the industry, a firm must grow in some directions to offset declines in others.

Although few firms may afford to discard the goal of corporate growth, a clear understanding of planned growth is important to management. Firms must develop relevant definitions of growth, improve their selection of internal and external growth opportunities, and act decisively and with full commitment. It is through managerial action alone that growth can evolve systematically from the planning stage to final implementation.

PART IX. FINANCIAL IMPACT OF ACCOUNTING

This section is concerned with three of the major areas in which accounting problems have a major financial impact on corporations. Events outside of the firm, such as new reporting requirements or price movements, lead to very serious internal decisions and to reporting problems. Changes in the way in which records are kept and responses of investors and lenders must be considered in all such decisions.

The 1968 article by Professor Robert K. Mautz deals with problems of reporting divisional sales of conglomerate and other diversified corporations. This basic article remains timely because of an SEC order that became effective in 1971. Among other things this order requires corporations with sales of $50 million or more to disclose in their annual reports the approximate percentage or amount of revenues and net income before income taxes and other items contributed by each line of business that accounted for 10 percent or more to its revenues or net income. The Federal Trade Commission also is continuing to press for line-of-business disclosure of operating results.

Professor Mautz summarizes the findings and recommendations of a Research Foundation of Financial Executives Institute study. The objective of the study was to determine the usefulness, practicability, and desirability of publishing corporate operating results on a detailed basis. Separate questionnaires were answered by (1) more than 200 financial analysts and investment advisors and by (2) more than 400 corporate executives. Meetings were held in various parts of the country with persons from both groups. The summary of the responses emphasized the hazards of disclosing financial data by divisions or by products.

The last section of the article presents five research-based recommendations for reporting by conglomerate and diversified companies. These recommendations reflect the areas of agreement among most users and providers of corporate financial data. First, companies that are unitary in nature should not be required to fractionalize themselves for reporting purposes. Second, companies that have a material degree of activity in more than one broadly defined industry should meet the extended disclosure requirements. Third, management itself is in the most informed position to separate the company into realistic components for reporting purposes. Fourth, the recommended disclosures may be presented in parts of the annual report other than in the formal financial statements themselves. Finally, the complexities of reporting diversified activities are so great that recommendations should be applied with judgment and flexibility by all concerned. Within this framework, diversified companies should report sales and relative contributions to profits of each major broad industry group.

Professor Robert M. Soldofsky offers a timely discussion of the impact of rising prices on net income, real income tax rates, and financing. The high rate of inflation in 1974 will affect corporate liquidity, capital expenditures, leverage, and other financial variables for years to come. The Financial Accounting Standards Board has urged experimentation in using price-level-adjusted financial statements in annual reports. Persistent, high-level inflation may well result in a requirement that corporations publish such statements regularly.

Soldofsky presents an illustration of *paper profits* that result from rising prices and their consequences. Paper profits are the difference between net income determined on the basis of conventional, historic costs and net income determined on the basis of current or opportunity costs. Income taxes expressed as a percentage of real net income rise rapidly with the rate of inflation. If the rate of inflation is steady, the real income tax rate tends to rise also if that inflation rate continues. He shows that most of the conventional net income is needed to maintain the stock of physical assets during inflation. A simple adjustment to price-level accounting without a change in the basis of computing income taxes will provide only very modest relief from financial pressures. The fiscal policy implications of the present historical-cost basis and a possible opportunity-cost basis for computing corporate income taxes are discussed.

When a company takes a financial bath, it recognizes or anticipates losses that have occurred or estimates losses that are likely to occur. The "bath" is said to depress current earnings and to correspondingly increase future earnings. A "big bath" is intended to get all of the bad news out of the way at once.

Professors Copeland and Moore in the article *The Financial Bath: Is It Common?* are concerned about the frequency with which corporations utilize discretionary accounting rules to take a bath, the background income and stock price movement at the time the decision is made to take a bath, and the relative and absolute size of the bath as it relates to adverse income and stock price movements for the company.

Some studies of financial baths have been done prior to the Copeland-Moore study. Their study covers the period 1966-1970, which appears to be representative based upon hindsight from 1975. A massive random sample and excellent statistical controls were used in the Copeland-Moore study. Three to seven percent of the sample firms took a bath each year. Statistical measurements confirmed that "bath" firms had significantly greater declines in income than nonbath firms in the year that the bath was taken, and that the bath firms had losses significantly more frequently than the nonbath firms before considering the discretionary accounting decisions that reported losses. The relationships between stock prices and income movements were tested but the results were not clear-cut on statistical or logical grounds.

Financial baths are a continuing phenomenon. For example, for 1972 Gulf Oil Corporation took a charge of $250 million for withdrawing from certain markets and after 1972, it was disclosed, they took another $25 million loss for currency revaluations. Early in 1975 Lockheed Aircraft was reported to be considering an $800 million write down for developmental costs on its L1011 aircraft. The Securities and Exchange Commission continues to call for more and timely information of accounting policies that affect financial statements.

29. FINANCIAL REPORTING BY CONGLOMERATE COMPANIES*

ROBERT K. MAUTZ †

Diversified companies with certain characteristics should report sales and the relative contribution to profits of each major broad industry group, according to the recommendations in the study conducted by the Research Foundation of Financial Executives Institute.

The report is the result of a year of intensive research by the Foundation to determine the usefulness, practicability, and desirability of publishing corporate results of operations on a more detailed basis than total company results. Its findings place stress on the necessity for management of a corporation, working within recommended guidelines, to make the determination of the information and group breakdowns which would be meaningful to investors.

"Management, because of its familiarity with company structure," states the study, "is in the most informed position to separate the company into realistic components for reporting purposes. To require reporting on some rigid basis might fractionalize a company into unnatural parts which could not fairly reflect the results of its operations."

The report suggests that companies which are unitary in nature, that is, which operate almost completely within a single broadly defined industry, or which are highly integrated, should not be expected to fractionalize themselves for reporting purposes, but companies which to a material degree have activity in more than one broadly defined industry should meet the extended disclosure requirements.

According to the study, a "material degree" means 15 percent or more of a company's gross revenue. No present system of industry or product classification appears ideally suited to the identification of broad industry groups, so considerable discretion to management in defining broad industry groupings is essential.

The study recommends that disclosures may be included in parts of the annual report other than the formal financial statements. Whether in narrative or tabular form, they should be grouped and should carry a clear indication of the limitation of their usefulness.

The findings have been released in summary form. The full report, including voluminous statistical data, will be released in late spring of this year.

The Financial Executives Research Foundation enlisted the assistance of representatives of the American Bar Association, the New York Stock Exchange, the Securities and Exchange Commission, the Investment Bankers

*From *Financial Executive* (February, 1968), pp. 46-63. Reprinted by permission.

†Partner, Ernst & Ernst; formerly Professor of Accounting, Graduate School of Business, University of Illinois.

Association, the Financial Analysts Federation, the National Association of Accountants, and the American Institute of Certified Public Accountants in providing information in the course of the study.

The study takes a financial or business point of view, reflecting the concern of financial executives for both the informational needs of investors and the welfare of present shareholders.

The summary report, including conclusions and recommendations, is as follows.

SCOPE OF THE RESEARCH

The purpose of this research, as stated at the inception of the project, ". . . is to complete an investigation of the usefulness, practicability, and desirability of corporate disclosure in published and other generally available reports, of the scope, nature, and results of operations on some basis more detailed than total company figures, for the purpose of making recommendations to interested parties respecting whether disclosure is desirable and, if so, the kinds and extent of such disclosure." This led to an early emphasis on diversification in general rather than to a study of conglomerate diversification in particular.

Efforts were necessary to determine:
1. The information needs of those who make investment decisions;
2. The extent of present internal reporting on a less than total company basis;
3. Any limitations on the usefulness of such internally reported data as conceived by:
   a. those who produce and use such data internally
   b. by those who would use them externally if made available,
4. The disadvantages to corporate shareholders if increased disclosures were to be made.

Two lengthy questionnaires were developed, tested, and mailed. The investors' questionnaire was answered by 218 financial analysts and investment advisors from widely scattered geographic locations and filling a variety of roles in the investment market. Of these, 77 percent were Chartered Financial Analysts.

The corporate questionnaire brought useful responses from 412 companies of varying sizes representative of all major, nonregulated industries. These included 66 of the 100 largest industrial corporations listed in the "*Fortune 500*" and 212 or 42.4 percent of the entire "500." Also included were 26 of *Fortune's* 46 "most diversified companies."

A number of meetings were held in various parts of the country to provide the research staff with opportunities to seek information from, and exchange views with, financial executives, financial analysts, fund managers, and industrial and public accountants. Studies were made of published annual reports, and relevant writings on the subject were examined.

Both the conceptual and the pragmatic aspects of the subject received attention in the study. At the same time that questionnaires were developed and distributed to secure information about internal reporting practices and the opinions of financial executives and financial analysts, efforts to identify and clarify concepts essential to the research were also undertaken.

Financial analysts were selected as the group to represent the views of all those who read and rely on reported corporate financial data. They seem to be satisfactory representatives of this point of view because, as a group, they include a diversity of positions and interests and because they include in their ranks some of the most sophisticated of all users of published financial statements.

Neither the importance nor the problems of the individual investor was overlooked. To the extent that the individual investor desires to make informed investment decisions, he needs the same information as the financial analyst serving an institutional investor. Hence, if the needs of the most sophisticated users are met, other investors should be supplied with at least as much information as they can use effectively.

Financial analysts have become an important factor in the investment market because that market has changed significantly in recent years. The amounts of available investment funds have increased dramatically with increased levels of affluence and as new methods of wealth accumulation have been discovered and developed. At the same time, industry has become more complex technically, financially, and organizationally. With great sums to invest in a highly complex market, fund managers have sought the most expert advice obtainable. Analytical methods developed to supply investment advice to major investors are soon adapted and made available to other portfolio managers and investors of all kinds. One result has been an institutionalization of the investment procedure involving careful research, recommendations based upon such research, and review of such recommendations for reasonableness and conformity with the decision maker's investment policy.

Using the term "conglomerate company" in the broadest sense, an attempt was made to conceptualize the common characteristics which establish a group of companies appropriately designated by that term as distinct from all other companies. Given the point of view of the study, attention was directed to those variables of interest to investors which would be influenced by various aspects of diversification. Thus the tentative definition adopted was essentially a definition of diversified companies. As proposed, the definition was conceptual and was accompanied by a caveat that modification might be necessary before it would be practicably applicable.

Other aspects given conceptual attention were the separation of a diversified company into reportable components, the nature and influence of costs common to two or more reportable components of a diversified company, and the effect of the pricing of transactions between such components. Tentative conclusions resulting from this portion of the study were:

1. No one basis of segmentation of diversified companies for reporting purposes appears to apply to all companies. This argues strongly for a flexible approach, perhaps even freedom, for management to select a basis appropriate to the specific company.
2. Because of common cost allocations and intra-company pricing, data prepared for management purposes could be misleading if supplied to others who are less well acquainted with the company and who may not know the purpose for which the information was prepared.
3. The relative importance of common costs in segment reporting tends to decrease as the breadth of the reporting segments is increased.
4. Disparate components may have so few intra-company transactions and such a small portion of common costs that these present no serious deterrent to the presentation of operating data for such components.

RESULTS OF THE CORPORATE QUESTIONNAIRE

Perhaps the overriding impression one received from the corporate questionnaires is the variety of responses to almost all questions and the lack of unanimity or even near unanimity on any important point. To those familiar with business, this comes as no surprise; to those not so familiar, it warrants considerable thought. The impact of this variety in business structure and practice is a strong argument for the flexibility which is incorporated in the final recommendations.

Most of the responding companies provide operating data for internal company purposes on the basis of organizational units, although this is done in a wide variety of ways and for a variety of internal control purposes. Organizational units were defined in the questionnaire as components of the company identifiable in terms of the company's organization chart, reporting operating data to some top management group, and accounting for 2 percent or more of the company's sales or gross revenue. The number of such units reported was generally less than ten, and only a very few companies listed more than 15. For some companies, a close relationship existed between organizational units and their major product lines, leading to the conclusion that in a broad sense they are organized on a product-line basis. For almost as many other companies, there was very little relationship between organizational units and products.

More than half the responding companies prepare complete income statements by organizational units, and most of the remainder provide substantial operating data, although somewhat short of a complete income statement. Fewer companies, although still a significant proportion, supply some operating information by products. Generally the amount of information supplied is less than that available by organizational units. Yet when queried as to the most suitable basis for reporting operating data on some basis more detailed than total company figures, almost as many chose a

TABLE 29-1

Percent of Assets Identified with Units Specified	Total Companies Responding on an Organizational Unit Basis		Total Companies Responding on a Product-Line Basis	
	Number	Per-cent	Number	Per-cent
Under 50%	48	11.9	158	41.0
50-59%	6	1.5	11	2.9
60-69%	20	4.9	23	6.0
70-79%	28	6.9	28	7.3
80-89%	51	12.5	46	11.9
90% and over	253	62.3	119	30.9
Totals	406	100.0%	385	100.0%

product basis as chose organizational units. (For use in answering the questionnaire, product or product line categories were defined by each respondent, the only requirement being that a product or product line account for 5 percent or more of a company's gross revenue.)

Common costs were reported to exceed 10 percent of sales by 38 percent of these companies which provide internal operating data on an organizational unit basis and by 57 percent of the companies which report operating data internally on a product-line basis. (Common costs were defined in these questions by specifically listing certain items of expense, all of which would be shown in an income statement after the determination of gross margin on sales or gross profit. Thus, common costs of production were excluded from consideration.)

Practices with respect to the extent of allocation of common costs and the number and variety of allocation bases used vary widely.

The impact of intra-company pricing does not appear to be as material as that of common costs. For 24 percent (92 of 382) of the companies which provide internal operating data on an organizational unit basis, internal sales amounted to 10 percent or more of total sales. For 37 percent (63 of 169) of the companies which report operating data internally on a product-line basis, internally used product amounted to more than 10 percent of total production.

A variety of pricing methods for intra-company transfers is used, often by the same company.

Responses to the corporate questionnaire indicate that a significant number of companies cannot identify a large proportion of their assets with either organization units or product lines (see Table 29-1). The word "identified" may have been misinterpreted by some respondents. It was intended to convey the idea of direct attribution without allocation or prorating. Some apparently read it to mean that the assets could be allocated on a reasonable basis. These results may, therefore, imply a greater ability to supply information about assets committed to individual organizational units and product lines than actually exists.

The corporate questionnaire results support the tentative conclusion reached in the conceptual study that if diversified companies are to be separated into parts for financial reporting purposes, a flexible approach is essential. This follows both from preferences expressed by respondents and because of practical problems in reporting.

Some questions asked for opinions about disclosure preferences under the assumption that disclosure would be required even if the respondent disapproved of such reporting in general. Preferences are shown below, but it should be noted that preferences of some companies are impracticabilities for others. A number of companies include more than 50 separate corporations, thus making corporate entities an unlikely basis for effective reporting. A number of those reporting on an organizational unit basis also indicated numbers of units too large to constitute a practicable reporting base. Some companies stated they do not now report internally on the basis of product lines and indicated serious problems if they attempted to do so (see Table 29-2).

TABLE 29-2

| | Responses | |
Preferred Bases to Be Used for Reporting	Number	Percent
Legal corporate entities	55	14.2
Organizational units	153	39.5
Products or services	132	34.1
Other	47	12.2
Total	387	100.0%

Different methods for reporting the results of operations on a less than total company basis (assuming that such reporting were required) were also found "most satisfactory" by significant numbers of the corporate respondents:

	Companies Responding	
In the statement of income	100	25.8%
In a footnote to the financial statements	33	8.5
In the text of the annual report	189	48.7
In some other way	66	17.0
	388	100.0%

While not covered in the questionnaires, a matter implied or discussed specifically in many conversations with management representatives and analysts is the importance of so segmenting the company that the reporting segments represent the company as an operative entity. Companies organize in various ways to achieve like results. Personnel available at critical moments, the sequence in which essential decisions are made, commitments made by previous managements, management judgment as to operating policies, and a host of other factors exert varying influences upon the way in which a given company is structured. Arbitrary segmentation might divide integrated and coherent activities in ways that would make reports about them so unrepresentative as to be misleading. Thoughtful segmentation into a company's natural components, with full awareness of the intimacy of coherent activities, can be accomplished only by those well acquainted with the organization and inner workings of the company.

Managements see a number of hazards in disclosing operating and other data for the segments of a diversified company. These include the possibility that:

1. Confidential information would be revealed to competitors about profitable or unprofitable products, plans for new products or entries into new markets, apparent weaknesses which might induce competitors to increase their own efforts to take advantage of the weakness, and the existence of advantages not otherwise indicated.

2. Information thus made available would cause customers to challenge prices to the disadvantage of the company.

3. Operating data by segments might be misleading to those who read it. Segment data prepared for internal management purposes often includes arbitrary judgments which are known to those using the data and taken into account in making evaluations. The difficulty of making such background information available and understandable to outside users is considered by many to be insurmountable.

4. The cost of providing segment data where it is not now prepared could be significant.

5. Uniform reporting categories would be established which might call for additional expense in recording and reporting and which, because arbitrarily defined, might not fairly represent the operations of the enterprise as a going concern. Some fear that establishment of arbitrary reporting requirements might in turn lead to arbitrary rules for business activity to make the required reporting possible.

These are the more important reasons why some managements expressed themselves as generally opposed to disclosing any operating information on some basis more detailed than total company figures. Many expressed a willingness to disclose sales data but nothing more, while a significant number indicated at least qualified approval of increased disclosure generally.

RESULTS OF THE INVESTORS' QUESTIONNAIRES

The investors' questionnaires indicate that analysts rate "maximum return in the long run from a combination of dividends and capital appreciation" as the most important investment objective with "maximum capital appreciation in the long run" as next. These two are by far the most important objectives for those responding to the questionnaire.

The most important company characteristics in attaining these objectives are indicated as growth potential, managerial ability, and profitability, in that order.

The return on common stock equity, return on total assets, and ratio of net income to sales were rated as the most useful indicators of profitability.

The preferred indicators of growth potential are growth of major markets, rate of growth in earnings per share, and research and development expenditures.

Managerial ability is best indicated by the growth of the company, the return on common stock equity, and the personal reputation of key personnel.

In summary, these responses stress the importance of information (A) descriptive of a company's activities, (B) indicative of its share of markets, and (C) showing its success in terms of net income and return on equity data.

Diversified companies constitute a special problem to investors because of their activity in different industries. To judge the future prospects of such a company, one must examine the company's activities industry by industry before they can be considered in combination. Responses indicate that a substantial number of analysts now attempt to analyze diversified companies on a segmented basis, including estimates of cost of goods sold and allocation of operating expenses to arrive at net income by segments.

Although analysts state that financial statements and other material in the annual report provide the leading sources of information in the analysis of conglomerate companies by segments, a substantial majority indicate that annual reports do not provide satisfactory clues to appropriate segmentation. This leads to a conclusion that investment decisions are based on calculations which may not fairly reflect the facts.

Analysts are aware that common costs present significant allocation problems, and a majority agree that the allocation of such costs to organizational units or to products may be misleading. Most of those responding indicated that the point at which segment profit figures lose their significance because of the influence of common costs is 10 percent of sales or less, and relatively few felt results were reliable which included common cost allocations in excess of 20 percent of sales. Similar questions concerning intra-company sales brought similar answers.

In those cases in which common costs or intra-company pricing are sufficient to destroy the significance of segment net income figures for analytical purposes, a substantial number of analysts indicated they would find useful a "defined profit" which is computed by subtracting direct expenses of the segment from segment sales.

No clear preference for one basis of common cost allocation versus other possibilities was indicated.

The items of information about the segments of a conglomerate company considered most important by analysts are sales or other gross revenue, net income, and operating income (sales less cost of goods sold, selling expenses, and general and administrative expenses). Some analysts indicated that total assets and net assets committed to the activities of the segments were also important.

For comparisons of segments of one company with similar segments of other companies or with other segments of the same company, net income, sales, and assets invested were considered the most important items of information, and in that order.

The bases most often mentioned as appropriate in determining the minimum point at which an organizational unit becomes significant enough to require separate reporting were sales, net income, assets employed, net income before allocation of common costs, and total costs and expenses. Regardless of the base selected, a substantial majority indicated that the measure should be under 20 percent, with the largest grouping at the 10 to 14 percent range. In answer to another question, most respondents indicated that the maximum number of segments to be reported for a typical company should be 11 or less.

Analysts indicated that audit by independent CPAs would add satisfactory objectivity to common cost allocations, to definition of segments for reporting purposes, and to the results of operations including intracompany transactions.

Based on the following summary, the conclusion appears that most analysts would prefer but not insist upon audited data for the segments of diversified companies.

COVERAGE OF SEGMENT REPORTS BY INDEPENDENT CPAs OPINION

	Total Responses	Percent of Responses
Essential	59	27.2%
Desirable	122	56.2
Immaterial	36	16.6
Total	217	100.0%

In contradiction to their preference for a relatively small number of reporting units, a substantial number expressed a preference for uniform definition of reporting segments on some product basis such as the Standard Industrial Classification. This reveals a basic unfamiliarity with the Standard Industrial Classification and with the disadvantages of reporting a functioning, viable organization in terms of arbitrary and, therefore, probably artificial subdivisions.

CONCLUSIONS

Sufficient examples were cited in the corporate questionnaire responses to add substantial weight to the contention that disclosure of profit on individual products might be advantageous to competitors and/or customers to the detriment of shareholders in the disclosing company. Assertions that inordinate amounts of management time might be required to respond to questions encouraged by additional disclosures also appeared to reflect valid fears based upon experience. Unquestionably, excessively detailed disclosures could provide aid and comfort to those whose interests are opposed to the interests of the shareholders. Illustrations cited, however, relate to disclosures about specific products or specific decisions, a degree of detail well beyond that suggested by responses to the investors' questionnaire or incorporated in the accompanying recommendations.

The difference in point of view between the most reluctant corporate representative and the most demanding financial analyst was an extreme one. The views of more moderate financial executives and financial analysts appear reconcilable. For diversified companies, the majority of the financial analysts seek reliable data as a basis for predicting the prospects of the company in the near and long-term future. Such data should reflect the operations of the company's components separately and in total as viable parts of a complete enterprise, not as minute, arbitrarily segmented pieces bearing little resemblance to the operating organization. No great extent of detail is desired; indeed, reasonable summarization is essential. At the same time, information indicating the major industries in which a single enterprise is active is necessary and data showing the extent of involvement and success in each are considered essential.

A careful review of the specific objections to additional disclosure cited by corporate executives finds few, if any, concerned with disclosures of this nature. If presented in appropriate terms, disclosures useful to investors ordinarily need not be harmful to the disclosing enterprise. In recognition of the possibility of harm to shareholders in unusual cases, consideration needs to be given to recognition of possible hardship cases where the disadvantages of disclosure exceed the benefits to investors. Also, because companies vary, reasonable freedom for the management of each company to seek and identify appropriate terms of disclosure appears essential.

The conceptual definition of a conglomerate company requires modification in two respects if it is to be adapted to practical problems of financial reporting. First, common usage requires recognition that the class of companies described in the definition is more appropriately referred to as diversified companies than as conglomerate companies. In general usage, the term conglomerate company is used more and more in a restricted sense to describe diversified companies containing disparate components typically obtained through business acquisitions.

Second, for all practical purposes, the type of diversification of significance for financial reporting purposes can be viewed as industry diversification. The tentative conceptual definition noted the possibility of internal diversification resulting from either management decentralization or nonintegrated operations and of external or market diversification because of differences in customers or products or because of geographical distribution of its assets. Conceptually, these are all possible; practically, with the exception of industry diversification, they are either unlikely to exist or extremely difficult to identify.

Managerial decentralization sufficient to permit a company to experience rates of profitability, degrees of risk, and opportunities for growth that vary within the company to any material extent are theoretically possible but highly improbable. Common ownership of the company's components is itself enough to forbid such a degree of decentralization to influence profits, risk, or growth opportunities for any significant period of time.

Diversified markets might influence the investment variables actually as well as theoretically, but the practical definition of markets presents untold difficulties. Pragmatic distinctions among customers or geographic area are elusive indeed, except for the domestic versus international classification which already is provided for by generally accepted accounting principles applicable to conglomerate and nonconglomerate companies alike.

Activity in different industries remains as the only practicable basis for identifying diversified companies. Even here difficulties appear. No single, inclusive industry classification appears to provide the well-defined, mutually exclusive categories needed. And if one were established, its application to all companies might well be undesirable. The operations of different businesses do not necessarily fall into the same well-defined, mutually exclusive categories. There are certain clearly disparate and separable activities such as newspaper publishing and steel making, for example, that might be combined under one corporate roof. But newspaper publishing and radio or television broadcasting may be joined harmoniously and become virtually inseparable for meaningful reporting purposes. Steel making may have a close tie to bridge building which, in turn, may find heavy construction of other kinds a natural direction for expansion. If such coherent activities were required to report separately from one another in order to fit some uniform system of industry categories, the reported results might ill reflect operational entities within a company.

Industry diversification may thus fall into disparate or coherent patterns, depending less on the specific industries involved and more on the organization and operation of the specific company. To require reporting on some strict industry basis might fractionalize a company into unnatural parts which could not fairly reflect the results of its operations.

Both analysts and companies found gross revenue, net income, and assets invested to be satisfactory bases for determining the point at which a segment of the company should be reported separately. Gross revenue, which was the basis favored by both groups, appears to have advantages over the others. Net income is certainly the most volatile measure of the three and, during periods of low net income for the total company, might be reduced to a point where almost any segment reporting a profit would constitute a material portion of total net income. Its use would also raise interesting questions about net losses, either for the total company or for the segments, as indicators of materiality. Assets committed to reporting segments provide a satisfactory measure only if a high percentage of assets can be identified with segment operations. Responses to the corporate questionnaire suggest that some companies find difficulty in so identifying any substantial portion of total assets.

This leaves gross revenue as the most reliable and easiest measure to apply. Disadvantages exist here also. There is no assurance that gross revenues will vary proportionately with assets invested. Conceivably, a segment which utilized as much as one half of the company's total assets might produce only a small portion of the total revenue and thus not be marked for separate reporting by a test based solely on gross revenue. This suggests the need for a supporting test. The guide might be an appropriate percent of gross revenue unless gross revenue is not proportional to net income or assets invested, in which case a more representative measure should be sought. Where assets invested cannot be determined with accuracy, approximations may be required for this purpose.

General agreement is indicated by both analysts and corporate managements with respect to the point at which a given segment becomes sufficiently material to merit separate reporting and the total number of segments to be so reported. The financial analysts indicated that materiality fell in the 10 to 20 percent range and indicated that gross revenue, net income, and assets employed were the preferred bases to which such measures should be applied. Responses to a similar question in the corporate questionnaire picked the same three bases and approximately the same percentage measure. A guide set at 15 percent of gross revenue (already accepted by the Securities and Exchange Commission as a significance test for certain purposes) with recourse to an equivalent portion of net income or total assets when revenue is an unsatisfactory indicator, appears reasonable.

In reply to a question directed at ascertaining the maximum number of segment reports for a typical company which can be utilized effectively for analytical purposes, analysts stated a preference for a relatively small number rather than a large number of reporting components. A substantial number indicated they could not use more than about a dozen, while 56 percent of those responding stated they would prefer to deal with only eight or fewer. Generally, the numbers of organizational units and product lines reported in the corporate questionnaire fell within this range. 85 percent of those responding listed less than ten organizational units. The numbers of products listed did not differ materially from the numbers of organizational units, indicating that whichever base is selected, results fall within the range preferred by analysts.

Both analysts and corporate executives indicated an awareness of the significance of common costs and the possibility that their allocation might produce results subject to misinterpretation. This might lead one to consider defined profit as the natural solution. The corporate questionnaire, however, reveals that many management representatives are not enthusiastic about a defined profit figure. Their objections question the desirability of describing any figure as "profit" before all costs and expenses have been deducted. They fear that readers will misinterpret such a figure and may conclude the company is far more profitable than it really is. Thus, although some accept the notion of defined profit for segment reporting, others prefer a net income figure either before or after taxes. To require either one of these for all companies would force some into a position they could justifiably protest as a hardship. A reasonable solution appears to be to leave the choice to the individual company management. Thus, a company would be permitted to report either a defined profit before the allocation of common costs or an income figure after the allocation of common costs providing (A) that there is full disclosure of the nature of the "profit" figure reported, and (B) that if income is chosen and the method of allocating common costs or pricing intra-company transactions significantly influences the reported income, the method for allocating any significant amounts of common cost and for determining any significant intra-company pricing is disclosed.

A combination of factors leads to the conclusion that the extended disclosures may be made acceptably elsewhere in the annual report than in the audited financial statements. Financial analysts do not feel the application of the independent CPA's opinion to this information is essential. Responses show a majority of company representatives prefer to report it elsewhere than in the financial statements, yet the results of the corporate questionnaire also suggest that a number of companies will submit the extended disclosures to their auditors for review, and, as experience accumulates, more companies will probably choose to do so. For the present, however, this can scarcely be viewed as a requirement.

The importance of freedom to experiment with a variety of methods of presentation is apparent. Individual companies will seek ways to present their diversified activities as effectively as possible and may employ a number of presentations before settling on the one they find most useful. Because the disclosure of the results of diversified activities on a less than total company basis will represent an innovation in the reports of many companies, there exists the possibility that some readers will utilize the data in ways for which they were never intended. To reduce this possibility as much as possible, the grouping of such disclosures with a warning note to those who read them should be beneficial.

RECOMMENDATIONS

A. Companies which are unitary in nature, that is, which operate almost completely within a single broadly defined industry, or which are highly integrated, should not be expected to fractionalize themselves for reporting purposes.

1. Unless a company has components which (a) operate in different industries, broadly defined, and (b) experience rates of profitability, degrees of risk, or opportunities for growth independent of other components, and (c) meet the test of materiality (as stated in B-2 below), the company should be considered unitary in nature.

2. Companies, or parts of companies, whose segments transfer substantial amounts of products to or receive substantial amounts of products from, or render substantial services to, other segments with which they are integrated in a product sense, should be considered unitary in nature rather than diversified.

B. Companies which to a material degree have activity in more than one broadly defined industry should meet the extended disclosure requirements in C following.

1. Activity in more than one broadly defined industry exists when a company either (a) receives gross revenue from, (b) derives income from, or (c) utilizes assets in industries subject to significantly different rates of profitability, diverse degrees of risk, or varying opportunities for growth.

   No present system of industry or product classification appears ideally suited to the identification of broad industry groups for reporting purposes. If any of the existing systems (including the Standard Industrial Classification at the 2-digit level) is applied without consideration of a company's historical development and the interrelated nature of its established activities, the disadvantages to shareholders may be substantial. Considerable discretion to management in defining broad industry groupings for the purpose of meeting the disclosure requirements in C is essential.

2. Ordinarily, a "material degree," as the term is used here, means 15 percent or more of a company's gross revenue. If the amounts of gross revenue are significantly disproportionate to the amounts of income from, or the assets employed in, diversified components, as compared to other components of the company, a more representative test of the materiality of the diversification should be used.

C. Management, because of its familiarity with company structure, is in the most informed position to separate the company into realistic components for reporting purposes. Therefore, management should determine the number and scope of a diversified company's reporting components and report the activities of those components within the following guidelines:

1. Identify and describe the components which are subject to separate reporting.
2. Disclose any significant changes from the previous period in the composition of the reporting components.
3. For each reporting component:
   a. Disclose sales or other gross revenue.
   b. Disclose the relative contribution made by each component to the income of the enterprise. The contribution to income made by each component may be calculated before or after the allocation of common or corporate costs but in any case should be clearly described. In the event of a change in the method of computing or reporting either gross revenue or the relative contribution to income of the reporting components, the change should be clearly described.
4. If the method of pricing intra-company transfers or allocating common or corporate costs significantly affects the reported contribution to income of the reporting components, the method used should be disclosed in general terms similar to the following:
   a. "Corporate expenses were allocated to the reporting components on the basis of a formula giving approximately equal weight to assets employed, sales, and number of employees."
   b. "Intra-company transactions are priced at close approximations of open market prices for similar products and services."

D. Disclosures recommended under C may be included in parts of the annual report other than the formal financial statements at the discretion of management. Whether in narrative or tabular form, they should be grouped and should carry a clear indication of the limitations of their usefulness. Words similar to the following may prove useful: "The data supplied in (specify pages, paragraphs, or schedules) presents certain information relative to the nature, principal types, and results of the company's diversified activities. No assurance can be or is given that they have been prepared on a basis comparable with similar data for other companies."

E. Because of the innovative nature of these recommendations and the innate complexities of reporting diversified activities, the recommendations should be applied with judgment and flexibility by all concerned. In those cases where management sincerely believes the recommended disclosures, if followed, would have a significantly adverse effect upon the interests of shareholders, a statement to this effect should be made in lieu of extended disclosures.

30. NET INCOME, FINANCING, AND RISING PRICES*

ROBERT M. SOLDOFSKY†

Prices in the United States increased an average of about 2 percent per year from the early 1920s until the mid-1960s. From 1966 through 1971, price increases were in the 3-6 percent range. Starting about mid-1971 a combination of domestic and international problems led to the longest and largest price increases this country has experienced as shown in Figure 30-1. For the most recent year, 1974, the Consumer Price Index rose at more than a 12 percent annual rate. Although the rate of inflation is likely to drop below the devastating level of 1974, another outburst of such rapid inflation before the end of the decade is quite possible.

Our military and economic commitments to orderly worldwide economic and political development, continuing international monetary turmoil, the energy crises, the intensifying problems in our cities, and other serious domestic problems all help to generate this bleak outlook.

Even with prices rising no faster than they have been in the United States, the consequences for the rate of growth of business income, the distortion of reported net income between companies and industries, the maintenance of technologically up-to-date plant and equipment, and financing the added investment related directly to price-level increases have been serious. Congressional and professional studies of this many-sided problem are frequent.[1]

My major concern in this brief article will be with the income statement rather than the balance sheet. The purpose is to explore in some detail the impact of generally rising prices upon the net income and financing of business firms. In order to achieve this objective, the level and meaning of net income against a background of prices rising at a specific rate—10 percent a year—will be sketched. In the next section the impact of conventional, historical-based costs upon net income, income tax payments, and income tax rates will be contrasted with the impact of a price-level-adjusted cost basis upon these critical factors. Although the differences in the net income and income tax implications of these two cost bases are important, the conclusion emerges that price-level-adjusted net income—if that concept became acceptable for accounting practice and income tax purposes—would provide business

---

°From *The Quarterly Review of Economics and Business* (Autumn, 1968), pp. 67-74. Reprinted by permission. Updated by the author in March, 1975.
†Professor of Finance, The University of Iowa.
[1]For example, Jules Backman and Martin R. Gainsbrugh, *Inflation and Price Indexes* (Washington: U.S. Government Printing Office, 1966), *Reporting the Financial Effects of Price-Level Changes, Accounting Research Study No. 6* (New York: American Institute of Certified Public Accountants, 1963); *A Statement of Basic Accounting Theory* (Evanston: American Accounting Association, 1966).

FIGURE 30-1

COMPREHENSIVE PRICE MEASURES
SEASONALLY ADJUSTED QUARTERLY

Change at Annual Rates

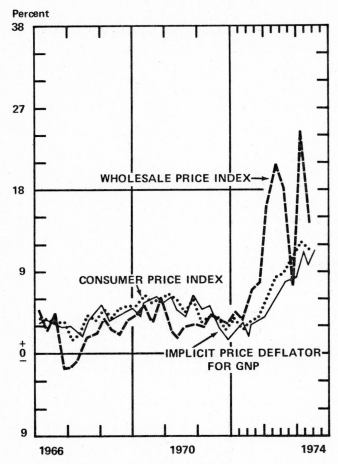

Source: Board of Governors of the Federal Reserve System.

firms with only a small part of the relief they seek from the pressures for outside financing during periods of sharply rising prices.

In the last section the relationship between fiscal policy and the acceptance of price-level-adjusted taxable income is discussed. Income tax regulations that do not accept price-level-adjusted costs are seen as providing an automatic stabilizer against some of those pressures which would push prices higher faster in an overheated economy. The implicit higher corporate income tax rate that develops under conventional accounting and income tax regulations tends to dampen capital investments in the right industries at the right time for fiscal policy purposes.

Under conditions of certainty, economic and financial decisions are made that will maximize net present worth or wealth. Even when prices are constant, new investments will not be made nor new products introduced unless the expected discount value of the net receipts stream is greater than the initial (or time-adjusted) outlay. When prices are rising at some known rate or amount, new investment will not take place unless the same condition prevails, namely, that there will be an increase in net worth or wealth. To state the same point in a slightly different way, within the capital-budgeting framework of analysis, matching requires the use of the time-adjusted value of money. In conventional accounting the time value of money is not a consideration in the matching process.[2]

Within the decision-making framework for capital budgeting, the analytical procedure is the same whether prices are constant or rising at some given rate. When prices are rising, the data on which the decision will be made will include the expected higher prices dated for each point in time at the appropriate and discounted rate. The latter is expected to increase enough to offset the rise in prices.[3]

One of the many problems that exist in the real world is that the selling price, the quantity sold, and the related costs are not known with a high degree of assurance. The certainty device of economic theory will be used in order to facilitate and to clarify the exposition of the way in which changes in costs flow through the accounting records and the impact of these flows of costs upon the net income and income taxes of the firm.[4]

NET INCOME AND RISING PRICES

First, the accounting process by which generally rising prices impinge on the net income of a firm will be illustrated. The amount of

---

[2]For a similar criticism of conventional accounting, see John W. Coughlan, "Industrial Accounting," reprinted in Hector R. Anton and Peter A. Firmin, *Contemporary Issues in Cost Accounting* (Boston: Houghton Mifflin Company, 1960), pp. 50-68. Alexander A. Robichek and Stewart C. Myers, *Optimal Financing Decisions* (Englewood Cliffs, N.J.: Prentice-Hall, Inc., 1965), pp. 11-16, also point out differences between net income based upon the conventional accounting and discounted-present-value approaches.

[3]As an aside, note that the controversy between the advocates of absorption costing and direct costing is undercut by the capital-budgeting or time-adjusted decision framework. Neither absorption costing nor direct costing faces the problem of the dating of costs and revenues squarely. The attempt to approximate the marginal-cost concept of static economic analysis, as discussed in most textbooks on price theory, does not help in deciding within a considerable range whether the decision or policy in question will aid in increasing the net present wealth or worth of the firm. Of course, so far as direct costing results in an income in each accounting period different from absorption costing, the market price of the company's stock may be affected.

[4]Briefly, under conditions of certainty, there is a one-to-one correspondence between anticipated events and their outcomes.

paper profits will be quantified in the case developed. Second, the impact of alternative cost assumptions on income tax amounts and rates will be specified in terms of the illustration.

The terms "paper profits," "fictitious profits," and "capital consumption taxes" are used widely, and their meaning should be carefully defined. Paper profits, which are associated with the rising price level, are the difference between net income determined on the basis of current or opportunity costs and net income determined on the basis of historical or book costs. The term "paper profit" is usually used to refer to this difference on a before-tax basis. The well known difficulty is that the before-tax paper profits are defined as taxable income for income tax purposes and are taxed as such. The consequences of paper profits for financing and determining rates of return on investment will be made clearer with the aid of an example.

Paper Profits Illustrated

Assume that a firm (the Able Corporation) has a six-month product cycle. Its product costs and other expenses are rising at 10 percent a year, which is very close to the rate at which the general price level is rising. The product and the productivity of Able Corporation do not change during the three-year period being considered. In Table 30-1 costs are shown in separate terms to approximate both conventional (historical cost) accounting and economic (current cost) accounting. The same quantity is sold in each of the six-month periods, and the rising sales dollars reflect the increases in the selling price, which is assumed to be rising at 5 percent every six months. Sales revenues are identical in terms of conventional and economic accounting.[5] In current- or opportunity-cost terms, the period and product costs would be reported as rising to reflect the market conditions exactly. In conventional accounting, depreciation is reported on the basis of the historical prices that are shown on the books of account. For the Able Corporation this condition is indicated by the constant $50,000 depreciation expense. In practice most of this depreciation element would be related to product costs and would be matched with realized revenues. The costs of material and labor reflected in the inventory or product would be incurred on the average approximately six months prior to the time of sale. Hence, in this example there would be a 5 percent lag in the material and labor cost components of the product cost on the conventional statement as compared with the statement of economic income. Some costs, primarily period costs, would be reported on (almost) a current basis in both statements. The greatest difference between the economic and accounting versions of taxable net income relates to depreciation of fixed assets.

---

[5]The time-adjusted differences in value between the date of sale and collection are disregarded at this point.

TABLE 30-1
DETERMINATION OF NET INCOME WHEN PRICE LEVEL IS RISING°

Period	Sales	Costs				Taxable Net Income	Income Taxes°°	Net Income
		Depreciation†	Material, Labor, Overhead††	Current	Total			
Conventional (Historical) Cost								
First year								
January 1–June 30	$550,000	$50,000	$350,000	$100,000	$ 500,000	$ 50,000	$20,000	$30,000
July 1–December 31	577,500	50,000	367,500	105,000	522,500	55,000	22,000	33,000
Total					1,022,500	105,000	42,000	63,000
Second year								
January 1–June 30	606,375	50,000	385,875	110,250	546,125	60,250	24,100	36,150
July 1–December 31	636,694	50,000	405,169	115,763	570,932	65,762	26,305	39,457
Total					1,117,057	126,012	50,405	75,607
Third year								
January 1–June 30	668,529	50,000	425,427	121,551	596,978	71,555	28,620	42,931
July 1–December 31	701,955	50,000	446,699	127,629	624,328	77,627	31,051	46,576
Total					1,221,306	149,178	59,671	89,409
Current Cost§								
First year								
January 1–June 30	550,000	52,500	367,500	100,000	520,000	30,000	12,000	18,000
July 1–December 31	577,500	55,125	385,875	105,000	546,000	31,500	12,600	18,900
Total					1,066,000	61,500	24,600	36,900
Second year								
January 1–June 30	606,375	57,881	405,169	110,250	573,300	33,075	13,230	19,845
July 1–December 31	636,694	60,775	425,427	115,763	601,965	34,729	13,892	20,837
Total					1,175,265	67,804	27,122	40,682
Third year								
January 1–June 30	668,529	63,814	446,699	121,551	632,064	36,465	14,586	21,879
July 1–December 31	701,955	67,005	469,034	127,629	663,668	38,287	15,315	22,972
Total					1,295,732	74,752	29,901	44,851

°Price and costs assumed to be rising steadily at 10 percent a year.
†Constant. No purchases made during this 3-year period.
††All costs and expenses for which there is a 6-month lag between date of acquisition or use and date of sale. Depreciation expense excluded.
°°Income tax rate at 40 percent assumed.
§Costs and expenses adjusted to current cost basis as of date of sale.

Notice that for the first six months taxable conventional-accounting net income and taxable net income on a current-cost basis are $50,000 and $30,000 respectively. The difference of $20,000 is the *paper profit*. When the income tax rate is set at 40 percent, the income tax on this $20,000 difference is $8,000 which is the difference between the income taxes in the two panels of Table 30-1. Table 30-2 shows depreciation as a percentage of receipts, net income, and assets for 15 different leading corporations representing a wide variety of industries.

TABLE 30-2

RELATIVE IMPORTANCE OF DEPRECIATION FOR LEADING CORPORATIONS IN SELECTED INDUSTRIES (1973 DATA)

	Depreciation as a Percentage of		
Corporation	Receipts	Net Income	Assets
American Telephone and Telegraph	14.2	111.1	10.5
International Business Machines*a*	13.4	92.8	11.4
Commonwealth Edison	11.5	78.7	3.1
UAL, Inc.*a*	9.9	369.7	7.8
Delta Airlines, Inc.*a*	8.0	127.7	8.9
DuPont deNemours*b*	7.9	72.4	8.8
Southern Pacific Transportation Co.	6.0	87.9	2.7
United States Steel*c*	5.1	109.9	5.2
Exxon*c*	4.4	46.5	4.5
Coca-Cola	2.7	27.3	4.2
General Motors*b*	2.5	37.8	4.4
Boeing	2.0	128.9	3.9
International Harvester*c*	1.9	67.9	2.8
Sears, Roebuck and Co.	1.0	18.7	1.2
Foremost-McKesson, Inc.	0.5	33.9	1.4

a Includes amortization.
b Includes obsolescence.
c Includes depletion.
Sources: *Moody's Industrial Manual, Moody's Public Utilities Manual,* and *Moody's Transportation Manual.*

Effect of Real Income Tax Rates

One complaint of companies that use relatively large amounts of fixed assets in their production is that their real income tax rate rises during periods of rising prices. The income tax paid in the circumstances described would be $42,000 for Able Company in the first year under existing accounting conventions and income tax regulations. The real rate of income taxes would be stated as the $42,000 divided by the $61,500 of real net income, or 68.3 percent as compared with the apparent or nominal rate of 40 percent. For the second year the effective income tax on real taxable income would be 74.3 percent. The increase in the second year is related to the method of accounting for depreciation. The increase in the real over the nominal tax rate amounts to about two thirds of the nominal income tax rate. Using the same illustration and considering the first year only, annual rates of price increases within a reasonable range and effective real income tax rates are as follows:

Annual Rate of Price Increase	Effective Real Income Tax Rate
6%	53.7%
8	60.0
10	68.3
12	79.6
14	94.0

Many prices of many types of industrial equipment and structures have been rising at more than 15 percent per year since 1970.

Another way of viewing this difference in income taxes is to state that it is a levy on the use or consumption of capital goods. If one of the axioms of accounting and business is that capital goods should be conserved, this axiom appears to be violated. The reported rate of return is of interest to managers, investors, and others.[6]

If the asset value of the firm were $1 million according to conventional accounting at the end of the first year, the conventionally computed rate of return would be 6.3 percent and income in current terms would be 3.7 percent when related to the same base. The difficulty with the latter computation is clear: the current-cost-based rate of return should be related to the market value of the assets. Determination of the latter value is more difficult although it is a part of the business of appraisers to make such estimates. Another way to attempt a market-validated rate of return is to relate the earnings per share of a company to the market value of its stock.[7] However, both the management and the stockholders should be at least as much concerned with the decision process for selecting investment opportunities and reviewing their individual results as they are with the aggregate results.

FINANCING AND RISING PRICES

A point that is often overlooked by those who take the position of outside critics of the financial system is the impact of price-level in-

---

[6]The stockholder also is not fully protected against inflation. The point made here is that the real income tax rate on the corporation rises and that corporate net income does not rise in proportion to the rising level price. For a discussion of this point and related problems, see Diran Bodenhorn, "Depreciation, Price Level Changes and Investment Decisions," *Journal of Business*, Vol. XXXVI, No. 4 (October, 1963), pp. 448-457.

[7]This rough-and-ready procedure has many obvious faults. The reported net income of companies reflects a host of accounting problems. The market price at a particular point in time may not be representative, and the yield for a given year may not be representative of past history or of future prospects.

creases on the problem of financing business. Using Table 30-1, for example, during the first year the conventional net income was $63,000. Some $36,000 of this amount must be used to finance the higher cost of goods sold next year and another $10,000 to finance the expected higher expenses. The difficulty has been simplified further in that the inventory valuation problem has been side-stepped, but the maintenance of inventory at the same physical level would also require more funds. The replacement of depreciating assets is also avoided temporarily. Even so, financing the higher expense levels absorbs well over half of the conventionally reported net income. If current cost accounting were used and were acceptable for federal income tax purposes, the outlay for income taxes would be less, but the same amount of funds would be absorbed to finance the higher expense levels. In fact, the amount of funds absorbed at the minimum would be over 70 percent of the correctly computed net income.

The remaining net income in either case would be available for such uses as financing expansion in real terms and for dividend payments or debt repayment. Periods of rising prices are most likely to be those during which firms would prefer to expand because they anticipate rising demand for their products and rising profit margins. Financing such expansion becomes a more difficult problem because most of the internal funds that might be used are absorbed to finance the price-level increases in costs and assets. When many (or most) firms experience such pressure to expand and seek to finance the expansion with borrowed funds, this latter factor alone operates in the direction of increasing the interest rate. Expansion by widely held firms could be financed by equity offerings as well as by borrowing, but many investigators have pointed out the great reluctance of industrial firms in general to offer new common stock.[8] Large numbers of firms do not know whether they are expanding up to the point (or even into the neighborhood) at which their internal rate of return on added investment is approximately equal to the added cost of funds. Speculation about the impact of added equity financing upon the firm's cost of funds, and the added impact of attempting further expansion upon the price level, would take this discussion too far afield. The concern here is to point out that rising prices intensify the financial problems of the firm. Price-level accounting practices which are widely discussed have numerous advantages, but their adoption would have only a small salutary effect upon the financing problem.

Caution should be exercised in using the illustrative numbers that have been presented; these amounts are intended to be realistic, but the proportions of current, lagged, and slowly responsive costs (such as

---

[8]For example, Gordon Donaldson, *Corporate Debt Capacity* (Boston: Harvard University, 1961), and Walter Heller, "The Anatomy of Investment Decisions," *Harvard Business Review*, Vol. XXIX, No. 2 (March–April, 1951), pp. 95-103.

depreciation) differ widely by company and industry. The illustration is also limited in other directions. Increases in the price level for three years only was illustrated; nothing was stated about how long the price rise had been under way or about how much longer it might be expected to continue before reversing itself. The rate of price change need not and should not be expected to be constant. The price changes for different classes of goods are likely to proceed at rates different from the average rate of increase.[9]

FISCAL POLICY IMPLICATIONS, ALTERNATE NET INCOME BASES, AND RISING PRICES

The use of accounting and income tax procedures that recognize net income computed on a current or market-price basis have important fiscal policy implications. First, the real income tax rates would be lowered, and this decrease would be most favorable for the heavier capital-using companies and industries. Income tax payments would tend to be lower, and the cash flow of corporations higher, during periods of more rapidly rising prices. The higher cash flow would be desirable from the point of view of facilitating corporate investment but would be destabilizing and tend to feed *demand pull* inflation.

Historical-cost depreciation tends to increase real income tax rates faster the greater the rate of price increases, and in that sense it is an automatic stabilizer. The higher real income tax rate impinges more on heavy capital-goods-using industries, but that effect is also in a stabilizing direction.

Many of those who favor price-adjusted depreciation point out that the revenue loss to the federal government would be small. For example, an executive of American Telephone and Telegraph Company suggested that only $2 billion dollars in revenue would be lost.[10] However, few would doubt that the federal government would maintain its expenditures level by either increasing taxes or borrowing. In the United States and in other nations of the world, historical-cost depreciation is almost universal. Revenue officials almost everywhere appear to be reluctant to condone the erosion of the income tax base and to face the higher explicit income tax rates that might be a likely consequence. Only in Sweden does the corporate income tax policy appear to be substan-

---

[9]E. Cary Brown demonstrates a number of similar but more complex situations. He illustrates and discusses the problems of asset-replacement values based upon depreciation, longer periods of time, and patterns of rising, falling, and sporadic changes in prices. *Effects of Taxation: Depreciation Adjustments for Price Level Changes* (Boston: Harvard University, 1952).

[10]Statement of Alexander L. Stott, comptroller of American Telephone and Telegraph Company, before the Committee on Ways and Means of the U.S. House of Representatives, quoted by Francis J. Walsh, *Inflation and Corporate Accounting* (New York: National Industrial Conference Board, 1962), p. 9.

tially modified and integrated into a fiscal policy rationally designed to influence the performance of the economy.[11]

Only when price level increases have been much larger than historically they have been in the United States have any nations enacted replacement or price-level cost depreciation relief, and then it was generally of a temporary nature. If more business costs were permitted on an escalator basis for tax purposes and if personal retirement incomes were also expected to be fully adjusted for price-level changes, the question might be asked, Who will stand up for maintaining a nearly constant price level? Who will stand up against inflation?

---

[11]Sidney Davidson and John M. Kohlmeier, "A Measure of the Impact of Some Foreign Accounting Principles," *Journal of Accounting Research*, Vol. IV, No. 2 (Autumn, 1966), pp. 183-212.

31. THE FINANCIAL BATH: IS IT COMMON?*

RONALD M. COPELAND†
and MICHAEL L. MOORE††

Recent business literature contains frequent references to a phenomenon called the *bath* which greatly affects the interperiod and intercompany comparability of financial statements. The bath is described as a "clean-up" of balance sheet accounts. Assets are written down or written off, and provisions are made for estimated losses and expenses which may be incurred in the future. These actions decrease income or increase losses for the current period while relieving future income of expenses which it would otherwise have had to absorb. In simple terms, taking a bath tends to inflate future income by depressing current income.

Some reporters claim that the bath is a common phenomenon, that it is used in a variety of different circumstances, and that it is detrimental to the financial community as a whole. These reporters castigate accountants for allowing such practices and they advocate corrective policies. Few studies have been made to determine the actual frequency of bath activity or the conditions under which companies take financial baths. This article reports on one study of the bath phenomenon and related policy recommendations.

Allegedly a bath should be taken during a period when the earnings of a company decline significantly, when the market price of a company's common stock declines significantly, and/or when there has been a change in the top management of a company. Consider the following examples found in the current literature:

• The seemingly classic example of the big write-down is in the works for Tyco Laboratories. President Arthur J. Rosenberg has already made a preliminary announcement that Tyco, whose stock has fallen from a high of $68.63 to last week's close of $7.37, expects to report a net loss of about $15 million vs. a profit of $2.3 million a year earlier. Included in the loss is, first, a write-down of $10 million in the value of the common stock in the two companies that Tyco had earlier purchased at much higher prices. Next, there will be a write-down of an undisclosed amount in several divisions that Tyco hopes to sell, and finally, a write-off of some of the $5 million in "goodwill" that Tyco is carrying in its books.[1]

*From *MSU Business Topics* (Autumn, 1972), pp. 63-69. Reprinted by permission of the publisher, Division of Research, Graduate School of Business Administration, Michigan State University.
†Professor of Accounting, University of South Carolina.
††Assistant Professor of Accounting, The University of Texas at Austin.
[1]"The Big Bath," *Newsweek*, 27 July 1970, p. 54.

• "There is a tendency for new management suddenly to become very pessimistic about the future of a product line or about the value of inventories," explains one CPA diplomatically. The new management trims out all the excess expenses it can find during its first year in office, blaming the low earnings on the old bunch.[2]

• Leonard Spacek, managing partner of a major CPA firm, recommends the bath when there has been an accumulation of inferior accounting practices "in order to clear the accounting tubes and to persuade management (often a new management) to lead a better life accounting-wise from then on."[3]

• Robert Amen, a vice-president of Combusion Engineering, Inc., recommended the bath as a tactic in a declining stock market. "Consider writing off those bad results you have been hiding for years. After all, if your stock is down 50 percent already, how much worse can it get?"[4]

• We had one single big write-off we decided that we should take. Once we decided on that, we tended to throw some other stuff in with it. I don't expect all the write-offs we took will stand up under Internal Revenue Service scrutiny. But even if we have to go back and reverse it sometime later, it can't do anything but help our shareholders.[5]

Motivation for a bath has its essence in the attitude, "So we got shellacked this time around. By making it a little worse, we can guarantee an improved income picture in the future. Why not get some benefit out of an existing fiasco?"

PREVIOUS STUDIES

Research on the bath is not extensive. The phenomenon itself, without the bath label, was mentioned by Barry E. Cushing[6] (housecleaning) and by Leopold Bernstein[7] (clean sweep). Renowned accounting pioneers W. A. Paton and A. C. Littleton allude to the problem of write-downs resulting from management's desire to improve future performance, and soundly denounce the practice as an unwarranted extension of the accounting concept of "conservatism."[8] But the act of

---

[2]"What *Are* Earnings? The Growing Credibility Gap," *Forbes*, 15 May 1967, p. 42.

[3]Leonard Spacek, *What is Profit?* (Cambridge, England: The Institute of Chartered Accountants in England and Wales, 1970), p. 26.

[4]"How C-E Gears its Financial PR to the Bear Market," *The Corporate Communications Report*, June 1970, p. 5.

[5]"The Year of the Big Bath," *Forbes*, 1 March 1971, p. 43.

[6]Barry E. Cushing, "The Effects of Accounting Policy Decisions on Trends in Reported Earnings Per Share" (Ph.D. diss., Michigan State University, 1969), p. 12.

[7]Leopold Bernstein, "Reserves for Future Costs and Losses; Threat to the Integrity of the Income Statement," *Financial Analyst Journal*, January–February 1970, p. 147.

[8]W. A. Paton and A. C. Littleton, *An Introduction to Corporate Accounting Standards* (American Accounting Association, 1940), p. 130.

bathing continues. Carl Devine observed in 1955 that accountants were allowing wholesale write-downs and that pressure from individual companies was increasing to allow further expansion of bath behavior.[9] In an empirical study released in the mid 1960s, Bernstein found "that there is a tendency, especially in years of loss or in cases of changes in top management, to over-provide for future losses, thus benefiting the results of future years."[10] In a later study Bernstein restated the same position:

> Management will often seize on a period in which losses or comparatively adverse results are reported to create such reserves (reserves for future costs and losses). A new management team will often desire to make a "clean sweep."[11]

In still another empirical study of the 1960s, Cushing investigated the effects of 580 accounting policy decisions on reported earnings per share, but discovered only ten that were consistent with a "house-cleaning" motive.[12] However, a recent *Forbes* article implies a much more widespread use of the bath and attributes the resulting effects of the bath to the stock market rise in early 1971.[13]

These research efforts and other related studies generally infer that the bath phenomenon has implications for three interrelated groups: the company's management, the accounting profession, and financial analysts. Whenever a bath experience is "discovered," some member of the financial press usually decries the growing credibility gap between managers and the public, and may even imply that such behavior will eventually destroy our free enterprise system. Accountants are castigated for failing to develop rules of evidence useful in measuring the timing and magnitude of losses or expenses to be recognized; suggestions frequently are made that their function or authority should be taken over by some agency such as the SEC if they can't improve their own self regulation. Financial analysts are warned that overcharges to income do occur, and that they should look beyond the accounting income numbers to ascertain the intrinsic value of a given company.

AN EXAMINATION

There is no conclusive evidence that the bath is a widespread practice or that it is becoming more common. We examined this point

---

[9]Carl Thomas Devine, "The Rule of Conservation Reexamined," *Journal of Accounting Research*, Autumn 1963, p. 312.
[10]Leopold Bernstein, *Accounting for Extraordinary Gain and Losses* (New York: Ronald Press Co., 1967), p. 126.
[11]Leopold Bernstein, "Reserves for Future Costs and Losses," p. 147.
[12]Barry E. Cushing, *The Effects of Accounting Policy Decisions*, pp. 70-73.
[13]"The Year of The Big Bath," p. 42.

along with various characteristics of those companies which appear to have taken a bath. For our study, we operationally defined a bath company as one which makes certain discretionary accounting decisions that reduce income before these decisions by 10 percent or more.[14] A discretionary accounting decision is made by management whenever it determines the existence of changed conditions which justifies a non-exchange adjustment. The discretionary accounting decisions include write-offs, write-downs, and provisions for future losses and expenses where the ultimate realization is not objectively determinable at the time the financial statement was issued. For example, our definition excludes cases where an asset was written down to net realizable value for a sale consummated after the fiscal year-end but before the financial statements were issued. We would include the case if the sale was consummated after the current year's financial statements were issued. References to discretionary accounting decisions in this article refer only to *income reducing* discretionary accounting decisions.

HYPOTHESES

We examined the relationships between income movements, stock price movements, and discretionary accounting decisions. Tests of discretionary accounting decisions made in a year of management change indicate that a strong relationship exists between changes in management and discretionary accounting decisions. These results are only briefly described here.[15] Three hypotheses were tested:

• *When companies make discretionary accounting decisions, the movement of their incomes (before discretionary accounting decisions) relative to prior years' income are no different than the year to year income movements of companies selected at random that did not have discretionary accounting decisions.*

• *When companies make discretionary accounting decisions, the proportion incurring losses before these decisions is no different from the proportion of companies incurring losses in a random sample that did not have discretionary accounting decisions.*

• *When companies make discretionary accounting decisions, the movements of their stock prices relative to prior year-end prices are no different than the year to year price movements of companies selected at random that made no discretionary accounting decisions.*

Because we knew nothing about the data in the population from which the sample was drawn, nonparametric tests were used to evaluate

---

[14]The 10 percent criterion is an arbitrary figure. However, Bernstein found that the modal area of practice suggests a border zone of 10 percent to 15 percent of net income after taxes as a point of distinction between what is material and what is not. See Bernstein, *Accounting for Extraordinary Gains and Losses*, p. 90.

[15]Michael L. Moore, "Management Changes and Discretionary Accounting Decisions" (Unpublished paper, The University of Texas at Austin, 1971).

our sample data. Since the hypotheses are directional, one-tailed tests were run—with a predetermined .05 level of significance.

THE SAMPLING PLAN

Requests: Annual reports to stockholders were requested from 1,000 companies selected at random from the 1,800 companies listed on the Compustat tape. These requests were for reports for 1966 through 1970, and they were mailed early in 1971; all reports received before the 1 June 1971 cut-off date were used in the analysis.

Responses: Reports were received from 907 companies, a 90.7 percent response rate. Most companies sent reports for the years requested if the reports were available. The total number of reports received was 3,761 and varied from 545 to 871 for the individual years from 1966 to 1970, inclusive.

EXAMINATION PROCEDURE

Each of the 3,761 reports was examined for the presence of extraordinary items which reduced income or increased a loss before extraordinary items by 10 percent or more.

There were 373 reports identified by this procedure. These reports were then closely examined for the types of extraordinary items present. Reports with extraordinary items which were entirely exchange transaction based were eliminated. Reports with exchange transactions and nonexchange adjustments (discretionary accounting decisions) were eliminated if the nonexchange adjustment did not reduce income by 10 percent or more. After these eliminations, 195 reports, representing 165 companies, remained. The numbers of potential bath companies classified by fiscal year-end are shown in Table 31-1.

TABLE 31-1

NUMBER OF REPORTS DETERMINED TO HAVE THE
BATH CHARACTERISTIC

Year	Total Reports	Bath Reports	Percentage Column 3 and Column 2
1970	765	58	7.58
1969	871	53	6.08
1968	822	34	4.14
1967	758	33	4.35
1966	545	17	3.12
Total	3761	195	

From the upward trend in the percentage in Table 31-1 it can be seen that the bath has become somewhat more prevalent over the five year period, based on the sample in this study. The percentage of companies having characteristics similar to what would be expected of a bath-taking company ranged between 3 and 7 percent. While this is not as great as some observers have estimated, it is more than enough to concern interested parties.

INCOME MOVEMENTS

The bath companies (companies with income reducing discretionary accounting decisions) were compared with a random sample of 100 companies selected from the 742 companies that reported no discretionary accounting decisions. The absolute percentage year to year movements of income (not including the discretionary accounting decision) was calculated using the income of the earlier year as the base. Absolute percentages were used to accommodate all cases, including those where income changed from a profit to a loss or from a loss to a profit. The absolute percentage movements of income for the random sample of companies were also calculated.

The Mann-Whitney U Test was used to test the first hypothesis and produced results as shown in Table 31-2.[16] This statistical technique tests whether two independent groups have been drawn from the same population. Except for 1966, companies making bath type decisions have significantly greater declines in income for the decision year than do companies not making these decisions. These data lend support to the notion that our sample companies were taking a bath.

TABLE 31-2

MANN-WHITNEY U TEST OF THE DIFFERENCES IN INCOME MOVEMENTS BETWEEN BATH COMPANIES AND NON-BATH COMPANIES (RANDOM SAMPLE)

Year of Interest	n_1	n_2	Value of U	Corresponding Z Value	Level of Significance
1970	58	100	1351	−5.41	0.0001
1969	53	100	1148	−5.76	0.0001
1968	34	100	1355	−1.76	0.0389
1967	33	100	719	−4.85	0.0001
1966	17	100	685	−1.28	0.1010

The second hypothesis examines the relationship between frequency of discretionary write-offs and the profitability of firms. A 2 X 2 contingency table was prepared for each of the selected years. The

---

[16]Sidney Siegel, *Nonparametric Statistics for the Behavioral Sciences* (New York: McGraw-Hill Book Company, 1956), p. 116.

tables were in the following format (where relatively heavy loadings in cells *a* and *b* indicate evidence of bath behavior):

	Loss Before Discretionary Accounting Decisions	Profit Before Discretionary Accounting Decisions
Number of companies with:		
Bath companies	*a*	*b*
(Random sample) Nonbath companies	*c*	*d*

Chi Square tests were used to analyze the data.[17] The Chi Square test may be used to determine the significance of differences between two independent groups when the research data consists of frequencies in discrete categories. For each year tested, the bath companies have a significantly greater proportion of losses than do the nonbath companies, supporting the bath hypothesis.

TABLE 31-3

RESULTS OF CHI SQUARE TEST OF SIGNIFICANCE OF THE NUMBER OF COMPANIES WITH LOSSES BEFORE BATH TYPE DISCRETIONARY ACCOUNTING DECISIONS

Year of Interest	Number of Bath Companies	Random Sample Companies	Bath Companies with Losses	Random Sample Companies with Losses	Value of x^2	Level of Significance
1970	58	100	16	7	10.91	0.0005
1969	53	100	19	2	30.71	0.0001
1968	34	100	10	5	12.85	0.00016
1967	33	100	9	4	12.70	0.00016
1966	17	100	3	4	°	0.0015

° Since the expected frequencies of the *a* and *c* cells were less than 5 the Fisher Exact Probability Test was used to calculate the probability. Sidney Siegel, Nonparametric Statistics for the Behavioral Sciences (New York: McGraw-Hill Book Company, 1956), pp. 96-104.

STOCK PRICE MOVEMENTS

The third hypothesis compared the bath companies with a random sample of 100 companies selected from the 742 companies reporting no discretionary accounting decisions. For each bath company and company in the random sample, the current and prior fiscal year-end stock

[17]Ibid., p. 104.

price was obtained from *Standard and Poor's Stock Guide*. The percentage change between these two figures was calculated and these percentage changes were inputs to the Mann-Whitney Test.

Table 31-4 shows the results of the Mann-Whitney U Test for each of the test years. Three of the five comparisons are significantly different, but these findings are difficult to interpret. We cannot determine nor logically derive whether stock prices were dependent on the movements of income, or vice versa. Also, the correlations between the stock price movements and income movements of the bath companies were rather high. Therefore it is entirely possible that the significance achieved in 1967 and 1970 could be largely attributable to income movements.

TABLE 31-4

MANN-WHITNEY U TEST OF THE DIFFERENCES IN STOCK PRICE MOVEMENTS BETWEEN BATH COMPANIES AND NONBATH COMPANIES

Year of Interest	$n2$	$n1$	Value of U	Corresponding Z Value	Level of Significance
1970	58	100	1374	−5.32	<0.0001
1969	53	100	1999	−2.50	0.0062
1968	34	100	1387	−1.60	0.0548
1967	33	100	1093	−2.90	0.0019
1966	17	100	703	−1.14	0.1271

Additional tests were run using information of the companies for which the third hypothesis could not be accepted. The purpose of these tests was to determine if any relationship existed between *a*) the relative magnitude of the discretionary accounting decision to equity in the company, and *b*) the relative magnitude of the discretionary accounting decision and the year to year stock price movements.

The assumptions underlying these tests are that adjustments of certain accounts could have a desired effect on future income and hence on certain indexes or ratios (such as rate of return or price/earnings). If an earnings decline was not perceived to be temporary, these adjustments could affect the size of the estimated future earnings stream. Kendall Rank Correlation tests were calculated, but the results also failed to provide any additional insight into the bath phenomenon.

CHANGES IN MANAGEMENT

The "Who's News" column of *The Wall Street Journal* for the years 1966 through 1969 was scanned in order to identify companies with changes in management. Almost 250 companies were identified as having changed some top management positions. Annual reports of 165 of the 246 potential management change companies were received upon request, and thirty-six were identified conclusively as representing a management change situation.

These thirty-six reports were examined for the presence of discretionary accounting decisions which reduced net income, and twenty-three were found with this condition. Comparisons were made between the thirty-six management change companies and two random samples of 100 each, the first with no known changes in management and a second with some changes in management personnel (but not enough to constitute a "management" change). A Chi Square test indicated that the management change firms had a significantly higher proportion of discretionary accounting decisions than found in either of the two random samples. Further analysis of the twenty-three management change firms with discretionary accounting decisions found twenty-one applying procedures that decreased income by more than 10 percent. Furthermore, the twenty-three applied seventeen cases of asset write-off or write-down, twenty-six cases of provision for future costs or losses, and six changes in accounting principles. These data strongly support the management change aspect of the bath phenomenon, but also indicate that total management change does not occur with great frequency.

CONCLUSIONS AND RECOMMENDATIONS

We attempted to determine (1) how frequently companies utilize discretionary accounting decisions to reduce income, that is, take a bath; (2) what are the economic conditions with respect to income or stock price movements that exist when discretionary accounting decisions are made; and (3) whether the size of discretionary accounting decisions is related to the magnitude of the adverse income or price movement. We also summarized some previous findings on the relationship between changes in management and discretionary accounting decisions.

Of 3,761 financial statements examined, 195 reports of 165 companies exhibited potential bath characteristics. For the years 1966 through 1970, inclusive, the relative amount of bath taking ranged between 3 and 7 percent. Another sample of thirty-six companies, drawn from 246 candidates with suspected management changes, indicated that twenty-three employed discretionary accounting decisions to decrease reported income. Appropriate statistical analysis indicates that there is a significant relationship between both income declines or management changes and discretionary accounting decisions, but the bath does not appear to be related to stock price declines. These data confirm that the bath phenomenon does exist, that it is less frequent than some observers estimated, but that it still is of sufficient size to be of concern to interested parties.

Since the bath affects interperiod and intercompany comparisons, corporate managers, accountants, and financial analysts all ought to be concerned. While managers may be tempted to insure better future results at the expense of a current poor showing, they should be aware of the potential credibility gap which may destroy their effectiveness in relating to stockholders or the investing public. Accountants should recognize that the bath results, at least in part, because they have failed to specify definitive rules of evidence for loss recognition, and that increased use of the bath will further erode the public faith upon which they rest their attest function. Financial analysts are directly affected by the lack of comparability which results whenever a bath occurs.

Our recommendations stem directly from our findings. Managers should not succumb to the temptation of taking a bath when conditions are "right": most other companies do not do it but rather state the results of operations as they are. Accountants should specify definitive rules of evidence for loss recognition, thus reducing management's temptation and the criticism to which they subject themselves whenever a bath occurs. And financial analysts should scream bloody murder whenever they find financial statements which abuse the sense of fair reporting. All of these groups do have a common goal, the creation of public reporting that is subject to interperiod and intercompany comparability, but it is only through concerted effort that this goal will be achieved.

PART X. INTERNATIONAL FINANCIAL MANAGEMENT

An increasing commitment to international business is one of the most significant changes occurring in the American economy. As foreign operations grow in relative importance, a stage is reached at which they can no longer be treated as isolated parts of the parent company's business. The articles in this section recognize the growing importance of the international business finance brought about largely by United States direct investment abroad. All three articles examine the various phases of international finance at the micro-level.

In his article, Professor Merwin H. Waterman argues that the problems of financial management of multinational corporations are not different from those of domestic corporations, but the answers to these problems are different. The problems of financial management that are unique to multinational corporations derive from the fact that their operations take place in two or more environments. Are there any theoretical peculiarities in foreign investment theory that require special justification? The answer is no, according to Waterman. However, the potential profit rate must be determined after including factors such as political stability, currency convertibility, marketing vagaries, nationalistic labor, and fund-raising restrictions.

The second part of the article deals with income administration and dividend policy which are complicated by many impediments such as taxes, exchange controls, and restrictions by the host country of managerial choice with respect to income administration in international business operations. In the field of finance, the separate nationalistic legal patterns and political philosophies influence the relations of business to the financial institutions and the use by business of the instruments and tools of finance. Based on his experience, he sums up, "it is not possible to generalize about financial markets and institutions or financial instruments and their use." For most multinational companies, the answer to banking problems would seem to lie in the establishment of relationships with both host country and international bankers. Gradually, American banking methods, systems, and philosophies are moving into other parts of the world, influencing the banking practices in foreign countries. As these changes take place, many nations are moving toward a united world economy as characterized by the European Economic Community, the European Free Trade Association, and the expanding participation by United States corporations.

The article by Professors Robbins and Stobaugh stems from research reported in their book, *Money in the Multinational Enterprise: A Study of Financial Policy.* The multinational enterprise can shuttle funds from country to country to take advantage of different tax, money-market, and currency relationships throughout the world. However, the authors' research reveals few attempts to integrate those elements into a system to take optimum advantage of them. Such failure may cost U.S. foreign direct investors as much as 25 percent of their foreign earnings. The authors employed a computer model as a multinational enterprise system to reveal the consequences of alternative financial policies related to intercompany loans and deferred credits, exchange risk, dividends, and the flow of funds between parent and subsidiaries.

The article by James R. Piper, Jr., summarizes the responses of 21 corporations to a research study which addressed two questions: (1) What type of variables do multinational firms attempt to analyze in evaluating foreign investment proposals? (2) Does the range of variables most often considered by a potential investor reflect an adequate, thorough approach to investment risk analysis in the foreign context? The study concludes that "many U.S. firms' overall approach to foreign investment decision-making is much less sophisticated than their comparable domestic approach."

32. FINANCIAL MANAGEMENT IN MULTINATIONAL CORPORATIONS*

MERWIN H. WATERMAN †

I.

Basically, the problems of financial management of multinational business are not different from those of domestic corporations; by "domestic" I mean those domiciled and operating in any single country of the world that I have so far encountered. After extended experiences in a variety of European countries and a brief visit to oriental ones, I have concluded that search for fundamental differences has been in vain. The problems are the same; it is only the answers that are different. It is true that my experiences have been confined to those countries that are generally labelled "capitalistic," where there is at least a semblance of free enterprise and where a substantial portion of the whole economy is characterized by a profit motivated private sector.

A simple classification of these universal business financial problems would be but 2-fold—the inside problems and the outside problems; there can be no others. Even the subclassifications under these two main heads are not many; let us say, for instance:

Inside problems such as,

1. Investment justification, by projects or business activities;
2. Control and efficient use of capital resources, particularly in terms of working capital management; and
3. Fund management, involving income administration and control, dividend policy; and

Outside problems such as,

1. Capital raising and relations with securities markets;
2. Relations with lending institutions, long and short term,
3. Owner-stockholder relations; and
4. Environmental conditions.

Obviously business problems do not fit only into any such watertight compartments, and if any one of the suggested subclasses tends to dominate all of the others in the international arena, it is environmental conditions— especially those in terms of the legal, political, institutional, macro-economic, traditional, and, yes, even moral factors.

ENVIRONMENTAL PROBLEMS

Really the problems of financial management unique to multinational corporations derive from the fact that their operations take place in two or

*Reprinted by permission from the January and March 1968 issues of the *Michigan Business Review,* published by the Graduate School of Business Administration, The University of Michigan.

†Professor Emeritus of Finance, Graduate School of Business, University of Michigan.

387

more environments. Even this characteristic is not solely one of the multinational units; so-called domestic business need not be very large before it begins to have to adapt itself to a variety of financial, legal, and economic conditions. So, it may be concluded that any study or analysis of financial problems under the "international" or "multinational" head must be largely a study of facts, conditions, instruments, and institutions bearing on financial management in a still segmented world. Any study of these phenomena would be dated before the pages could be numbered; the winds of change are scattering the facts like chaff. Perhaps, however, we can identify the general direction of the winds in some instances, even though observations may be hazardous as predictions of the future.

What may be helpful and what this analysis will try to accomplish by example and experience is to indicate to the financial manager or student some of the kinds of variables he may expect to encounter in foreign business. Wherever possible comparisons between countries or environments will be used to alert the reader and to help him to interpret the conditions as he finds them on the day when his own problems arise. It is certain the answer to a single actual problem encountered during 1968 or subsequently will be of little practical application to solutions of future problems. To the extent possible the discussion will be kept multinational; i.e., applicable to the financial manager of any international business located anywhere. The fact that the author is an American with a special interest in American business in Europe will undoubtedly intrude and color the presentation, but we hope it will not be miscolored by this interest.

INVESTMENT JUSTIFICATION

Modern, efficient financial management has learned to emphasize the importance of the allocation of capital resources by some kind of rate of return or valuation process as applied to decisions on capital commitments. Here is not the place to present the variety of methods of comparing various investment alternatives nor the occasion for trying to set standards of investment goals in terms of cost of capital or otherwise. It is sufficient to say that in most acceptable approaches to these problems the element of risk plays a significant role. Profit and profit potential are closely related to and dependent upon the risk of an enterprise or projects in our capitalistic system, and the amount of this profit (or potential) is necessarily related to the amount of capital resources put out at risk. It is then the problem of the decision maker to judge whether the rate of return (potential) on the investment is sufficient to compensate for the risk entailed—in light of alternative opportunities.

Are there any theoretical pecularities in foreign investment theory that require special justification? I would say, "No," because I think that adequate consideration of the risks involved will result in an intelligently determined potential profit rate (or discount rate) which, when applied to estimated profits or payout, can provide the basis for judgment, just as in case of decisions with respect to home-side investments. Actually some currently existing worldwide companies don't know which investments to call "home-side;" in a sense they are all "foreign," and there is no reason why any of the acceptable techniques of investment justification could not be used to sort out or rank the alternative opportunities according to the risk rate investment relationships.

The solutions are not made simpler by saying that these are the same old problems; when we say that the rate of return or discount rate can be made to reflect the risk, keep in mind how difficult that expression is even in the simplest one-country situation. Then compare it with a multi-country decision where each environment has its own variables and unknowns in such areas as political stability, currency convertibility and exchange control, marketing vagaries, nationalistic labor and investment ideas, and capital raising restrictions. All that management needs to do is equate all these things and express them in a rate of return (or discount) on what they think will be the investment commitment, and the office boy can give the answer on the calculator! That's all!

SPECIAL EXCHANGE RISKS

Perhaps some special and practical words of warning might be added to the theoretical considerations with respect to the application of "payout period" or "discounted cash flow" methods of investment analysis and justification as applied to multinational situations. Generally within our own country it can be assumed that the results of a business investment can be "paid out" and that "cash" will "flow." These assumptions make sense of the mathematical logic of discounting and give some credence to the element of timing of the investment return. But as an owner or shareholder in a business that is earning or generating cash beyond the borders of our country, you may take a dim view of all this going on behind a wall of nationalistic restrictions—economic or political. The mathematical logic of discounting reduces to minuscule the dollars, the pounds, the francs (Belgian, French, or Swiss), the deutschmarks, the lire, or the yen that you may never get, or whose receipt for your benefit may be indefinitely postponed. Just try discounting $1 million of annual potential that you might get for an indefinite period beginning in 15 years. In perpetuity and beginning right now the annual million would be worth $10 million, if discounted at 10 percent; but, all of that coming after 15 years until foreverafter [sic] would be worth only roughly one quarter of the total, or $2.5 million. So, you would have to project a substantially higher ultimate return on undistributed earnings to reach the value justification of $10 million at 10 percent.

It has been said to me that only the very large, diversified corporation can afford to take the risks of foreign investment, particularly in those countries where inflation risks so readily turn to actualities. Such large companies may be better able to take risks. Perhaps they may be more skilled at evaluation, or have taxable income from other sources that help them to absorb losses, or know better how to cope with problems of expropriation, devaluation of currency, and other problems of foreign management. But isn't it a matter of degree? A capital-intensive industry perhaps would require such large unit investments as to overextend a small concern, but even such a business may have the possibility of hedging the risk with funds borrowed in host country currencies (and payable in same) which might so minimize that particular risk of inflation as to reduce the investment exposure.

Thus, may we leave this investment justification problem with the comment that there is very little new under the sun, but also with a recognition of the extreme difficulty of evaluating risks of foreign investment. This has real meaning in terms of financial management, because it demands skill, knowledge, and experience that come neither from studying books nor discussing cases. It's a "know how" requirement coupled with a "know what" that must go with the essential "know why." As the number of countries and environments increases, somewhere it becomes impossible for one person or staff to handle foreign affairs with one hand while handling domestic with the other; specialization or a series of specializations becomes necessary to keep abreast of the facts and environmental changes. The essentials of the coordinating and decision-making functions will not change; the principles can remain firmly established, but the implementation of financial policy with respect to investment justification in foreign lands must rest on an even wider range and variety of facts than many of us are accustomed to assembling and assimilating.

FINANCIAL CONTROLS IN MULTINATIONAL BUSINESS

More frequent, though perhaps less romantic than decisions to build a new plant in a foreign country, are those daily decisions affecting the management of a company's working capital. This pertains to all of its forms—inventory, receivables, and cash. What are the factors in a multinational business environment that affect the management of working capital, and what tools, instruments, and schemes need to be considered to the end of increasing the efficiency of that management? What reasonably can be done either to increase the numerator of the profit/investment fraction or to decrease the denominator, since either will move to maximize the utilization of capital resources and increase the rate of return thereon.

Generally speaking, it would seem that decisions regarding inventory management would be most closely related to rationalization of production in a multinational company; material would be stored in the place and form and processed where the costs of processing and carrying would be minimized. However, one offsetting factor will be the tariff, and it may prove to be more economical to ship bits and pieces in export for assembly elsewhere, thus changing the locale of the financing problem if not its magnitude. In England and on the European continent it seems often to be easier and cheaper to finance working capital than plants and equipment. During the 1966 period of credit restriction in England, there was for a time a priority indicated by government policy in favor of loans for "working capital" purposes. If it is possible to relate working capital requirement to the export potential of a national unit of a multinational concern, loans may become cheaper or easier to get within the framework of credit policy guidelines or the more complete credit controls such as have existed in France— at least until very recently. It is doubtful, therefore, whether the financial problems of inventory can be isolated within the international picture; certainly they do not exist in a vacuum, but the controller or financial manager can do some thinking in terms of inventory management—both with respect to ways of keeping the amount down and in minimizing the costs of carrying.

WORKING CAPITAL PROBLEMS

With respect to this whole matter of working capital finance, the internal control and mobility possibilities of the components seem worth mentioning in some detail. Inventories have their possibilities as mentioned above. Receivables perhaps even more so can be, shall we say, juggled? Particularly are intra-company, inter-country receivables sources of interesting potentials for management. Receivables are generated when company X in country A ships to its sister company Y in country B, both X and Y subsidiaries of company Z. Eventually there will probably be a transfer of funds in payment in the opposite direction, but when? It depends on whether, at least for the time being, it is easier or cheaper to get capital in country A or B; if in A, then company X can hang on to its receivables in either open book form or in the form of notes or bills until management directs payment. So-called receivable financing may be especially a cheap source of finance, because in European countries there is a predilection for discountable bills. Particularly for those bills originating from an export transaction, as implied here, favorably low or subsidized rates of interest are often available. (Of course, this latter facility applies both to export to outsiders and to sister companies.) Relations of company A shipping to another sister C in country W may be such that C has or can get all the money it needs cheaply, so prompt payment of the bill is called for and the company C carries the load as an inventory financing problem.

Beyond this matter of relative cost that can be affected by judicious receivable-payable financing, there are matters of exchange restrictions in some areas; even France with its 1967 liberalization of controls has seemingly changed only from a "no, but" situation to a "yes, but" one. Transfers of substantial amounts of funds must still be explained. There are still definite limits and restrictions on foreign exchange in so many non-European areas that special long term commitments may become involved, and this is a problem not of working capital but of permanent (more or less) finance.

The difficulties of Krupp in Germany came from inadequate solution to these problems. The degree of flexibility and maneuverability that can be achieved by a multinational corporation dealing among countries with monetary restrictions is very great; literally, by anticipation or postponement of payments among units, the methods and locale of financing can be directed so as to take fullest advantage of markets and to avoid the effects of many restrictions. It would seem that the greater the number of intra-company, inter-country transactions, the greater the opportunities. A smaller company with only one foreign branch or subsidiary, for instance, would not have the same benefits of diversification and choice of movement available to it.

MANAGEMENT OF CASH

Cash, as such, is generally considered the most useless and sterile asset on a company's balance sheet—necessary as a lubricant to operation but containing no motive power. Particularly since World War II, the management of cash funds by most business corporations has received much greater attention in order to minimize these sterile amounts and to direct these amounts into some earning form while retaining them in reasonably liquid form readily available for management use. In the multinational business the opportunities and risks of fund management assume new proportions. Within the category that we usually see on a balance sheet labelled "cash and marketable securities" can now be counted:

1. Cash, in various currencies
2. Bank deposits
   a. in various currencies
   b. with various maturities (or withdrawal restrictions)
3. Certificates of deposit
   a. in various currencies
   b. with various maturities (or withdrawal restrictions)
4. Marketable securities
   a. in various currencies
   b. with various maturities (or withdrawal restrictions)
   c. secondary market liquidity.

Almost daily the conditions pertaining to the world's security and money markets are changing. In the United States within the last few years, the "uneconomy" of demand deposits in noninterest paying commercial bank accounts has been overcome by the purchase of "Certificates of Deposit" (CD's) carrying varying rates of interest for maturities from one month to 12; these are now also available in European centers through U.S. bank branches. There is even talk of sterling CD's in England as a British Prices and Incomes Board report suggests a range of deposits of varying size and maturity with varying interest rates. ("Bank Charges," Cmnd. 3292, HMSO.) Thus even within the category of bank deposits, the fund manager has numerous alternatives involving risks and profits.

In most currencies the exchange risks can be hedged by buying forward cover—at a cost—i.e., deposits in pounds sterling can be hedged by selling pounds for future delivery; or if it is deutschmarks you want, buy them now and take them later, getting less or more as your pounds go up or down in value related to the marks. The technicalities of these forward trans-actions are not within the scope of this presentation. Suffice to say that there are costs of brokerage, the risk costs reflected in the differential price of currency for future delivery, and the carrying costs of the deposit. Against these costs can be balanced the benefit of the hedge plus any interest received on the deposit and, of course, the less quantifiable need to maintain funds in more or less liquid form in various markets and currencies. Again, we may conclude that this area of fund management on an international basis is a very complicated one requiring very special skill and knowledge of market institutions and instruments.

These considerations of working capital management are really only suggestive—suggestive of the many directions in which the financial manager must turn to survey the whole of the opportunities to make the most efficient use of the capital resources under his control. The compli-cations involved rightly suggest the need for specialists in money markets by countries, in tax implications of various moves, in legal and political problems of fund movements, and in the economics of foreign exchange transactions. Unless a firm is large enough itself to afford such specialists, it could better depend on the services of institutions such as commercial, merchant, or investment bankers.

Another interesting dimension of financial operations of this type is their market effect. As more and more multinational corporations react to their own needs and to the costs of meeting them, the increasing number and scope of transactions should sharpen the international money markets and tend to bring them closer together. Certainly it could be expected that businesses themselves will become an influence through their exchange and fund operations. When a company such as Dow Chemical opens its own bank (Dow Banking Corporation) in Switzerland and buys an interest in another in the Netherlands, you have a further example of direct partici-pation of business in the financial markets.

II.

In the January issue of the *Review*, a bit was said about the solutions of financial management problems that are more or less unique to multi-national corporations. It was emphasized—particularly in problems of working capital management—that environmental conditions affect the answers to the problems, although the financial theories and principles are the same as at home. In this article, I have tried to set down some things to watch for in other areas of financial management and control; again, this is not an all-inclusive study of events and institutions. Rather, the items are suggestive of the types of considerations that must be included in any man-agement's decision-making process.

INCOME ADMINISTRATION AND DIVIDEND POLICY

By tradition (and taxation) there seem to be separate problems of income or profit administration in multinational corporations, although we all recognize that it is only "funds" that can be administered or their flow directed. If this fact of life is accepted, then we must agree that it is really impossible to distinguish between capital funds and profit funds. When one sees the pounds, francs, deutsche marks, lira, or yen that he may have in the bank or cash drawer, those that may have come from the issue of securities look surprisingly like the ones that resulted from profitable (or not) commercial transactions, such as the sale of goods or services. In all countries it is true that funds available for administration are affected by income taxes, and thus income administration or determination becomes an important matter. In some countries what is done with the actual funds, paid out or kept in the business, also affects available funds via the corporate tax or personal tax withholding route. Even in our simplest domestic enterprise, one scarcely orders lunch without considering the tax implications. When the movement of funds across country boundaries between jurisdictions that have different tax laws begins to take place, the implications and complications increase in more than geometric proportion. It will not be possible to discuss these tax impacts in detail here. I can only emphasize their importance and the need to consider them in each and every individual decision involving income or fund administration. Some general examples will be cited but nothing inclusive.

The object of business, be it domestic, foreign, or multinational, is ultimately to bring through to the owner or shareholder funds representing return on or of his investment. The timing of the receipt of those funds by the owner introduces the discounting process and develops values both for funds that will be taken out and those that may be left in the business to generate future profits (and funds). In the multinational corporation funds for distribution to the shareowners must come through to the treasury of the corporation, either the parent of foreign subsidiaries or the home office of branches abroad. Here the complications begin again.

Within many countries there are impediments to managerial choice with respect to fund administration in purely national businesses as well as in the local units of multinational concerns. Germany's tax law is such that a rate of only 15 percent[1] is paid on the annual income equivalent of dividends paid out, whereas 51 percent is paid on the balance of taxable income. (Remember when the United States had a discriminatory federal income tax on "undistributed profits" in 1937?) The reports of Ford-Werke Aktiengesellschaft show that they have been paying out in common dividends an amount equal to 100 percent of the previous year's profits. Then these amounts have been loaned back to Ford-Werke by parent Ford, and

---

[1]Equivalent, actually, to 23.44 percent, because the tax on distributed profits is not treated as a deductible expense but as undistributed income (taxed at 51 percent).

lately (1964-1965) these loans have been capitalized by allocation to "legal reserve." In this case the company had to balance the costs (in U.S. income tax) of taking the money home and sending it back as loan capital subject to a German capital issue tax, against the differential tax impact of a so-called reinvestment of earnings program. So, round Robin Hood's barn they went to accomplish an increase in Ford-Werke equity in tune with the company's capital expansion.

Another choice sometimes to be made is that between moving funds from the foreign subsidiary to the ultimate dividend paying parent by means of royalty payments, management fees, or franchise fees—rather than by dividends. Insofar as such fee payments are expensable (for tax purposes) in the host country of the subsidiary, the decision will rest on a comparison of the income tax rates applicable in the subsidiary host country and the parent host country, respectively. Maneuvering of intra-company, inter-country pricing becomes a means of tax minimization and has led even to the establishment of pure sales companies in so-called tax haven countries in order to concentrate profits in the lowest tax area. Obviously when any of these movements of funds or "income" reach a sufficient magnitude, some jurisdictions will consider them as tax evasion rather than just a tax minimization move and react accordingly. Within the confines of The European Economic Community, at least, there are hopes and some expectations that standardization and uniformity in tax statutes and procedures will ultimately change these possibilities of maneuvering profits, or at least remove the tax motivation.[2]

As a matter of contrast, consider some such complicated U.S. domestic situation as the American Telephone and Telegraph Company with its dozens of subsidiaries scattered throughout the country, operating in 48 states and the District of Columbia. Within the entire A.T.&T. system it is possible to rationalize the management of funds on an overall basis. For one thing, there are no tax implications of fund transfers as far as federal income taxes are concerned; they are assessed and paid on the basis of a consolidated tax return. Funds are moved from subsidiaries to parent as dividends on shares owned or interest on loans and advances. Generally, share ownership is at or near 100 percent of each subsidiary, so only nominal amounts are syphoned out of the system to minority interests where dividends are distributed. Decisions for such moves then can be made on the basis of an overall, national system policy and on fund requirements for expansion and debt payments of the several subsidiaries, debt payments of the parent, and dividends to ultimate parent company shareowners.

Among multinational corporations freedom of fund movement in some instances may be restricted by exchange controls or direct control

---

[2]A good summary of European (EEC) country tax characteristics is contained in *The Development of the European Capital Market*, Chap. 14, Annex, European Economic Community Commission, Brussels, November 1966.

on capital movements with no distinction between funds as profit or capital. All these factors create problems for the financial manager; he must be aware of them and have his tax and corporate counsel at hand to participate in decisions. It is not difficult to find, in addition to the outright governmental restrictions or directives on the movement of funds from country to country, political pressures all the way up to guidelines designed to achieve the same ends. Even the United States is limiting capital movements abroad by taxes and by trying to encourage homeward movements of profits by counting earnings left abroad as a "capital movement" in that direction.[3] The use of private business as an instrument of public policy by government fiat may not be palatable, but it's an old game and becoming ever more popular when a government itself can not effectuate its own policies. This may be another example of what is known as the modern "political economy" with which we must live, which we must interpret and to which we must react to the best of our ability. Late in 1966 U.S. corporations in Germany had to borrow very expensive D-Marks (at rates as high as 8 percent) because Europe-dollars were not available, because the U.S. branch banks were sending the dollars home to help on the government-created credit squeeze, whereas Germany had a tax on new foreign money coming in which was designed to stave off an inflationary condition caused in large part by their own lack of control over German state security issues for financing expansion programs. (That's a good German sentence; read it again, because it expresses the complex interrelations.) And so it goes; irrationalities introduced by government economic controls and balance of payment manipulations are everyday facts of life that are continually shifting the scene in which financial operations must be carried on.

The problems of budgeting and financial control as we know them in a domestic business become more than usually insoluble in the multinational corporation. There must be budgets for country-by-country operations; these must reflect company pricing and payment policies—intrasystem. Tax considerations and government fund movement restrictions must be counted in, and somehow all of these must be coordinated with the company's expansion policy at home and abroad, its dividend hopes and expectations, and its alternative sources of funds, at home and abroad. It is this last item of interest to which I now turn: sources of funds, at home and abroad.

FINANCIAL MANAGEMENT—INSTITUTIONS AND INSTRUMENTS

The business environment of the world is just about as segmented as the political environment; in some respects even more so. The variety and divergency of political entities bring with them their institutions and instruments

---

[3]The new 1968 U.S. regulations applicable to Europe call for a program limiting the annual investment of earnings of such overseas operations to 35 percent of each company's average *total* investment during the years 1965 and 1966. The permissive percentage is 65 percent for Britain, Canada, Japan, Australia, and oil-producing nations. No funds at all can be sent to continental Europe from the United States.

applicable to their commercial activities. In the field of finance, the separate nationalistic legal patterns and political philosophies and goals definitely influence the relations of business to the financial institutions and the use by business of the instruments and tools of finance. Based on my only brief forays into the Far East—Hong Kong, Taiwan, and Japan—this presentation cannot reflect any great depth of understanding of financing in those areas. Longer professional exposure to southern Italy was now eight years ago, and this has not been followed up. The Scandinavian countries have never yet been included, nor have Latin American ones, in any visit—even for sightseeing. However, on the basis of experience limited primarily to England and Central Europe, it is possible to come up with one generalization, namely, *it is not possible to generalize about financial markets and institutions or financial instruments and their uses!* Tendencies and contrasts perhaps we can talk about, but again they are only things for the financial manager to watch out for, pointing the way for him to plot his course in handling the affairs of the multinational corporation.

Banks and Bank Loans

In the United States the financial manager is more or less accustomed to thinking of his banker(s) first when he needs funds—almost regardless of purpose. Bank borrowing may shortly or ultimately be refinanced in the form of a security issue—bond or equity—if the capital need is sufficiently permanent. But such is the nature of bank/business relationships that short, medium, and even fairly long term bank loans are things to be considered in financial planning. This is not quite so true in Europe, at least as far as the so-called commercial banks are concerned. They are more tuned to the short-term advances for commercial transactions (domestic or foreign), and they just love security, either in the form of a wide balance sheet margin in current assets or an actual pledge of assets. A Sf.50,000 gold bar would undoubtedly get you a Sf.40,000 loan from a Swiss bank if pledged as security, and the loan might even be renewed at the end of a year! Of course, this is exaggerated, but it does exemplify the extreme in contrast to the frequent habit in the U.S. for banks to negotiate a loan to a concern, not ignoring security but depending heavily on the basis of a budgeted payout period that would meet a schedule of maturities. A Swiss bank might extend itself to two or three years for a native Swiss concern, but not for a loan across its borders—where many of them go.

Loans to finance exports will usually be unquestioned, but other loans might be interpreted as contributing to undesirable expansion and internal inflationary influences and thus be subject to restraint. One multinational concern arranged for very satisfactory bank credits (in some instances at subsidized rates) in a number of European countries on the basis of the export of components hither and yon. One can easily sense the possibility of using a bank to finance an export deal so that the company can import! After all, it is the financial manager's job to match the overall fund disbursements of his company with receipts from all sources.

The Europe overdraft scheme for making bank advances to customers is, in many respects, a handy gadget. Arrangements for overdrafts can be made as long as they are within bank or government policy limits in England and on the Continent; borrowers pay interest only on the amounts and for the time that funds are actually borrowed. This is in contrast to the formality of the promissory note which is the typical instrument for borrowing from U.S. banks and which requires not only payment of interest for the period of the note(s) but also usually involves the requirement that some percentage of the loan be left on deposit with the lending bank—5, 10 or 20 percent, depending on the tightness of the market. Yet this latter instrument is a contract in definite terms. On the other hand, overdraft privileges may be subject to change almost without notice, there being no specific maturity on which the borrower may depend. The budget plans of a multinational corporation could be substantially upset by vagaries of call by lending banks, if it had this exposure in several different countries. Overdraft privileges may run for years, although they are considered "short term" loans, but then one day they may be reduced as the result perhaps of bank policy or government fiat. The latter was the case in England in the summer of 1966 when the government asked the banks to impose credit restrictions.

Another variant, while not exclusive to the overdraft, is the tied interest rate that is characteristic of it; interest is usually x percent above the bank rate or discount rate. (This type of deal also exists in the U.S. when interest on a formal loan may be expressed as x percent above the prime rate in New York.) A borrower may find it an advantage to use the overdraft scheme which does not relate his borrowings so much to his ability to pay from generated funds but just to his balance sheet position. He may also be willing to take the risks implied in the looser overdraft arrangements.

Generally speaking, it makes sense for a foreign concern or subsidiary thereof to use some banking facilities in host countries. U.S. branch banks sometimes find resistance to their efforts to get accounts even from subsidiaries of U.S. companies with which they have homeside relations. Relationships developed with host country bankers may have been well-established before the appearance of the U.S. branch or they may have existed for long when the subsidiary was acquired. In some environments it is customary for a company to include on its letterhead the name of its bank affiliation. It is considered good business to have local (or host country) banking relationships where a business lives and operates. The desirability of such a relationship seems obvious, but the problem may be one of adequacy of facilities. In England one of the "big five" could probably handle most situations, or one of the "big three" in Germany; but in the Netherlands one of the reasons for bank mergers has been to create sufficiently large institutions to carry the requirements of large, multinational firms. In France, likewise, there have been recent mergers which may improve the competitive position of the banks there vis-à-vis multinational banks.

But it isn't always size; it's sometimes the service concept. Otherwise why would Bache and Co. think it could successfully open a bank (not a large one) in Frankfurt, Germany, right under the noses of the Deutsche and Dresdner banks? (Mostly, at the moment, because it can be a member of the Stock Exchange.) Or how could Dow Chemical Company be able to show a good year operating a brand new bank in Zurich, supposedly the "bankingest city" in the world? For most multinational companies or even just international ones, the answer to banking problems would seem to lie in the establishment of relationships with both host country and international bankers. In some instances these may be one and the same. Some English banks are opening in the U.S. and have old establishments in other parts of the world. At least one Dutch bank is again moving out across borders after a lengthy hiatus in the foreign and colonial activities of the Netherlands. The top six or seven U.S. banks may have the most branches throughout the world, but others are developing, so the choice is not limited. The origin and flow of transactions by a multinational company would seem to indicate an important test of U.S. banking choice; do the banks have branches where the business is, and are their facilities modern and adequate?

Term Loans

Mention was made of the fact or tendency of English and European banks not to go in for term loans. Perhaps one reason why the opposite has been true in the U.S. is that the latter environment does not always include so-called merchant banks. Merchant banking in Europe and in England is probably older even than commercial banking as we think of it today. Longer term credits and advances were needed in the old days to finance transactions through slower trade channels and to carry risky trade ventures. That type of lending became the province of merchant bankers who are still doing business at the old stand. In America, investment bankers tended to cater to the long-term needs by acting as middlemen for sale of securities to the general public; there is some of this in Europe, yes, but there is still more left for institutional and merchant bank financing. The commercial banking function has remained more or less separate from that of merchant banking. On the Continent the two are often combined in a single firm but with the functions separate. In Holland and Germany, more than elsewhere, the bankers tend to be all things to all people—commercial, savings, investment, and merchant bankers.

Facilities for furnishing intermediate-term capital in Europe are presently in a further stage of development. In England the major banks own the equity in Industrial and Commercial Finance Corporation (I.C.F.C.) which is now quite well established in the business of furnishing capital—both debt and equity—to smaller- and medium-size enterprises. Further institutionalization of this market is occurring on the Continent; in

France the Bank of America and the Banque de Paris et des Pays-Bas have joined to form a medium-term lending unit. A more than Common Market move is indicated by the recent establishment of an international institution under joint ownership of Barclays Bank of England, Banque National de Paris, Algemene Bank Nederland, and the Dresdner Bank of Germany. It is presumed that this investment type operation will cater to and serve multinational concerns. It is probable that some of these modernization moves would have taken place anyway, but some credit must be given to the aggressive competition of the U.S. banks that have moved abroad in all directions with a special emphasis on the European situation and with their concept of the term loan. They have moved not only by way of branches, the number of which has multiplied 7-fold since 1958, but they have also bought varying proportions of ownership in native banking establishments. The number of U.S. banks with branches overseas reached 14 in 1966 (from seven in 1958), and the number of branches rose from 119 to 244 in this 8-year period.[4] Seventeen other banks have established overseas subsidiaries under the Edge Act sections of the Federal Reserve Act.

Influence of American Methods

One way or another, what may be called American banking methods, systems, and philosophies are moving and will continue to move into other parts of the world. Local and multinational businesses will find new banking concepts based more and more on service to business with less emphasis on banking for banking's sake. In the fall of 1967, banks in the Netherlands started a bank checking system. The Prices and Incomes Board in England suggested that British use competitive deposit rates and service facilities. Belgian bankers are learning the hows and wherefores of term lending. There are German bankers who will privately admit that it might be a good idea to separate out from their institutions the functions of brokerage, underwriting, and industrial stock ownership which have for so long characterized their commercial banks. In Switzerland a banker says, "No, we are not interested in extending our services; we are quite happy and doing well enough as we are," but one wonders how long the banks in this little country, whose chief attraction to world capital is shelter, will continue to do well if the Common Market really develops and becomes stabilized. With more or less worldwide competition becoming the order of the day, a market orientation of management in the field of banking may leave the self-satisfied at the post.

Any conclusion regarding banks and their contributions to the solution of the financial problems of the multinational business must await developments. Either native country banks will grow and offer services compatible

---

[4]Robin Pringle, "Why American Banks Go Overseas," *The Banker* (November, 1966), p. 722.

with internationalization of business, or foreign banks that do respond to the needs of their customers (capital users) will make the greater share of loans and profits. The financial manager who expects these changes to take place overnight is wrong; the banking habits, customs, and laws are slow to change. It will be some time, for instance, before open book credit in commercial or consumer transactions in Europe will replace bills and cash. The banks will need to educate their respective customers in the use of the services they can offer, just as some multinational businesses may need to educate the banks with respect to the kind of service they need and expect. The next few years should be interesting and dynamic. A view of changes that have actually taken place between two visits—1958 and 1967—promises that more will be forthcoming in the banking field as well as in other phases of finance. The EEC's special study of "The Development of the European Capital Market" (the so-called Segré Report) points out that shortcomings of the European capital markets "are due not so much to insufficient savings as to the impossibility of adjusting correctly supply and demand on markets that are too narrow."

FACTORS IN INTERNATIONAL FINANCE

Now the recent and more stringent restrictions on foreign loans by U.S. banks, particularly to finance operations in Europe, will upset further the development of anything that can be called international finance. These regulations will tend to force European financing of European operations whether to be accomplished by European banks or by U.S. bank branches from their foreign dollar or foreign currency deposits.

The need within the banking systems to provide these adjustments is emphasized by the fact that one new medium for so doing has entered the scene—the Euro-dollar deposits. U.S. dollars owned and deposited in Europe (including England) are loaned hither and yon, even having been sent to America to help relieve the credit storage there in late 1966. These funds are loaned from bank to bank and from bank to industrial user. This whole operation represents a money market over and above the existing and fragmented national ones. Another start at an attempted European solution to the financing of intercountry projects may be the newly formed Societe Financiere d'Europ, which was mentioned above, even though it may operate more in the area of term loans rather than in the servicing of commercial transactions. Anyway, it is an international organization there to accomplish whatever jobs its management may find or imagine, and imagination in such a spot will be a big asset. As multi- and international businesses develop on the new scales characterized by such as the EEC, the EFTA, and the greatly expanding participation by U.S. corporations, it is as if there were a vacuum being created in the money and banking system. This vacuum will be filled by something; in our day it will probably not be an international monetary system or unit, but with advent of full convertibility, it can as well be done by multinationally recognized institutions.

33 THE PROFIT POTENTIAL OF MULTINATIONAL ENTERPRISES*

SIDNEY M. ROBBINS†
and ROBERT B. STOBAUGH††

Among the principal attributes of a multinational enterprise are (1) it commands a common pool of resources and (2) it is capable of responding to a common strategy. Indeed, from the point of view of maximizing its profit potential, the *distinctive aspect* of the multinational enterprise is that it is a *system* operating in a multiplicity of economic environments with varying tax rates, costs of money, and currency values. Yet few enterprises try to integrate the financial links available to them into a grand design that embraces all elements of the system. As a result, for all U.S. foreign direct investors, the potential savings to be made by improving their financial policies appear to be about one-quarter of their total *foreign* earnings, an improvement of some $3 billion in 1972 and presumably more in subsequent years.

UNEXPLOITED PROFIT OPPORTUNITIES

To understand the financial practices of multinational enterprises, extensive interviews of one day to several weeks were conducted with the financial executives in the home office, regional offices, and foreign subsidiaries of 39 out of 187 enterprises that met the definition of multi-nationality[1] and with governmental, banking, accounting, and legal experts in the United States and abroad. In addition, the unpublished records of scores of firms and the published records of almost 200 firms were studied.

This investigation showed that a major reason for the failure of many enterprises to exploit fully their profit opportunities arises from their lack of understanding of the meaning of the system concept to a multinational organization. Almost half of the 187 multinational companies do not have sufficient overseas experience to recognize how funds may be shuttled over the financial links interconnecting the units of their

---

°Reprinted with permission from the Fall, 1973 issue of the *Columbia Journal of World Business*, pp. 140-153. Copyright © 1973 by the Trustees of Columbia University in the City of New York.

†Professor of Finance, Graduate School of Business, Columbia University.

††Professor of Business Administration, Harvard Business School, Harvard University.

[1]For purposes of the study, a multinational enterprise is defined as one appearing on the *Fortune* 500 list in 1964 or 1965 and having had manufacturing facilities in six or more foreign countries by the end of 1963.

system so as to be limited and the financial managers of its foreign subsidiaries to function without close direction from the parent. The operating pattern is one in which each subsidiary tends to conduct its business independently—"every tub on its own bottom."

Reflecting this provincial attitude, an official of one such firm shrugged off the influence of taxation on the dividend policy of its foreign subsidiaries. "I don't think that's a prime consideration. And I don't think our tax people are involved with any decisions to declare or not to declare a dividend." Contrast this point of view with that of the official of a more sophisticated firm who, when asked to explain the variations in his company's dividend policies from country to country, put it this way: "Particularly in the developing countries, where we have low tax rates, we like to keep our dividends low. It helps our effective tax rates. In a new subsidiary with a small capital stock, if the tax rate is low enough we might forego dividends for ten years and get loan repayments instead. In a very high-tax country, on the other hand, we try to have a very heavy payout."

Somewhat over half of the 187 companies had sufficiently important foreign operations and experience in managing them to recognize the need for centralized control to coordinate the various units of the system. But even here there are problems. The system may have become so large that rather than try to grapple with its intricacies, the easier if less potentially profitable course of using simplifying rules is pursued. As an illustration, the availability of overdrafts has an important effect on the manner in which foreign subsidiaries handle their cash and investments. Following this policy, the overseas units of one large multinational enterprise not only use overdrafts extensively but also are likely to apply any excess cash to reduce their overdraft position rather than to seek new short-term investment outlets.

On the other hand, another firm with more flexible policies does not place a similar automatic reliance on overdraft privileges. Instead, it favors a strategy that cuts costs by taking advantage of interest-rate differentials, and, therefore, it may even frown upon the use of overdrafts, despite their convenience, if less expensive sources are available elsewhere in the corporate system.

Other factors may inhibit a firm from making full use of its system's potential. For example, there may be government restrictions on the movements of capital; the desire to act like a "good citizen" in the host country may immobilize funds locally; the need to maintain cordial relations with financial institutions may lead to borrowing at higher rates than necessary. But when such circumstances prevail, it is relatively unusual for the management of the multinational enterprise to weigh the cost and benefits that underlie each decision affecting financial policy to seek the optimum solution. For one thing, most U.S. firms simply have not reached this degree of sophistication in their conduct of their overseas activities.[2] Then again, or perhaps reflecting this same factor, their record-keeping often is not adequate to permit decisions of this sort to be made.

For these reasons it was impractical to determine optimum profit-making procedure on the basis of the actual records of a firm even when it was willing to disclose this information in some detail. Accordingly, to reveal the consequences of alternative financial policies, a computer model of a multinational enterprise system was employed.[3]

MODEL OF A MULTINATIONAL SYSTEM

The operations of the hypothetical firm of the model cover four consecutive years. The firm is of medium size having foreign sales of $200 million in the first year, gradually expanding to $320 million in the fourth year. A real-life enterprise of this magnitude would have quite a few units—say a dozen or so—but, for convenience, the model used has only three units:

1. Company A, the parent, located in a developed country designated as Country A
2. Subsidiary B, also located in a developed country, designated as Country B
3. Subsidiary C, located in a less developed country, designated as C

The structure of the model is expressed by some 400 linear equations that include all of the financial connections between each unit of the system and the outside world. Links between units of the system are shown in Figure 33-1, and the financial connections between each unit of the system and the outside world are typical of those existing in the real world. The equations can be solved on a computer by using the conventional procedures of linear programming; the solution indicates the financial policies that will meet a given objective, which must be specified by the operator of the model. Of the various objectives employed in the solutions, the most common was "obtain the maximum amount of consolidated profits after taxes for the system over the whole four-year period." The solution offered by the model indicates the set of financial policies that will meet the desired objective.

To make the simulation as realistic as possible, financial constraints similar to those imposed by institutions, governments, or customs were

---

[2]In addition to the technical complexities (an enterprise with 24 subsidiaries and ten financial links between each member of the system would have 3,000 intercompany financial links), there also is the problem of evaluating subsidiary management when profits are shifted from one member to another; see Sidney M. Robbins and Robert B. Stobaugh, "The Bent Measuring Stick of the Multinational Enterprise," *Harvard Business Review.*

[3]This model was constructed by Daniel Schydlowsky.

fixed, such as principal (and interest), or they are fixed in terms of sales of services or goods, such as royalties and accounts receivable. Distributions in the "flexible" category, notably dividends, ordinarily may be varied.[5] The distinction is loose because the intimacy of the contracting parties makes it easy to modify the agreements, while the overseeing eyes of governments sometimes inject rigidities into otherwise "flexible" dividend policies. It therefore is sometimes difficult to tell which withdrawal form may be adjusted more easily and with minimum repercussions. But, at least in theory and often in fact, the distinction exists and is recognized by management in developing programs of withdrawal.

One means of taking into account the differences between contractual remittances and dividends is to have the subsidiary meet the contractual requirements as they become due and to use dividends as the residual channel. For large firms, this method of operation provides a convenient rule-making base. To handle varying conditions, it permits concentration on dividend policy, which, for a big system with many subsidiaries, is difficult enough. At the same time, such a guiding rule deprives the firm of the opportunity of manipulating other important fund flows to take advantage of changing financial relationships.

The budgets of multinational enterprises indicate the total amount of funds to be withdrawn and in many cases the form of the withdrawal. The decision on the amount and form is so important that it is ordinarily made by management in the headquarters.[6] Nevertheless, although management generally considers some mix of methods in effecting withdrawals, very few firms consider all the possible avenues available and formulate a program to maximize the system's profits after taxes. To the extent that an overall withdrawal policy exists, it is likely to be geared to a particular subgoal such as minimizing taxes or maximizing the parent's liquidity. Forming a policy for the whole system that takes into account all relevant objectives has proven too complicated for the multinational enterprise to follow.

HOW THE MODEL MOVES FUNDS TO THE PARENT

The model uses all the methods available to it to move funds—a strategy most multinational firms do not follow. The flows that occur between the parent and the subsidiaries to maximize net profits after taxes are summarized in Table 33-4. To make the table manageable,

---

[5]For this distinction see Michel Z. Brooke and H. Lee Rammers, *The Strategy of Multinational Enterprise: Organization and Finance.* New York: American Elsevier Publishing Company, Inc., 1970.

[6]For further support of this conclusion, see Irene W. Meister, *Managing the International Financial Function*, Business Policy Study No. 133. New York: National Industrial Conference Board, 1970.

TABLE 33-4

FLOW OF FUNDS BETWEEN PARENT AND SUBSIDIARIES
($ MILLION)

Years	Subsidiary B				Subsidiary C			
	1	2	3	4	1	2	3	4
Cash sales at arm's-length prices	16.0	17.6	19.4	21.3	10.0	11.0	12.1	13.3
Transfer pricing	−3.2	−3.5	−3.9	−4.3	−2.0	−2.2	−2.4	−2.7
Change in receivables	2.5	—	—	—	−2.5	4.0	−4.8	4.8
Royalties	4.0	7.8	5.0	6.0	1.7	5.5	2.0	6.7
Management fees	—	1.0	—	—	—	—	—	—
Interest	2.4	2.0	1.7	1.4	5.1	1.7	6.2	1.2
Short loans	—	—	—	—	−78.6	78.6	−120.5	120.5
Long loans	−60.4	10.1	8.4	7.1	−51.1	8.5	7.1	6.1
Dividends	—	—	—	—	—	3.8	55.3	—
Total	−38.7	35.0	30.6	31.5	−117.4	110.9	−45.0	149.9

Note: Positive figures are flows from subsidiaries to parent. Negative figures are flows from parent to subsidiaries.

subsidiary-to-subsidiary flows were not included, nor were flows between each of the units and the outside world included.

Table 33-4 provides a broad perspective of the major fund movements that took place. In it, the positive figures are the transfers from subsidiaries B and C to the parent; in the first row it is indicated that in all periods cash moves from both subsidiaries to the parent as a result of arm's-length sales transactions. The negative figures are transfer prices, thereby in effect generating a reverse movement of funds from it to the subsidiaries.

The parent and subsidiary C enter into substantial short-term lending arrangements because of the advantages gained by exploiting the sharp differentials between the two areas in tax and interest rates and by taking advantage of exchange-rate relationships. The tax and interest factors predominate in years 1 and 3 when the parent grants substantial amounts of low-interest loans to C. The exchange-rate factor is dominant in years 2 and 4 when C repays these loans, thereby shifting liquidity to the parent as a means of protecting against devaluation.

In the world of the model, the corporate tax structure renders it undesirable for C, whose tax rate is only 30%, to pay any more than the minimum allowable royalties, management fees, or interest to the parent, unless a devaluation occurs, as in years 2 and 4. On the other hand, there is incentive for B to make the maximum allowable value of such payments to the parent, thereby displacing taxable income from a 60% to a 50% jurisdiction. But in fact, B pays the minimum allowable royalties and management fees except in year 2, when devaluation occurs. This seemingly unusual behavior on B's part apparently is caused by the liquidity needs of B.

Despite the fact that subsidiary C is in a country where the tax rate is higher than that prevailing in the country where the parent is located, B does not use dividends as a withdrawal device at all. On the other hand, the model elects an odd course for subsidiary C. Note that in year 3 the parent lends $120.5 million to subsidiary C, which at the same time pays $55.3 million in dividends to the parent. By this means, the model is able to maximize system earnings while at the same time maintaining required liability standards.

THE DIVIDEND POLICY OF A SYSTEM-ORIENTED FIRM

As might be expected, it was impossible to find a firm that could be used to illustrate the intertwining relationships of all fund movements elected by the system to shift funds on balance to the parent. As mentioned previously, it is rare for the management of even sophisticated multinational enterprises to develop a comprehensive policy of this sort, and, moreover, their worldwide records ordinarily are not designed to show all this to-and-fro shuttling. But since dividends are the most widely used device to bring back funds to the parent, the policy of Delta, a medium-sized firm that made adroit use of this method in the movement of funds, will be described.

Delta's dividend policy provided for the integration of the flow of funds into its organizational structure and for their concentration at the U.S. parent. In 1965, the U.S. parent owned a Canadian operating company, a British operating and holding company which was the major foreign subsidiary in the system, a European holding company, and a holding company in Panama. The British, European, and Panamanian holding companies were the top units in three subsystems, each including manufacturing as well as sales subsidiaries. Within this organizational arrangement, two types of international flows of dividends occurred. One was to the U.S. parent from its British and Canadian companies, and these dividends constituted the parent's major source of income from overseas operations. The other type of dividend flow was to the holding companies from subsidiaries held by them.

Table 33-5 indicates that the foreign dividends received by the U.S. parent were equal to about 20% of its operating profits; these dividends were not negligible but were not enough to affect significantly the parent's own dividend policy. Most of the foreign dividends came from the British subsidiary, primarily from its own operating profits rather than from dividends paid by the units below it. Part of the foreign dividends received by the U.S. parent were reinvested in foreign operations in the form of equity and loans, for each year the parent either increased its investment in its foreign holding companies or made loans directly to operating subsidiaries.

TABLE 33-5

DIVIDEND MOVEMENTS WITHIN DELTA ENTERPRISE
($ MILLIONS)

	1963	1964	1965
U.S. Parent			
Operating profit	13.4	18.5	16.2
Foreign dividends received	3.2	3.3	3.3
U.K. Subsidiary			
Operating profit	12.4	16.7	12.3
Dividends received	.1	.4	.3
Dividends paid to United States	2.3	2.8	2.8

Source: Unpublished company records.

IMPLICATIONS FOR THE MULTINATIONAL ENTERPRISE

As a firm's operations extend across international boundaries, it must deal with circumstances that it did not encounter when its operations were confined to the United States. Among other things, it must learn new methods of financing a chain of subsidiaries strung over the globe; it must deal with a variety of currencies, the values of which—whether fixed by agreement or floating—are not stable over time; and it must move funds among subsidiaries to take advantage of changing financial conditions and eventually back to the parent in the United States where the bulk of its stockholders are located.

It has been described how the multinational computer model functions in each of these areas in its rigorous quest to maximize profits for the entire system. It was not possible to find a parallel illustration drawn from real life. Instead, an account of how different firms acted in a reasonably optimal manner in each of the areas had to be given.

When U.S. companies first went overseas, they left their foreign subsidiaries largely to their own devices. With increased sophistication, the firms became aware of the desirability of providing direction to their distant units to enhance the profitability of the entire system. For this purpose, the firms have tended to concentrate on particular areas and have either continued substantially to ignore the others or to guide them by rules.

In the formulation of optimal strategy, an analytic chain is linked together to determine the successive effect of each financial transaction. Even in the simple equations on which the model is based, this chain is sufficiently complex to result in enormous difficulties in obtaining an optimal solution without the assistance of a computer, and unexpected optimal solutions often emerge. So it is not surprising that in the real world, the maze of interrelationships embodied in a firm's intricate web of subsidiaries forces managers to adopt various compromise solutions rather than to strive for a system optimum using all possible financial links. There is little question that these compromises are made at the expense of profits. For example, under an optimal policy, consolidated profits after taxes from the model are $471 million, which is 16% higher than when the subsidiaries were permitted to operate at arm's length without direction and 8% higher than when operations were simplified by adoption of various rules for shifting funds.

The unique potential of the multinational enterprise lies in its ability to shuttle funds to take advantage of different tax, money-market, and currency relationships throughout the world. It is clear that different firms have learned to handle certain financial practices so as to exploit these differences effectively. This concentration on separate practices simply is a stage in their development until, like the computer model, they learn to formulate integrated programs that achieve optimal results for their corporate system.

As managers improve their ability to use intercompany financial links and as governments become more aware of their use, a new sphere for bargaining between the multinational enterprise and the state can be expected. The enterprise will be seeking greater permissiveness to shift profits and move funds, and the state will be agreeing provided certain conditions are met—such as the firm's importing more capital, exporting goods, and not moving such large amounts of funds that the currency value will be jeopardized. Accordingly, important requirements for the multinational executive of the future will be his ability to take the system point of view in planning intercompany financial links and his skill in negotiating with government officials to obtain the freedom to use these links in implementing his ideas.

(This article stems from research reported in the authors' recently published book, *Money in the Multinational Enterprise: A Study of Financial Policy* (New York: Basic Books, Inc., 1973). This research was conducted as part of the Harvard Business School's Multinational Enterprise Study, which was financed partially by the Ford Foundation.)

34. HOW U.S. FIRMS EVALUATE FOREIGN INVESTMENT OPPORTUNITIES*

JAMES R. PIPER, JR.†

Despite heady references in the business literature concerning the trend toward corporate multinationalism, the fact remains that many U.S. firms—large and small—approach foreign investment opportunities with much less sophistication and confidence than they exhibit in the domestic environment. This is particularly true when the prospective investment relates to a less developed country.

A surfeit of conceptually glamorous models and approaches has poured forth in recent years claiming to offer the decision maker a more systematic approach to his foreign investment decision problem. But few such models have been preceded by an attempt to establish more precisely just what those problems are. In surveying a number of foreign investment and feasibility studies made by U.S. firms, this article attempts to identify some recurring soft spots and problems in a typical foreign investment analysis.

The concept of risk implies uncertainty about the outcome of an event, which is a function of the interaction of variables affecting the event. The intelligent risk taker is one who presumably has identified these variables, and has performed some kind of analysis upon the variables in order to predict how they will affect the outcome. The U.S. manager considering a domestic investment decision perhaps best fits this characterization of the intelligent risk taker. The nature of the immediate environment surrounding his potential investment (that is, the U.S. domestic economy) has reduced the number of variables in his risk analysis. In other words, the relative stability of the U.S. political, social, economic, and legal milieu reduces such factors to constants for all practical purposes. The decision maker thus begins with a smaller and less complex series of variables which he must subject to analysis. Moreover, since the social-legal-political environment is relatively constant, he is able to focus upon what are largely commercial variables. These often are relatively easy to quantify and to investigate from abundant and available statistical data. In short, the domestic investor, confronted with a relatively small number of decision variables and the prospect of being able to analyze those variables in a rational way, has a reasonably good chance of becoming an intelligent risk taker, that is, of identifying and measuring an investment risk.

°From *MSU Business Topics* (Summer, 1971), pp. 11-20. Reprinted by permission of the publisher, Division of Research, Graduate School of Business Administration, Michigan State University.

†Management Consultant, Theodore Barry and Associates.

The same chances of success, however, are most often greatly reduced when the manager considers expansion into foreign markets, particularly in the developing areas. Two factors complicate his risk analysis in this case: (1) the social, political, and legal variables dormant in the U.S. investment decision are activated. These are often difficult to identify and to deal with in quantitative form; and (2) the commercial variables become more difficult to quantify in the absence of sophisticated economic and commercial data.

Thus, in the absence of successful precedents or guidelines for a systematic approach to the foreign investment decision, the company's decision methodology may range from the rational to the emotional and irrational. *Business International*, for example, surveyed a large number of U.S. firms of diverse background concerning their primary motivation for making an investment commitment abroad. Four principal factors emerged:

1. an outside proposal that cannot be easily ignored, for example, from a foreign distributor or an existing or potential customer;
2. fear of losing a market;
3. the bandwagon effect, for example, "Everyone is investing in the Common Market, why don't we?"
4. an active search by the advanced international corporation planning to establish its most effective presence in every market of every size.[1]

The wide diversity of investment decision approaches which such influences suggest is apparent. As one corporate executive observed, "Indeed, at times it seems there is no path leading to a logical decision that an investment makes sense or that the project is worth the effort."[2] For many companies the criticism is well founded. Within such companies the absence of a widely accepted, systematic approach to the foreign investment decision often leads to an extensive commitment based upon what Robert Stobaugh has called "a combination of inadequate information and intuition."[3]

A seasoned executive might smile at Stobaugh's complaint and ask what else is new. The experienced manager certainly understands that information and unquantifiable judgment (or "intuition") are the ingredients of virtually every significant, real-world decision, foreign or domestic. He thus may be prone to dismiss any line of reasoning which argues for the unique problem of the decision maker in the international environment.

---

[1]"How Firms Make Decisions to Invest Abroad," *Business International*, 9 September 1966, p. 287.

[2]Simon Williams, "Negotiating Investment in Emerging Countries," *Harvard Business Review*, January-February, 1965, pp. 89-99.

[3]Robert B. Stobaugh, Jr., "How to Analyze Foreign Investment Climates," *Harvard Business Review*, September-October, 1969, pp. 100-108.

For some of the reasons suggested above, however, the analogy between the domestic and foreign investment decision problem may be specious. In the case of the domestic decision, while the information may be incomplete, the manager can insure that the collection and analysis of the data is thorough, and based upon the proven business principles which stem from a century of American industrial experience. In the case of the foreign investor, it is not only the information but also the analytical tools themselves which are inadequate. *The decision maker, by virtue of habit, custom, and training, is prone to analyze the foreign investment within the same framework as previous domestic investments, utilizing the same assumptions, analytical tools, and intuitions that have brought investment success in the considerably less complicated domestic environment.*

While a number of normative approaches and conceptual models have been suggested as a means of handling the foreign investment decision problem more systematically, little effort has been devoted to identifying more precisely current thinking and practice as exhibited by actual firms in an operating environment.

REVIEW OF CORPORATE INVESTMENT SURVEYS

This article summarizes a preliminary research effort concerning twenty-one corporations which addressed two questions: What kind of variables do companies attempt to analyze in evaluating foreign investment opportunities? Does the range of variables most often considered by a potential investor reflect an adequate, thorough approach to investment risk analysis in the foreign context?

Two complementary approaches to data collection were involved: The first was a sample of "fifty-fifty" pre-investment studies—actual feasibility studies as opposed to preliminary surveys—made by U.S. corporations under the sponsorship of the now superceded AID Foreign Investment Survey Program.[4] The second approach utilized follow-up personal interviews with selected international executives to determine the significance of the trends identified in the survey sample.

Until the beginning of fiscal year 1971, the Agency for International Development administered a program of assistance to U.S. companies seeking investment opportunities in underdeveloped countries. One service offered was the "fifty-fifty survey," whereby a qualifying company could undertake an investment study in any country designated by AID as underdeveloped. If as a result of the study the company made a positive investment decision, it then bore the full cost of the

---

[4]The "fifty-fifty" program was phased out at the end of fiscal year 1970. Under the administration of the new Overseas Private Investment Corporation (OPIC) a revised, more selective program has been initiated, with OPIC paying up to 80 percent of investment survey costs.

survey. If the company decided not to proceed with the investment, AID assumed half the survey cost, and the study became government property. The file of negative decision studies available at the agency and the questionnaire responses from firms which had made positive investment decisions were used to analyze the issues raised in the introduction to this paper.

TWO CRITERIA

In order to reduce the influence of irrelevant variables upon the analysis, an attempt was made to select a reasonably homogeneous group of investment studies from the diverse files available. The two criteria used in this selection were: (1) a food production-food processing-agricultural support investor; and (2) a Latin American investment opportunity. Although the use of these criteria limited the quantity of the available research data considerably, such a provision seemed necessary to support any conclusions based upon synthesis and generalization.

From 1962 through fiscal 1969, 317 "fifty-fifty" investment studies were conducted, forty-one of which resulted in positive investment decisions. Approximately 150 additional studies were terminated or withdrawn for unexplained reasons with no claims made against AID support. Of the remaining 130 negative decision studies, sixteen qualifying under the criteria discussed above were available at AID. These constitute a substantial part of the data base for this paper. In addition, firms which had made positive investment decisions as a result of pre-investment surveys sponsored under the AID program were solicited by mailed questionnaire to participate in the survey. Five firms responded to the questionnaire, leaving the total survey base heavily weighted (sixteen of twenty-one) in favor of negative decision surveys.

There is a possibility that a substantial difference in character exists between positive and negative decision surveys. In fact, the data presented later in this paper seem to indicate that investment surveys resulting in positive investment decisions were generally characterized by consideration of a greater number and variety of decision variables. The possible explanations for this are: (1) a more thorough approach to investment analysis by firms more seriously committed to the foreign investment idea; (2) questionnaire "noise" generated by five positive decision firms who were perhaps seeking to present a favorable image of their approach to foreign investment analysis. In this regard, it is most important to remember that while the actual studies were available for review in the case of the negative decision surveys, positive decision surveys were not available, and firms which had conducted such surveys were asked only to respond to a questionnaire regarding the variables analyzed in their surveys; and (3) some combination of these two.

IDENTIFICATION OF DECISION VARIABLES

The investment survey program of AID took a flexible and open-ended approach to the individual investment study, providing no format, standards, or specific criteria by which the company must structure its research project. As a result, the sixteen studies of interest in this article varied in terms of individual character, format, style, and overall quality (the latter being a subjective judgment of the authors). Nevertheless, in characterizing the discussion and analysis contained in each individual investment survey in terms of specific decision variables, such diversity did not present a significant problem. A discussion of estimated return on investment, for example, was relatively easy to identify regardless of the specific context in which it was presented. Still, some interpretation and judgment were necessary in order to construct a useful framework for generalization.

In essence, an informal content analysis was carried out upon the texts of the sixteen surveys. This analysis led to the identification of thirty-eight decision variables utilized in one or more surveys which were grouped into categories as indicated in Table 34-1.

The numerical indicators (1 through 38) in Table 34-1 represent their respective variables in the data presented in Table 34-2. It should be emphasized that Table 34-1 represents a complete list of the kinds of variables considered in the studies which were surveyed; it does not represent an attempt to develop an ideal, conceptual listing of most significant variables. Some items in Table 34-1 may appear only in a single study, and may not necessarily be of great, theoretical significance; conversely, there may be significant decision variables which all the studies overlook, and which, therefore, do not appear in Table 34-1. The reader should bear these considerations in mind when interpreting the data which follow.

The list of variables developed from the content analysis was sent to twenty-two companies which had conducted investment surveys resulting in positive decisions. These firms were asked to identify from that list the variables which they felt they had addressed in their surveys.

One additional variable was suggested among the questionnaire responses: "communication and travel 'distance' from the home offices." This item is listed as number 39 in the data matrix of Table 34-2.

Company names and dates and locations of investment studies are not listed in this article. The list of survey subjects and countries is representative of the character of both the survey and questionnaire samples:

Cattle operations   Honduras
Fertilizer plant   Dominican Republic
Juice concentrate plant   Argentina

TABLE 34-1

DECISION VARIABLES IDENTIFIED IN SIXTEEN INVESTMENT STUDIES

Financial Considerations
1. capital acquisition plan
2. length of payback period
3. projected cash inflows (years one, two, and so forth)
4. projected cash outflows (years one, two, and so forth)
5. return on investment
6. monetary exchange considerations

Technical and Engineering Feasibility Considerations
7. raw materials availability (construction/support/supplies)
8. raw materials availability (products)
9. geography/climate
10. site locations and access
11. availability of local labor
12. availability of local management
13. economic infrastructure (roads, water, electricity, and so forth)
14. facilities planning (preliminary or detailed)

Marketing Considerations
15. market size
16. market potential
17. distribution costs
18. competition

19. time necessary to establish distribution/sales channels
20. promotion costs
21. social/cultural factors impacting upon products

Economic and Legal Considerations
22. legal systems
23. host government attitudes toward foreign investment
24. host attitude toward this particular investment
25. restrictions on ownership
26. tax laws
27. import/export restrictions
28. capital flow restrictions
29. land-title acquisitions
30. inflation

Political and Social Considerations
31. internal political stability
32. relations with neighboring countries
33. political social traditions
34. Communist influence
35. religious/racial/language homogeneity
36. labor organizations and attitudes
37. skill/technical level of the labor force
38. socioeconomic infrastructure to support American families

Corn production and marketing	Central America
Wholesale produce marketing	Central America
Poultry plant	Brazil
Citrus fruit processing	Brazil
Vegetable processing	Brazil

The participating firms ranged in size and character from a $1.5 million grocery wholesaler to the agricultural chemical division of a *Fortune* "500" industrial company. The typical firm encountered in this survey was a medium-sized food packaging or processing company with sales in the $15-25 million range.

Table 34-2 represents a matrix of investment surveys versus the range of identified decision variables, indicating the frequency with which each decision variable appears among the entire set of investment studies.

TABLE 34-2
MATRIX OF INVESTMENT SURVEYS AND DECISION VARIABLES

Decision Variables

Category	#	A	B°	C°	D°	E	F°	G°	H	I	J	K	L	M	N	O	P	Q	R	S	T	U	Number of Times Considered
Financial	1	X	X		X		X	X	X	X	X	X			X	X	X	X		X			14
	2	X	X	X	X		X	X	X	X	X	X	X	X	X	X	X	X		X	X	X	19
	3	X	X	X	X	X	X		X			X	X	X					X	X			12
	4	X	X	X	X	X	X		X			X	X	X					X	X			12
	5	X	X	X	X	X	X	X	X	X	X	X	X	X	X	X	X	X	X	X			19
	6		X		X		X	X	X	X	X												8
Technical and Engineering	7	X	X	X	X	X	X	X	X	X	X	X	X	X	X				X	X	X	X	19
	8	X	X	X	X		X	X	X	X	X	X	X	X	X				X	X		X	18
	9		X			X	X		X	X	X								X				7
	10	X	X	X	X	X	X	X	X	X	X	X	X	X	X	X	X	X	X	X	X	X	20
	11	X	X				X	X		X	X	X						X	X	X	X		11
	12				X	X	X	X	X									X	X				7
	13	X	X	X	X	X	X	X		X	X	X	X	X	X			X	X			X	16
	14	X	X	X	X	X	X	X	X	X	X	X	X	X	X	X						X	18
Marketing	15	X	X	X	X	X	X	X	X				X	X	X				X	X			13
	16	X	X	X	X	X	X	X		X			X		X	X				X			12
	17	X	X	X	X	X	X	X	X		X	X	X	X	X							X	14
	18			X	X	X			X	X					X					X			8
	19	X								X													2
	20	X		X	X				X					X						X		X	7
	21	X	X					X		X													4
Economic and Legal	22	X	X	X	X		X	X							X		X						8
	23	X	X	X			X	X	X		X	X		X	X		X						10
	24	X	X	X		X		X					X	X		X							8
	25	X	X	X	X		X		X				X	X		X	X						9
	26		X	X	X	X	X	X	X				X		X	X	X						11
	27			X				X									X						3
	28			X			X	X						X			X						5
	29	X		X			X	X	X			X	X			X	X					X	X	12
	30		X	X		X		X					X	X									6
Political and Social	31	X		X	X	X	X	X															6
	32	X			X																		2
	33	X			X																	2
	34	X	X	X	X	X	X	X			X				X						X		10
	35	X			X																		2
	36	X	X	X	X																		4
	37	X	X	X	X																		4
	38		X	X				X															3
Management	39		X																				1
Total		29	28	26	26	25	24	22	19	17	16	16	15	15	13	13	11	11	11	11	9	9	

*Questionnaire responses.

TENTATIVE FINDINGS

The data in Table 34-2 have been arranged to assist the reader in understanding some of the generalizations we formed as a result of the analysis. The major tentative findings are discussed below.

With very few exceptions, political and social considerations (variables 31-38) received only slight attention. In actual fact, these variables received even less attention than Table 34-2 indicates. For example, although the table shows that investment survey A addresses seven of eight political-social considerations, it does not indicate that only four out of approximately 160 pages of text were devoted to these factors. The sole negative decision survey with an in-depth analysis of legal-social-political considerations devotes approximately 100 pages out of 362 to a discussion of issues which fall within the framework of political and social consideration. All questionnaire respondents however, indicated a relatively high degree of interest in economic, social, and legal and political variables. The contrast with negative decision surveys is interesting in this regard.

Finally, although survey *H* contains no explicit discussion of political considerations, variables 31, 33, and 34 are so checked because the firm imposed a moratorium on its study in the spring of 1966 pending the outcome of the national election in the Dominican Republic in June. One can only suppose that management would have considered the return to power of a Bosch administration as an unhealthy investment signal (Bosch lost the election, but the company decided against investment for other reasons). Thus, the study implicitly acknowledged the importance of socio-political considerations.

In sum, the data seem to support the hypothesis that social and political factors tend, in general, to be treated with the same lack of concern in the foreign context as they are in the domestic. The reasons for this unconcern are open to conjecture, but it does not seem reckless to suggest that a combination of procedural inertia (that is, the habit of ignoring political and social considerations in the domestic environment) and lack of expertise is a prime cause in the neglect of such factors.

Marketing considerations received relatively little attention. This is perhaps the most surprising generalization to be drawn from the data. Nevertheless, Table 34-2 clearly suggests that marketing is often a secondary, tertiary, or—in two cases—virtually non-existent consideration. Table 34-3 indicates that financial and technical-engineering considerations received primary attention, with marketing following a distant fourth.

TABLE 34-3

NUMBER OF VARIABLES CONSIDERED PER STUDY

Category	Average Number of Variables Considered per Study
Technical and Engineering	5.5
Financial	4.0
Economic and Legal	3.3
Marketing	3.0
Political and Social	1.6
Management	0
Total	17.4

What accounts for the apparent neglect of marketing considerations? The question is open to speculation, but a closer analysis of the survey suggests some clues which point toward at least one answer.

Each investment survey began with an objective which was limited by the national boundaries of the country in focus. For example, a study might be entitled *Feasibility of a Poultry Processing Plant in Argentina,* but no survey was entitled "Optimal Locations for Poultry Processing in South America," which would suggest a range of alternative locations by country, and so forth. It is also worth noting that a number of companies identify their original source of interest in a country. One cites a general interest article in a popular magazine as the source of its interest in cattle ranching in Brazil; another says it merely "heard" from business associates about the potential fertilizer market in the Dominican Republic. In other words, the one-country orientation of all these studies, the absence of comparative data, the often superficial or negligible market research contained therein, and the tendency toward exclusive interest in financial and technical feasibility suggest that market existence is largely a presumed postulate *before* a study ever begins.

There is little evidence in most of these studies of the influence of the kind of sophisticated marketing viewpoint which increasingly has characterized American domestic commerce since World War II. The approach might be characterized in general, perhaps, as the early-twentieth-century view of marketing: "Let's build a plant, make a product, then worry about selling it." It is difficult to accept what appears to be such a primitive approach to marketing considerations in the underdeveloped environment. Yet, there is ample evidence elsewhere of the same kind of phenomenon occurring within the management structure of top U.S. corporations. The collapse of Litton Industries' twelve-year-old, $240 million investment in Greece is partially explained by one Litton executive as being just such a case:

> Litton just plain didn't know too much about the facts of life in Greece. They hadn't done their homework. Their advertising was way out of proportion. . . . In other words, Litton should have studied Greek customs, history, economics . . . and other pertinent structuring before going out to sell.[5]

The corporate behavior pattern thus far discussed, that is, the emphasis on financial and technical considerations to the relative exclusion of socio-political and economic and legal considerations, and the neglect of marketing factors, poses an interesting paradox. On the one hand evidence points toward the tendency of many firms to adhere closely to domestic decision-making patterns in excluding consideration of socio-political and economic-legal variables; on the other, the

---

[5]"The Litton-Greece Nation-building Experiment—Why Did It Go on the Shoals?" *Government Executive,* February, 1970, pp. 58-59.

tion of the current status of foreign investment decision making. This research points toward a most important general conclusion for which ample other evidence exists, but which still is not widely accepted because it sharply conflicts with the traditional lore of American business efficiency. *In general, many U.S. firms' overall approach to foreign investment decision making is much less sophisticated than their comparable domestic approach.* The former is often characterized by a lack of breadth in consideration of important variables, a biased perspective, and by lack of adequate preparation.

In addressing these problems in more specific terms, at least three areas seem to require particular emphasis in the future: (1) the need to recognize and to develop acceptable methodologies for the evaluation of important political, social, legal, and economic variables; (2) the need to develop effective substitute approaches to the market research and analysis requirement in light of the frequent irrelevancy or inapplicability of domestic approaches; and (3) the need to build balance and breadth into the structure of the study of investment possibilities.

The key to future improvement of investment decisions in foreign markets, particularly in the Third World, may lie in the motivation generated by the inevitable increase in competition. In the past, the sheer power, dynamism, and momentum of U.S. business virtually insured its success in almost any underdeveloped foreign environment. As competition, particularly from Europe, becomes more significant, the recognition of shades of difference and finer distinctions with regard to investment alternatives becomes more important as well. Yet, if the investment studies reviewed in this paper are representative, it seems fair to suggest the capabilities and methodologies necessary for making such distinctions have not kept pace with the need.

Moreover, a final issue suggests itself in considering the non-comparative, one-country approach which still seems to characterize foreign investment analysis. Despite the contrary opinion of the executives interviewed in this study, it still seems defensible to argue that the studies reviewed here only touch on the most significant phase of the study—comparative analysis of alternative investment locations. Popular magazine articles and hearsay from friends hardly seem appropriate bases for narrowing a range of investment choices to a single country, yet the practice, apparently, is not uncommon. In any case, a major step in the development of a more sophisticated approach to foreign investment analysis is the necessity for American business to overcome, or at least become aware of, the limitations of the single-country conceptual framework.